THE IDEAL OF A RATIONAL MORALITY

The Ideal of a Rational Morality

Philosophical Compositions

MARCUS GEORGE SINGER

CLARENDON PRESS · OXFORD

OXFORD
UNIVERSITY PRESS

Great Clarendon Street, Oxford OX2 6DP

Oxford University Press is a department of the University of Oxford.
It furthers the University's objective of excellence in research, scholarship,
and education by publishing worldwide in

Oxford New York

Auckland Bangkok Buenos Aires Cape Town Chennai
Dar es Salaam Delhi Hong Kong Istanbul Karachi Kolkata
Kuala Lumpur Madrid Melbourne Mexico City Mumbai Nairobi
São Paulo Shanghai Taipei Tokyo Toronto

Oxford is a registered trade mark of Oxford University Press
in the UK and in certain other countries

Published in the United States
by Oxford University Press Inc., New York

© in this volume Marcus George Singer 2002

British Library Cataloguing in Publication Data
Data available

Library of Congress Cataloging in Publication Data
Singer, Marcus George, 1926–
The ideal of a rational morality: philosophical compositions / Marcus George Singer.
p. cm.
Includes bibliographical references and index.
1. Ethics. 2. Rationalism. I. Title.
BJ1012 .S48 2002   171'.2—dc21   2002030848
ISBN 0–19–825021–5 (alk. paper)

1 3 5 7 9 10 8 6 4 2

Typeset by Hope Services (Abingdon) Ltd.
Printed in Great Britain
on acid-free paper by
Biddles Ltd
Guildford & King's Lynn

For
Karen Beth
and
Debra Ann

If it was not such an awful thing to say of anyone, I should say that she meant well.

The Way of all Flesh

In the disturbances caused by scarcity of food, the mob goes in search of bread, and the means it employs is generally to wreck the bakeries.

Ortega y Gasset

PREFACE

> To do philosophy is to explore one's own temperament, and yet at the
> same time to attempt to discover the truth.
>
> Iris Murdoch

Even though they were written over a considerable period of time, the
essays in this book bear some unity of theme and interconnect in one way
or another. Most relate fairly directly to the ideas developed in the first
four: rationality, justification, proof, truth, and principle in morality,
ethics, and moral philosophy, and the indispensability of certain necessary
and ineradicable presuppositions of moral thought and enquiry—which
comes out particularly in Chapters 1 and 4. Other chapters, without dealing with these topics directly, relate nonetheless. Thus, the essays on 'Race
and Racism', 'Institutional Ethics', 'Judicial Decisions', and 'Moral Issues
and Social Problems' interrelate in various ways, possibly not obvious on
first inspection. Racism is a social institution constituting a moral issue
generating a social problem, and is capable of being illuminated, if not
eradicated, by judicial opinions.

  Chapter 13, on the moral philosophy of John Stuart Mill, is basically a
discourse on the nature of happiness, a topic which has been at the forefront of ethical discussion since its origins, and which is illuminated by
what Mill says about it (though this is not apparent on a cursory reading of
Mill). I include it here because I have something fresh to say about it, stimulated by Mill's writing, which I find perennially fresh and provocative,
largely because he was not enamoured of what Emerson called 'a foolish
consistency', was not constantly looking over his shoulder to make sure that
what he is saying today is in agreement with what he said yesterday.[1] This

---

  [1] There was a time when one could suppose that just about every literate person would recognize this allusion to Ralph Waldo Emerson's essay 'Self-Reliance'; not so any longer. The reference is to the oft misunderstood statement, which I quote—and annotate—as follows: 'A
foolish consistency is the hobgoblin of little minds, adored by little statesman and [little] philosophers and divines. With [such] consistency a great soul has simply nothing to do . . . Speak what
you think now in hard words and tomorrow speak what tomorrow thinks in hard words again,
though it contradict every thing you said today.' Emerson, as he foresaw, has certainly been misunderstood on this point, and when I first read this passage I misunderstood him myself. It took
a while before I realized that the consistency Emerson is referring to is really a form of conformity, conformity to what one has said in the past. John Stuart Mill, thankfully, was not guilty of

chapter is thus an essay in the theory of value, an essential component of a full theory of morality, a topic also at the centre of Chapters 6 and 7.

Some of the material included herein may seem fairly elementary. I can understand the sentiment, but the judgement is premature. The first four or five sections of Chapter 6, for example—'Value Judgements and Normative Claims'—might be thought to succumb to that indictment. However, what at first seems elementary is not so at all, is rather an essential preliminary to some points and some distinctions not at all elementary and of considerable importance. In order to make some advance on received ideas it is sometimes necessary to build on them. Nonetheless, this chapter does contain a brief introduction to the basic problems and terminology of ethics.

My aim throughout is to be philosophical without being technical, and that ought to be possible. I regard it as not only possible, but necessary; for I regard philosophy as properly not a branch of the arcane or the occult, but, potentially at least, a branch of literature, an art, and also to some extent a science, though hardly an exact one and not a science of nature. Some use of technical apparatus is sometimes unavoidable, but in philosophical as distinct from logico-mathematical writing that ought to be the exception, not the rule. I am aware that I have not always succeeded in achieving my aim. But 'A man's reach should exceed his grasp, or what's a heaven for?'

Information on the original setting of these essays is provided in the Additional (lettered) Notes at the end of individual chapters, along with some afterthoughts and responses to comments. Most of the essays have been only slightly altered; a few, however, have been extensively revised, some so extensively as almost to have been rewritten, though the threads of identity remain. The Additional Notes also contain some supplementary essays, in particular though not solely on norms and principles, on common sense, on values, and on the Golden Rule.

The main problem I faced was determining which pieces to include and which to exclude. I am currently planning another work responding to some of the many comments and criticisms that have appeared on my book *Generalization in Ethics*, and have accordingly decided not to include herein any papers bearing mainly on generalization or universalizability, though the basic idea does pop up from time to time. The ordering

this sort of 'consistency', which equals conformity, something few of his critics have understood. There may be no need to provide an exact reference for the quotation, there are so many editions available of Emerson's writings. However, I have quoted this passage from *The Complete Essays and Other Writings of Ralph Waldo Emerson*, ed. Brooks Atkinson (New York: Modern Library, 1940), p. 152.

arrangement chosen is not chronological but thematic, so far as I could achieve thematic order. Still, the essays are self-contained and can be read in any order. There is some repetition, not always undeliberate; I did eliminate some, but not all. The distinction between positive and personal morality, for instance, plays an important role in both Chapter 1 and Chapter 5, and a number of things said in the one are also said in the other; I have not tried to achieve elegant variation by struggling to avoid repeating the wording. Besides, repetition adds emphasis, and 'in philosophy as in music, emphasis is of the essence'.[2] Alternatively, repetition may be, also as in music, 'simply part of invention itself, a restating of themes so that variations may be explored'.[3]

In these days when the pronouns 'he', 'him', and 'his', used to refer indefinitely, are frowned on as 'sexist', it is sometimes a matter of some difficulty to find an adequate way around that, no standard and acceptable usage having yet been devised. The expression 'he/she' is ugly, awkward, and stilted, as is the converse expression 'she/he', not to speak of the unspeakable 's/he'[4] (or the unsayable 'h/she'). Let these be reserved for bureaucratic forms and questionnaires. And to move back and forth between 'he' and 'she' from one sentence or paragraph or chapter to another, in an effort to show that one is an especially sensitive person, merely jars and generates confusion and is an abomination of style. I have dealt with this matter in various ways in these essays, but have made no special effort to change my usage of the indefinite third-person-singular pronouns in papers of some time ago, before 'sexism' became the vogue word it has became. This sort of after-the-fact revision is also awkward and stilted.

The role of the copy editor is generally not well understood, so the important work of the copy editor often goes unheralded and may all too often be unappreciated.[5] But not by me. I am pleased to acknowledge the invaluable copy-editing of Jane Wheare, who saved me (and the reader) from some egregious blunders of statement and style, which became obvious once she pointed them out. And I have over the years learned a great deal from my friend A. Phillips Griffiths (known to all and sundry as Griff),

---

[2] Morris R. Cohen, 'Some Difficulties in Dewey's Anthropocentric Naturalism', *Studies in Philosophy and Science* (New York: Holt, 1949), p. 140.

[3] Angeline Goreau, *New York Times Book Review*, 27 May 2001, p. 22, in a review of Anita Brookner, *The Bay of Angels*.

[4] Try saying it aloud.

[5] The following observation is especially apropos here: 'Copyeditors, by and large, are invisible people. Yet next to authors themselves, they are the most important persons in the production of books' (Francis Paul Pushka, 'Livia Appel and the Art of Copyediting', *Wisconsin Magazine of History*, 79(4) (summer 1996), p. 364.

especially about institutions and institutional ethics, and it is a pleasure to acknowledge that here. Mark Timmons has been a great source of advice in deciding what to include. It was his idea to include 'The Golden Rule', which I had been thinking would fit better in the context of generalization in ethics. But I have great respect for Mark's judgement, so here it is. It provides another example of the way in which a fundamental moral principle can be defended against misunderstandings and objections, in the process discovering both its implications and its limitations. Other acknowledgements are provided where appropriate.

I have the feeling that this book contains an excessive number of footnotes, a certain defect of style and a disease of the modern age. (The ancient writers had no need of footnotes; they had no one to refer to.[6]) Even though I realize that, ideally, every footnote should have a justification, I fear I have honoured this doctrine more in the breach than in the observance, and I have not been able to emulate the example of Gilbert Ryle—who maintained, among other things, that a footnote should never be used to advance the argument, that this is out of place in a note, and who is undoubtedly right on this point, and who managed, even in a scholarly work, to stick to the idea of avoiding footnotes, sometimes by some pretty transparent and even clumsy expedients, through thick and thin. Still, the footnotes can all be ignored with no damage to understanding or to the clarity or cogency of the argument.[7]

Young authors contributing to *Mind* during Ryle's tenure as editor were often admonished on just such points and others of a stylistic nature. In 1953 he acknowledged a paper I sent him thus: 'Dear Singer, Thanks for your paper, which I shall use, though I am afraid not for some time. I have removed a number of "ands" from the beginnings of your sentences, which are quite clearly not wanted. The practice of beginning sentences with "and" I think stems from Moore, and it is one I much dislike.' I thanked

---

[6] I find some comfort in the following observation on footnotes which appears in a story by Saul Bellow, a Nobel laureate, in what is itself referred to as 'a sort of extended footnote': 'I have always had a weakness for footnotes. For me, a clever or a wicked footnote has redeemed many a text' ('Ravelstein', *New Yorker*, 1 November 1999, p. 96). Even though the story is written in the first person, as by a narrator named Chick, I take the observation as the author's, made through his narrator. And the observation embodied here clearly demands to be in a footnote rather than in the body of the text, though I doubt if it is wicked.

[7] Cf. Michael Gershon, *The Second Brain* (New York: Harper Collins, 1998; paperback edn., 1999), p. 208: 'Serotonin receptors in the gut have been a little like ants at a picnic. First you have one, and then before you know it, you are swimming in them.' Footnotes have become something like ants at a picnic—I do not know about serotonin receptors—especially if one composes on a computer. There are only three alternatives: either provide certain information in notes, or cram it into the text, or don't provide it at all. No one solution works for all works.

him for his courtesy but could not resist saying that I doubted that I had acquired this habit from Moore, whose style of writing I did not much care for, and was pretty sure I had picked it up from Hemingway, whose style I much admired, and added, 'I hope some day to write a philosophical essay in the style of "The Killers"'. Ten years later, when Ryle was my host at Magdalen College, he introduced me as 'Professor Singer from America, who told me once he hoped some time to write a philosophical paper in the style of Hemingway's "The Killers". Ha ha! Pretty good, what?' That was quite a memory he had. Unfortunately—or perhaps fortunately—I have never been able to fulfil that early ambition.

I hope the compositions that follow are readable nonetheless.

MGS
Madison, Wisconsin
3 December 2001 and 23 April 2002

ACKNOWLEDGMENTS

I am pleased to acknowledge permission to reprint granted by the proprietors of works in which these essays originally appeared: the American Philosophical Association for Chapter 1; *Philosophy in Context* for Chapter 2; the Royal Institute of Philosophy for Chapters 3 and 6 and 10–13; the Society for Value Inquiry for Chapter 4; the *Revue Internationale de Philosophie* for Chapter 5; the Wisconsin Academy of Sciences, Arts and Letters for Chapter 7; *Philosophia* for Chapter 8; and *Criminal Justice Ethics* for Chapter 9.

CONTENTS

Citations and Abbreviations

1. The Ideal of a Rational Morality 3
   Additional Notes and Comments 29
2. On Truth in Ethics 34
   Additional Notes and Comments 42
3. Moral Theory and Justification 43
   Additional Notes and Comments 48
4. The Methods of Justice: Reflections on Rawls 50
   Additional Notes and Comments 82
5. Ethics and Common Sense 84
   Additional Notes and Comments 120
6. Value Judgements and Normative Claims 123
   Additional Notes and Comments 151
7. Moral Worth and Fundamental Rights 152
   Additional Notes and Comments 158
8. On Race and Racism 159
   Additional Notes and Comments 187
9. Judicial Decisions and Judicial Opinions 190
   Additional Notes and Comments 212
10. Institutional Ethics 214
    Additional Notes and Comments 237
11. Moral Issues and Social Problems 239
    Additional Notes and Comments 260
12. The Golden Rule 264
    Additional Notes and Comments 284
13. Mill's Stoic Conception of Happiness and Pragmatic Conception
    of Utility 293
    Additional Notes and Comments 313

Index 315

CITATIONS AND ABBREVIATIONS

The following works, cited with some frequency in the text, are identified here to avoid unnecessary duplication:

Aristotle, *Nicomachean Ethics*. The translation I use most frequently is the one by W. D. Ross (1915), available in the standard Oxford University Press edition of the works of Aristotle and also in numerous reprints.

The Cambridge Dictionary of Philosophy, ed. Robert Audi (Cambridge: Cambridge University Press, 1995; 2nd edn. 1999).

Encyclopedia of Ethics, ed. Lawrence C. and Charlotte B. Becker (New York and London: Garland, 1992), 2 vols. (2nd edn., London and New York: Routledge, 2001), 3 vols. Most of my references have been updated to the second edition.

The Encylopedia of Philosophy, gen. ed. Paul Edwards (New York: Macmillan and Free Press, 1967), 8 vols.

Hume, David, *A Treatise of Human Nature* (1739, 1740), ed. L. A. Selby-Bigge (Oxford: Clarendon Press, 1888).

Kant, Immanuel, *Groundwork of the Metaphysic of Morals* (*Grundlegung zur Metaphysik der Sitten*) 1785, trans. H. J. Paton, in *The Moral Law* (London: Huchinson's University Library, 1948).

Mill, John Stuart, *On Liberty* (1859), quoted both in the World's Classics edition (Oxford: Oxford University Press) and the Everyman's Library edition.

—— *Representative Government* (1861), quoted in the World's Classics edition (Oxford: Oxford University Press).

—— *Utilitarianism* (1863), quoted in one chapter from the Library of Liberal Arts edition, in another from the Everyman's Library edition. I typically cite these three works of Mill by reference to chapter and paragraph number.

Murphy, Arthur E., *The Uses of Reason* (New York: Macmillan, 1943).

—— *Reason and the Common Good* (Englewood Cliffs, NJ: Prentice-Hall, 1963).

—— *The Theory of Practical Reason* (La Salle, Ill.: Open Court, 1965).

The Oxford Companion to Philosophy, ed. Ted Honderich (Oxford and New York: Oxford University Press, 1995).

Rawls, John, *A Theory of Justice* (Cambridge, Mass.: Harvard University Press, 1971; rev. edn. 1999). Cited sometimes as *TJ*, sometimes as *Theory*, from the first edition only, except where otherwise specified.

—— *Collected Papers*, ed. Samuel Freeman (Cambridge, Mass.: Harvard University Press, 1999). Cited as *Papers*.

—— *The Law of Peoples* (Cambridge, Mass.: Harvard University Press, 1999).

The Routledge Encyclopedia of Philosophy, gen. ed. Edward Craig (London and New York: Routledge, 1998).

Sidgwick, Henry, *The Methods of Ethics* (London: Macmillan, 1st edn. 1874; 7th edn. 1901). Cited as *Methods*.

——*Essays on Ethics and Method*, ed. M. G. Singer (Oxford: Clarendon Press, 2000).

Singer, Marcus G., *Generalization in Ethics: An Essay in the Logic of Ethics* (New York: Alfred A. Knopf, 1961). Cited as *Generalization*.

——(ed.), *Morals and Values* (New York: Charles Scribner's Sons, 1977).

Tawney, R. H., *Equality* (London: George Allen & Unwin, 1931; 4th edn. 1952).

——*The Acquisitive Society* (London: G. Bell, 1921; (New York: Harcourt, Brace, 1920, with different pagination).

The Ideal of a Rational Morality

1

The Ideal of a Rational Morality

1. The Systematic Ambiguity of 'Morality'
2. Positive and Rational Morality
3. Provisions of Rational Morality
4. Philosophical Proof
5. Proving Moral Principles
6. The Concept of Moral Freedom

It has been said that every young American wants to grow up to be president. But that was never true of me. The height of my ambition was merely to be president, someday, of the Western Division of the American Philosophical Association. Alas, I never made it, though I came close. Just as I was about to be promoted from Vice-President of the Western Division to its presidency, the Western Division disappeared, to be replaced by a hitherto unknown entity entitled the Central Division, and I found then that I have the distinction, such as it is, of being the first president of the Central Division. Well, so much for ambition.

As Ernan McMullin has pointed out,[1] the presidential address is a special occasion, at least for the speaker; for it provides a special and indeed unique opportunity—and also, I cannot forbear adding, responsibility. A presidential address is not—or ought not to be—just another paper, though any one may turn out to be just another presidential address. And I feel oppressed by the demand to say more than I have time—though I hope not more than I have reason—to say. This being so, I shall borrow liberally—always, of course, with the consent of the author—from material already published, and also from work in progress, not already published, and present for the most part a summary or sketch or overview, meant to be intelligible to the ear. And if you think that some essential argument is

---

[1] Ernan McMullin, 'The Goals of Natural Science', *Proceedings and Addresses of the American Philosophical Association*, 58(1) (September 1984), p. 37.

missing, content yourself with the thought that it is here, only unexpressed.[2]

Yet I want to say something first about the very idea of a presidential address. In selecting a topic, a theme, a manner, I have not lacked for advice, a great deal of it useful—except for the fact of their mutual incompatibility. I had no idea there were so many theories of what a presidential address should be, each with something to be said for it. Though I am not about to give a presidential address on presidential-address theory, I did for a time contemplate that as a fitting accompaniment to our essentially reflective activity. I have had in mind throughout the exalted image of philosophy expressed by Gilbert Highet: 'Beneath every serious dispute in the world of scholarship lies a judgment of value; and when that point is reached, science and scholarship must bow their heads in silence. Only one voice may still be heard: the voice of philosophy. There speaks reason.'[3] Although that is a great and moving aspiration, those of us more closely connected with the clamour of philosophical debate may find it hard to say, when a philosopher speaks, 'There speaks reason'—especially given the unwanted presence of ideology in the philosophizing of so many of our colleagues. But as for philosophy itself—as distinct from philodoxia, the love of opinion—yes, that is the ideal, 'There speaks reason', and it is an ideal worth every effort to forward and to pursue.

Thus I am impelled, by a process almost beyond choice, to talk about the ideal of a rational morality—in which speaks reason—and in the process will say something about proving and using moral principles, the principle and province of conscience, the essential role of decisions, and moral freedom. In short, a sketch of a moral theory. And that it is about morality, or in ethics, seems only fitting considering my past offences in this area, where I have, I have been told, become expert at committing subtle fallacies (and others not so subtle).

1. THE SYSTEMATIC AMBIGUITY OF 'MORALITY'

In 1924 there appeared a symposium volume entitled *Our Changing Morality*; among the authors was Bertrand Russell, who contributed a

---

[2] A number of points made in brief and undoubtedly dogmatic fashion are taken in summary fashion from sections of a book under way now for a number of years, some others are from an unfolding project of reconsidering the theory of generalization in ethics (see below, nn. 14 and 15).

[3] Gilbert Highet, *Man's Unconquerable Mind* (New York: Columbia University press, 1954), p. 96. Cf. pp. 93, 89.

piece called 'Styles in Ethics'. The book dealt mainly with changes in the status of women and attitudes towards marriage, divorce, and sexual relations. Now there is no doubt that sexual morality has changed and has been changing, and if the authors thought it had changed a great deal by 1924, they, as we all know now, hadn't seen anything yet, and maybe, in the same parlance, we haven't seen anything yet either—though it is hard to imagine what else there is to see. However, if morality is changing, how can there be a single true morality? Indeed, can there be any true morality?

There can. There can because the concept of morality is systematically ambiguous. It can mean either positive morality, or personal morality, or true or rational morality.[4]

What is called positive morality could also go under the name of conventional or received or accepted or customary morality, and, by a sort of anomaly, positive morality is largely negative. Positive morality is the customary or accepted morality of a given group at a given time. This also is an ambiguous conception. The positive morality of a given group consists in the rules or principles or standards the members of the group generally follow in their conduct, whether or not they profess to or are even aware of them. But it also consists in the standards the group professes to follow or believes it follows, whether it actually does or not. As we all know, practice does not always follow precept, and precept does not always determine practice. For some purposes it would be important to emphasize this ambivalence; I shall not stress it at the moment. By positive morality I mean some combination of these. Thus the positive morality of a group is its conventional morality, in the sense of the standards most members of the group normally follow or profess to follow or believe they follow or think they should follow, in their own conduct and in their criticism of their own conduct and the conduct and character of others. The precepts of positive morality are the precepts that are taught to the young and supported by characteristic forms of social pressure, such as expressions of approval or disapproval, acceptance or ostracism. There is no doubt there is such a thing, even though we are not always aware of what it is until we find ourselves criticizing it, or perhaps departing from it.

[4] Here and in the next section I make use of some ideas, even unto the exact wording, expressed in Ch. 9, 'Judicial Decisions and Judicial Opinions', and in Ch. 5, 'Ethics and Common Sense'. Of course, the distinction between positive and personal morality has been developed by many writers, especially Herbert Hart and Neil Cooper (see References, below), and my idea of a rational morality bears some resemblance to what Kurt Baier in *The Moral Point of View* referred to as true moralities; cf. e.g. p. 183. On rational morality see also Peters, *Reason and Compassion*, pp. 22–3, 66, 71, 76–7, 79, 114. (And, as I found out later on, some ideas presented here appeared earlier in C. S. Lewis's *Mere Christianity* (New York: Macmillan, 1960), which includes Lewis's *The Case for Christianity* of 1943, in the preface and chs. 1–3.)

When we criticize the morality of our own society, we do so, at least in the first instance, on the basis of our own personal moral standards, which perhaps we think should become the standards of the group but which clearly are not in actuality. One's personal morality consists in one's own ideas of right and wrong, which sometimes do guide one's conduct, and if they do not guide one's conduct, at least they guide one's judgement of others. Here also we must distinguish between the standards one professes to follow and the standards one actually does follow, and here also by personal morality I shall mean some combination of these. But personal morality must be distinguished from positive morality because we recognize that our personal morality is not always congruent with the morality of the group to which we belong. If a group has attained that level of civilization at which individuality is discernible, it will contain people who have ideas of right and wrong not always congruent with those of the group, which sometimes puts them in the position of being critical of or in conflict with the group to which they belong. And of course a person's morality is not just a set of principles; it is a complex of conduct, character, and values— that is, things a person regards as important. It includes the person's moral beliefs, but is not restricted to them. It reflects the person's character and is expressed in the person's conduct, both overtly and in more subtle forms. One's morality is expressed in one's conduct even in cases where it does not determine the conduct; where, for instance, one acts contrary to one's morality. For such conduct gives rise to feelings of guilt or shame or remorse, which are expressions of one's morality (as on occasion they are expressions of one's fear of breaching positive morality or public opinion). But in distinguishing one's personal morality from the morality of one's society the emphasis is on the standards that are part of one's own idea of right and wrong, whether in agreement with one's society's or not.

I doubt if many if any would deny the distinction between positive and personal morality, and the account I have given is fairly standard. (There are of course problems about how exactly they are to be defined, as there are problems about how they interrelate and how they ought to.) I have not distinguished between manners, morals, and mores, nor have I said anything about the role played by customs, traditions, and laws. Nor will I. What I must get to is the existence of rational morality, which may seem more dubious. Yet its reality is not far to seek. It is a presupposition of any criticism of positive morality, past or present. It is presupposed in our critical moral judgements, those based or thought to be based on reasons, that there is a rational or true morality that our judgements represent. The existence of rational morality should be manifest to anyone who has ever had a change of mind on a moral matter. 'I used to think that was all right, and now I see that it is wrong' (or, 'I used to think that was wrong, and now I no longer think so') represents the form of such a change of mind. What one is thinking in such a case is that the judgement previously made is false, though once believed true, and that it is corrected by the judgement that is now held and believed true. Thus one has a conception of a more rational morality which, though elusive, is an essential presupposition of the process of thinking about one's change of view, or even having one. Where one has a belief that the positive morality of one's group (which, say, approves of slavery or torture or a caste system or apartheid or a lower wage scale for females than for males) is unjust or wrong or unjustified, one has a belief that this conventional morality ought to change and that the change ought to be in the direction of a more rational, equitable, justified arrangement. What one thinks in such a case is not just that conventional morality does not correspond to one's own personal morality (though confusion on this matter is rife in practice, with some thinking that that is sufficient for refutation, when all that it does is pit one outlook against another), but that it cannot be approved of at the bar of rational morality.

Thus whenever one criticizes some precept or practice, not with mere irritation or aversion or anger but on the basis of reasons, one is appealing to an idea of a rational morality which provides the basis for the criticism. And at least a glimpse of this rational morality is provided to anyone who has ever changed his or her mind on a moral matter for what one regards as good reason. 'I was mistaken,' one thinks, 'I was in error. It is hard to realize this, and even harder to admit it. But if I am to be honest with myself, if I am to be able to maintain a sense of my own integrity, I must admit that I was mistaken, I was in error.' In thinking this one is necessarily thinking that something that was once and perhaps for a long time a part of one's personal morality has to this extent changed, and that the change is in the direction of a more rational or correct morality.

What is essential to this process is that the change of mind be thought to be rationally based, that it not be conceived of as something resting solely on whim. What I am claiming is that we cannot make sense of a change of moral *belief* or *judgement* or *opinion* apart from the conception of a rational or true morality. A change in one's tastes or preferences is of a different order and is not a change of moral belief. I used not to like broccoli, now I do; I used to like squash, now I don't; at an early age I liked strawberry ice cream, and after a while no longer did. (And I am not wholly inconstant in my food tastes: I do not now and never have liked Brussels sprouts.) But whether or not I think I understand the causes of this change of taste, I do not for a moment think of it as something rationally based or that my later preferences are more rational or correct than my previous ones. (There are, to be sure, cases in between, where a change in taste is brought about by a conviction that some substance is harmful, as where one gives up smoking. These are changes that are not merely changes in taste or preference but are mixed.)

In matters of taste or preference, as distinct from matters of judgement and opinion, the concepts of truth and falsity, of being correct or incorrect, are not involved. (The conception of 'good' and 'bad' taste provides a complication here, but I am thinking of taste in the primary, gustatory sense, not in the aesthetic sense.) If I think I am 'changing my mind' (to use the conventional characterization), I do not think of it in terms of a change in likes or dislikes or preference or inclination. I think that I have progressed from believing something false to believing something true, or at least to believing something more rationally based. Thus, in changing one's mind and in having the idea that one previously was mistaken in what one believed, one has the conception of a rational morality which is presupposed in the very process of thinking about and attempting to describe the change in opinion. Thus it is evident that the idea of a rational morality is involved both when we think some criticism of positive morality is rationally based—and not just something we don't like—and also when we recognize the phenomenon of changing our minds on a moral matter, which itself involves a change in our personal morality. And these three conceptions of morality, so different and yet in some ways so similar, may well involve one another.

2. POSITIVE AND RATIONAL MORALITY

Positive morality, then, is the morality we find around us. We are born into a culture and acquire its moral outlook as we acquire its language. We are in this sense creatures of traditions and institutions, and morality is one of the institutions that mould us. The existence of positive morality is a social fact, as indubitable as any social fact can be, even though just what it requires or permits is not always clear or indubitable, and in some cultures, such as ours, is easily confused with public opinion, which is variable, unstable, and transitory, and can be played upon by demagogues, propagandists, and advertisers. The more heterogeneous the society the more complex or confused the requirements of positive morality are. We are also born, or enter freely, into various groups or associations or subcultures, and these can have moralities different in important respects from that of the wider society. This creates conflicts and engenders moral problems, and helps generate a sense of personal or individual morality, which sometimes only appears to be individual but is really only another species of positive morality, that of a subculture. It turns out to be hard to avoid the influence of positive morality, and it may not be avoidable altogether.

Is morality an institution? It is often said to be. But it is also said to be the basis on which institutions can be judged or criticized, and it is hard to see how it can play both roles at once. Our distinction enables us to see. Positive morality is an institution; personal morality is a social and psychological fact, hardly an institution, except in the impossible case of a society of absolute individualists. But rational morality is not and cannot be an institution. It is the basis for all fundamental criticism of social institutions, including the institution of positive morality. In his *On Liberty* Mill was criticizing not just law and not just opinion, but also the positive morality of his time and place, as he did in *The Subjection of Women*. But he did this from a position partly inside that society and partly outside, a perspective supplied in part by the positive morality of his society, which allowed such fundamental criticism to take place, and partly by the perspective of his complex form of utilitarianism, which was put forward not as itself a form of positive morality but as something to modify it and eventually to replace it—and a very radical replacement it would have been.

The rules of positive morality and the attitudes they engender are often narrow, vicious, stupid, and cruel. They can be the results of ignorance, superstition, prejudice, fear, and folly, can embody taboos and desiccated habits, can be oppressive, intolerant, and unjust. But we can make such judgements only from the perspective provided by a more rational morality. Positive morality cannot by itself distinguish fundamental moral rules, essential to the survival of the society and the welfare of its members (such as the rules prohibiting murder, assault, mayhem, enslavement, rape, robbery, and gross dishonesty), from local rules, which vary across time and space and which constitute the part of morality that is felt as changing, sometimes giving rise to feelings of being adrift. But there is also no doing without positive morality. It is because we are brought up in a culture that has a morality that we are enabled to acquire a morality of our own and hence the capacity to improve on the morality of the group. No doubt an individual can do without a morality, for a time, as an individual can do without a language, but no society can. One of the tests of any proposed change in morality is whether it could serve as the morality of a group and work and find acceptance, in actual practice and not just in the imagination of the theorist. The received morality is what is generally accepted and conformed to, almost as something natural and certainly as something habitual. Nothing can replace it that is not capable of becoming habitual and seeming natural.

Let us return now to the book of 1924 on *Our Changing Morality*. The distinction between positive and rational morality, though implicit in some of its discussions, was nevertheless not explicitly recognized. The editor, for instance, starts by speaking of 'the subject of sex', says that 'men and women are ignoring old laws. In their relations with each other they are living according to tangled, conflicting codes', and then speaks of 'the gap that was left when Right and Wrong finally followed the other absolute monarchs to an empty nominal existence somewhere in exile'.[5] But this is double confusion: between morality and sexual morality, and between rational and positive morality. When right and wrong follow other absolute monarchs to extinction or exile we have Hitler's gas ovens or Stalin's Gulag or more up-to-date torture chambers. Here evidently right and wrong are being identified with the dictates of a narrow social code, and that is the mistake of moral parochialism.

Russell also was involved in this confusion. He says, accurately, that:

> In all ages and nations positive morality has consisted almost wholly of prohibitions . . . The Jews . . . prohibited murder and theft, adultery and incest, the eating of pork and seething the kid in its mother's milk. To us the last two precepts may seem less important than the others, but religious Jews have observed them far more scrupulously than what seem to us fundamental principles of morality.

But this already incorporates a distinction, unrecognized, between positive morality, which varies with time and place and class and religion and can be or seem largely irrational, and 'fundamental principles of morality', which make implicit claim to rational status, a claim that makes no sense apart from the conception of rational morality. And Russell sees no incongruity in going on to recommend 'lines of argument by which it is possible to attack the general belief that there are universal absolute rules of moral conduct'. Again we have confusion between positive and rational morality, and between morality as such and sexual morality. Thus Russell says: 'Broadly speaking the views of the average man on sexual ethics are those appropriate to the economic system existing in the time of his great-grand-father.' Yet he doesn't hesitate to juxtapose remarks on 'popular morality' with claims about 'the morality that ought to exist', nor does he hesitate to proclaim that 'Sexual morality, freed from superstition, is a simple matter

---

[5] Freda Kirchwey (ed.), *Our Changing Morality* (copyright 1924) (New York: Albert and Charles Boni, 1930), pp. v, vi; the passages by Russell are on pp. 3, 11, 12, 14.

... Relations between adults who are free agents are a private matter, and should not be interfered with either by the law or by public opinion, because no outsider can know whether they are good or bad.' This claim nay be perfectly sensible, even correct—and it is certainly one that most people in this society who regard themselves as advanced would today accept—but it is not so as a report on popular or positive morality. It is both an expression of Russell's personal morality and a claim, stemming from that personal morality, of what a rational sexual morality would be. But this admits the distinction that has been clouded over.[6]

The positive morality of our society, as we know, has changed enormously, especially on matters relating to sex. But attitudes relating to sex have changed before, and can change again, back to a state of greater rigidity. That our views on these matters are now different is no proof that our present attitudes are sounder, no matter how much we think they are. Fashion rules and fashions change even among intellectuals; advanced thinkers as well as professed rebels against society are not immune from its influence, may be even more prone than others to confuse the dictates of current intellectual fashion, sanctioned by peer pressure, with the provisions of rational morality, as they claim to have an outlook more advanced than that of the ignorant and uncultured masses. But that something is accepted, even by our own special in-group, is no proof that it is right. If we are rational on such matters we recognize that our present attitudes, though they have evolved from earlier ones, can still be wrong, and must rest, if they are to be rational, on something firmer than present attitudes or current acceptance, even if they are the attitudes of people who agree with us.

Hume's conclusion that 'the rules of morality . . . are not conclusions of our reason' has generated much controversy.[7] Yet, though his premises are questionable, his conclusion is true, in the main. For Hume was writing about positive morality, not about rational morality, of which he had no conception, and the rules of positive morality are not, let us face it, 'conclusions of our reason', or anyone else's either. Hume thought this a good thing, regarded morality much as Wittgenstein regarded language, as

---

[6] I am not here attempting to show anything about the moral philosophy of Russell, which, for all his well-deserved eminence as a philosopher, is something he had little talent for, and I now drop the reference. I wanted it only as an example. But I recognize the possibility that I may be misinterpreting him and that even if I am not I may receive a sharp rap on the knuckles from zealous members of the Bertrand Russell Society. Russell makes much of a distinction between an ethics of rules, which he doesn't like, and an ethics of ends, which he does. I regard the distinction as incoherent.

[7] David Hume, *A Treatise of Human Nature*, bk. III (1740), pt. I, sect. I, para. 6, p. 457.

perfectly in order as it is.[8] Some of us, however, are not so sanguine about natural developments, think there are ways in which positive morality has improved over the years, and possibly also ways in which it has retrogressed. One of the suppositions of rational morality is that rational thought and discussion is one of the ways in which positive morality can be improved, though improvement is bound to be slow and no one can be sure how much of it is ever due to rational processes. The question is not whether the rules of positive morality are conclusions of our reason, but whether they can withstand rational scrutiny, and what sort of rational scrutiny is appropriate to the rules of morality.

It is interesting that on this matter Hume and Bradley were much in agreement. For Bradley insisted that 'There is . . . no need to ask and by some scientific process find out what is moral, for morality exists all round us'.[9] But immorality also exists all round us. Bradley's claim is true of positive morality, and understood thus is both true and a valuable observation. Positive morality, however, is not self-sufficient and can be corrupted. It is no accident that the title of the next chapter of Bradley's *Ethical Studies* is 'Ideal Morality', but ideal morality does not exist all round us. If we have in mind ideal or rational morality, there *is* need to ask and find out what is moral.

3. PROVISIONS OF RATIONAL MORALITY

The ideal of a rational and true morality, then, is presupposed in our critical moral judgements, those based on reasons, and also in the phenomenon of changing our minds on a moral matter, where this is regarded as not a matter of whim or taste but as something resting on reasons. The expression 'changing our minds' is a curious one, containing a curious ambiguity. It sounds like something we do deliberately and on volition, like changing our shoes or our selection from a dinner menu. Sometimes, when we are merely choosing a course of amusement, or are in a situation where there is no question that we can choose what to do—as in choosing to go to the circus or a concert or a movie or stay home instead—we can

---

[8] Ludwig Wittgenstein, *Tractatus Logico-Philosophicus* (1922), 5. 5563. Max Black, *A Companion to Wittgenstein's 'Tractatus'* (Ithaca, NY: Cornell University Press, 1964), supplies other references on p. 305.

[9] F. H. Bradley, *Ethical Studies*, p. 187. Cf. Bradley's *Collected Essays* (Oxford: Clarendon Press, 1935), i. 122: 'I am speaking of the world and morality as we know them. I recognize no other criterion. The world of our fancies and wishes, the home of absolute categorical imperatives, has no place in legitimate speculation.'

decide one way one moment and then 'change our minds' the next, and this is a matter of volition or whim, having no more basis in reason or necessity than choosing to change our clothes. But when we are exercising judgement about what is true or what is right, the language of 'changing our minds', though perfectly natural, is nonetheless deceptive. The true relation is that our minds are changed, but we do not choose to change them. Though our judgement may in the end actually rest on whim, we cannot think so or we could not think of it as a judgement on a matter of what is true or what is right. We necessarily think of it as something over which we have no control but which we must go along with. If you and I are discussing some matter on which we disagree, and I come to think that you were right and I was wrong, I may describe the phenomenon that occurs by saying 'I have changed my mind', but that is just a *façon de parler*; you have changed my mind, or, rather, your argument has, and I have no more control over that, as distinct from the admission of it, than I do over your argument itself. Here is genuine necessity, the true home of determinism, the power of reason.

It is something of this phenomenon, with which every philosopher, and every rational person, has to be familiar, that I have in mind in talking about rational morality. But so far we have caught merely a glimpse of it, and we want more than a glimpse. More than a glimpse can be had, and I go on to give some account of its contents, principles, structure, and limits.

The following are some central provisions of a rational morality:

(1) A rational morality rests on principles, which provide its basis.

(2) These principles are capable of rational proof, though this proof might not be evident to all who are rational.

(3) Some of these principles are fundamental, others subsidiary, established by reference to the fundamental principles.

(4) A rational morality contains rules of conduct, more specific than principles, which in turn rest on reasons, reasons that relate to the principles.

(5) The principles of a rational morality allow for different rules for different conditions, and provide the basis for determining justified exceptions to the rules.

(6) But some of the rules are fundamental and changeless, as long as human beings retain certain essential features, such as being mortal, capable of being deceived and taken advantage of, capable of feeling pain. Such rules relate to the condition of being human, a presupposition of their applicability.

(7) The rules and principles of a rational morality must be acceptable in human conditions and relate to human purposes, not to purposes that are

made up a priori having no relation to the realities of human life. This is consistent with great variety of human conditions and purposes and values, as it is consistent with certain uniformities.

(8) The principles and fundamental rules of rational morality must apply to all human beings in all societies, and can be excepted or inoperative only under conditions that they themselves allow for.

(9) Judgements made in a rational morality are made on the basis of reasons and on knowledge of the relevant facts—though this is perhaps a feature of rational moral persons rather than of a rational morality itself.

(10) It is not necessary that specific moral judgements on concrete cases made within a rational morality be conclusively supported or even in agreement. As a matter of principle, conclusive reasons are rarely, if ever, available. Thus it may be reasonable for one person to think that some action is right in some situation, and for another to think something else right in that same situation; given that each judgement is reasonable, there will be reasons for each; given the impossibility of attaining conclusive reasons (which would rule out variability of judgement), each would be justified in acting, and judging, on his or her own judgement.

(11) The rules and principles of a rational morality leave a realm of moral freedom, where it is open to each person to decide and act as he or she thinks best or wants or is inclined, without breaching any rule or principle of rational morality. This will occur even in situations that are felt to be moral and to generate moral problems. That is to say, there is a realm of moral freedom where each person must decide individually what to do, and no right answer can be deduced or otherwise obtained from the principles. The opposite state is one of moral fanaticism, where it is supposed that in every situation there is just one course of action that is morally right and that this is or must be uniquely determined by the principles. This is the fallacy of exclusive rightness.

(12) It follows that in a rational morality in most situations what specifically ought to be done, as distinct from what ought not to be done, is not deducible from the principles. One must decide.

In listing some of these provisions of a rational morality I have had in mind some things Holmes said about law. 'It is revolting', Holmes said, 'to have no better reason for a rule of law than that so it was laid down in the time of Henry IV'. One difference between law and morality is that a rule of morality cannot be laid down, though it can, if not fundamental, be established in a community by acceptance and occasionally by agreement.

But the idea is the same. It is revolting to have no better reason for a rule of morality than that so it has been since time immemorial. That is the reason that often operates in customary morality; it cannot operate in rational morality. To have no better reason for a rule of rational morality is an impossibility, though if everyone else accepts and acts on a certain rule that may be a reason for doing the same.

Holmes also observed that

a body of law is more rational and more civilized when every rule it contains is referred articulately and definitely to an end which it subserves, and when the grounds for desiring that end are stated or are ready to be stated in words[10]

Again, although there are differences between a body of law and a morality, Holmes's second observation also has application to morality. Thus: 'a [morality] is more rational and more civilized when every rule it contains is referred articulately and definitely to an end which it subserves, and when the grounds for desiring that end are stated or are ready to be stated in words'. This, though it is put more teleologically than I would think best, comes close to the ideal of a rational morality. We are still some way from the ideal of a rationalized legal system, and even farther from the ideal of a rational morality. But we are now closer at least to an idea of what it is.[11]

At times I have spoken of the *existence* of rational morality, at other times of the *ideal*. Is it in existence or is it an ideal? In part, both. When I speak of its existence, I do not mean that there is some place, say Rationalia, where rational morality is accepted and practiced. I mean that the idea of it is available to us, that the idea is not self-contradictory and neither fiction nor figment, and that there are occasions when it is embodied in conduct and character. But mainly I want to emphasize its status as an ideal. It is not now fully existent and most likely cannot become fully existent. When we talk about positive or personal morality, we are talking about something that already exists. But rational morality can never exist as the morality that

[10] Oliver Wendell Holmes, jun., 'The Path of the Law', 10 *Harvard Law Review* (1897), at p. 469, in *Collected Legal Papers* (New York: Harcourt, Brace, 1921), pp. 187, 186. Holmes's statement of when 'a body of law is more rational and more civilized' omits—but perhaps it merely omits to mention—one essential consideration. The condition mentioned can be met by a repressive and immoral body of law, if only it is in this way rationalized. Efficiency is only an indirect virtue, and by itself has no value. For this ideal to be genuinely an ideal instead of a monstrosity, it must be understood to be in accordance with fundamental and justifiable moral principles.

[11] The ideal of a rationalized legal system is only analogous to the ideal of a rationalized morality, and it is easier to see how a rationalized legal system can be brought about or approximated to than how a rationalized morality can be brought about. But one way is by rationalizing the body of law of a society, since morality is in so many ways dependent on law.

people have in the way positive and personal morality do. When we talk about rational morality we are talking about something that does not as such already exist but that, to some degree and to some extent, ought to. We can describe it in general terms and delineate its general features. The progress of moral philosophy itself is an attempt to carry out this project, and we cannot predict the specific results of future enquiry. And clearly rational morality is better than existing positive and personal codes, and in that sense desirable. Hence rational morality is ideal because it is not now actual, is better than what is actual, worth aiming at, and capable of some realization, even if not in full.

By rational morality I do not have in mind, even though I refer to it as ideal, what some philosophers (e.g. Bradley, Lindsay, Lamont) have called 'ideal morality', morality beyond the morality of justice or claims and counter-claims, a morality of service and self-effacement. I am not sure whether such a morality is ideal, or whether it is for human beings or for saints. An ideal to be serviceable must be anchored in the actual and the possible.

4. PHILOSOPHICAL PROOF

One fundamental principle of rational morality is that one's conduct and one's judgements should accord with one's principles; the opposite is hypocrisy. This principle is not unknown in positive morality, but it is breached as often as the principles on which a group behaves differ from the principles on which it professes to behave, and that also is not unknown. Since the very same ambiguity affects personal morality, with occasional twinges of conscience and feelings of guilt if not shame, it is evident that this *principle of coherent principle* is already felt, even if dimly, therefore recognized even if breached. But, allowing for occasions on which one might be justified in practicing something other than what one preaches, no morality can be rational that does not abide by this principle.[12]

---

[12] It would not be too difficult to establish that this principle of coherent principle, or principle of accordance between principles and conduct, is involved in positive morality, since it is so often appealed to and implicitly conceded. If so, then positive morality presupposes rational morality—a result that strikes me as surprising and a counter example to Burke's thesis that no discoveries are to be made in morality (Edmund Burke, *Reflections on the Revolution in France* (1790), Everyman's Library edn. (London: Dent, 1910), p. 83.) Now, if positive morality presupposes rational morality, and if rational morality presupposes positive morality (I think I have already shown how), then they are conceptually (though not existentially) polar or interdependent. I

This principle links with the principle of justice—the generalization principle—and also with the Golden Rule. For the Golden Rule directs us to judge and determine our conduct on the same standards we use in judging the conduct of others, whether we are affected by it or not.[13] The generalization principle, which states that what is right for one person must be right for any similar person in similar circumstances. is still liable to misconceptions, some of them identical with misconceptions of forty years ago, some of them ingenious innovations. (Some years ago I embarked on a project of reconsidering the theory of generalization in ethics; I have still some way to go.[14] But I have seen no objections to

---

suggested earlier that the three conceptions of morality involve one another. This is part of the argument for that suggestion. There is a brief account of polar concepts in 'Some Reflections on Rights: Human, Natural, Moral, and Fundamental', *Transactions of the Wisconsin Academy of Sciences, Arts and Letters*, 72 (1984), at p. 63.

In 'allowing for occasions on which one might be justified in practicing something other than what one preaches', I was allowing for the shred of truth in Sidgwick's doctrine of esoteric morality: 'it may be right to do and privately recommend, under certain circumstances, what it would not be right to advocate openly; it may be right to teach openly to one set of persons what it would be wrong to teach to others; it may be conceivably right to do, if it can be done with comparative secrecy, what it would be wrong to do in the face of the world' (Sidgwick, *Methods*, p. 489 ff. But cf. p. 484: 'And whatever is it right for him to do himself, it is obviously right for him to approve and recommend to other persons in similar circumstances'.) Sidgwick's discussion, in bk. IV, chs. 4 and 5, of the problems involved in attempting to reform positive morality on the basis of rational considerations is still by far the best of any known to me; a classic and invaluable source on this topic. That Sidgwick's discussion revolves around utilitarianism as the basis of rational morality is merely incidental, not essential.

[13] This is argued in Ch. 12, 'The Golden Rule'.

[14] For instance, in 'The Principle of Consequences Reconsidered', *Philosophical Studies*, 31 (1977), pp. 391–410; 'On Pollocks Dilemma for Singer', *ibid.* 38 (1980), pp. 107–10; 'Consequences, Desirability, and the Moral Fanaticism Argument', *ibid.* 46 (1984), pp. 227–37; 'Gewirth's Ethical Monism', in E. Regis, jun. (ed.), *Gewirth's Ethical Rationalism* (Chicago, Ill.: University of Chicago Press, 1984), pp. 23–38; 'On Gewirth's Derivation of the Principle of Generic Consistency', *Ethics*, 95 (January 1985), pp. 297–301; and 'Universalizability and the Generalization Principle', in Nelson Potter and Mark Timmons (eds.), *Morality and Universality* (Dordrecht: D. Reidel, 1985), pp. 47–73. I hope I am not catching the disease of referring over and over to my own writings. I regard this as a special occasion, with special prerogatives and special responsibilities. This must also be my explanation, and apology, for the extraordinary, and outrageous, number of footnotes. When once caught up in footnote fever it is hard to get over it. In general, every footnote should be justified beyond any reasonable doubt, and then, if necessary, should if at all possible be integrated into the text. The special conditions of this address made that not at all possible, and when once a rule is breached, it is like a dam bursting—so here they are. I deliberately do not speak to the matter of justification. This is, as I said, a special occasion, and if everyone on just such an occasion were to go footnote wild the consequences would not be disastrous. Unfortunately, too many of our colleagues think every occasion is just such an occasion—which is absurdly false—or else they do not recognize the rule, which is a pity. The consequences for philosophical writing—if writing is the word—*are* just about disastrous, and get worse all the time, as philosophers try to ape lawyers or scientists, and too often manage only to combine the worst features of each. For some further observations on this matter I refer the reader to 'The Principle of Consequences Reconsidered' (just cited), p. 409 n. 2. Of course, there

the generalization *principle*, as distinct from the generalization *argument*, that I regard as anywhere near being valid, though not all are easy to answer.[15])

The principle of justice is also involved more or less clearly in positive morality—depending on how enlightened the positive morality we have in view is with respect to fundamental principles. Now my argument for this principle was, basically, that it is involved in all moral reasoning and all genuine moral judgement—moral judgement based on reasons rather than whim or preference. Given this—it is a large given—we have all the proof of it we can ask for or need.[16]

There is an obvious relation between the generalization principle and the golden rule. But years ago when I first wrote about this topic, I did not get the relationship straight. Now, a number of years later, I think I may finally have it straight, but I do not want to get into that again here and now.[17] Both principles are involved in Golden-Rule thinking, an essential component of moral reasoning. Golden-Rule thinking helps bring out the rational character of rational morality. Hans Reiner, a German philosopher of the phenomenological school, has provided the most discerning account of the rationality of the Golden Rule that I have seen, and I paraphrase and abbreviate it here.

The Golden Rule implies that 'I should order my conduct consistently with my judgements of the conduct of others'. In doing so it 'presupposes a moral standard' and also 'gives us a standard to judge our own conduct by in referring us to our judgements of similar conduct on the part of others'. It thus refers us 'to a norm that it does not . . . explicitly contain, but

is no good reason to make the avoidance of footnotes itself a form of fetishism, as Ryle in his later writing was I think inclined to do, along with reviewers for *The New Yorker*. It is well to remember that the best part of Karl Popper's *The Open Society and its Enemies* may well be the notes at the end.

[15] The generalization *principle* states that what is right or wrong for one person must be so for any similar person in similar circumstances. The generalization *argument* (which is indifferently either an argument or a principle) states that if the consequences of everyone's acting in a certain way would be undesirable then no one ought to act in that way without a reason. Some reviewers—why, I cannot fathom—did not see the difference. The *generalized principle of consequences* states that if the consequences of a certain kind of action would be in general undesirable then it is wrong in general to act in that way. This also, though distinct from the generalization argument, has sometimes been confused with it—though in this case the excuse is more plausible.

[16] This argument was developed in *Generalization*, chs. 2 and 3.

[17] In *Generalization* it was stated (p. 16) that the golden rule is an immediate consequence of the generalization principle; in 'The Golden Rule' it was stated that the golden rule is at the basis of the principle of justice (= the generalization principle). This discrepancy was deftly pointed out by Martin Scott-Taggart in 'Recent Work on the Philosophy of Kant', *American Philosophical Quarterly* 3 (July 1966), sect. 9, pp. 198 ff., which has also some interesting coverage of Reiner (cf. n. 18).

that each of us takes for granted'. As Reiner puts it: 'Every one of our judgments about the conduct of others . . . presupposes a moral norm'; consequently, 'we must have long ago *acknowledged* some norms to be valid . . . What we have in consequence is a moral *a priori* to order our conduct by; an *a priori* that is admittedly neither formulated nor proved in the abstract, but that we still previously acknowledged to be valid in certain applications. Our acknowledging this', Reiner adds, 'is of greater importance than any philosophical proof'.[18] I myself regard these observations, which bring home to us what we already think and must think, as providing a philosophical proof, and a proof of the strongest possible kind. And the 'world-wide dissemination of the Golden Rule' shows that it is acknowledged independently of language and of culture, and is consequently a principle both of rational and of positive morality, acknowledged even when it is violated. Violations of it typically occur when people who mistreat others do not think of them as people, or simply do not care, and this is a failure of imagination and sympathy as well as of moral discernment.[19]

5. PROVING MORAL PRINCIPLES

I have argued, though only in a cursory way, that a moral principle can be proved by showing it to be involved in all moral judgement and moral reasoning, and that this can be proved true of certain principles. This, however, is a very severe and restrictive test. Other sorts of proof are possible and necessary.

An article of over forty years ago opens with the argument that

ultimate ethical principles must be arbitrary. One cannot derive conclusions about what should be merely from accounts of what is the case; one cannot decide how people ought to behave merely from one's knowledge of how they do behave. To arrive at a conclusion in ethics one must have at least one ethical premiss. This

---

[18] Hans Reiner, *Duty and Inclination: The Fundamentals of Morality Discussed and Redefined with Special Regard to Kant and Schiller* (The Hague: Martinus Nijhoff, 1983), pp. 278, 288; cf. pp. 209–10.

[19] Tocqueville has some singularly acute observations on this phenomenon in *Democracy in America*, vol. ii, bk, III, ch. 1, entitled 'How Customs are Softened as Social Conditions Become More Equal'; for instance: 'At the time of their highest culture the Romans slaughtered the generals of their enemies, after having dragged them in triumph behind a car; and they flung their prisoners to the beasts of the Circus for the amusement of the people. Cicero, who declaimed so vehemently at the notion of crucifying a Roman citizen, had not a word to say against these horrible abuses of victory. It is evident that, in his eyes, a barbarian did not belong to the same human race as a Roman' (New York: Vintage Books, 1954), ii. 177.

premiss, if it be in turn a conclusion, must be the conclusion of an argument containing at least one ethical premiss. And so we can go back, indefinitely but not for ever. Sooner or later, we must come to at least one ethical premiss which is not deduced but baldly asserted. Here we must be a-rational; neither rational nor irrational, for here there is no room for reason even to go wrong.[20]

The argument is fascinating, even though the general point is a familiar one; it is also mistaken. The author, Brian Medlin, claims that this account of 'the logic of moral language' cannot be resisted by argument. But that is false. Let us simply restate the argument, replacing 'ethical' by 'logical' throughout and making similar changes where appropriate. Presto:

ultimate logical principles must be arbitrary. One cannot derive conclusions about what must be merely from accounts of what is . . . To arrive at a conclusion in logic one must have at least one logical premiss. This premiss, if it be in turn a conclusion, must be the conclusion of an argument containing at least one logical premiss. And so we can go back, indefinitely but not for ever. Sooner or later, we must come to at least one logical premiss which is not deduced but baldly asserted. Here we must be a-rational; neither rational nor irrational, for here there is no room for reason even to go wrong.

Now any argument to the conclusion that 'ultimate logical principles must be arbitrary' must have something wrong with it; it makes use of those very same principles of logic that it declares to be a-rational. One thing wrong with it is the assumption that argument to ultimate principles must take the same linear form as argument to less ultimate conclusions, namely deduction from premises of the same type, and this easily leads to the seductive infinite regress regress. Another error is the assumption that 'to arrive at a conclusion in ethics'—presumably this means a conclusion about a moral matter—one must deduce it from an ethical premiss. Moral judgements are judgements, not deductions; they are not themselves deduced; they can be supported, defended, argued for or against, justified or criticized, but not deduced. The linear-inference idea has the further implication that *no* principle could be ultimate, for it must be either arbitrary, in which case it is not established, or else deducible from another, which must in turn then be ultimate, *und so weiter.*[21]

Consider the following similar argument: 'Proof will not do [for acquiring knowledge of right and wrong], for since you may prove some moral

[20] Brian Medlin, 'Ultimate Principles and Ethical Egoism', *Australasian Journal of Philosophy*, 35 (August 1957), p. 111.

[21] I take the term 'linear inference', and something of the conception, from Bernard Bosanquet, *Implication and Linear Inference* (London: Macmillan, 1920), esp. pp. 21 ff.

judgments only by assuming others, all moral judgments cannot be proved.'[22] On this argument, not all moral judgements can be proved, because in every argument some have to be assumed. But this also would imply that *none* can be proved. And this also proves nothing; for, again, the same argument can be reframed with respect to logical claims, and would then imply that nothing whatever can be proved. If nothing whatever can be proved, then the conclusion of this argument cannot, yet it claims to be itself a proof. A 'proof' that nothing can be proved is no proof at all; so the argument that we cannot have proof on matters of right and wrong is fallacious.

The operative idea in these accounts—it is a fairly standard one—is that a moral principle cannot be proved because in the process it would have to be deduced from other moral principles, which supposedly generates the infinite regress difficulty or else is somehow circular. I have now argued that all-embracing sceptical arguments of the kinds just considered are fallacious. But this is still not enough. Something more is wanted, something more positive—a valid and substantial argument to a fundamental moral principle. It is to me surprising that it has been thought for so long that such an argument cannot be supplied. For it can be and has been.

From among several available alternatives I select for presentation one developed by Hardy Jones. Jones's argument is based on Sidgwick's procedure in *The Methods of Ethics*, and is in essence and in outline as follows:

Premiss 1: If conflicts and confusions in common-sense moral judgements can be clarified and resolved by some principle P, and if these judgements can be systematized and explained by P, then P is an ultimate moral principle.

Premiss 2: Conflicts and confusions in common-sense moral judgements can be clarified and resolved by the Q principle, and the Q principle can explain and systematize these judgements.

Therefore: The Q principle is a fundamental moral principle.

Jones pointed out that neither premiss is itself a moral principle, 'so a fundamental moral principle can be established by means of premises . . . not themselves . . . moral principles'.[23]

Sidgwick thought this form of argument established the principle of utility as fundamental. Whether it does this depends on whether the

---

[22] Jonathan Harrison, 'Moral Scepticism', *Aristotelian Society*, suppl. vol. xli (1967), p. 203.

[23] Hardy Jones, 'Are Fundamental Moral Principles Incapable of Proof?', *Metaphilosophy*, 10 (April 1979), pp. 155, 156.

second premiss is true of the principle of utility, and that is another enquiry. The same form of argument could establish as fundamental any moral principle that accomplished the task called for by the first premiss. And whether the argument works in any case depends on whether the major premiss truly states the conditions sufficient for establishing some principle as fundamental, and that also is another enquiry. The point is that the argument is substantial and valid, and the premisses are not them-selves moral principles. Proof in ethics is available without circularity or infinite regress.[24] The argument for it is of course not simple. But why should it be supposed to be?

I move on to another line of argument for establishing moral principles, albeit subsidiary not ultimate ones, which illustrates logical relationships among them and shows that rational morality has a logical structure.[25]

Consider any moral rule, say the rule that lying is wrong, and let us sup-pose that it is established. If it is established, it is not as a rule that holds in every instance, but as one that holds generally or presumptively. Lying is sometimes justified, and if this provision is not recognized, we can make no sense of conflicting rules and claims. Consider now the principle that every violation of a moral rule must be justified, and the further principle that one is never justified in doing something that is presumptively wrong merely by the fact that one wants to. It follows that one is never justified in doing something that is generally wrong merely for the sake of doing it. Hence, from the rule that lying is generally wrong it follows that lying for the sake of lying is always wrong. And this is readily generalized: given any moral rule to the effect that some kind of action is generally wrong, it fol-lows that it is always wrong to do an act of that kind just for the sake of doing it.[26]

---

[24] The following is a good example of the received approach: 'In ethical argument, as in all other types of argument, the series of validating premises cannot regress to infinity. There must be some premises which themselves are not validated—and which presumably not only cannot be but do not need to be validated. These are "axioms", as it were, of a deductive system. Any ethical validation must therefore assume certain prescriptions which themselves cannot be valid-ated.' This last is the most though not the only fallacious move, but there is no doubting the siren-like character of this argument (John Ladd, *The Structure of a Moral Code* (Cambridge, Mass.: Harvard University Press, 1957), p. 142.)

[25] The essence of this argument is in *Generalization*, pp. 121–2, 214, 337–8.

[26] Cf. O'Brien in George Orwell's *Nineteen Eighty-Four* (New York: Harcourt, Brace, 1949), p. 267: 'The object of persecution is persecution. The object of torture is torture. The object of power is power.' O'Brien, quite evidently, was ignorant of fundamental moral laws. But we knew that on other grounds. With everything else so inverted in Newspeak, it would be surprising if rational morality were not. Of course, Orwell tells us that the words '*honor, justice, morality* . . . had simply ceased to exist' (p. 308) and 'there were no longer any laws' (p. 8), though there was certainly punishment. (Is it *possible* that there were no longer *any* laws?)

It also follows that there are universal absolute rules of moral conduct, and that it is possible to formulate universal moral laws that have no exceptions. We just have. To be sure, I have said nothing about the standard of proof on which I am relying, or on the standards of proof that are appropriate—and there is in every proof a standard of proof that is presupposed. This is matter for a larger work not essentially summary in character.

6. THE CONCEPT OF MORAL FREEDOM

I want now to say something about how moral principles can be used, and their limitations. The application of principles to concrete cases, especially difficult or controversial ones, constitutes the classical and difficult problem of casuistry, now due for another hearing. There is a tendency on the part of philosophers, especially those enamoured of game-theoretic considerations, to look for some sufficient, infallible, and complete action guide.[27] There is and can be no such thing. Moral principles only circumscribe an area of moral freedom. They do not tell us what to do within this area. They only determine its parameters. If there is something that it is wrong to do, that is something that ought not to be done; if there is something that it is wrong not to do, that is something that ought to be done. But in most circumstances of life we have to choose between or among alternatives that are neither wrong to do nor wrong not to do; we are in the area of moral freedom, and we must decide what to do or what we ought to do—and take the responsibility and the consequences of so deciding. Within this area one has the right to do as one thinks best or as one pleases or is inclined, and whatever one does within those parameters is not only morally right but does not require justification. The demand that one always justify one's conduct is often taken as the typical demand of moral philosophy. It is not, it is only the typical demand of inveterate moralizers and moralistic busybodies. Its typical expression takes the form of moral fanaticism, the encrusted and caked-over idea that everything we do requires justification. That is false.[28] Something requires justification only

---

[27] For instance: 'By a *complete principle of action* I mean a function whose domain includes every possible situation in which a person might find himself and whose values include every possible action he might perform. A complete principle determines an action for every possible situation' (David Gauthier, 'The Impossibility of Rational Egoism', *Journal of Philosophy*, 71(14) (15 August 1974), p. 441). But there are no 'complete principles of action', never have been, couldn't be, and it wouldn't be a good thing if there were.

[28] This point has been seen and put nicely by J. R. Lucas in 'Discrimination and Irrelevance', *Aristotelian Society Proceedings*, lxxxvi (1985/6), pp. 312–15, 317. Cf. *Generalization*, 111–12.

if there is some prima-facie reason to think that it breaches some moral rule or principle. Actions within the parameters of moral freedom by definition do not; what requires justification is the demand that they be justified, and it cannot get it. This is not a merely epistemological point; it is morally wrong to demand justification of an action in the area of moral freedom, since the demand itself is an interference with moral freedom, is a terrible precedent for moral education, and has no place in a rational morality. (This is, incidentally, one significant disanalogy between ethics and epistemology. What we do does not normally require justification; what we believe does. Normally we have the right to do what we please; we do not normally have the right to believe what we please.) This point is summed up in the 'Mind-Your-Own-Business Principle', within its limits as fundamental and undeniable as the 'principle of factual relevance': 'Do not judge without knowing the facts'; and also one on which there is a great deal more to be said, though I am not now about to say it.

One of my favourite characters in all literature is Moreland, in Anthony Powell's *Dance to the Music of Time*, who, though he has decided opinions on just about everything, from the management of world affairs to how other people should conduct their lives, is unable to decide what to order from a menu, so that his friends end up ordering for him. Although there may be some process he could go through to become more decisive when faced with a bill of fare, he did not need a course in assertiveness training, and there is surely no set of principles from which he could deduce a decision on what to order. (But a 'deduced decision' is surely no decision at all.) And there are problems involving the interests of others that can similarly be resolved only by deciding, where if one waits too long one loses the opportunity to decide. Someone in love with two people who cannot have both—at least in matrimony—cannot determine whom to marry by derivation from any set of moral principles, positive, negative, personal, or rational. No doubt this is not a moral problem, even though there are moral relationships involved, but there are moral problems of this same order. There is the example presented by Sartre, the most persistently discussed example in recent moral philosophy, of the young man in France during the Nazi occupation who tries to decide whether to go off to join the Free French or to stay home to care for his mother. But one reason our young man (whose name, let us say, was Pierre) cannot easily decide is that he is ignorant of relevant facts about what is going on around him at the moment and of what will happen as a consequence of deciding one way or the other. Sartre mentions the possibility that if Pierre goes off he might get stranded in Spain or be stuck at a desk job, not something he was aiming at. However, Sartre does not mention the possibility that if he goes off he might get caught in a Nazi dragnet and hanged, nor the possibility that if he stays behind he might get drafted into the German army and sent to the Russian front.[29] If either one of these could be known to be in the offing, the decision would be relatively easy; if both are, it is worse, and Pierre has then only the choice of being shot or being hanged. But no moral principle will decide that either.

Yet this does not show that moral philosophy is somehow deficient. Neither does it show that in every moral situation one must decide for one-self on the basis of instinct or feeling and that there is no criterion apart from the value that one supposedly in this way creates for oneself for deter-mining whether one's action is right. Nonsense. If Pierre had hit on the stratagem of shuffling his mother off this mortal coil and then with a free heart setting out for England, no matter how unencumbered by remorse he felt himself to be his decision would have been wrong, decidedly. Of course, our Pierre would not even have thought of doing a thing like that. He already accepted certain moral principles that made this abstract possi-bility morally and therefore emotionally unavailable. There are 'objective criteria' available even though they do not decide for us.

Pierre's situation illustrates what I mean by the area of moral freedom. Within the parameters circumscribed by fundamental rules and principles, he is free to decide what he ought to do; as long as he stays within these parameters, whichever choice he makes will be justified. (I am here ignor-ing the possibility of in-between solutions such as staying home and join-ing the local Resistance.) Coming down, after long deliberation, on one side of the question or the other, the choice may well seem to the agent as though it is what he 'ought' to do. This is natural enough. For the situation is one in which one has the right to act in one way or the other, so that either course of action is morally permissible, and the psychological phe-nomenon of this being felt as 'what I ought to do' does not gainsay this. It shows only that one feels the choice is morally sanctioned, and so it is; it is only not morally required. In such a situation, what one ought to do, within the limits of moral principles, is what one feels one ought to do, and this can be equivalent—in fact, if not psychologically—to what one is, all things considered, most inclined to do.

---

[29] Jean-Paul Sartre, *Existentialism and Human Emotions* (New York: Philosophical Library, 1957) pp. 24–6. I discuss this and some similar problems in 'Imperfect Duty Situations, Moral Freedom, and Universalizability', in William C. Starr and Richard C. Taylor (eds.), *Moral Philosophy: Historical and Contemporary Essays* (Milwaukee, Wisc.: Marquette University Press, 1989), pp. 145–69, and my brief discussion here is in large part drawn from there.

Imperfect duty situations fall within the area of moral freedom. Kant defines a perfect duty as one that allows no exception in favour of inclination. An imperfect duty then is one that allows exceptions in favour of inclination. Kant maintains that the maxim of refusing to help others who are in need of help when one is not in need of help oneself cannot be willed to be universal law. I have argued elsewhere that this is sound,[30] and will here only suppose that it is, for the sake of illustration. This would establish the duty to help others who are in need of help. But the duty is imperfect, meaning indefinite, not determinate. From the rule itself it cannot be determined whom is to be helped, under what circumstances, to what extent, in what way, and at what cost. It is up to the agent to decide this, and the agent *must* decide. There is no way to answer these questions by deduction from basic rules or principles, which determine only the parameters of these duties, what ought not to be done not what ought to be done in a situation of imperfect duty. One decides for oneself on the basis of one's interests and sympathies and inclinations. How one decides will reflect one's character and values, and no doubt there is advice of a general kind to be offered on such matters as well, but I do not deal with such matters here. I also do not deal with the special case of one who needs help in deciding. There are all sorts of agencies around to offer *such* help.

Here is where value theory and judgements of character come in. But no one has yet discovered (though some have claimed to) a workable and justifiable formula (much less a universal one) for helping or giving—either whom to give to or how much to give. We are reduced to judgements such as 'stingy' or 'generous', 'sensible' or 'foolish', 'thoughtful' or 'selfish'—often made without knowledge of the circumstances. The matter is especially complicated where there is large-scale deprivation, because no one person's giving can be effective unless coordinated with that of others, and the questions 'What ought I to do, if others do the same?' and 'What ought I to do, given that others will not do the same?' come to the fore. But I am not about to launch here on these problems connected with generalization in ethics.

The concept of moral freedom is essential for dealing with the problems otherwise presented by the principle of conscience: 'Everyone ought to do what they think they ought to do'.[31] Sidgwick thought this principle, or

---

[30] *Generalization*, pp. 267–74; 'Reconstructing the Groundwork', *Ethics*, 93 (April 1983), at p. 574.

[31] This is usually stated in the form: 'Everyone ought to do what he thinks he ought to do'. But as so stated there is a suggestion—obviously absurd—that it does not apply to females, that is, to human beings normally referred to by the pronouns 'she' and 'her', or else that another principle, in which 'he' is replaced by 'she', must be stated to cover this other half of humanity—also

something very like it, self-evident, formulated it in a number of contexts. For instance: 'It is a necessary condition of my acting rightly that I should not do what I judge to be wrong'; 'It is our duty to do what we judge to be our duty'; and 'No rule can be recognized, by any reasonable individual, as more authoritative than the rule of doing what he judges to be right.'[32]

But on this principle of conscience, taken without restriction, if we judge it to be our duty to hurt or eliminate people we do not like, then it would be our duty to hurt or eliminate people we do not like, and this apparently objective principle of conscience or autonomy would eliminate all objectivity, and all rationality, from morality. It is a great favourite with undergraduates, who are given to saying, as though it summed up all moral wisdom, 'I can't say it's wrong for you, I can only say it's wrong for me; everyone has to decide for himself what is right or wrong, for himself'—which is an exact quotation of an inexact thought. This anarchic idea is regarded as a principle of tolerance, and actually recommended on moral grounds. None the less, it is confusion. We have here the inchoate moral wisdom of 'Don't make judgements—it's wrong', which is, it is evident, incoherent. (There is a notion about, fairly recent, that there is something wrong with being 'judgemental'; and so there is, if being judgemental is understood as making judgements when they are out of place. A judgemental person is one who is constantly judging others even in situations where judgement is not called for. 'Never make judgements' does not follow from 'Don't be judgemental'. Yet the two are often confused.)

Apply now our concept of moral freedom. The principle of conscience embodies an unstated restriction to such situations. One who is in such a situation already accepts basic principles defining the situation as what it

absurd. I have come to realize the point of trying to avoid the use of 'he', etc. in this double way, where it is not too inconvenient or clumsy to do so, even if this involves some ungrammar. The rules—the positive morality—governing the use of the pronoun 'he' and kindred expressions are in process of change, at least partly in response to reasoned complaint, and we cannot now be certain what they will turn out to be. But further resistance is futile, since the 'sexist' use of 'he', etc. is now just as jarring as circumlocuted attempts to avoid it. Better to sin against grammar than against one's mother, one's sisters, and one's aunts, especially since you know that eventually grammar will go along.

[32] Sidgwick, *Methods*, pp. 344 n., 345, 394. Brenda Cohen has an interesting discussion of this principle, which she calls the principle of non-dogmatism, in 'An Ethical Paradox', *Mind*, 76 (April 1967), pp. 250–9. Cf. Santayana, *The Life of Reason*, vol. v, ch. 9, pp. 240–1: 'to suggest that a rational being ought to do what he feels to be wrong, or ought to pursue what he genuinely thinks is worthless, would be to impugn that man's rationality and to discredit one's own. With what face could any man or god say to another: Your duty is to do what you cannot know you ought to do; your function is to suffer what you cannot recognize to be worth suffering? Such an attitude amounts to imposture and excludes society; it is the attitude of a detestable tyrant, and any one who mistakes it for moral authority has not yet felt the first heart-throb of philosophy.'

is. Everybody ought to do what they think they ought to do, but only in a situation of moral freedom and within the moral parameters—that is to say, as long as they do not do anything determinately wrong. And this does not give moral title to anyone to do something determinately wrong if only he can bring himself to think it right. This is perfectly compatible with an extrapolation from the negative principle of conscience, 'Nobody should ever be required to act against his or her conscience', a principle that is fundamental—though of course not ultimate—in any rational morality.

We are now in a position to see the element of truth in a number of widely held though narrowly based accounts:

(1) Not all ethical statements are true or false. Some merely express feelings or attitudes or inclinations—in particular those unsupported by reasons and those expressing the resolution of a problem in a situation of moral freedom. Hence there is some vindication for emotivism.

(2) Not all moral judgements are objectively based, nor can we expect unanimity on matters where there are reasonable things to be said in different directions. Hence there is *some* vindication for subjectivism; for there are some situations where it applies.

(3) Some moral problems are to be decided by deciding, rather than by reasoning from general principles, and there are situations where there is no objectively right answer independent of the wishes or inclinations or values of the one deciding. Hence there is some vindication for existentialism.

(4) In certain situations what is right is relative to the standards of a particular culture and cannot even be understood apart from those standards. This is, actually, only an application of the axiom that the character of every act depends on the circumstances in which it is done. Nonetheless, it provides some vindication for relativism—some, but not much.

(5) There are situations in which there is no one right answer, objective and the same for all, to the question 'What ought I to do?', and these situations are more numerous than has been supposed. Hence there is some vindication for moral scepticism—some, but not much.

Yet all such views are examples of *hasty* generalization in ethics.

On the other hand, such one-sided views have clouded over the ideal of rational morality. Their merits have consisted in the stimulus they have provided to reflective thought, the merits of good false hypotheses. From the point of view of philosophy, if not from the point of view of morality, these merits are considerable. If scepticism didn't exist, we should have to invent it—and very often we have.

We should note, however, that the ideal of rational morality has been made available to us only through the work of philosophers, and practically every element in the idea is due to this ongoing, even sacred, tradition. Without reflective thought on morality, which is moral philosophy whether practiced by professed philosophers or not, though there would certainly have been morality, there would have been no improvements in morality, hence no moral progress—this is true even though some instances of moral progress have been won only at immense costs in blood and pain. Since they enter into this tradition, even unwillingly, some debt is owed even to professed irrationalists and immoralists—whether they would like it or not. It is the tradition of moral philosophy, and the practice of morality, that has made the idea of rational morality possible and available. We are the present beneficiaries of this work, often carried on in great agony of spirit, and we must also regard ourselves as carrying on a tradition which, though in essence the same, will be in substance somewhat different—and, we can hope, better—for our having assumed this responsibility, which is to humanity, morality, rationality, and philosophy itself. I cannot think of any commitment or any calling that is higher, more noble, more exhilarating, or more important.[33]

ADDITIONAL NOTES AND COMMENTS

A. 'The Ideal of a Rational Morality' was originally delivered as the presidential address before the eighty-fourth annual meeting of the Western (now Central) Division (or the First Annual Meeting of the Central—formerly Western—Division) of the American Philosophical Association, in St. Louis, Missouri, 2 May 1986. (The American Philosophical Association is organized as a federation of three Divisions, Central, Eastern, and Pacific. The Western Division was first organized in 1900, was then called the Western Philosophical Association, took the name Western Division in 1920, and changed its name to Central Division in 1986. Hence the remark in the first paragraph.) Originally published in *Proceedings and Addresses of the American Philosophical Association*, 60 (September 1986), pp. 15–38; reprinted here with a few verbal changes.

[33] My appreciation to Claudia Card, Don Crawford, Hack Fain, and Lester Hunt, who, hearing a précis of some early points, persuaded me to make that my topic. This, of course, by the conventional rules of positive academic morality, makes them responsible, collectively if not individually, for all excesses, of omission as well as commission. I am grateful also to Kurt Baier and John Silber for some very useful advice of a general sort; it would be ungrateful to try to determine just how much responsibility they bear, in consequence, for the results, but it is considerable.

B. An ideology, in my conception of it, is a set of ideas masquerading as ideals serving as a false front for economic interests or other interests with which the holder of the ideology identifies, and an ideologue is one who defends at all costs the selected ideology against anyone and anything taken as being against it. Ideology, consequently, is the pathology of philosophy, which at its best is free and unfettered enquiry, aiming at truth and clarified understanding, and not at defending some preconceived set of ideas or the social order or programme thought to rest on them.

I have found the following account especially illuminating:

The term 'ideology' as a substitute for 'ideal' came into general currency through its use by the Marxists to designate the status of a particular sort of ideal—that which serves as a rationalization or idealistic false front for class interests and bias. It is the combination of the pretension to disinterestedness (in the moral rather than the scientific sense) with the fact of a determining bias whose special claims the ideology portrays as universal values, that gives an ideology its peculiar status. The Marxists held, of course, that in a class society the ruling ideas will necessarily be the ideals of the ruling class and will justify as right and reasonable whatever that class finds to be useful and expedient. In the classless society such ideological bias will presumably wither away since the classes whose struggle it projected on the plane of ideals will disappear. Since the time for that happy eventuality, however, seems still remote, we are likely for some time to have to deal with a world in which the exposure of ideals as 'ideologies' will be a favorite form of social criticism in advanced Leftist circles. The notion of ideology can be generalized, however, and such generalization has been found of use for other purposes than those of Marxist controversy. It is not only the economic interest that leads men to present their less reputable wants under the guise of universal rules of reason or to discover just those particular rules of reason that will suit their controversial purposes.[34]

C. I should emphasize that by 'incoherent' I do not mean self-contradictory. Sometimes 'incoherent' means inconsistent with itself, but not generally. As I am using the term here, to say that something is *incoherent* is to say, roughly, that it

---

[34] Arthur E. Murphy, *The Uses of Reason*, pp. 205–6; cf. pp. 264–70. A very clear example—practically a paradigm case—of an ideology, consequently of an ideologue, is provided by the following series of events: when the non-aggression pact was negotiated between Nazi Germany and the Soviet Union in 1939 on the eve of World War II, members of the Communist Party of the United States switched their stance of opposition to Nazi Germany, which they had previously characterized as a fascist country, to one of neutrality as between Britain and France, on the one side, and Germany on the other, saying they all were imperialist countries with no difference between them; until Hitler invaded the Soviet Union, in June 1941, at which point the party line shifted to ardent and all-out support, not only of Holy Russia, but of Britain in what up till then had been its lonely fight against Nazism, so that the character of the war, in this ideological estimation, shifted back to one of opposition to fascism, and in 1942, after the United States entered the war, the operative slogan became 'Open Up that Second Front'. And the members of the CPUSA all—or almost all—acted with good intentions. A number of members who bounced back and forth in this way between 1939 and 1941 later quit the party after Khruschchev's 1956 revelations about Stalin's crimes, some after the Soviet Union's invasion of Hungary in 1956. And some, of course, never did.

makes no sense, does not fit together in a coherent whole. I explained this distinction in 'Incoherence, Inconsistency, and Moral Theory', *Southern Journal of Philosophy*, 20(3) (1982), pp. 389–405.

D. On 'philosophical proof' (p. 19). This *is* just the way in which a philosophical proof differs from a mathematical or scientific proof, and a philosophical proof *is* a logical proof, even though it does not conform to the standard and conventional pattern of deduction from known or certain premisses. Whatever is presupposed in all proofs is thereby proved, even though it is not 'deduced'.

E. The concept of presuppositions is analysed in depth in 'The Presuppositions of Inference', in Kenneth R. Westphal (ed.), *Pragmatism, Reason and Norms* (New York: Fordham University Press, 1998), pp. 111–44. And I provided a detailed analysis of polar terms in 'Polar Terms and Interdependent Concepts', *Philosophic Exchange 1990–1991*, nos. 21 and 22, pp. 55–71.

F. A brief article on 'Universalizability', summing up some of the most prominent ideas about it, may be found in *The Cambridge Dictionary of Philosophy*, pp. 822–3; 2nd edn., pp. 940–1. R. M. Hare presents a distinctly self-centered account of his conception of universalizability in the *Encyclopedia of Ethics*, ii. 1258–60 (2nd edn., iii. 1734–7).

G. In *Beyond Deduction* (New York and London: Routledge, 1988), Frederick L. Will has presented an illuminating and fascinating view of the nature and role of norms or standards. Will particularly emphasizes the way in which norms that govern conduct are modified in the course of being applied, so that they are constantly undergoing modification. I should not deny this, except to remark that *moral principles*, as I am conceiving of them, are not modified in this way. The procedure Will describes applies to moral rules and standards, and to legal rules and principles, not to moral principles. Moral principles are *sui generis*. (This conception is developed in *Generalization*, ch. 5.)

H. Not only are moral principles *sui generis*, on my conception they are a priori—though this is a relativized a priori, relative to the nature of human beings and the conditions of human life. They thus contrast with legal principles and such principles as the principles of engineering.

I. There are other senses of the term 'principles', or, to put it another way, principles of different kinds. Some writers like to dwell on the sense in which a person is said to 'have principles' or 'not have principles'. There is no doubt that there is such a sense. But it is not in this sense, in which I can have principles that you do not have, and in which one can say 'It's against my principles', and in which one's principles (or lack of them) are thought of as defining one's character, that principles are a priori, and I am not speaking of principles in this sense, the possession sense. The relation between these two senses may be illuminated by noticing that a person who is said to have no principles, or to be unprincipled, is one who does not accept or recognize, or govern his or her conduct by, the principles of morality. In other words, an immoral person. Moral philosophy has no control over this. It is not clear whether anything does.

REFERENCES

Some notes are linked to references supplied here. I also list here some other items, not otherwise referred to, that were either especially useful in preparing this chapter or are important on the topic of positive and personal morality.

ACTON, H. B., 'Tradition and Other Forms of Order', *Proceedings of the Aristotelian Society*, liii (1952–3), pp. 1–28.

AUSTIN, JOHN, *The Providence of Jurisprudence Determined* (1832) (London: Weidenfeld and Nicolson, 1954), pp. 11–12, 124–9, 157–64.

BAIER, KURT, *The Moral Point of View* (Ithaca, NY: Cornell University Press, 1958), ch. 7, sects. 1 and 2, pp. 173–83. (One of the best accounts ever given of the character of rational morality, but for this account one must range beyond the brief reference just given.)

BRADLEY, F. H., *Ethical Studies* (1876), 2nd edn. (Oxford: Clarendon Press, 1927) essays V and VI; also p. 338.

COOPER, NEIL, 'Two Concepts of Morality,' *Philosophy*, 41(155) (January 1966), pp. 19–33. (An especially interesting account, from which I have learned much.)

DEVLIN, PATRICK, *The Enforcement of Morals* (London: Oxford University Press, 1965), chs. 1 and 6.

DURKHEIM, EMILE, *Moral Education* (1925), trans. E. K. Wilson and H. Schnurer (Glencoe: Free Press, 1961), part I, 'The Elements of Morality'. (Cf. p. 20: 'We must take care lest we impoverish morality in the process of rationalizing it.' Yes, that is right.)

HART, H. L. A., 'Legal and Moral Obligation', in A. I. Melden (ed.), *Essays in Moral Philosophy* (Seattle, Wash.: University of Washington Press, 1958), pp. 100 ff.

—— *The Concept of Law* (Oxford: Clarendon Press, 1961), pp. 165–73, 252, 196, 254.

—— *Law Liberty and Morality* (London: Oxford University Press, 1963), pp. 17–24, 68–77, 82.

HAYEK, F. A., *The Constitution of Liberty* (Chicago, Ill.; University of Chicago Press, 1960), ch. 4. (A penetrating account.)

—— *The Road to Serfdom* (Chicago, Ill.: University of Chicago Press, 1944), pp. 57–8, 211–12. (A close examination would be required to determine whether these two works by Hayek present the same doctrine with regard to the matter with which we have here been concerned.)

KEKES, JOHN, 'Moral Conventionalism', *American Philosophical Quarterly*, 22 (January 1985), pp. 37–46.

LAMONT, W. D., *The Principles of Moral Judgement* (Oxford: Clarendon Press, 1946), chs. 2 and 6, and p. 61.

LEMASTERS, E. E., *Blue-Collar Aristocrats* (Madison, Wisc.: University of Wisconsin Press, 1975), chs. 5 and 6: 'Battle of the Sexes' and 'The Sexual Way of Life'.

LINDSAY, A. D., *The Two Moralities* (London: Eyre & Spottiswoode, 1948).

LUCAS, J. R., 'Discrimination and Irrelevance', *Proceedings of the Aristotelian Society*, lxxxvi (1985/6), pp. 307–24.

MacIver, R. M., and Page, Charles H., *Society* (London: Macmillan, 1953), chs. 7–9.

Peters, Richard S., *Reason and Compassion* (London: Routledge & Kegan Paul, 1973). (Especially interesting on the concept and development of rational morality.)

Santayana, George, *The Life of Reason*, v. *Reason in Science* (New York: Charles Scribner's Sons, 1905), chs. 8–10, esp. pp. 211–12, 239, 240, 251.

Sibley, W. M., 'The Rational versus the Reasonable', *Philosophical Review*, 62 (October 1953), pp. 554–60.

Sidgwick, Henry, *The Methods of Ethics*, pp. 164, 215, 458–9, 464–5, 480, 484.

—— *The Elements of Politics*, 3rd edn. (London: Macmillan, 1908), pp. 23–4 and ch. 13.

Stephen, James Fitzjames, *Liberty, Equality, Fraternity*, 2nd edn. (London: Smith, Elder, 1874), ch. 4, and pp. 209–10. (This probing critique of Mill strikes me now as somewhat more penetrating and sensible than it did when I first read it some years ago, at least in the chapter here listed.)

Whitely, C. H., 'On Defining "Moral"', *Analysis* 20(6) (June 1960), pp. 141–4.

2

On Truth in Ethics

In the previous chapter I sketched an account of how moral principles can be proved, and said something also about how they can be used, as well as their limitations. But why, one might wonder, so much emphasis on the proof of moral principles? Well, a principle that is proved, or shown capable of proof, is assuredly rational; and if there is a kind or sense of morality whose first principles are shown capable of proof, that is rational morality, and such an argument helps fill out our sketch of the idea of rational morality by providing us with more than just a glimpse of it. Further, if proofs can occur within morality, as in the proof of subordinate principles—moral laws—that adds to the claim, and the identity, of rationality. Finally, if it is shown that these principles, and genuine moral judgements in general, are also capable of truth, we have the two requisites, proof and truth, sufficient for the rationality of morality.

On the matter of moral truth, the truth of moral judgements or value judgements and normative claims, we touch on a knotty topic, the long-standing question 'What is Truth'?, which cannot be dealt with adequately short of a full-scale enquiry into the nature of truth. Something, however, can be said about it in short compass, sufficient, in my judgement, for filling out the idea, and the ideal, of a rational morality.

A considerable number of philosophers have expressed doubts about whether moral judgements—claims, rules, principles, standards, precepts, statements—can be true or false. Bertrand Russell is only one of these, though undoubtedly one of the most prominent. And, not surprisingly, he has put the matter in a way that is especially perspicuous and that can be fairly taken as representative. 'A judgment of fact', Russell said, 'is capable of a Property called "truth", which it has or does not have quite independently of what any one may think about it . . . But . . . I see no property, analogous to "truth", that belongs or does not belong to an ethical judgment. This, it must be admitted, puts ethics in a different category from science.'[1] But

[1] Bertrand Russell, 'Reply to Criticisms', in *The Philosophy of Bertrand Russell*, ed. Paul Arthur Schilpp (Evanston, Ill.: Library of Living Philosophers, 1946), p. 723.

while it may be admitted that ethics is in a different category from science, it is not for this reason.

One property that 'ethical judgments' can have that is 'analogous to truth'—indeed, is a hallmark of it—is actually mentioned in the passage. There are innumerable moral principles or propositions that are true independently of what any one may think about then. Here are just some examples; it would be tedious to provide many. It is true that rape is wrong, no matter what anyone thinks about it; the fact would not be altered if the victim should later come to think it right; for it was still rape when it occurred, and rape is always wrong and it is wrong irrespective of the intentions or the moral beliefs or the later claims of the perpetrator. And I am not begging any genuine question here. Does anyone seriously doubt this? Torture for the sake of torture is always wrong, and the proposition that it is always wrong is another moral proposition true independently of what anyone may think about it. (It is true that I have provided no argument yet. Though I think argument is really unnecessary on these points, it is actually easy to provide. Read on.) Now I seriously doubt that Russell was thinking about such obvious matters when he set down what he did; he was, more likely, thinking of controversial matters. I will get to these shortly, but it needs emphasizing—apparently over and over again—that not all moral judgements are controversial; some are so obvious that we tend to ignore then, especially when we are theorizing about morality. No one denies that rape is wrong. The accused rapist only denies that what he did was *rape* or that it was *he* that raped. It is also dubious that Russell in the passage quoted was intending to bring out sane differences between ethical judgements of specific cases and ethical principles of greater generality, but the point would hold even so.

These examples, incidentally, show also that there are 'universal absolute rules of conduct',[2] something else Russell thought was false, a stance on which he has had a lot of non-sceptical company. Thus, Carl Wellman, hardly an ethical sceptic, has said: 'I find myself unable to formulate any ethical generalizations that seem to me true universally, and I can always think of exceptions to principles asserted by my friends.'[3] It is true that there are a great many ethical generalizations that are not exceptionless, but I think my friend Carl Wellman was simply not thinking of examples of the right sort. 'Torture for the sake of torture is always wrong' is true universally, without

---

[2] Bertrand Russell, 'Styles in Ethics', in Freda Kirchway (ed.), *Our Changing Morality* (copyright 1924) (New York: Albert and Charles Boni, 1930), p. 11.

[3] Carl Wellman, *Challenge and Response: Justification in Ethics* (Carbondale, Ill.: Southern Illinois University Press, 1971), p. 11; cf. p. 30.

exception, and the same is true of 'Cruelty for the sake of cruelty is always wrong', and these are representative of a large class, which can be obtained by a recipe not difficult to formulate. Thus: (1) take any moral rule to the effect that some kind of action is generally wrong (such as the rule that lying is generally wrong—which, curiously, is, as it is stated, exceptionless); apply now the principle that any breach of a moral rule requires justification, and (3) apply also the principle that one is never justified in breaching a moral rule, or in doing something that is generally wrong, by the fact that one wants to; (4) notice now that doing something simply because one wants to is identical with doing it for its own sake (so that, in our example, lying simply because one wants to is identical with lying for the sake of lying); and (5) it follows, without exception, that it is always wrong to do for its own sake, or simply because one wants to, something that is generally wrong, so that it follows that it is always wrong to lie for the sake of lying—whether it causes much or even any harm is irrelevant—always wrong to steal for the sake of stealing, always wrong to torture for the sake of torture, and so on, indefinitely.[4] We thus have a number of examples of 'universal absolute rules of conduct'.

Russell was attempting to distinguish judgements of fact, as he called them, from ethical judgements, and I should not deny, as it is now fashionable to do, that there is a distinction, only it does not lie in the source claimed, namely that ethical judgements are not true or false independently of what any one thinks about them. However, the analogy between these kinds of judgements may not be something simply overlooked but rather something actually denied. So let us proceed to another argument, in my judgement more significant. In a paper of a number of years ago I argued that there are certain formal properties of truth essential for deduction, implication, and logical relations generally. My target then was the pragmatic conception of truth as satisfaction or effectiveness, which fails to preserve these essential formal properties and hence can make no official sense of deductive relationships, which nonetheless it presupposes and makes use of.[5] My object now is to bring out that ethical statements or judgements are 'capable of truth' in this sense as well.

Three formal properties of truth are these:

---

[4] This argument was first presented in *Generalization*, pp. 121–2, 337–8, and is sketched in Ch. 1 above. To underline a point parenthesized above, we have here an argument to show that torture for the sake of torture is always wrong, and though not an argument nonetheless a recipe for showing that rape is always wrong.

[5] 'Formal Logic and Dewey's Logic', *Philosophical Review*, 60(3) (July 1951), pp. 375–85, at 378–9.

(i) Deduction, or entailment, is truth-preserving—from true propositions only true propositions are deducible. No true proposition entails a false proposition. This is an interesting and important respect in which truth and falsity are not parallel, and provides a way of distinguishing between truth and falsity. Entailment is not falsity-preserving; it is not the case that from false propositions only false propositions follow. And this distinction between truth and falsity is just as applicable to moral claims as to statements of fact.

(ii) Where P is any proposition (whether factual or moral), if it is true that P then P, and if P then it is true that P.

(iii) Truth is timeless—if a proposition is true then it is always true, and it makes no difference whether the proposition is one of fact or of logic or of morality.[6]

Although truth may be ascertained differently in ethics, and the obstacles to obtaining it may be greater or of a different dimension, its formal properties are the same regardless. From the proposition that rape is wrong, which is true, only true propositions follow; since it is true that it is always wrong to inflict pain for the sake of doing so, it follows that it is always wrong to inflict pain for the sake of doing so, and conversely; and the truth that wanton torture is always wrong is timeless, even if there was a time when it was not recognized and even if there are people who do not recognize it now, as, unfortunately, there are. It is true 'independently of what any one may think about it'.

This condition of timelessness, however, is subject to the constraint that it applies only to beings who are capable of being tortured or of feeling pain. But this is only to say that it must be applicable. If human beings or living organisms were incapable of being tortured or terrorized or of being killed or of feeling pain, then there would be no occasion for the proposition ever to be uttered or appealed to. But if the beings we are imagining were capable of having a conception of pain, then the proposition would still be true, only conditionally. Analogously, in a world in which there was no light at all, colour propositions would not be false, only inapplicable, and almost certainly unknowable.

[6] Here is one difference, which need not always be emphasized, between propositions and statements. A statement such as 'It is hot out today' can be true at one time and false at another; such a statement is an incomplete statement or expression of a proposition, which would specify date, time, and place. For example, 'It is [or was] hot in Madison, Wisconsin, USA, at 3 p.m. on 16 May 2001 cannot sensibly be regarded as true at one time and not true at another. That 'hot' is a vague and relative term is irrelevant: to see this, replace it by an exact specification of temperature.

I conclude that truth in ethics is what it is elsewhere in its formal properties; that is, in its essential respects. It is irrelevant to this point, though still an interesting question, to ask what if anything true moral propositions correspond to or what they are true of. Even if their truth does not consist in their correspondence to anything, it would not follow that they are incapable of truth. Truth in logic does not consist in correspondence either; that is, correspondence to facts of this world, but this does not show that logical propositions are incapable of being true, and it would be self-defeating to suppose it did. And if we postulate a world of logical facts that true logical propositions are to correspond to, we can just as readily postulate a world of moral facts that true moral propositions correspond to. The procedure is otiose, since there is no means of access to this world except through these very propositions themselves. Now, this might seem to mark off a difference between facts, on the one hand, and 'logical necessities' and morality on the other. But it is far from settling the matter. As Sidgwick pointed out in dealing with this very same question:

even in the case of our thought about 'what is', though error may lie in want of correspondence between Thought and Fact, it can only be ascertained and exposed by showing inconsistency between Thought and Thought, *i.e.* precisely as error is disclosed in the case of our Thought about 'what ought to be'.[7]

This, however, merely opens another line of enquiry, and I am willing to concede that truth in ethics is ascertained differently from the ways in which truth is ascertained in other areas, such as the sciences, everyday life, and logic. This would not show that there is no such thing as truth in ethics, or that moral propositions are neither true nor false. We should beware also of supposing, as is too often done, that truth is identical with knowledge of the truth, so that if we do not know or cannot know (or cannot be certain) whether some proposition is true, then it is not true. This is outright nonsense. All that follows is the trivial proposition that we do not know it to be true. There can be, there almost certainly are, unknowable truths. And even though what is taken as known at one time is later, on the basis of some new theory or discovery, judged not to be true, this does not show—and has no tendency to show—that 'truth is relative', as some easygoing relativists apparently suppose.

One of the reasons Russell espoused scepticism about truth in ethics is that there is so much controversy about (certain) ethical and of course political matters. (Another is that he was never able to answer the objec-

---

[7] Henry Sidgwick, *Philosophy, Its Scope and Relations* (London: Macmillan, 1902), p. 247.

tions brought to bear by Santayana on Russell's early ethical view expressed in his 1910 essay on 'The Elements of Ethics', in which Russell was presenting in his own elegant way a version of the ethical theory he had acquired from Moore.[8]) But that there are differences of opinion on some matter does not show that the matter is incapable of truth or falsity; and that the differences of opinion may be ineradicable has no such tendency either. It is true that on many moral matters there are deep-seated differences of opinion. This does not show that the differences of opinion are on matters incapable of truth, hence really matters of preference, not opinion. There is a tendency, it is true, in the moral area as in the political area, for such differences to be settled by a process that amounts more to terminating or getting over them than it does to proving anything—a vote, a court decision, negotiation, mediation, arbitration, a shift of interest to something else (and sometimes, as Russell neatly put it, 'by rhetoric, brass bands, and broken heads'[9]). This shows only that the ways in which such differences of opinion are and have been settled can vary from those that have, ostensibly, proved most effective in the physical and biological sciences. But this establishes no distinctive difference between ethical and other matters. There are controversies in the sciences that get settled by shifts of interest or the disappearance of an older generation or a shift in the climate of opinion, and not by the rational procedures of disinterested sifting of evidence so extolled—and rightfully so—by philosophers, at least rational philosophers, and scientists alike.

There are, indeed, many questions of fact that we can be certain will never be settled to everyone's satisfaction, though there is a fact of the matter and also no doubt that of a pair of contradictory propositions one is true and the other false. One reason this occurs is that as time goes on evidence gets so difficult to obtain; in other cases the matter becomes politicized. 'Who killed President John F. Kennedy?' is a prime example of such a politicized question. Was it Lee Harvey Oswald acting alone (the official answer), or were there several killers operating independently of one another, or was there a conspiracy of some kind? It is now impossible to tell with certainty, and the number of nuts as well as sane investigators with pet theories shouting their certitudes adds only to the general clamour and

---

[8] Bertrand Russell, 'The Elements of Ethics', in Russell's *Philosophical Essays* (London: George Allen & Unwin, 1910), repr. in Wilfrid Sellars and John Hospers (eds.), *Readings in Ethical Theory* (New York: Appleton-Century-Crofts, 1952). The essay by George Santayana is 'Hypostatic Ethics', in *Winds of Doctrine* (London: J. M. Dent, 1913), pp. 138–54; G. E. Moore, *Principia Ethica* (Cambridge: Cambridge University Press, 1903).

[9] Russell, loc. cit. n. 2.

not to the general enlightenment. This question has been thoroughly politicized, hence thoroughly obscured. The chance that there will ever be a non-controversial and certain answer established by scientific means is now practically nil. Yet *there is a right answer*, even if we don't know what it is, and one of the propositions about the matter is true and the others false. Though if something is known it must be true, something can be true without being known or even knowable.

The question about John Kennedy is one of an enormous class of politicized questions of fact which have right answers that will almost certainly never be known. Yet in the folklore of human society such questions will after a time come to be regarded as 'settled', simply because there is an accepted answer that is taught in the schools and imbibed in the culture, and thus what 'everyone' believes—despite the fact that at an earlier time they were the subjects of intense controversy; yet it would be fatuous to suppose that this accepted in the sense of received answer has been established in the sense of being proved true.

Now the situation with respect to controversial moral matters is in no essential respect different from this. There is only some tendency to think, perhaps through the influence of Hume and possibly also Kant, that provability is an essential and unbridgeable difference between questions of fact and questions of morals.

Yet I am not maintaining that truth means the same thing in application to moral judgements and judgements or claims of other kinds. Whatever the meaning of 'what truth means', it may indeed be the case that truth means something different (identity of formal properties being taken for granted) in application to moral *principles*, which are abstract and general, from what it means in application to moral *judgements* about specific cases. If we take seriously the character of moral judgements, as distinct from statements of fact (though the distinction is certainly not crystal clear nor is the line unbreachable), we may come to see that such judgements have a different logic. I shall merely suggest here what I mean by this. What I have in mind is that the ordinary distinction between truth and probability, between truth and justifiable belief, which is absolute with respect to ordinary statements, tends to break down in application to moral judgements, especially those with a future reference. There is no clear distinction between the claim that someone's action is justified and the claim that it is right, as there is a clear distinction between the claim that sane proposition is probable—or that one is justified in believing it—and the claim that it is true. As a proposition can be both probable and false, so one can be justified in believing something that is false. But a similar distinction tends to break down in application to moral judgements. If one is justified in doing something then one acts rightly in doing it, though this does not entail that the action will 'turn out right' or is the action hindsight would have chosen. To put it shortly, truth is independent of evidence, while justified belief is not; on the other hand, both acting justifiably and acting rightly are dependent, not on evidence (which is the wrong word in the context of moral judgement) but on the reasons available at the time of acting. This difference, however, has no tendency to show that truth is not applicable to moral judgements.

There is one curious fact here, which I mention without yet being fully cognizant of its implications. Moral judgements of complex particular cases seem to have a different logic from abstract moral principles, and even though relations of deducibility hold (as I argued earlier), in a complex case what ought to be done is not something simply deducible from general principles. In such situations application is not deduction, and judgements—sound or sensible judgements—are not deducible. They can be supported, argued about, rejected, or affirmed, but not deduced. For what is deduced is not itself a *judgement*. If you *deduce* your 'judgement', you have performed a deduction, not formed a judgement. Yet none of this goes to show that the judgement made or that one is searching for cannot be *true*. It relates only to how one can discover or determine whether it is true and how one can establish its truth.

I mention just one more analogy between facts and morals in relation to truth. Peirce maintained that the trait most vital to science is 'the sincere desire to find out the truth, whatever it may be'. But this is also the trait most vital to ethics. P. G. Hamerton termed this trait disinterestedness and maintained that it is the highest intellectual virtue. By disinterestedness Hamerton meant the disposition 'to be ready to accept the truth even when it is most unfavorable to ourselves'; and he argued that 'the endeavor to attain it . . . is a great virtue, and of all the virtues the one most indispensable to the intellectual life'.[10] But it is also the virtue most indispensable to the ethical life and to ethical enquiry, which is postulated on the possibility of attaining the truth, even when the truth does not correspond to our desires. And with this we come full circle.

---

[10] Charles Sanders Peirce, *Collected Papers*, ed. C. Hartshorne and P. Weiss (Cambridge, Mass.: Harvard University Press, 1934), 5.584 (i.e., vol. 5, para. 584, p. 57); Philip Gilbert Hamerton, *The Intellectual Life* (1873) (Boston: Little, Brown, 1902), pt. II, letter 3, pp. 65, 68.

ADDITIONAL NOTES AND COMMENTS

A. The substance of 'On Truth in Ethics' was originally conceived of as part of my presidential address, was omitted for reasons of space and time. Originally published in *Philosophy in Context*, 16 (1986), pp. 11–16; revised for publication here.

B. The following passage, attributed to Adolf Hitler, should be considered carefully by philosophical 'no-truth' theorists: 'a new age of magic interpretation of the world is coming, of interpretation in terms of the will and not of the intelligence. There is no such thing as truth, either in the moral or in the scientific sense.'[11]

---

[11] Quoted in *Condemned to Freedom*, by William Pfaff (New York: Random House, 1971), p. 90, 'as quoted in Hermann Rauschning, *Hitler Speaks*' (London: Eyre & Spottiswoode, 1939). Normally it wouldn't matter who said it, what matters is what is said; but in this case the source has a special poignancy. Did Hitler actually say this? I don't know, but it sure fits the champion of 'thinking with your blood'.

3

Moral Theory and Justification

I here present some observations on some observations John Rawls makes in *A Theory of Justice* on, first, moral theory and, second, justification and proof. These Rawlsian observations are both intriguing in themselves and stimuli to more extensive study of justification and proof in ethics.

1. MORAL THEORY

In a section on Moral Theory, Rawls says:

The notion of reflective equilibrium . . . is a notion characteristic of the study of principles which govern actions shaped by self-examination. Moral philosophy is Socratic: we may want to change our present considered judgments once their regulative principles are brought to light. And we may want to do this even though these principles are a perfect fit. A knowledge of these principles may suggest further reflections that lead us to revise our judgments. This feature is not peculiar though to moral philosophy . . . For example, while we may not expect a sub-stantial revision of our sense of correct grammar in view of a linguistic theory the principles of which seem especially natural to us, such a change is not inconceiv-able, and no doubt our sense of grammaticalness may be affected to some degree anyway by this knowledge. But there is a contrast, say, with physics. To take an extreme case, if we have an accurate account of the motions of the heavenly bod-ies that we do not find appealing, we cannot alter these motions to conform to a more attractive theory. It is simply good fortune that the principles of celestial mechanics have their intellectual beauty. (pp. 48–9)

It may be granted that we cannot alter the motions of the heavenly bodies, either to conform to a more attractive theory or for any other purpose. We can nonetheless alter our '*account* of the motions of the heavenly bodies' to conform to a more attractive theory, even if the accepted account is accu-rate; for we can always replace one accurate account with a different but still accurate account—accurate, that is, so far as our observations and theories go. And the analogy with ethics holds up here as well. Rawls says: 'we may want to change our present considered judgments . . .'. But it would be better and more accurate to say: 'we may find the need to change our present considered judgments . . . '. If our judgements are genuinely considered, wanting to change them is out of place; what we want is not what we consider when we are considering them. This language sounds too wilful and is in the context misleading. But even though we may find the need to change our considered judgements, this does not mean that we can change the moral facts about what is right and wrong. Rawls of course is not operating with a notion of moral facts; on his constructivist account there can be no moral facts. This, however, is not an assumption that can blithely be made but something to be established, and to operate without the assumption of moral facts does not prove there are none.

Now, changing our considered judgements is analogous to changing our account of the motions of the heavenly bodies. Furthermore, the assumption that there are moral facts—assuming that 'assumption' is the right word—fits this situation very nicely and precisely. To try to change the moral facts—which I regard as impossible—is analogous to changing the motions of the heavenly bodies, which only God can do. But even if God can change the motions of the heavenly bodies, not even God can change basic moral facts about right and wrong. The most that God can do, in some devilish mood, is to change or distort our perception of these facts, but that is to affect our judgements, and not the facts they are about.[1] No moral theory can change the moral facts, for example that it is always wrong to lie for the sake of lying, kill for the sake of killing, torture for the sake of torture, and these are without any doubt whatever fixed moral facts. These could conceivably change—or, rather, become inapplicable—if there were a drastic change in the nature of the beings to whom moral laws apply—if, for instance, human beings were to change so drastically in their powers of discernment that they could not possibly be deceived by a lie, or if they became so immune to pain that they could not possibly be tortured. But that is not a change that we can bring about, even with the most optimistic forecasts for genetic engineering. And this holds true even though we can discover these moral facts, and that they are moral facts, only through moral theory.

---

[1] Some slight qualification may be needed here. God could so change the nature of human beings and of living organisms generally as to make then immune to harm, to murder, lies, theft, and so on. This conceivable though far-fetched change would differ somewhat from distorting 'our perception of moral facts', would result in there being no moral rules against harming, murder, lies, theft, and so on. There could be no conception of such acts, which not only could not be conceived of, could also not occur. There could also be no morality.

How 'Socratic', then, in the sense Rawls specifies, is moral philosophy? The analogy with grammar is, I think, unfortunate. For our sense of correct grammar is, in the end, something conventional. The grammar of one language differs, like its vocabulary, from that of another language, and the grammar of a given language changes through time. If a community of language users were to decide to change some features of the grammar of their language they could do so, just as they could decide to change some features of their vocabulary. This might generate confusion inconsistency and resentment—and the change might take time to be effective—but it is possible. No community, however, can by law or convention or custom or decree or any other means decide to change the morality of an action or institution and succeed in this. All they can change is their view of it, though even this must seem forced and would lead to considerable cultural displacement.

With moral facts in the picture, along with moral judgements and moral theory, the analogy with celestial mechanics holds up well. For we need a theory even to have an account of the motions of the heavenly bodies. I do not maintain this on the ground, which I regard as specious, that all facts are theory-laden—itself a heavily theory-laden theory. But the facts of the heavenly bodies are paradigm theory-laden facts. The theory in question may be rudimentary, but it is nonetheless theory on the basis of which we identify the same heavenly body as Jupiter, Mars, the sun, or the moon— or, rather, identify the spots and phenomena observed in the sky as continuous and the same heavenly bodies.

I conclude that the contrast here developed between moral philosophy and physics breaks down, as does the analogy drawn between ethics and grammar, moral theory and linguistic theory. I conclude also that even though the passage provides no explicit role for moral facts, it still allows for them. But what they are and that they are—these are other matters.

2. JUSTIFICATION

In his discussion of justification, Rawls says:

justification is argument addressed to those who disagree with us, or to ourselves when we are of two minds. It presumes a clash of views between persons or within one person, and seeks to convince others, or ourselves, of the reasonableness of the principles upon which our claims and judgments are founded. Being designed to reconcile by reason, justification proceeds from what all parties to the discussion hold in common. Ideally, to justify a conception of justice to someone is to give him a proof of its principles from premises that we both accept, these principles having in turn consequences that match our considered judgments. Thus mere proof is not justification. A proof simply displays logical relations between propositions. But proofs become justification once the starting points are mutually recognized, or the conclusions so comprehensive and compelling as to persuade us of the soundness of the conception expressed by their premises. (580–1)

Although there is much here that is tied to the particular terms of Rawls's own moral theory, there is also much that is abstractable from that context and of interest in its own right. I am especially interested in the idea that justification 'presumes a clash of views', and what is said about the relations between justification and proof, one of the very few discussions of their relations to be found anywhere.

One problem with the first idea is that it does not draw a sharp enough distinction between making up one's own mind and trying to persuade or convince another. In trying to resolve a problem, come to a decision, make up one's mind, one characteristically starts from uncertainty and attempts to proceed to certainty (or at least a feeling of certainty). This process presumes neither prior disagreement nor that one is 'of two minds'. However, attempting to convince another—to justify something to another—is characteristically a situation arising out of disagreement, and can be characterized as a clash of opposing certainties (or as a clash between certainty and uncertainty). From this point of view, then, there is an important difference between making up one's mind and attempting to convince another, between (to use the language of justification) justifying something to oneself and justifying something to another, or attempting to convince oneself and attempting to convince another.

There are, to be sure, occasions when one's own feeling of uncertainty results from one's being of two minds, from an inner clash of opposing certainties. But this is by no means essential either to uncertainty or to justification. In general, it is false that 'justification is argument addressed to those who disagree with us'. Though it can be, it need not be, unless we are prepared to call a case where one person is certain of something and another uncertain one of disagreement. But this would be a stretcher. To be in doubt about something one need not accept a contrary view.

Rawls evidently thinks of justification as necessarily justification *to*. He speaks always of justifying something *to* someone. He evidently thinks of justification on the model of persuading or convincing. There is no doubt that justification is often justification to someone, and in this way analogous to persuading or convincing. But this is not so always or necessarily.

Persuading or convincing is always in this way necessarily relative to persons; there can be no persuading or convincing without someone who is persuaded or convinced or on whom the attempt is being made. But there is no similar necessity for justifying. Justifying is not necessarily relative to persons in this way. 'Persuasion' and 'conviction' are psychological terms; 'justification' is not. It is always a person who is persuaded or convinced, just as there is always something of which that person is persuaded or convinced. But it is not, in the same sense, a person who is justified; there is something—some action, some practice—that is justified, and it may be, on occasion, that it is justified *to* some person, though that seems a rather roundabout way of saying that someone accepts its justification. (This statement may need a slight qualification: sometimes and in some uses it is a person who is justified—a person can be justified in believing something, doing something, and so on. This does not gainsay the point being made. A person is not justified in the same sense in which a person is convinced.)

It is possible that the conception of justification as necessarily relative to persons derives from the conception of justification as always occurring in a debating context. But that does not justify either conception. These conceptions—or misconceptions—however, are fairly widespread. The ideas Rawls presents about justification and proof, on the other hand, are not. Rawls says 'mere proof is not justification'. One more often hears it said that mere justification is not proof. It is not that the latter idea is clear; only that it is more common. But the idea that 'a proof simply displays logical relations between propositions' is both idiosyncratic and out of place. Here proof is taken as identical with derivation or deduction, and this is taking the mathematical model too far. There is proof outside mathematics—which is where a proof is often defined as a string of formulae logically related to one another by the rules of the system in question—and outside mathematics this idea is not one of proof at all. Where characterization of it rises to articulateness, it would be called simply derivation, and the relations between deduction and proof have still to be determined. Proof in mathematics is not the most suitable model for proof in ethics. To 'prove' a formula in mathematics one need simply deduce it from the axioms or show how it is to be deduced. But that is not to prove it, that is, to prove it true; it is to prove, not *it*, but the proposition that it is thus derivable. A genuine proof does more than simply display logical relations; it actually proves some conclusion—that is, shows it to be true—whereas a mere derivation, which is what one has in geometry, does no more than display logical relations.

To depart now from this misguided and misleading mathematical analogy, to prove something is to prove it true, and there is thus an inextricable connection between proof and truth. If something is known it must be true; just so, if something is proved it must be true. There is no such connection between justification and truth. One reason is that justification has a wider range than truth—actions can be justified, though they cannot be proved (meaning that the concept of proof does not apply to actions). Another is that—accepting for the moment the convention that a proposition (or a principle) can be justified (which is really a misconvention)—a proposition can be justified (that is, one can be justified in accepting it) without its being true. Here is one clear-cut difference between justification and proof, which the passage in question ignores. From this perspective, justification links more closely with probability than with truth. A justified belief is one that it is reasonable to hold in relation to the evidence.

There is a suggestion in the last sentence in our passage ('proofs become justification once . . . the conclusions [are] so comprehensive and compelling as to persuade us of the soundness . . .') that 'justification' is a psychological term, since 'persuasion' is. 'Proofs become justification' when we are persuaded of something, is the way it seems to read; but this idea is neither proved nor justified nor persuasive. Although it is true that we often speak of proving something *to* someone, and in that context and in that sense seem to conflate proving with persuading or convincing, this is not essential to proof but only an accident of it. ('You've proved it to me' means 'I accept your claim'; similarly with 'You've justified it to me'.) Something can be proved or can be a proof, just as something can be true, without anyone's being persuaded of it or accepting it. Similarly something can be justified without anyone's believing it or accepting it.

The relations between justification and proof thus remain to be delineated.

ADDITIONAL NOTES AND COMMENTS

A. The substance of 'Moral Theory and Justification' was, like the previous chapter, originally conceived of as part of my presidential address, and was omitted for the same reasons. First published in *Philosophy*, 62 (1987), pp. 517–22; slightly revised here.

B. In *The Law of Peoples* Rawls makes explicit his conception of 'justification' as a process that takes place in the public arena. Thus he says: 'Public justification is . . . argument addressed to others' (p. 155). Note the emphasis on public justification—

that is, argument or discourse in the political arena—and, again, this does not appear to differ much if at all from persuasion or conviction, except perhaps to indicate that the process is one that appeals to the reason of the members of the audience, whereas persuasion, especially persuasion as practiced by advertisers, public-relations people, 'spin doctors', and propagandists, appeals to emotions—feelings, desires, and aversions.

4

The Methods of Justice: Reflections on Rawls

1. Sidgwick and the Contract Tradition
2. Some Presupposed Principles
3. Choice and Contract
4. Further Presuppositions—Maximization and Primary Goods
5. Desert and Redress
6. Applications—Judgements of Justice
   Appendix: Sources and Antecedents

Rawls's *Theory of Justice*[1] is so well known that there is no call for a review of it of the ordinary kind. It does not follow, however, that there is no call for a further review. For Rawls's *Theory of Justice* is so large, so complex, and so comprehensive that, like a mountain, there is no one point of view from which it can be fully comprehended. It presents different aspects and features from different points of view, which vary in size and significance as one continues to view it. All the more reason, then, for viewing it again. For there is constant challenge, and infinite prospect of reward. Rawls speaks at the end of seeing our place in society *sub specie aeternitatis*, and of combining all social and temporal points of view into one (p. 587). This is an expressive though impossible aspiration, and is itself the expression of a point of view. There is no similar position for regarding *A Theory of Justice*, which must be regarded, I have finally concluded, as not only a seminal but also a noumenal work. It is in this spirit that I offer some reflections on it.

---

[1] John Rawls, *A Theory of Justice* (1971). All page references, unless otherwise specified, are to this work, and are given parenthetically in the body of the text. In the Appendix there is a brief account of some antecedent works and writers with which Rawls's ideas have a special affinity; this should have some historical interest. Rawls has since revised his work; for details, see note C, pp. 82–3.

1. SIDGWICK AND THE CONTRACT TRADITION

Many years ago, in one of his first published writings, Rawls said: 'Morals is not like physics; it is not a matter of ingenious discovery but of noticing lots of obvious things and keeping them all in reasonable balance at the same time.'[2] True to his own prescription, Rawls has noticed lots of things, some of them obvious and some not, and tried to keep them all in reasonable balance. This is a source of some difficulty, and in both these respects there is a striking resemblance between Rawls's *Theory of Justice* and Sidgwick's *Methods of Ethics*.

One could, of course, detail many other points of resemblance, but right now I want to detail some points of difference; for present purposes these are more significant.

First of all, Sidgwick was defending utilitarianism, while for Rawls utilitarianism is the main opponent; Rawls's theory is presented as 'an alternative superior . . . to the dominant utilitarianism of the tradition' (p. viii). (How far Rawls—like common sense?—is himself unconsciously utilitarian is another matter altogether.) Further, although their views about method in moral theory are in one important respect very much alike, in other important ways they are vastly different. They are similar in recognizing the need of moral theory to account for and systematize and coordinate the moral beliefs we start with—what Sidgwick calls common-sense morality and Rawls calls our considered judgements of justice (§9). But this important point of agreement goes along with, and may obscure, two important points of disagreement. It is a fundamental part of Sidgwick's theory that there are necessary moral truths, synthetic a priori principles, that underlie the morality of common sense and are sufficient to establish that morality is rational. Such a view is emphatically not a part of Rawls's theory. 'While some moral principles may seem natural and even obvious,' he says, there are great obstacles to maintaining that they are necessarily true, or even to explaining what is meant by this . . . There is no set of conditions or first principles that can be plausibly claimed to be necessary or definitive of morality and thereby especially suited to carry the burden of justification' (p. 578). A further point of difference is this. Sidgwick is concerned with this world and moral problems as they arise in it. 'As moralists', he says, 'we naturally inquire what ought to be done in the actual world in which we live'.[3] It is Rawls's view that we must determine what perfect just-ice would be if we are to be able to say anything sensible and determinate about justice in this world. Hence the theory he constructs is an 'ideal theory', assuming strict compliance and consequently a well-ordered society—a world very far removed from the actual world in which we live: 'The principles of justice (in lexical order) belong to ideal theory. The per-sons in the original position assume that the principles they acknowledge, whatever they are, will be strictly complied with and followed by everyone. Thus the principles of justice that result are those defining a perfectly just society, given favorable conditions' (p. 151). For Sidgwick, the question is 'What is a man's duty in his present condition?'; consequently 'The inquiry into the morality of an ideal society can . . . be at best but a preliminary investigation, after which the step from the ideal to the actual, in accord-ance with reason, remains to be taken.'[4]

Rawls's differences with utilitarianism are put in a number of different ways, but one most illuminating way is provided by his concept of 'the pri-ority of right' (p. 31). Though Rawls repeatedly explains what he means by this, it is best understood by contrast, and the contrast is nicely provided in the following passage by William James:

Every *de facto* claim creates in so far forth an obligation . . . Take any demand, however slight, which any creature, however weak, may make. Ought it not, for its own sole sake, to be satisfied? If not, prove why not. The only kind of proof you could adduce would be the exhibition of another creature who should make a demand that ran the other way. The only possible reason there can be why any phenomenon ought to exist is that such a phenomenon actually is desired.[5]

Not so here. On Rawls's view, claims and demands must themselves be in accordance with principles of right and justice if they are to be entitled to satisfaction: 'The principles of right, and so of justice, put limits on which satisfactions have value . . . interests requiring the violation of justice have no value. Having no merit in the first place, they cannot override its claims' (p. 31).

This difference defines precisely the distinction between the utilitarian and the non-utilitarian points of view. And in maintaining the priority of the right over the good, and that this priority can be accounted for on prin-ciples that can themselves be accounted for, Rawls is squarely within the Kantian tradition in ethics.

---

[3] Sidgwick, *Methods*, p. 19. [4] *Methods*, pp. 19–20.
[5] William James, 'The Moral Philosopher and the Moral Life', in *The Will to Believe and other Essays* (New York: Longmans, Green, 1897), p. 195. This work is discussed at length in Ch. 11, 'Moral Issues and Social Problems'.

It is possible, however, to accept the priority of right—the Kantian tradition—without at the same time accepting another perhaps even more central feature of Rawls's theory, the extension of the idea of the social contract to the first principles of justice and morality themselves, which places it in the 'contractarian tradition' (p. 32). Though Rawls thinks of them as going together, and writes of them in the same setting, there is no necessary connection between them. The only connection is historical: they both in fact have been opposed to utilitarianism, as utilitarianism has been opposed to each. But they are separable as well as distinguishable. Let us assume, with Rawls, that 'the persons in the original position would reject the utility principle' (p. 29); it does not follow that those who reject the utility principle must also accept the idea of the original position and the idea that the principles of right and justice can be understood as the object of a social contract. Though the idea of the social contract in politics is attractive, it has, I think, no status in establishing the fundamental principles of justice and morality. This, at any rate, is what I shall argue first.

2. SOME PRESUPPOSED PRINCIPLES

'The main idea of justice as fairness' is that 'the principles of justice are those that would be agreed to by rational persons in an original position of equality' (p. 438). 'Since all are similarly situated and no one is able to design principles to favor his particular condition, the principles of justice are the result of a fair agreement or bargain' (p. 12).

Hence justice as fairness is conceived of as a theory that 'generalizes and carries to a higher level of abstraction the traditional conception of the social contract' (p. 3; see also p. 11). There can be no doubt that it does, and the idea is ingenious. But traditional conceptions of the social contract were all attempts to explain the *political* order, to provide the basis of *political* principles and of *political* obligation, while here the conception of a contract, an original agreement in an initial situation, is used as a basis for generating the principles of morality and justice themselves, the very framework of the political order. And the question presents itself whether it makes any literal sense to think of the principles of *morality* as themselves the objects of choice or agreement. For the traditional contract conception has its setting in a framework of moral principles presumed to be already known or accepted. But a contract conception of the principles of morality themselves would at least appear to have no setting in which to operate. And yet it needs one.

It turns out that this required setting is provided by certain principles that Rawls presupposes, apparently unwittingly, as binding and fundamental; principles that are not themselves chosen but are rather the preconditions of any such choice or agreement.

It is presupposed, for one thing, that one is bound by one's agreements. 'Having acknowledged certain principles and a certain way of applying them, we are bound to accept the consequences' (pp. 99–100). But why are we bound to? The principle seems obvious enough, but it also seems obvious that it cannot get its binding power on the basis of a choice or agreement. For it is presupposed by all agreements or 'original choices'. Similarly: 'When we enter an agreement we must be able to honor it even should the worst possibilities prove to be the case. Otherwise we have not acted in good faith' (p. 176). This clearly is a principle *presupposed* in the original position, and not one generated by it. And this point is confirmed by the statement that 'the concept of a contract has a definite role: it suggests the condition of publicity and sets limits upon what can be agreed to' (p. 175). The concept of a contract is one that persons in the original position originally have, and it is one that in turn is governed by principles that are not themselves the object of choice or contract, but rather govern the choices that can legitimately be made. This then is a limitation on the generalizability of the contract model.

What is perplexing about this is that Rawls does not seem to recognize that he is antecedently presupposing the principle that promises or agreements are binding and ought to be kept. For he sets out to derive it, as a principle of morality for individuals (as distinguished from a principle of justice for institutions). Thus he says that 'the principle of fidelity . . . the principle that bona fide promises are to be kept . . . is a moral principle, a consequence of the principle of fairness' (p. 346). Indeed, 'it is but a special case of the principle of fairness applied to the social practice of promising' (p. 344). The principle of fairness, which 'must itself be chosen, since a complete theory of right includes principles for individuals' as well as principles for institutions (p. 108), is the principle that 'a person is under an obligation to do his part as specified by the rules of an institution whenever he has voluntarily accepted the benefits of the scheme or has taken advantage of the opportunities it offers to advance his interests, provided that this institution is just or fair, that is, satisfies the two principles of justice' (pp. 342–3). So 'the principles of justice apply to the practice of promising in the same way that they apply to other institutions' (p. 345). But this cannot be. Apart from the fact that the practice of promising cannot itself be said to be just or unjust, it is a practice and a principle that is already presupposed in the original position, so that the principle that promises ought to be kept is already presupposed in the argument by which it is derived from the principle of fairness. The choice made in the original position constitutes an agreement, which amounts to a promise, and one is supposed to be bound by this agreement—no matter what, in perpetuity.

So the principle that one ought to abide by one's agreements is already presupposed as a principle that persons in the original position will accept and abide by, apart from and prior to any agreement on principles of justice. This helps make sense of the notion of an agreement on the two principles. But this is not the only moral principle presupposed in the initial situation. It is also assumed that 'one has no title to object to the conduct of others that is in accordance with principles one would use in similar circumstances to justify one's actions towards them' (p. 217). Now the principle taken for granted here is what Sidgwick called *the* principle of justice and I have called the generalization principle: what is right (or wrong) for one person must be right (or wrong) for any similar person in similar circumstances. This principle, which I regard as more fundamental, though also more formal, than any Rawls is in a position formally to acknowledge, is presupposed throughout the whole theory. But it is not a principle that can be explained as one that would be chosen or agreed to in the original position, since it is and must be presupposed in any such choice or agreement.

Further, it is said that: 'A principle is ruled out if it would be self-contradictory, or self-defeating, for everyone to act upon it. Similarly, should a principle be reasonable to follow only when others conform to a different one, it is also inadmissible. Principles are to be chosen in view of the consequences of everyone's complying with them' (p. 132). Although this condition appears in a section dealing with 'formal constraints on the concept of right', and is itself listed as a formal constraint on principles rather than a principle itself, it nonetheless takes for granted a principle that I some time ago called the generalization argument. Why is a principle inadmissible that is reasonable to follow only when others conform to a different one? The only ground that can be given for this is that it is unfair, because in violation of the generalization principle. Again, if we ask why 'principles are to be chosen in view of the consequences of everyone's complying with them' we are given no answer, although the position is reaffirmed a few pages later, when it is said that: 'The evaluation of principles must proceed in terms of the general consequences of their public recognition and universal application, it being assumed that they will be complied

with by everyone' (p. 138).[6] It is startling that there is no discussion in the
book of the difficulties that attend any position of this kind—as though the
propositions just quoted are self-evident. They are not. It is true that it is
said that these conditions are 'not justified by definition or the analysis of
concepts, but only by the reasonableness of the theory of which they are a
part' (p. 131), but an appropriate enquiry to this end never appears.

So some principles are presupposed in the original positions and therefore are not themselves chosen. A further perplexity in this connection is
why the principles of rational choice are not themselves chosen. Moral
theory, and consequently the theory of justice, is regarded as part of the
theory of rational choice (pp. 172, 16). But if 'the principles of social
choice, and so the principles of justice, are themselves the object of an original agreement', as they are said to be (p. 28), then why not the principles
of rational choice themselves? Rawls says quite plainly that they are not
(p. 446), but I do not find his reasons very convincing. He believes that
'since each person is free to plan his life as he pleases', there is 'no necessity
for an agreement upon the principles of rational choice', and correspondingly no need for 'unanimity concerning the standards of rationality'
(p. 447). I should not have supposed that there was any connection at all.
Let each person be free to plan his life as he pleases; this gives no one the
freedom to determine by his planning that his plan of life is rational. It is
true that different, even incompatible, plans of life can be rational. But to
determine this we need a concept of and standards for rationality, which
people have not the power to make up as they go along, as they have the
power to make plans.

Be this as it may, the original choice or agreement is to be made, not simply to achieve certain ends, but also in accordance with certain principles,
not themselves chosen. These include the principles of rational choice
themselves, and also the generalization principle (which I still regard as *the*
principle of justice), the generalization argument, and the principle that it
is unfair not to keep an agreement once it is made or to enter into one without the settled determination to keep it. This places definite limitations on
the range and reach of a contract theory for moral principles themselves.

---

[6] Another example: 'The exercise of the right of dissent, like the exercise of rights generally, is
sometimes limited by others having the very same right. Everyone's exercising this right would
have deleterious consequences for all, and some equitable plan is called for' (p. 375). The condition of universality is simply that 'principles must hold for everyone in virtue of their being moral
persons', so that they are 'universal in application' (p. 132) . This is not the same as saying that 'a
principle is ruled out if it would be self-contradictory, or self-defeating, for everyone to act upon
it'.

For these principles, being presupposed in the original choice situation, are not themselves the objects of choice or agreement, nor could they be. This being so, the theory has no explanation for some principles and modes of reasoning fundamental to ethics and on which it must rely.

3. CHOICE AND CONTRACT

So far I have been proceeding as though it is a matter of indifference whether one speaks of a choice or a contract in the original position. Rawls himself speaks indifferently of choosing, adopting, accepting, or agreeing on the principles of justice. But it is not really an indifferent matter. While choice in the original position may be full-bodied or genuine choice, agreement in the original position cannot be full-bodied or genuine agreement. Even if there is room for choice, there is no room for contract.

The reason is that 'bargaining in the usual sense' (p. 139) has no place in the original position, because of the veil of ignorance, and it has no place in the scheme because 'the parties have no basis for' it. Since 'no one knows his position in society nor his natural assets . . . no one is in a position to tailor principles to his advantage . . . they cannot identify themselves either by name or description' (pp. 139–40). But then the concept of agreement, or of contract, turns out to have no literal place either. If there is no basis for bargaining there is no basis for contract. I do not mean that there must in fact be an actual process of bargaining or negotiation for there to be an agreement or contract. I mean only that there must be room for such a process. (It is worth brief notice that another word for 'contract' is 'bargain'.) Since, given the veil of ignorance, 'no one is able to formulate principles especially designed to advance his own cause . . . each is forced to choose for everyone' (p. 140). This may be so. But it is nonsense to speak of each *agreeing* for everyone.

Why, then, is the notion of a contract or an agreement brought in at all? There are a number of related reasons. Rawls is attached to the contract tradition because he thinks that it must be, and can only be, some sort of contract theory that can effectively be pitted against utilitarianism. And the notion of contract plays an explicit and definite role in the theory: 'It suggests the condition of publicity and sets limits upon what can be agreed to. Thus justice as fairness uses the concept of a contract to a greater extent than the discussion so far might suggest' (p. 175). Hence the concept of agreement, or of contract, is brought in to provide a basis for the idea that the parties in the original position have a commitment to abide by their decisions. But from what does this commitment derive? The mere choice of a principle does not commit one to abide by it. Hence the idea of a contract has work to do. If one has agreed, then one is bound. Yet the notion of agreement in the original position, even though it is essential for the theory, has no independent criterion for its application. The operative principle is: 'If there is choice, then there is agreement'; the principles that would be chosen by one person in the original position would, by definition, be agreed to by all:

Since the differences among the parties are unknown to them, and everyone is equally rational and similarly situated, each is convinced by the same arguments. Therefore, we can view the choice in the original position from the standpoint of one person selected at random. If anyone after due reflection prefers a conception of justice to another, then they all do, and a unanimous agreement can be reached. (p. 139)

Such a principle, of course, has no application anywhere else. On the contrary, the assumption that the 'deliberations of any one person are typical of all' (p. 263) is altogether false in actual situations.

Hence the notion of agreement is imported from outside into a context in which it can have no literal sense, and this is done in order to provide a basis for commitment: 'Since the original agreement is final and made in perpetuity, there is no second chance. In view of the serious nature of the possible consequences, the question of the burden of commitment is especially acute' (p. 176). But if one is simply *choosing*, there is no burden of commitment at all. 'Having acknowledged certain principles and a certain way of applying them, we are bound to accept the consequences' (pp. 99–100). One is not normally bound by one's choices. The metaphor of a contract is taken over from contract theory in order to convey the idea, which otherwise would not be conveyed, that persons in the original position are bound to abide by their agreements, that is, their choices. It is *as though* they agreed. Consequently, although 'the original position is a purely hypothetical situation' (p. 120), the original contract is not hypothetical at all—it is metaphorical.

In a later article, replying to objections, Rawls emphasizes that the concept of a contract is essential to the argument, and that the concept of choice is not the only one required. 'The concept of a contract (agreement) is essential', he says, 'to the argument from the strains of commitment [which] has an important place in justice as fairness'.[7] This I take as con-

---

[7] Rawls, 'Reply to Alexander and Musgrave', *Quarterly Journal of Economics*, 88 (November 1974), p. 650; *Papers*, p. 249. This is an important paper, containing a valuable summary by Rawls of the essence of his argument, in the light of a number of comments made up to that time.

firming the reservations I have just expressed. I do not deny that the concept of a contract is essential to Rawls's argument. I deny that he has any literal right to it. Of course the concept of choice is not sufficient, notwithstanding the importance attached to the theory of rational choice. But the concept of a contract, even though it is required, is not literally available. In the context the notion of a contract is only a metaphor. Consequently the commitment or obligation that it is brought in to support is only a metaphor.[8]

If I am right on this, then the principles of justice cannot be regarded as objects of contract. Can they be regarded as objects of choice? Rawls obviously thinks that they can, and that 'in this way conceptions of justice may be explained and justified' (p. 16). On this matter also I have my reservations. If my previous argument is correct, the principles of justice that Rawls sets forth, as fundamental as they are, can be conceived of as chosen only if certain other principles, even more fundamental, are presupposed—including the principle that one has the obligation to abide by one's agreements. The idea is undeniably expressive, but there are further difficulties in the way of conceiving of the principles of justice and morality themselves as, literally, objects of choice—as being what they are because they are chosen, or would be chosen, in the original position. We can choose to act on, or abide by, certain principles, and in that sense can choose the principles on which we act, but we cannot, in the original position or out of it, choose that the principles we act on or choose to act on be right or valid. We cannot, in other words, make them right by our act of choosing. For if the principles of morality could be chosen, and be what they are because they are chosen, then whether an action is right or an institution just would be a matter of choice, and it is not. We can acknowledge that some practice is just, but our acknowledgment is not what makes it so.

Rawls thinks that 'it is clear that the contractarian idea can be extended to the choice of more or less an entire ethical system, that is, to a system including principles for all the virtues and not only for justice' (p. 17). I have my doubts, given these constraints on the concepts of choice and

---

[8] My colleague Jon Moline has argued, in an unpublished paper, 'Perspectives on Principles: A Modified Myth of Er', that 'Rawls' contractarian line is a useless appendage to his theory of justice' on the ground that the veil of ignorance reduces 'the alleged plurality of persons in the original position to an undiscerning sameness'. Although my grounds—that a genuine contract implies the possibility of bargaining—are somewhat different from his, as is my conclusion (since I do not regard the notion of a contract as here useless, but rather unavailable), I am pleased to acknowledge my indebtedness.

contract, whether it even extends to the principles of justice. Perhaps Rawls is prepared to accept, when he says that 'principles of justice can be conceived of as principles that would be chosen by rational persons' (p. 16), that they can be conceived of as chosen only in some metaphorical sense, and perhaps this is all that he means. After all, he does not say that they *are chosen* or *were chosen*. He says that they can be *conceived of* as chosen. But I do not think so. Too much rests on the concepts of choice and contract for them to be literally conceived of as metaphorical. I think that what Rawls means when he says that they 'can be conceived of' as objects of choice is only that the choice is hypothetical. Thus he says: 'The undertakings referred to are purely hypothetical' (p. 16). But if this idea is metaphorical it cannot be hypothetical.

There is no denying the force in this idea. It provides an almost automatic solution to the problem of stability (§76); a conception of justice that would be accepted by rational persons in suitable conditions for making such determinations is one that would tend to be regarded as acceptable, since it would tend to 'engender in human beings the requisite desire to act upon it' (p. 455). Thus, to argue from the outset that the true principles of justice are the ones that would be accepted under suitable conditions by persons in a position to know what they are accepting is to give them a measure of initial acceptability.[9] It would certainly be hard lines if the true principles of morality and justice were principles that no one could abide by in the ordinary circumstances of life. Yet we have to admit, I think, that this *might* be so, and that the true principles of justice and morality might not be ones that we can expect many people to abide by; by itself this would not diminish their status as standards. It would be better if a conception of justice were stable and meshed with human psychology and the conditions of human life, but if it is not that is not a conclusive point against it. Further, there is a serious question whether a conception of justice that would be accepted, and therefore acceptable, in the original position, is thereby one that would be accepted in the actual conditions of life. I do not mean to trade here on the idea that an agreement (so called) in the original position is hypothetical (so to speak), which has led some to question how this choice or agreement can be binding on persons in everyday life, who were

---

[9] Compare the following passage from an essay by George W. Ball on a matter dealing with international relations: 'A world order enforced by the common support and action of major world powers—which is, in essence, the formula for peacekeeping contemplated by the United Nations Charter—can operate effectively only if it rests on a body of rules to which these nations agree' ('The Disenchantment with Kissinger', *Saturday Review*, 12 June 1976, p. 20).

never involved in the agreement.[10] The question I am raising is whether the conditions of human life correspond in the right way to the conditions imposed on the original position. For the conditions imposed on the original position are hard in some ways even to imagine. It is not impossible, but it is certainly difficult, to imagine being in a situation in which we (meaning all of us) have knowledge of the laws of nature, economics, and psychology, yet are ignorant of who we are, of our interests and inclinations, and of the historical conditions in which we live. And the question suggested by this difficulty relates to the wider question, to which I turn in due course, of the applicability of Rawls's special conception of justice, formulated for ideal theory, to the practices of everyday life—in other words, to the applications of justice.

4. FURTHER PRESUPPOSITIONS—MAXIMIZATION AND PRIMARY GOODS

I have argued that justice as fairness presupposes certain fundamental principles that cannot be accounted for on the perspective it provides, and that cannot literally be objects of choice or agreement. What we have now to notice is that there are other presuppositions of a substantive nature that a theory of first principles should rather provide a basis for.

Notice, for example, the conception of basic liberties introduced in connection with the first principle of justice, the principle of equal liberty:[11]

---

[10] As, for example, in the following passage: 'It seems obvious that hypothetical contracts agreed to by hypothetical individuals in a hypothetical situation cannot bind me. How could they, when what I myself *would* have done (but did not) cannot bind me. *Had* a particular student asked me to direct his research, I might have promised him to do so; given that I made no such promise, however, I am now under no obligation to him. Therefore, if I am not bound by a hypothetical contract that I myself would have made, I am surely not bound by a hypothetical contract that certain mythical creatures make' (Hans Oberdiek, 'Review of Rawls: A Theory of Justice', *New York University Law Review*, 47 (November 1972), p. 1022). Rawls, as so often happens, anticipates this question in the text, when he says: 'It is natural to ask why, if this agreement is never actually entered into, we should take any interest in these principles, moral or otherwise. The answer is that the conditions embodied in the description of the original position are ones that we do in fact accept' (p. 21). I take this to mean that, given that we do in fact accept the conditions embodied in the original position, we accept the principles that 'would be agreed on in the original position' as the principles to abide by. So it is not a matter of being bound by a contract made by somebody else, but of being bound by principles that we would, if we thought about the matter carefully enough, regard as binding.

[11] In its provisional formulation: 'Each person is to have an equal right to the most extensive basic liberty compatible with a similar liberty for others' (p. 60).

The basic liberties of citizens are, roughly speaking, political liberty (the right to vote and to be eligible for public office) together with freedom of speech and assembly; liberty of conscience and freedom of thought; freedom of the person along with the right to hold (personal) property; and freedom from arbitrary arrest and seizure as defined by the concept of the rule of law. These liberties are all required to be equal by the first principle, since citizens of a just society are to have the same basic rights. (p. 61)

We may grant that this list is, in its setting, rough and provisional. It is also in substance admirable. But I cannot forbear remarking that it reads something like a manifesto of the American Civil Liberties Union. One would expect a book on first principles to provide a basis for such claims, not simply to incorporate them without question. These are, of course, the values—the liberties—to which we in this society pay lip-service, the values of liberal democratic society. No doubt Rawls takes the judgements that these are the basic liberties of citizenship, and that they should be equal, as among the considered judgements of justice that a theory of justice must square with. But again, a theory of first principles should go further than just this. It should, one would think, at least search for some basis.

I emphasize this because the list is biased, in two ways. It is, first, set out as the liberties of citizens. But 'citizen' is a political term, whereas 'person' is a moral term, and the principle of equal liberty is not restricted to *citizens*; it applies to all *persons*. Second, the rights mentioned are all *against government*. There is nothing said about other liberties and rights which are just as basic, and which governments are instituted to protect, such as the right to freedom from assault or other interference from others.

We would seem to have here the manifestation of an unconscious bias rather than any conscious principle, but this becomes especially important in connection with Rawls's striking and intriguing notion of primary goods, which are defined as 'things which it is supposed a rational man wants whatever else he wants' (p. 92), or 'things that every rational man is presumed to want' (p. 62). 'The primary social goods', Rawls claims, 'are rights and liberties, opportunities and powers, income and wealth' (p. 92). (There are other primary goods, such as 'health and vigor, intelligence and imagination', which are *natural* as distinct from *social* primary goods; and self-respect, which is regarded as central (p. 62).) But what is the evidence that these are things that a rational person must be supposed to want if he or she wants anything at all? It is, in fact, just assumed. And the assumption rings plausible for us because it expresses the values of a consumer-oriented society. It is for this reason, I think, that duties and responsibilities, burdens and sacrifices, are never thought of as primary goods. Assuming, with Rawls, that 'the good is the satisfaction of rational desire' (p. 93), one can have a rational desire for responsibilities and burdens, as well as, on occasion, relief from them. It is surely not obviously irrational to want to have duties and responsibilities, if one wants anything at all. And if wanting primary goods 'is part of being rational' (p. 253), then duties and responsibilities must be primary goods.

Rawls goes on to say, further, about primary goods, that: 'Whatever one's system of ends, primary goods are necessary means. Greater intelligence, wealth and opportunity, for example, allow a person to achieve ends he could not rationally contemplate otherwise' (p. 93).[12] This is generally so, but not always, and really should not be assumed in this wholesale fashion. The assumption reflects further, in my estimation, the influence on Rawls's thinking of classical political economy and the derived assumptions of utility theory. No doubt greater intelligence, wealth, and opportunity are ordinarily valuable as means to the achievement of predetermined ends, but greater intelligence may prevent me from having ends I might otherwise have, and greater wealth may cause me not to strive as hard as I otherwise might and consequently not to develop talents I otherwise might develop. So they can have effects—adverse effects—on both my ends and my means.

Rawls operates with a maximizing assumption: Primary goods, whatever they are, are things it is rational to want more of rather than less. Thus: 'While the persons in the original position do not know their conception of the good, they do know, I assume, that they prefer more rather than less primary goods. And this information is sufficient for them to know how to advance their interests in the initial situation' (p. 93). The last sentence explains why the assumption is made. Even with the severe restrictions on particular knowledge imposed by the veil of ignorance, the parties in the original position can know what they want and what function of them would advance their interests. But, though the assumption seems plausible as well as minimal, I do not think it withstands scrutiny. The whole tenor and tendency of this conception is hedonistic rather than stoic. To want more wealth than one needs is not a sign of rationality, but of greed, and a rational person would recognize that too much of a good thing can bring with it other things that one would not want—as with Midas, who got more wealth than, as the saying goes, he bargained for. I think the only

---

[12] There is some incidental confusion here. Self-respect, which is central ('the most important primary good' (p. 440)) 'is necessary if they are to pursue their conception of the good with zest and to delight in its fulfillment' (p. 178). But this makes it, like health, necessary as a condition, not as a means.

blanket assumption we are entitled to make on this matter is that it is rational to want a certain amount, it is rational to want a sufficient amount,
sometimes it is rational to prefer more rather than less, and sometimes it is
rational to prefer less rather than more. The principles of arithmetic have
no application to goods, not because goods are hard to quantify, but
because they have a different logic, and growth and development in this
context is not a simple matter of increased quantity. Thus, in order to know
whether it is genuinely rational to want more than a certain minimal level
of some primary good one would have to know what that good is and
something of the circumstances.

There is—in addition to duties and responsibilities—another important
set of primary goods that for some reason also goes unmentioned in
Rawls's account. I refer to satisfying work and, a closely related value, a
matching of interests and abilities. A well-ordered society, whatever else it
is,[13] is one that would provide the opportunity for such challenge and ful-
filment to all its citizens and would place a proper value on this, perhaps
the most important of social primary goods, a nearly essential condition
for self-respect and an essential condition for social order. Rawls supposes
that in a free-market economy 'citizens have a free choice of careers and
occupations' (p. 272), but the forces that operate in a market system
(though they may make for efficiency, and may, all things considered, be as
just as is feasible) are often felt as coercive, and as restrictions on freedom.
Ideally, the determinant of occupation would be talent and interest; and
market factors, as they have actually been experienced, are no more reliable
in arranging the requisite matching than the directives of an efficient 'com-
mand society' (p. 272).[14] Remember, a theory of justice is intended to be
an ideal theory, which is to present a 'conception of a just society that we
are to achieve if we can' (p. 246), and 'it is ideal theory which is fundamental' (p. 241).

Rawls does have a concept of 'meaningful work', which, though it goes
undefined, is put to work at least once: 'It is a mistake to believe that a just

---

[13] A well-ordered society is one 'in which everyone accepts and knows that the others accept
the same principles of justice, and the basic social institutions satisfy and are known to satisfy
these principles' (p. 454).

[14] I am not here denying anything of importance that Pawls says about a free-market system.
In particular, I regard his observation that there is no necessary connection between a free-
market system and private ownership of the means of production (p. 271) (whether it is original
or not I do not know) as both sound and profound. A market arrangement may have the advantage of efficiency, as Rawls claims, and may also, all things in actuality considered, be the most
equitable available. But it is not as likely to bring about a match of interests and abilities as a system directed to that end, supposing one could be devised that would work.

and good society must wait upon a high material standard of life. What men want is meaningful work in free association with others, these associations regulating their relations to one another within a framework of just basic institutions. To achieve this state of things great wealth is not necessary. In fact, beyond some point it is more likely to be a positive hindrance, a meaningless distraction at best if not a temptation to indulgence and emptiness' (p. 290). These last remarks would appear to agree with my previous point about wealth, summed up in the allusion to that classical miser Midas. But the emphasis is all off, and I cannot avoid the suspicion that on this matter at any rate Rawls is saying one thing in one context and something else in another. The difference principle, both before and after all, 'is, strictly speaking, a maximizing principle' (p. 79).[15] Though there

---

[15] I should remind you that the Difference Principle, the first part of the second principle, states that social and economic inequalities are to be arranged so as to be to the benefit of the least advantaged—optimally, so as to be to the advantage of all, but 'the advantage of the least advantaged' is Rawls's essential criterion. I am impelled to observe that there is some ambiguity and confusion about it. In A *Theory of Justice* the Difference Principle is distinct from, though associated with, the maximin rule, which 'tells us to rank alternatives by their worst possible outcomes: we are to adopt the alternative the worst outcome of which is superior to the worst outcomes of the others' (pp. 152–3). The maximin rule is brought in as part of the (deductive) argument for the principles of justice. Thus it is said that 'it is useful as a heuristic device to think of the two principles as the maximin solution to the problem of social justice. There is an analogy between the two principles and the maximin rule for choice under uncertainty' (p. 152). Clearly on this account there is a distinction between the maximin rule and the difference principle, as there is between the maximin rule and the two principles taken together. There is only 'an analogy' between them. Yet in his 'Reply to Alexander and Musgrave' (cited *supra*, n. 7), Rawls throughout equates the first part of the second principle to 'the maximin criterion' (pp. 639, 641, 642; *Papers*, pp. 238, 240, 241). Why? Well, this paper was written for economists. There is some suggestion that the difference principle (now renamed the maximin *criterion*) is the fundamental feature of the conception of justice. Rawls actually says that 'in one form or another the difference principle is basic throughout' (p. 83). And the general conception of justice ('All social primary goods . . . are to be distributed equally unless an unequal distribution of any or all of these goods is to the advantage of the least favored' (303; also 62, 83)) is just a generalized form of the difference principle, a point made explicit on p. 83: 'the general conception is simply the difference principle applied to all primary goods including liberty and opportunity and so no longer constrained by other parts of the special conception'. One might be led to infer from all this that the maximin *rule* is basic throughout. But one shouldn't. It is the maximin *criterion*, which is equivalent to the difference principle, that is basic throughout. Unfortunately, the expression 'the difference principle' is never actually defined in the book. The term first appears in the table on p. 65, and Rawls thereafter proceeds as though it is obvious what the expression refers to (see Rawls, 'Some Reasons for the Maximin Criterion', *American Economic Review, Papers and Proceedings*, 44 (May 1974), pp. 141–6; *Papers*, ch. 11). In his discussion of the 'thin theory of the good' Rawls says: 'Rational individuals, whatever else they want, desire certain things as prerequisites for carrying out their plan of life. Other things equal, they prefer a wider to a narrower liberty and opportunity, and a greater rather than a smaller share of wealth and income' (p. 396). The 'other things equal' clause here would seem to suggest some modification of the maximization assumption. But just what modification is it, and just what function does it serve? One might as well say 'they prefer just the right amount to too much'. My conjecture is that the 'other things equal' clause here indicates only some hesitation. Again, in his discussion

are a few hints to the contrary, Rawls's developed view on this matter would appear to be the one expressed in the following passage:

The persons in the original position try to acknowledge principles which advance their system of ends *as far as possible*. They do this by attempting to win for themselves *the highest index of primary social* goods, since this enables them to promote their conception of the good most effectively whatever it turns out to be ... Put in terms of a game, we might say: *they strive for as high an absolute score as possible*. (p. 144; italics added)

Very late in the book, though perhaps not in the writing of it, Rawls says: 'Let us suppose ... that happiness (defined in terms of agreeable feeling) is the sole good. Then, as even intuitionists concede, it is at least a prima facie principle of right to maximize happiness' (p. 562). This indicates that Rawls regards it as at least a prima-facie principle of right to maximize good. I do not, and I have yet to see the warrant for this claim. Perhaps it can be explained in other ways: the context is one in which Rawls is bringing out the difference between the perspective provided by justice as fairness and that involved in any teleological or 'dominant-end' conception. But to me it presents itself as another vestige of unconscious utilitarianism.

Nothing that I have said is intended to diminish the importance or the value of the notion of primary goods. The idea is ingenious, and plays a role (especially in connection with what Rawls calls the thin theory of the good (pp. 396, 433–4)) in preserving and sustaining the priority of the right over the good. But Rawls never really questions his standard list of primary goods. He relies on it, over and over, as canonical, and seems to 'take [it] as established' (p. 434) for this reason alone. 'Their claims', he thinks, 'seem evident enough' (p. 434), but I do not think so, and I take this as further supporting my contention that Rawls is making certain assumptions of principle and of substance that his theory, on the contractual terms it provides, cannot account for.

---

of the rationality of the parties in the original position, Rawls says: 'Of course, it may turn out, once the veil of ignorance is removed, that some of them for religious or other reasons may not, in fact, want more of these goods. But from the standpoint of the original position, it is rational for the parties to suppose that they do want a larger share, since in any case they are not compelled to accept more if they do not wish to, nor does a person suffer from a greater liberty' (p. 143). This last point is true of a rational person, but outside of the original position the assumption of rationality cannot be sustained, and many persons suffer from a greater liberty than they can manage. Thus, in view of what I said before, I do not think that this point establishes that it is rational for the parties to suppose that they want a larger share—no matter what the goods are.

5. DESERT AND REDRESS

In addition to advancing a deductive argument, intended to show that the two principles of justice are the principles that would be accepted in the original position, Rawls also argues that these principles are supported 'by a comparison with our considered judgments of justice' (p. 152). This is in line with his important methodological point that our principles and consequently our theory of justice must match our considered judgements of justice in reflective equilibrium (pp. 19–20; §9). I regard his view on this methodological point as sound both in principle and detail; and it has not, I think, been sufficiently appreciated, by those who do not think so, that the considered judgements—akin to facts—against which we test our principles—theory—are not necessarily particular judgements only, nor are they necessarily more concrete and particular than the principles devised to account for them.[16] Although such 'facts' may be particular judgements about particular cases, they may also be abstract and general. Thus we must note that general principles can be themselves 'fixed points' of our considered judgements—'ones that we seem unwilling to revise under any foreseeable circumstances' (p. 318)—for among our considered judgements of justice are some to the effect that a certain general principle holds. Now, one such principle is the principle of desert, that it is right and proper that persons be happy in accordance with virtue, and that there are persons who deserve to suffer for what they have done. This sort of notion is sometimes referred to as poetic justice, and it is, I think, so referred to because it occurs so rarely in this imperfect world. Nonetheless, it is a common-sense moral principle, the exact meaning and scope of which have yet to be determined.

But, although the principle of desert is a common-sense principle, it is rejected by justice as fairness, on the ground that it 'would not be chosen in the original position' (p. 310). This has a certain incidental interest, for either the principle of desert is not a fixed point in our constellation of considered judgements or, even though it is, justice as fairness rejects it. This then shows how Rawls's methodology can lead him to modify judgements

[16] That considered judgements can be of any level of generality is made explicit by Rawls in his Presidential Address, 'The Independence of Moral Theory', *Proceedings and Addresses of the American Philosophical Association, 1974–5*, xlviii. 8: 'People have considered judgments at all levels of generality, from those about particular situations and institutions up through broad standards and first principles to formal and abstract conditions on moral conceptions' (repr. in *Papers*, p. 289).

that he had to begin with, and is not simply a device for sanctifying moral opinions that he wants to hold on to independently of the theory. But the situation is troublesome. For I find that the principle of desert is one of the fixed points in my set of considered moral judgements, and I also find it a basic principle of common sense (as does Rawls). Therefore the arguments against it would in my estimation have to be overwhelmingly powerful to carry conviction, and I do not find that Rawls's arguments against it have anywhere near this kind of power. His arguments against it presuppose ideal theory, strict compliance, and a well-ordered society (p. 312), and of course 'in this case we may assume that everyone is of equal moral worth' (p. 312). Clearly in ideal theory one person will have no greater moral worth, no greater desert, than another. But in the world in which we actually live persons do manifest different degrees of moral worth and do deserve different things. This raises again the question of the relevance of justice as fairness to the actual world in which we live. It may be admitted that the principle of desert is not fitted to be a 'first principle of distributive justice', since 'it cannot be introduced until after the principles of justice and of natural duty and obligation have been acknowledged' (p. 312). It may also be admitted that it is basically a principle of retributive rather than of distributive justice (p. 315). But it does not follow that it is false or unacceptable or to be rejected, and one is entitled to be wary of any theory that would simply reject it out of hand.

It is noteworthy that although the principle and the notion of desert are in this way criticized and rejected, nonetheless desert plays a role in connection with another principle that Rawls finds more acceptable, which he calls the principle of redress. This is 'the principle that undeserved inequalities call for redress; and since inequalities of birth and natural endowment are undeserved, these inequalities are to be somehow compensated for' (p. 100). There would be no point in this principle if deserved inequalities also called for redress, because then all inequalities would; so the statement of this principle presupposes that the concept of desert can be applied and make sense. Rawls says that the principle of redress is plausible 'only as a prima facie principle, one that is to be weighed in the balance with others . . . But whatever other principles we hold, the claims of redress are to be taken into account. It is thought [we are not told by whom; presumably this signifies its status as a fixed point in our constellation of considered judgements] to represent one of the elements in our conception of justice' (p. 101). I should have thought that precisely similar things would be true of the principle of desert. The difference appears to be that desert or moral worth can find no place in the standpoint defined by the original position, and in a conception that emphasizes ideal theory, strict compliance, and a well-ordered society.

In addition to presupposing the prima-facie soundness of the principle of redress, Rawls takes for granted certain limits to the concept of justice, determined by what he calls natural facts. Thus:

> The natural distribution [of talents and circumstances] is neither just nor unjust; nor is it unjust that men are born into society at some particular position. These are simply natural facts. What is just and unjust is the way that institutions deal with these facts. (p. 102)

I am not about to disagree with this judgement. I call attention to it only as something taken for granted, as a considered judgement of justice—or perhaps as a judgement of the limits of justice—which provides part of the background of the theory, one of its basic presuppositions, and not one that the theory itself can establish or account for. And it is important to notice that it is not a judgement shared by all. These may be natural facts, but it is not itself a natural fact that natural facts are not themselves either just or unjust. It is a moral judgement, and it must be recognized that it is a moral judgement that is as subject to change and reconsideration as any other, just as what is unalterable or not within our power to change is subject to change, through developments in technology, along with our estimates of them as so placed. (It may not at the moment be within the power of human beings to determine the talents and capacities of the newborn, but it may someday be, and that day may not be far off.) The person who is miserably ill all his life may well regard this as unfair or unjust. Similarly for the person who loses a parent or a child at an early age. It may be admitted that 'no one deserves his greater natural capacity nor merits a more favorable starting place in society' (p. 102). But by the same token no one deserves the misfortune of being ill or disfigured or disabled, and one may very well regard these misfortunes as injustices. If there are natural duties (§19), along with natural facts and natural primary goods, why can there not be natural injustices? No matter how well ordered the society, the disadvantages imposed by disabilities will be *felt* as injustices, and will be a source of dissatisfaction.[17]

---

[17] Mr Henry Chester, in Somerset Maugham's story 'Sanatorium', a decent, considerate, agreeable man, who gets tuberculosis in the prime of life, for no reason that he can understand, fits this case exactly—or almost exactly: 'It seemed to him a cruel and unjust trick that fate had played upon him. He could have understood it if he had led a wild life, if he had drunk too much, played around with women or kept late hours. He would have deserved it then. But he had done none of these things. It was monstrously unfair . . . "I'm going to die, and God damn it, I don't want to die. Why should I? It's not fair."' This is how he felt. It made him and those around

Rawls's general view on this matter is that if a situation is unalterable, then there can be no question of its justice or injustice:

It is a natural fact that generations are spread out in time and actual exchanges between them take place only in one direction. We can do something for posterity but it can do nothing for us. The situation is unalterable, and so the question of justice does not arise. What is just or unjust is how institutions deal with natural limitations and the way they are set up to take advantage of historical possibilities. (p. 291)

But what is puzzling is how this conception would be supported if challenged. If 'the criteria for justice between generations are those that would be chosen in the original positions' (p. 292), then why are not the criteria for the limits of justice? It appears that no *arguments* can be given for this position, since 'in a contract theory arguments are made from the point of view of the original position' (p. 104), and, unless I have completely misunderstood Rawls on this matter, arguments on *this* matter cannot be given from the point of view of the original position. So such conceptions are part of the framework of the theory, of its fundamental presuppositions, for which it cannot officially offer support.

Withal, a question naturally arises about the justice of the principle of redress itself. 'The principle holds that in order to treat all persons equally, to provide genuine equality of opportunity, society must give more attention to those with fewer native assets and to those born into the less favorable social positions. The idea is to redress the bias of contingencies in the direction of equality' (pp. 100–1). I think this is simply wrong. What requires redress, if anything does, is not natural inequalities, but *inequities*, and the fact of inequalities is not by itself an adequate guide to inequities. A person born with a cheerful disposition who possesses an innate capacity

---

him—especially his wife—miserable. Rawls alludes to such a situation, in one of his rare instances of irony, when he denies that the refusal to 'acquiesce in injustice is on a par with being unable to accept death' (p. 102). But it may be. It depends on how young and active one is, and how much unhappiness is caused by the injustice. (Suppose this is reworded just a bit. Suppose someone is *able* to accept death, but *refuses* to?) Henry Chester has a change of heart at the end: 'I don't mind dying any more. I don't think death's very important, not so important as love. And I want you to live and be happy. I don't grudge you anything any more and I don't resent anything. I'm glad now it's me that must die and not you. I wish for you everything that's good in the world. I love you.' But this shows only that he had a change of heart, and saw how unjustly he had been treating his wife. It does not show that he had not been treated unjustly by fate. And I do not regard this point as merely picturesque. I think he had been. There are those whom fate has treated miserably, but not unjustly. (To be sure, it could be argued, fairly plausibly, that to say that fate or life has treated one unjustly is literally senseless, as committing a category mistake. But this point, to be sustained, requires a theory as to the scope and limits of the concept of justice.)

to enjoy life is beyond a doubt better off, and will live a more satisfying life, than one born, like Jaques, with a penchant to gloom and melancholy, or one like Malvolio, who is 'sick of self-love' and 'tastes with a distempered appetite'. These are natural inequalities, they are no doubt not deserved—supposing that the idea of desert has any application here—but I can think of no reason whatever why such inequalities should be compensated for. And if the claim that they should be is implied in 'an egalitarian conception of justice' (p. 100), as Rawls seems to suggest, then I can only think that such a conception is mistaken.

6. APPLICATIONS—JUDGEMENTS OF JUSTICE

Now we must turn to the 'pressing and urgent matters . . . the things . . . we are faced with in everyday life' (p. 9). What application do the principles of justice, or the concepts and methods by which they were generated, have to such problems?

The principles of justice are not themselves applicable to individual situations or specific moral problems. They apply only to institutions, or the basic structure of society.[18] Furthermore, Rawls's special conception of justice (the two principles of justice in priority order) is meant to apply only in the imagined and artificial situation of ideal theory, hence to the basic structure of ideal society. 'Strict compliance is one of the stipulations of the original position' (p. 245). For Rawls has set out to determine what perfect justice would be, or what 'a perfectly just society would be like' (p. 8). And he has done this because he has taken it for granted that ideal theory is 'the fundamental part of the theory of justice' and also 'essential for the nonideal part' (p. 391).

How is it essential and in this way fundamental? Rawls suggests two ways: The principles of justice that belong to ideal theory 'set up an aim to guide the course of social reform' (p. 245). And 'the ideal part presents a conception of a just society that we are to achieve if we can. Existing institutions are to be judged in the light of this conception and held to be unjust to the extent that they depart from it without sufficient reason' (p. 246).

---

[18] The following passage makes this explicit: 'Neither principle applies to distributions of particular goods to particular individuals who may be identified by their proper names. The situation where someone is considering how to allocate certain commodities to needy persons who are known to him is not within the scope of the principles. They are meant to regulate basic institutional arrangements' (p. 64).

I find both these ideas implausible. An 'aim to guide the course of social reform' is relevant only if it is attainable, and the sort of arrangement envisaged in ideal theory, though it is constructible, is not really attainable. For the same reason, judging 'existing institutions . . . in the light of this conception' does not strike me as feasible. Since no existing institution exists in a society that is well ordered, in the sense required, and in which there is strict compliance, they all fall short, and it would follow that all existing institutions are unjust. This is not what is wanted, but it is, on these assumptions, what we must get. For how are approximations to an unattainable ideal to be gauged?

Rawls has concentrated on principles for the basic structure because he regards the problems this presents as more important, more fundamental, and more tractable: 'It is too much to suppose that there exists for all or even most moral problems a reasonable solution. Perhaps only a few can be satisfactorily answered. In any case social wisdom consists in framing institutions so that intractable difficulties do not often arise' (pp. 89–90). This is very acute. Nonetheless, even though the principles of justice do not apply directly to individual situations, there are some passages in the book that suggest that the original position may be regarded as providing a perspective from which individual cases can be viewed and particular problems resolved. Thus it is said that 'one or more persons can at any time enter this position, or perhaps, better, simulate the deliberations of this hypothetical situation, simply by reasoning in accordance with the appropriate restrictions' (p. 138). Again: 'it is important that the original position be interpreted so that one can at any time adopt its perspective' (p. 139). This suggests that the original position may not be simply and solely what it was introduced as, a hypothetical situation for determining the basic principles for regulating the social order, but may also be a perspective that we can adopt, or simulate, at any time to resolve or settle concrete questions of conduct. And this suggestion is borne out by the following passage:

When we try to simulate the original position in everyday life, that is, when we try to conduct ourselves in moral argument as its constraints require, we will presumably find that our deliberations and judgments are influenced by our special inclinations and attitudes. Surely it will prove difficult to correct for our various propensities and aversions in striving to adhere to the conditions of this idealized situation. But none of this affects the contention that in the original position rational persons so characterized would make a certain decision. This proposition belongs to the theory of justice. *It is another question how well human beings can assume this role in regulating their practical reasoning.* (p. 147; italics added)

Here the suggestion is unmistakable that it is possible in everyday life to simulate the original position in dealing with practical questions or engaging in practical reasoning about concrete questions of conduct; and that, so far as we can, we ought to, since the constraints of the original position are those required for moral argument to be moral and rational. We are not informed just how this is to be done, and in fact it is suggested that this is another question. So far as I have been able to determine, it is a question that is never again taken up. Still, it is a point that is worthy of consideration, whether it is elaborated in the book or not.

There surely are difficulties in the way of applying the perspective of the original position to the solution of concrete problems of conduct. One is that, as Rawls himself suggests, it is extraordinarily hard to simulate an ignorance one doesn't have, especially when one's own interests and attitudes are concerned. Another is that it is by no means obvious that whether one would be benefited or harmed by some line of conduct—something that behind the veil of ignorance one wouldn't know, and therefore something that on this position one shouldn't know—is irrelevant for determining its morality. But a third difficulty is that, to bring back a point from before, behind the veil of ignorance 'the parties have no basis for bargaining in the usual sense' (p. 139). It would be more accurate to say that they have no basis for bargaining in any sense. But this then would preclude bargaining, negotiation, as a method of settling moral disputes. It is, of course, conventional to think this, but I think unwise. It should be recognized that, provided the situations of the contending parties are not too unequal, negotiation is a form of pure procedural justice (p. 86),[19] surely as fair and as reasonable as gambling. After all, whether two persons in a dispute resort to a flip of a coin to settle it is itself subject to negotiation.

Still in all, as an interpretation of what Rawls is actually saying about the original position, the suggestion I have just developed is not supported by any overwhelming weight of evidence, and may not be supported by any evidence at all. It seems more likely that Rawls's considered view is simply that the original position can be used to generate principles, which in turn will be used to settle problems and disputes. After the principles for the basic structure have been determined, the parties in the original position

[19] Pure procedural justice is defined as follows: 'pure procedural justice obtains when there is no independent criterion for the right result: instead there is a correct or fair procedure such that the outcome is likewise correct or fair, whatever it is, provided that the procedure has actually been followed ... A distinctive feature of pure procedural justice is that the procedure for determining the just result must actually be carried out; for in these cases there is no independent criterion by reference to which a definite outcome can be known to be just ... A fair procedure translates its fairness to the outcome only when it is actually carried out' (p. 86).

are to acknowledge principles for individuals—for determining the duties and obligations of individual persons—in order 'to establish a complete conception of right' (p. 110). 'Once the full set of principles, a complete conception of right, is on hand, we can simply forget about the conception of original position and apply these principles as we would any others' (p. 116). This suggests that the original position is not intended to be a perspective for solving problems and settling disputes in actual concrete cases, but is to be used only for generating the principles for settling them. For once the rules are on hand, the veil of ignorance must be completely lifted or they could not be applied (p. 199): 'In judgments of justice . . . at the judicial and administrative stage . . . all restrictions on information are dropped, and particular cases are to be decided in view of all the relevant facts' (p. 499). On the other hand, even with a 'full set of principles on hand' there will be problems of conduct that cannot be settled merely by the application of a principle, largely because the problems are themselves generated by conflicts or obscurities of principle. Rawls himself raises the question: 'How are these duties to be balanced when they come into con-flict . . . ?', and points out that 'there are no obvious rules for settling these questions' (p. 339). He does 'not know how this problem is to be settled, or even whether a systematic solution formulating useful and practicable rules is possible. It would seem that the theory for the basic structure is actually simpler' (pp. 339–40). This echoes the idea, expressed earlier, that few if any moral problems can be satisfactorily settled, so the main prob-lem is to frame institutions in such a way that intractable problems do not arise (pp. 89–90). This supposes, we may note incidentally, that intractable problems arise basically from faults of institutions and not from traits of human nature, and we may justifiably wonder if that is true.

In any case, the question 'whether a systematic solution formulating useful and practicable rules is possible' is a question of ethics into which the book does not delve. The question whether 'the contractarian idea can be extended to the choice of . . . an entire ethical system' (under the name 'rightness as fairness'), as Rawls had earlier alleged (p. 17), is thus left open. Let us turn, then, from questions of casuistry to questions of institutional ethics, and consider the question of whether some institution is just. Now what we have to notice right away is that whenever we ask such a question about an actual institution we are in partial-compliance theory. The sup-position on which 'the principles of justice are chosen' (p. 245), namely that they will be strictly complied with, is not operative. How, then, can the principles of justice apply in these circumstances, so different from the ones in which they were adopted?

I must emphasize that the question is not, as is suggested at one point, 'whether and in what circumstances unjust arrangements are to be tolerated' (p. 351). The question is: Are these arrangements (which would be unjust under ideal circumstances) just or unjust (in these circumstances)? And the question whether unjust arrangements are to be tolerated is not itself an institutional question. It is a question of individual (or collective) conduct.

In his own discussion of such matters (or of the related though not identical question whether there is any duty to obey an unjust law), Rawls makes the crucial assumption that 'the context is one of a state of near justice, that is, one in which the basic structure of society is nearly just, making due allowance for what it is reasonable to expect in the circumstances' (p. 351).[20] It is not fully clear to me what a state of near justice implies, or how we are unambiguously to determine whether a situation is one of near justice or far, and I am afraid that actual disputes on institutional matters will quickly bog down in this detail. But, apart from this—which is really a question of individual and not of institutional ethics—I have become convinced, and the study of this work has helped convince me, that the determination of whether or not some institution or social order is just cannot, for the most part, be made in isolation and abstraction. One must consider it in its setting and against its historical background, and in the light of the customs and traditions that are part of the life of the community in which the institution operates.

Even if we suppose that as an account of what perfect justice would be Rawls's account is perfectly sound, it still would not provide a touchstone for automatically 'appraising institutions and for guiding the overall direction of social change' (p. 263).[21] Judgements of justice, it would appear,

---

[20] A nearly just society is defined a little later as 'one that is well-ordered for the most part but in which some serious violations of justice nevertheless occur . . . I assume that a state of near justice requires a democratic regime' (p. 363). This last remark is worth pondering. For one in Iraq, say, or Afghanistan or North Korea, what light is thrown on what ought to be done by Rawls's special conception of justice?

[21] Rawls maintains that the two principles 'define an ideal basic structure . . . toward which the course of reform should evolve' (p. 261). In this respect his view is remarkably like that of Mill, in *Representative Government*, who advances a theory of the levels of civilization, or the necessary stages of social progress, which, I suspect, Rawls is in large part echoing. Says Mill: 'Even personal slavery, by giving a commencement to industrial life . . . may accelerate the transition to a better freedom than that of fighting and rapine. It is almost needless to say that this excuse for slavery is only available in a very early state of society . . . The Egyptian hierarchy, the paternal despotism of China, were very fit instruments for carrying those nations up to the point of civilization which they attained . . . An ideal must be constructed of the form of government most eligible in itself . . . It would then be possible to construct a theorem of the circumstances in which that form of government may wisely be introduced; and also to judge, in cases in which it had better not be introduced, what inferior forms of polity will best carry those communities through

must be mediated by information about the setting and antecedent arrangements. Rawls himself suggests this when he says: 'A distribution cannot be judged in isolation from the system of which it is the outcome or from what individuals have done in good faith in the light of established expectations. If it is asked in the abstract whether one distribution of a given stock of things to definite individuals with known desires and preferences is better than another, then there is simply no answer to this question' (p. 88). But the context here is one in which Rawls is making a point about pure procedural justice: that the procedure determining the outcome is vital and 'there is no independent criterion for the right result' (p. 86). The suggestion is much more explicit in the following passage:

Which of these systems and the many intermediate forms most fully answers to the requirements of justice cannot, I think, be determined in advance. There is presumably no general answer to this question, since it depends in large part upon the traditions, institutions, and social forces of each country, and its particular historical circumstances. The theory of justice does not include these matters. (p. 274)

And this:

The theory of justice does not by itself favor either form of regime . . . The decision as to which system is best for a given people depends upon their circumstances, institutions, and historical traditions. (p. 280)

Rawls is here making a point about the choice of economic systems: that the choice of a politico-economic system, such as socialism or capitalism, is not determined by the theory of justice. But this suggests, though I do not recall that it is ever discussed in the work, that the application of the principles of justice may *in general* be dependent on such matters.

Consider what is said about slavery. Rawls has all along taken it for granted that slavery is an unjust institution, and in fact slavery has provided one of the main examples serving to distinguish his theory, in its moral import, from utilitarianism. For one of the standard objections to utilitarianism is that it could sanction or even require slavery, where this would maximize utility or increase the average benefit: 'Utilitarianism may seem to be a more exalted ideal, but the other side of it is that it may authorize the lesser welfare and liberty of some for the sake of a greater happiness of others who may already be more fortunate' (p. 573).

the intermediate stages which they must traverse before they can become fit for the best form of government' (*Representative Government*, ch. ii, pp. 174, 176, 178). Rawls's special conception of justice, which is 'the form that the general conception finally assumes as social conditions improve' (p. 83), is thus analogous to Mill's ideally best form of government. There is among the many points of difference one prominent one: Mill's ideally best form of government is not unattainable.

It turns out, however, that even in justice as fairness slavery can have a justification, when considered in relation to its background setting, what existed before, or what would exist otherwise. Thus:

Slavery and serfdom . . . are tolerable only when they relieve even worse injustices. There may be transition cases where enslavement is better than current practice. For example, suppose that city-states that previously have not taken prisoners of war but have always put captives to death agree by treaty to hold prisoners as slaves instead. Although we cannot allow the institution of slavery on the grounds that the greater gains of some outweigh the losses to others, it may be that under these conditions, since all run the risk of capture in war, this form of slavery is less unjust than present custom . . . The arrangement seems defensible as an advance on established institutions, if slaves are not treated too severely . . . None of these considerations, however fanciful, tend in any way to justify hereditary slavery or serfdom by citing natural or historical limitations. (p. 248)

This passage indicates that Rawls is prepared to recognize that the background setting has to be taken into account in judging the justice of a particular institution in a particular setting. The example has a certain oddity, however, in that slavery is, in my judgement, a paradigm case of an institution that is always and everywhere unjust, and it must therefore be regarded as an exception to the general rule. Disputes on this may well turn on how slavery is defined. I am thinking of slavery as defined by Kant's principle of personality. On this conception slavery is a special case, involving the legal ownership of persons, of treating human beings merely as means to ends in which they cannot share and not as persons with ends of their own. So I do not agree that holding prisoners of war as slaves would be, as Rawls suggests, 'less unjust' than putting them to death. It would be, I agree, other things equal, more humane, and therefore better; but this does not make it just, or even less unjust. Rawls makes the judgement depend on a prior treaty—a contract—but I regard the treaty as irrelevant. It can lead to more humane practices on the part of contending city-states, but, as I argued earlier, cannot make a practice just that is otherwise unjust. The injustice of slavery flows from its intrinsic nature; and what persons would agree to, in good times or bad, cannot alter this.

But I am led by these reflections to a conclusion so surprising that I must stop to ponder it, for, if my argument is sound, then it follows that although an institution may be unjust it is not thereby necessarily unjustifiable, and it must follow as a further consequence that we must distinguish, in considering an institution, between its being just and its being justifiable. Justice, according to Rawls, is 'the first virtue of social institutions' (p. 3). As such, it is 'uncompromising' (p. 4), and it 'denies that the loss of freedom for some is made right by a greater good shared by others. The reasoning which balances the gains and losses of different persons as if they were one person is excluded' (p. 28). One would think from the uncompromising nature of these remarks that there could be no justification for an unjust institution. But this apparently is not so. And this raises explicitly the question, not dealt with in the book, of the precise relation between justice and justification.

In any case, if the historical background is vital in judgements of justice—and I am satisfied that, except for such exceptional cases as slavery, it is—then comparison with the abstract ideal of perfect justice is, if not altogether irrelevant, certainly problematic. There is, it appears, no direct application of the principles of justice to institutions, just as there is no direct application of them to concrete conduct.

So, in the end, we come back to the point of the beginning; 'As moralists we naturally inquire what ought to be done in the actual world in which we live . . . The inquiry into the morality of an ideal society can therefore be at best but a preliminary investigation, after which the step from the ideal to the actual, in accordance with reason, remains to be taken.'[22] We may hope that Rawls, who is as aware as anyone of the 'pressing and urgent' nature of these matters, will before too long turn his attention directly to them. As it stands at present it is evident that, whereas the application of the first principle of utilitarianism is fairly clear, though beyond a doubt problematic, the application of the first principles of justice as fairness is obscure, assuming there is any at all.[23]

APPENDIX—SOURCES AND ANTECEDENTS

The principle of equal liberty—'Each person is to have an equal right to the most extensive basic liberty compatible with a similar liberty for others'—is foreshadowed in Kant and Spencer. Curiously, although Rawls acknowledges the precedence of Kant, and is generally more than generous in acknowledging just about anything that could be regarded as an indebtedness, he totally ignores Spencer—with one exception, itself curious. In the little-known paper 'Justice as Reciprocity', an expansion of the famous 'Justice as Fairness' that Rawls prepared

---

[22] Sidgwick, *Methods*, pp. 19–20.
[23] Among the many persons from whom in the course of this enterprise I received great stimulation, help, and counsel I must single out for special thanks and acknowledgement Claudia Card and Hans Oberdiek.

for distribution in classes, there is in n. 3 a glancing reference to Spencer: 'If the principle of equal liberty is commonly associated with Kant . . . it can also be found in works so different as J. S. Mill's *On Liberty* (1859) and Herbert Spencer's *Justice* (Pt. IV of *Principles of Ethics*), London, 1891.' Though the other references appear in the corresponding footnote of 'Justice as Fairness', the reference to Spencer does not, and—oddest of all—Spencer is never once referred to in *A Theory of Justice*.[24] Given the other resemblances to Spencer, to be detailed in a moment, one can only speculate on what led to this omission and de-emphasis.

Spencer's formula of justice, or, as he also calls it, 'the law of equal freedom', is: 'Every man is free to do that which he wills, provided he infringes not the equal freedom of any other man' (*Justice*, § 272, p. 46). He had first formulated it in his *Social Statics* (London, 1851), chapters 4–6, and at that time was writing without knowledge of Kant's *Rechtslehre* (1797), as he acknowledges in an appendix to *The Principles of Ethics* (ii. 437–9). Rawls has a special section (§40) on 'The Kantian Interpretation of Justice as Fairness', and goes to great lengths to bring out what he takes to be the Kantian character and background of his theory. The debt to Hobbes will, I take it, be obvious to anyone who has read Rawls's earlier papers, even though it is somewhat submerged in the book (only four index references), since Hobbes, and the reading of Hobbes, is now so very much in vogue. But Spencer is now little known and little read. So some comparisons may be instructive.

As we know, Rawls explicitly restricts his first principle to institutions, or rather, to the basic structure of society. Spencer does not. 'The law of equal freedom', Spencer maintains, 'is the law in conformity to which equitable individual conduct and equitable social arrangements consist' (preface to *Principle of Ethics*, p. viii). Rawls rightly sees, and through his work has helped us to see, that principles that apply to institutions or to the social order generally have no obvious or immediate application to individuals. And what we find in Spencer is that his first principle is, in practice, as distinct from his theory, applied to institutions and to the establishment of basic rights; not directly to the morality of individual conduct. For this purpose secondary principles, involving ends, are brought in. Spencer explicitly says: 'Individual or private morality, as distinct from social or public morality, is not to be entered upon in the following pages.'[25]

As we also know, Rawls's theory of justice is an ideal theory, presuming strict compliance and a well-ordered society (pp. 245–6, 351). Consequently he has nothing to say about punishment—retributive justice—and only on occasion deals with such topics of 'nonideal theory', involving 'partial compliance', as civil disobedience and conscientious refusal (§§ 53–59), and then only to illustrate

---

[24] 'Justice as Reciprocity' was finally published in *Utilitarianism: John Stuart Mill: With Critical Essays*, ed. Samuel Gorovitz (Indianapolis, Ind.: Bobbs-Merrill, 1971); n. 3 is on p. 244 (in *Papers*, ch. 10, p. 193). The reference for 'Justice as Fairness' is *Philosophical Review*, 67 (April 1958), p. 166 (*Papers*, pp. 193, 48–9).

[25] *Social Statics* 1st edn. London, 1851; New York: Robert Shalkenbach Foundation 1970), pt. 1, ch. 3, para. 10, p. 66.

applications. Spencer is the only prior philosopher I know of who adhered even more strictly and rigidly to such a conception (with the possible exception of Plato). Sidgwick did not, as is amply shown by the controversy he engaged in with Spencer on just this point.[26] Neither did Kant. Though Kant's principles presuppose the possibility of an ideal realm of ends, and postulate it as something to be aimed at as a duty, the Categorical Imperative was put forward as the principle actually governing and appealed to in the judgements made in everyday life and as the principle to be used as a touchstone to decide problems of conduct. The same is true of the classical utilitarianism of Bentham and Mill.

Consider now Spencer, at present in the limbo of disdain that a credulous society reserves for theorists admired by rugged individualists and robber barons, supposed defenders of the status quo:

Morality professes to be a code of rules proper for the guidance of humanity in its highest conceivable perfection. A universal obedience to its precepts implies an ideal society . . . A system of pure ethics . . . entirely ignores wrong, injustice, or crime, and gives no information as to what must be done when they have been committed.[27]

In the later *Data of Ethics* (1879) Spencer says:

Ideal conduct such as ethical theory is concerned with, is not possible for the ideal man in the midst of men otherwise constituted. An absolutely just or perfectly sympathetic person, could not live and act according to his nature in a tribe of cannibals. Among people who are treacherous and utterly without scruple, entire truthfulness and openness must bring ruin . . . There requires a certain congruity between the conduct of each member of a society and other's conduct . . . We must consider the ideal man as existing in the ideal social state . . . only when they co-exist, can there exist that ideal conduct which Absolute Ethics has to formulate, and which Relative Ethics has to take as the standard by which to estimate divergencies from right, or degrees of wrong. (p. 280)

That there are differences, even in the midst of these resemblances, does not make the resemblances less striking. Right along this line, Rawls maintains (as we further know) that 'ideal theory . . . is fundamental' (p. 241), since he is asking what a perfectly just society would be like' (p. 8).

It is not necessary to detail other points of resemblance. There are some. For instance, both Rawls and Spencer regard a free-market system as both efficient and just, as being in accord with the requirements of equal liberty, and thus are not regarded with approval by party-line socialists, who confuse a free-market economy with the institution of the private ownership of the means of production. And of course there are differences. There are many differences. To mention just one, Rawls regards government as necessary and desirable, even in ideal theory, while Spencer is a famous no-government theorist. I will not strain patience reciting others. What is striking are the resemblances.

---

[26] *Methods*, pp. 18–22.
[27] *Social Statics*, lemma 1, sect. 3, p. 36; pt. 1, ch. 1, sect. 3, p. 52.

Now, Rawls's second principle of justice is a combination of two, the difference principle and the principle called 'the liberal principle of fair equality of opportunity' (p. 83), also called 'the principle of open positions' (p. 84) and 'the principle of fair opportunity (p. 87). This is the principle that social and economic inequalities are to be arranged so that they are attached to offices and positions open to all under conditions of fair equality of opportunity (p. 302), and the difference principle, which 'is basic throughout' (p. 83), is the principle that 'social and economic inequalities are to be arranged so that they are to the greatest benefit of the least advantaged' (pp. 83, 302).

Antecedents to these principles, as Rawls states them and comes to understand them, are not so readily obvious. But the principle of fair equality of opportunity, or at any rate something closely resembling it, plays a prominent role in Tawney's *Equality*. Rawls refers to Tawney just once in the book, in a passing footnote in connection with what he calls the liberal interpretation of the two principles—an interpretation he rejects—which adds 'to the requirement of careers open to talents the further condition of the principle of fair equality of opportunity' (p. 73). I don't profess to understand this, perhaps because I unconsciously disagree with it, perhaps because I don't read Tawney in the way that Rawls suggests that he should be read. Perhaps we are merely reading different sections of Tawney. As I read him, Tawney says the following:

Inequality of power is inherent in the nature of organized society, since action is impossible, unless there is an authority to decide what action shall be taken, and to see that its decisions are applied in practice. Some measure, at least, of inequality of circumstance is not to be avoided, since functions differ, and differing functions require different scales of provision to elicit and maintain them. In practice, therefore, though inequality of power and inequality of circumstance are the fundamental evils, there are forms of each which are regarded, not merely with tolerance, but with active approval . . . Inequality of power is tolerated, when the power is used for a social purpose approved by the community, when it is not more extensive than that purpose requires, when its exercise is not arbitrary, but governed by settled rules, and when the commission can be revoked, if its terms are exceeded . . .

No one thinks it inequitable that, when a reasonable provision has been made for all, exceptional responsibilities should be compensated by exceptional rewards, as a recognition of the service performed and an inducement to perform it . . . The sentiment of justice is satisfied, not by offering to every man identical treatment, but by treating different individuals in the same way in so far as, being human, they have requirements which are the same, and in different ways in so far as, being concerned with different services, they have requirements which differ. What is repulsive is not that one man should earn more than others . . . It is that some classes should be excluded from the heritage of civilization which others enjoy . . . What is important is not that all men should receive the same amount of pecuniary income. It is that the surplus resources of society should be so husbanded and applied that it is a matter of minor significance whether they receive it or not.[28]

---

[28] R. H. Tawney, *Equality*, ch. III, sect. iii, pp. 117–18.

As I read this again, it begins to look not only like an antecedent of the principle of fair equality of opportunity, but also like an antecedent of the difference principle, and in a form in which, in my considered judgement, it is more nearly acceptable. But this is another matter altogether.

ADDITIONAL NOTES AND COMMENTS

A. Some time ago, shortly after John Rawls's *Theory of Justice* appeared, I told him that I had half-expected him to call his book *The Methods of Justice*. He said: 'Mark, I'll leave it to you to write that.' So I did. Originally published in the *Journal of Value Inquiry*, 10 (1976), pp. 286–316; reprinted here with excisions and revisions, and the omission of the original Appendix II. Rawls's papers have now been collected in *Collected Papers* (1999), which I cite in some of the notes. I have another extended discussion of Rawls in 'Justice, Theory, and a Theory of Justice', *Philosophy of Science*, 44(4) (December 1977), pp. 594–618. Rawls responded to one of the points in the latter in 'Kantian Constructivism in Moral Theory', *Journal of Philosophy*, 77 (September 1980), repr. in *Papers*, pp. 353–6. Rawls remarks (p. 353 n. 16): 'It should not be supposed that Singer's own position is that of a rational intuitionist. I simply suppose that a rational intuitionist would make this objection.' In case there should be any doubt on the point, my position is not that of a 'rational intuitionist'.

B. An extensive guide to the mass of literature on Rawls is J. H. Wellbank, Dennis Snook, and David T. Mason (eds.), *John Rawls and His Critics: An Annotated Bibliography* (New York: Garland, 1982). Even this is now somewhat outdated. And I have some qualms about its accuracy. The abstract it provides of the present paper is, in one respect, quite wrong. Thus its opening sentence is: 'Argues that a hypothetical social contract has no binding power and hence no status in establishing principles of justice'. That is not my argument at all; it is, rather, an argument I consider and reject, and it is a point made in the review of *Theory* by Hans Oberdiek cited on p. 61. So this is puzzling.

C. Rawls first revised *A Theory of Justice* for the German edition in 1975, revisions that were then incorporated into other translations (of which there have been a considerable number), and finally for the English-language edition in 1999. I have decided not to update my references here to the revised edition. This paper is included here not primarily for its discussion of Rawls but for the opportunity it provides to develop my own view of the importance of inescapable moral presuppositions and a priori principles in ethics. Rawls had previously modified some of his views (in fact, they have been under almost continual modification and revision) in other writings, such as *Political Liberalism* (New York: Columbia University Press, 1993) and *The Law of Peoples*—for example, his view of primary goods. In *Peoples* he says (i) 'the aim is to realize and preserve just (or decent) institutions, and not simply to increase, much less to maximize indefinitely, the average level of wealth', and (ii) 'Surely there is a point at which a people's basic needs (estimated in primary goods) are fulfilled' (pp. 107, 119). In the first edition of *Theory* everyone is said to aim at maximizing his or her stock of primary goods; I doubt if the difference here is to be attributed to the shift from thinking of justice for individuals, in *Theory*, to thinking of justice for peoples, in *Peoples*, since Rawls has also modified his view of primary goods in the revised edition of *Theory*. There is no need to detail the changes here. The preface to the revised edition provides a synopsis of revisions.

D. As noted in the text, Rawls says (*TJ*, p. 132) that 'A principle is ruled out if it would be self-contradictory, or self-defeating, for everyone to act upon it'. But I did not note in the text Rawls's further remark (p. 251) that

It is a mistake . . . to emphasize the place of generality and universality in Kant's ethics. That moral principles are general and universal is hardly new with him; and as we have seen these conditions do not in any case take us very far. It is impossible to construct a moral theory on so slender a basis.

It may be that these conditions do not take us very far—I do not argue that here—but we cannot do without them, and neither can Rawls's theory of justice. I leave for another place comment on this interpretation of Kant.

E. I quoted a passage from William James's 'The Moral Philosopher and the Moral Life' only to help explain Rawls's concept of 'the priority of right', and I do not wish to reinforce the general impression that James was a utilitarian. He was not.

5

Ethics and Common Sense

1. Ethics
2. Some Views of Common Sense
3. Common Sense and Common Knowledge
4. Morality
5. Common Sense on Common Sense
6. Common Sense and Positive Morality
7. Common Sense in Ethics
8. Lessons of Common Sense in Ethics
9. Ethics in Common Sense
10. Deficiencies of Common-Sense Morality
    Coda

> It was as though some huge force were pressing down upon you—
> something that penetrated inside your skull, battering against your
> brain, frightening you out of your beliefs, persuading you, almost, to
> deny the evidence of your senses . . . Not merely the validity of experi-
> ence, but the very existence of external reality was tacitly denied by
> their philosophy. The heresy of heresies was common sense.
>
> George Orwell, *Nineteen Eighty-Four*

What are the relations between ethics and common sense? This is not a
question that has been often pursued, and that not because of a lack of
interest in ethics. Although philosophers of various persuasions have had
some harsh things to say about common sense, there remains a deep-seated
grudging respect for it, and even philosophers can be occasionally gratified
at the thought that common sense may be on their side. How else account
for the occurrence of such titles as 'The Common Sense of the Exact
Sciences' and 'Common Sense in law'? Outside philosophy as well of course
there is persistent appeal to it; thus books appear claiming to be, for
instance, 'The Common Sense Book of Dog and Puppy Care' or 'The
Common Sense Book of Love and Marriage', and a book entitled *The*

Common Sense Book of Baby and Child Care has had enormous worldwide circulation. This is, surely, not simply because of its title, but because it lived up to it. One of the most influential political tracts ever penned was entitled *Common Sense*, and the author of that work (Thomas Paine), when he soon after issued a work entitled *The Crisis*, adopted the pseudonym 'Common Sense'. Here was a great political revolution fought under the banner of and in the name of common sense. It is intriguing that one most popular counter to *Common Sense* was entitled *Plain Truth*, for there really should be no clash between common sense and plain truth. But sometimes, evidently, there is.

There manifestly is such a thing as common sense. Its existence would be denied (in Bradley's apposite phrase) 'only by a fool or an advanced thinker'. But what is it, what does it consist in, how can it be ascertained, what judgements (if any) does it lead to, and what is its value? It is not easy to say. Common sense can be very elusive when made the object of direct attention. What is requisite here is careful observation and reflection more than deduction and argument, and it is still hard to be sure that one has it straight. I am aware of the dearth of explicit argument in what follows. Yet the argument is implicit in the interpretation that animates the observation. I have been plagued throughout by the question, natural to a philosopher, of how I know what common sense is and what it would say on one matter or another. But it has occurred to me more than once that it is common sense, which I cannot suppose I altogether lack, that tells me so. Without common sense we can get no adequate or accurate conception of common sense. With it we can get at least some. In William James's felicitous phrase, it is the 'natural mother-tongue of thought'.[1] As such, though it is both elusive and allusive, it is neither invisible nor ineffable.

A method for determining authoritatively and precisely just what common sense holds and consists in has yet to be discovered, and it may be that there is none. It seems likely, indeed, that common sense holds nothing precisely. Method in this area, such as it is, consists in being tuned to nuance, to association, to hints and suggestions rather than to clear-cut meaning and logical necessity. But from this mass of observations, and on the basis of common sense itself—or what I take to be common sense itself—I derive certain conclusions, which I set out here for future reference:

(1) Common sense is essential to ethics, but not sufficient for it;
(2) Ethics is also essential to common sense, which is an inherently practical capacity;

---

[1] William James, *Pragmatism* (New York: Longmans, Green, (1907), p. 181.

(3) Common sense is basically conservative, not innovative, and can be oppressive, and consequently on its own terms requires supplementation and correction by ethical thinking;
(4) Developments—improvements—in ethics that lead to improvements in morality lead to improvements in common sense by leading to improvements in common-sense morality.

I turn first, then, to an account of ethics; for this is somewhat plainer and at the same time has some interesting ambiguities of its own.

1. ETHICS

Ethics relates to conduct and character and, in a wider sense, values, where a person's values are understood as what that person thinks important. The term has two main senses. In one sense, ethics is a branch of theory: the study of the principles, standards, and methods for distinguishing right from wrong, good from bad, and better from worse. In another sense, a person's ethics is that person's code of conduct, as a group's ethics is the group's code of conduct; or is that person's character (which in turn relates to that person's 'code of conduct'). Thus if we speak of a person's ethics we might be speaking about (1) that person's ethical theory or ideas, or (2) the code of conduct that person follows, or (3) the code of conduct that person professes to follow, or (4) that person's character (which is in turn an amalgam of conduct and profession). Ethics thus relates to morality as well as values (since what a person thinks important will affect that person's conduct and character), and in some uses is indistinguishable from it. Although in philosophical discussions it is more usual to speak of ethics in the theoretical sense, as the theory of morality, even in philosophical discussions the code-of-conduct sense is present, even if not always noticed. We can thus speak of ethics in the theoretical sense and in the code-of-conduct sense, and morality approximates to the latter.

But 'morality' also sustains a systematic ambiguity. It can refer to either (a) positive morality, the morality of a group or society or culture, or (b) personal morality, the morality of a given person, which can depart from the morality of that person's society, more or less.

These distinctions can be taken as representing the common sense of the matter, even though common sense itself does not explicitly make them, since the distinctions are drawn from common or ordinary usage and are typical in their overlapping and intersecting, characteristics that would no doubt be outlawed in a logically perfect or scientific language but which are indicative of insight into interconnections and relations that more precise usage would obscure. Ordinary language is often a guide to common sense—at least the common sense of the time and place—as is idiom. Idioms are certainly ordinary language if anything is (thus we speak of 'verbal agreement' meaning oral agreement, and no one has trouble with that usage), and are guides to ordinary thinking, as sometimes they are guides to non-thinking. A standard prejudice, fallacy, myth, or misconception can be enshrined in idiom and hence in common sense, or what is taken to be common sense. One of the problems is that it is so often hard to distinguish here—as elsewhere—between reality and appearance, between common sense and what is taken to be (or what 'passes for common sense').

Now, I have undertaken to present some reflections on ethics and common sense. And it is sensible, and it is certainly philosophical, to begin such reflections by trying to get straight on what common sense is. But, typically, philosophers have expressed many different views about common sense and have placed conflicting values on it. This suggests that common sense, if one thing, is something complex, and that it may, indeed, be more than one thing. And so, as we shall see, it is.

2. SOME VIEWS OF COMMON SENSE

The diversity of opinion on common sense is easy to illustrate, and it should be instructive to do so. C. D. Broad's indictment of common sense is well known:

Very little can be done for common-sense . . . *Any* theory that can possibly fit the facts is *certain* to shock common-sense somewhere; and in face of the facts we can only advise common-sense to follow the example of Judas Iscariot, and 'go out and hang itself'.[2]

Almost as well known is Bradley's somewhat less emphatic verdict on it:

I see no way . . . by which the clear thinking which calls itself 'Common Sense' and is satisfied with itself, can ever be reconciled to metaphysics . . . I do not mean the doctrine of any one school, but . . . all speculation which is at once resolved to keep

---

[2] C. D. Broad, *The Mind and its Place in Nature* (London: Routledge & Kegan Paul, 1925), pp. 184–6.

its hold upon all sides of fact, and upon the other hand to push, so far as it can, every question to the end. For 'Common Sense' it will remain that the final result of reflection will seem not only out of harmony with experience but in collision with sound thought. And for 'Common Sense' also it will remain that we shall be able to live only so far as, wherever we feel it to be convenient, we can forget to think.[3]

It is unusual to find Broad and Bradley in agreement on anything, but they seem in agreement here, and in disagreement with the well-known view of Moore that 'The 'Common Sense view of the world' is, in certain fundamental features, *wholly* true'.[4]

But we have not here to adjudicate that dispute. We are to determine the relations of common sense to ethics. And for this we must take another view of the matter. A strong clue is provided by Bergson, who points out that

Common sense . . . bears on our intercourse with people. We cannot help observing that a man may be a first-rate mathematician, or an expert physicist, or a subtle psychologist, as far as self-analysis goes, and yet completely misunderstand the actions of other men; miscalculate his own and perpetually fail to adapt himself to his surroundings, be, in a word, lacking in common sense . . . Common sense may be impaired while the reasoning faculties remain intact . . . Common sense . . . or as it might be called, social sense, is innate in normal man, like the faculty of speech, which also implies the existence of society and which is none the less prefigured in individual organisms.[5]

If common sense bears on our intercourse with people, as it does, then it certainly has something important in common with ethics, which also bears on our intercourse with people. It is this practical element in common sense, common sense as a practical faculty, that we have here to deal with. This was recognized by Reid, when he said: 'In common language sense always implies judgment. A man of sense is a man of judgment. Good sense is good judgment. Nonsense is what is evidently contrary to right judgment. Common sense is that degree of judgment which is common to men with whom we can converse and transact business.'[6] When Reid adds that 'it is common to all men . . . whom we can . . . call to account for their conduct', the connection with ethics should become manifest.

---

[3] F. H. Bradley, *Essays on Truth and Reality* (Oxford: Clarendon Press, 1914), p. 444.

[4] G. E. Moore, 'A Defence of Common Sense' (1925), in *Philosophical Papers* (London: George Allen & Unwin, 1959), p. 44.

[5] Henri Bergson, *The Two Sources of Morality and Religion* (New York: Henry Holt, 1935), ch. 2, p. 96.

[6] Thomas Reid, *Essays on the Intellectual Powers of Man* (1785), essay 6, ch. 2, ed. Woozley (London: Macmillan, 1941), pp. 330–1.

Whately observed that 'Common-sense is . . . an exercise of the judgment unaided by any Art or system of rules: such an exercise as we must necessarily employ in numberless cases of daily occurrence; in which, having no established principles to guide us . . . we must needs act on the best extemporaneous conjectures we can form. He who is eminently skillful in doing this, is said to possess a superior degree of Common-Sense.'[7] Notice here the emphasis on the native unaided judgement, the connection between sense and judgement, and the emphasis on the relation to practice. However, though Whately conceives of common sense as 'an exercise of the judgment unaided by any art or system of rules' and gives it high marks in the matter of application, he goes on to argue that where there are established rules to be had they are always preferable to what he then comes to speak of as 'conjectural judgements', and he claims that this is supported by the universal testimony of mankind. Thus, he says, 'Common-Sense is only our *second-best* guide . . . the rules of Art, if judiciously framed, are always desirable when they can be had':

the generality have a strong predilection in favour of Common-Sense, except in those points in which they, respectively, possess the knowledge of a system of rules; but in these points they deride any one who trusts to unaided Common-Sense. . . . Each gives the preference to unassisted Common-Sense only in those cases where he himself has nothing else to trust to, and invariably resorts to the rules of art, wherever he possesses the knowledge of them.

And therefore, he claims, 'it is plain that . . . systematic knowledge' is universally regarded as preferable 'to conjectural judgments'.[8] But Whately's claim here is not as clear as it ought to be. For it is admitted that common sense is needed in the application of the rules of the art in question. And common sense itself need not be regarded as 'unassisted' or 'unaided'. An exercise of judgement 'unaided by any art or system of rules' is not identical with 'conjectural judgment' or mere conjecture. It is a practical capacity. And there often are rules at work, rules resulting from experience and the exercise of judgement, that are not formulated or framed as an explicit system. None of us can recite the rules we use in conversing in our native tongue, though there are rules at work. The attempt to formulate them precisely and accurately has so far baffled the minds of the most intelligent computers. It may very well be that neither language nor common sense operates on the principles of a deductive system.

---

[7] Richard Whately, *Elements of Logic*, 9th edn. (London: John W. Parker, 1851), preface, pp. xi–xii.

[8] *Elements of Logic*, p. xii.

3. COMMON SENSE AND COMMON KNOWLEDGE

We can find various views of common sense. What is most elusive is the common-sense view of common sense. 'Common sense' is an expression of almost infinite nuance. Common sense is spoken of as having a view of the world, as having a language, as having conceptions of various things, as having a morality, perhaps even values, as having its own point of view, its own business and its own distinctive standpoint, and we find references to common-sense propositions and beliefs, even common-sense know-ledge—often called common knowledge—common sense as issuing ver-dicts and pronouncements, as governing people, and as, all told, being nearly an omnipresent phenomenon. It is all very well to be told that 'we must not be slaves to common sense'.[9] But it is on balance more important not to be slaves to a misconception or misuse of it. Common sense itself is almost inescapable, though it may be ignored or flouted, and some con-ception of it is almost inevitable, though the term is so elastic it is hard to have a consistent view of it.

Common sense was originally conceived of as an internal sense that con-stituted the common bond of the 'five basic senses' (as they were thought to be), and it was spoken of as 'the common sense'. This sense of 'common sense' is not now current, since the physiology underlying it has been given up. But there is sense in it nonetheless. For it is *common* sense, so-called, that provides us with the ability to learn from and by the other and more orthodox senses and by and from experience.

In common usage there are two main senses of common sense. In one sense it is ordinary, normal, average understanding—common under-standing—without which one is foolish or incompetent or even insane. In the other, common sense is thought of as good, sound, practical sense. In the first sense, a person who lacks common sense is a person who lacks sense, who is witless, dim-witted, or stupid. In the second sense, a person who lacks common sense does not lack sense—is not stupid or incompet-ent—but lacks *good* sense, a certain sagacity, a special capacity for success-fully ordering his or her own life and practical affairs and for dealing with people. It is one of the anomalies of common sense that, in one sense, com-mon sense is something common, while, in another sense, common sense is something uncommon. Sometimes, indeed, it gets praised as 'uncom-

---

[9] A. J. Ayer, *Metaphysics and Common Sense* (San Francisco, Calif. Freeman, Cooper, 1970), ch. 10, p. 160.

mon' sense. Why the capacity in question should, in this latter sense, be called by a name that implies that it is *common* does not appear, and it seems a paradox oddly inconsistent with common sense. Yet this ambiguity, though on many occasions of no moment, can be a source of insight as well as trouble. For this reason, though often I shall speak of common-sense without making this differentiation, sometimes I speak simply of sense, other times of good sense. Even so, to speak of something as sense is normally to express praise; 'sensible' is a positive term of appraisal.

Common sense, in the sense of sense, since it is common to the members of a community and to some extent common to humans (or else supposed to be) gives rise to conceptions, beliefs, and theories about the world which often go under the heading of common knowledge. This generates another meaning of common sense, which is sometimes understood as either common knowledge or the source of common knowledge. But what is common knowledge, and how is it to be determined whether something is or is not a matter of common knowledge? The concept has caused confusion, though it does not need to. Morris Cohen has eloquently expressed the disdain of the scientific philosopher for what parades as common knowledge (and is often, as we shall see, only folklore under an alias):

Obviously [the 'obviously' is interesting] the great body of what we regard as common knowledge (as distinct from rational science) of any age is funded out of traditional teachings, superstitions, and ancient metaphysics, as well as the personal impressions and opinions developed in us by our fragmentary partial experience. The tragic inadequacy of the result, the fact that it is full of error and illusion, is the primal source of the failure of human effort and aspiration. The history of magic, witchcraft, and other superstitions throughout the ages indicates that there is hardly an offspring of human fancy too absurd to be regarded as a fact by immense multitudes of men. Have not men for ages believed and do not millions even now believe it to be a fact that children get sick when the evil eye is cast on them or that they get cured when the proper words (or prayers) are pronounced? Scientific method is a systematic effort to eliminate the poison of error from our common knowledge. If common knowledge were entirely wrong in substance and method, science could not have any base from which to start or any certain direction in which to proceed. It would be impossible for science to arise out of common experience and reflection if the latter did not contain the seeds of truth as well as the noxious weeds of error and illusion.[10]

Cohen goes on to say that common sense is 'a mixture of sense and illusion, of enduring truth and superstition', and that 'even its truth is . . . vaguely and

---

[10] Morris R. Cohen, *Reason and Nature* (New York: Harcourt, Brace, 1931), p. 79.

inaccurately expressed'. And this is only one thing worth noticing about this passage. Another is the way in which common sense and common knowledge are thought of interchangeably. Still another is the fact that 'common knowledge' is not itself a precise conception. It is a term of reference and not of attribution. Something can be a matter of 'common knowledge' and not be true, and in that sense not be knowledge. Thus what is called common knowledge is often not even supposed to be knowledge, only common myth and illusion. Yet, as Cohen implies, it is not entirely wrong in substance and in method. If it were, the error could never be detected.

This is brought out in an account Russell has given of common knowledge, supplied in the context of an account of philosophic method:

In every philosophical problem, our investigation starts from what may be called 'data', by which I mean matters of common knowledge, vague, complex, inexact, as common knowledge always is, but yet somehow commanding our assent as on the whole and in some interpretation pretty certainly true . . . We are quite willing to admit that there may be errors of detail in this knowledge, but we believe them to be discoverable and corrigible by the methods which have given rise to our beliefs, and we do not, as practical men, entertain for a moment the hypothesis that the whole edifice may be built on insecure foundations.[11]

For Russell this 'mass of common knowledge' affords the starting-point and the 'data for . . . philosophical analysis', and in the process it can be radically transformed, even though Russell believes that it cannot be *in toto* overturned.

Common knowledge, or what is so called, thus appears to be of two broad kinds. In one sense, it is the so-called 'common knowledge' of a given community or a given time, and is what is called received opinion, which is opinion, not knowledge (and is what is orthodox among the orthodox and unadventurous). (Folklore, of which more anon, fits here very well.) In a second sense, common knowledge is genuine knowledge shared by all or nearly all humans in virtue of their common humanity and their common human sense and capacities. It is the latter that Moore is referring to when he says that 'the Common Sense view of the world' is 'in certain fundamental features, *wholly* true'. I shall not here recite the details of what Moore calls the 'Common Sense view of the world'. The distinctive feature of Moore's argument is his claim that if something is a feature in the common-sense view of the world, it follows that it is true. I have been altogether unimpressed by critiques of Moore's argument—usually provided

[11] Bertrand Russell, *Our Knowledge of the External World* (1914), (London: George Allen & Unwin,1926), pp. 72–3.

by philosophers who would have us believe the analogue of the proposition that Achilles, no matter how fast he runs, can never catch the tortoise—and regard it as established beyond any reasonable doubt. Yet, as Moore is himself quick to point out, the phrase 'common sense belief' is 'extraordinarily vague' and 'there may be many' common-sense beliefs that 'are not true'. The common-sense beliefs Moore is calling part of the common-sense view of the world, then, are those beliefs that are forced upon human beings with sense by the fact of living in the world and having senses to enable them to find out something about it. Such are the beliefs that fire burns and that snow is cold and that ice melts when heated and that one needs to eat to live. Such beliefs as these, the primary beliefs of common sense, are beyond doubt true, and are also such that anyone who set out to deny them would at the same time be presupposing them and others like them. This in my judgement is the permanent source of wisdom in the philosophy of common sense as expressed by Reid and developed later by Sidgwick and Moore. It is such beliefs, related intimately to common sense and unavoidable through its exercise, that deserve to be called common knowledge in a sense in which that is still knowledge.

It is such beliefs that Hume called natural or instinctive, beliefs 'we embrace by a kind of instinct or natural impulse, on account of their suitableness and conformity to the mind'; but Hume, as we know, regarded natural beliefs as unreasonable even though we are caused by the constitution of our nature to take them for granted.[12] On the present view they are not unreasonable, when understood in their proper scope and context; there is much greater chance of error in the abstruse reasoning Hume used to derive his scepticism with regard to reason and the senses than there is that these natural beliefs that are essential for survival are false. Hume talks as though reason would really demonstrate the proposition that Achilles can never catch the tortoise, no matter how much faster he runs, though nature by some quirk somehow brings it about that we cannot help believing, contrary to reason, that Achilles somehow does overtake the tortoise.

There is still a third sense of common knowledge, one that appears in the law. Here common knowledge is information shared by such large numbers of ordinary people in the ordinary course of life that judicial notice is taken of it, so that it is admitted to the record of a trial without proof or testimony. Proof or testimony on such matters would be otiose as contrary to common sense.

---

[12] David Hume, *A Treatise of Human Nature* (1739), ed. Selby-Bigge (1888), bk. I, pt. iv, sect. 2, p. 214; cf. pp. 183, 184, 187, 216, also sect. 7, pp. 267–9.

Common knowledge, then, or what is taken to be such, is knowledge that is general, prevalent, widespread, such that one would be entitled to presume that another person in the same community shares it. And a common-sense belief is a belief that a person of sense cannot help forming in and through the very process of living in the world, which is, so far as has yet been discovered, the only place available for living. Sidgwick put the point well, though his way of putting it is not widely known: 'There is this advantage in putting questions from the point of view of Common Sense: that it is, in some degree, in the minds of us all, even of the metaphysicians whose conclusions are most opposed to it.'[13] I have no doubt whatever that this is an advantage, and not just in general philosophy, but in ethics and also in morality.

4. MORALITY

It is now time to refine the distinction between positive and personal morality. The positive (or conventional or customary) morality of a given group consists in the rules or principles the members of the group generally follow in their conduct in the belief that they ought to, or else the principles they profess to follow or believe they follow. This distinction is necessary because, as we all know, practice does not always coincide with precept. But the precepts of positive morality are the precepts that are taught to the young and supported by characteristic forms of social pressure, such as expressions of approval or disapproval, acceptance or ostracism. Yet only in the most primitive (or the most tyrannical) and most homogeneous societies, if anywhere, is such teaching and such pressure successful in moulding everyone to the same form. Individual differences still obtrude, giving rise to personal morality. A person's morality is not just a set of principles; it is a complex of conduct, character, and values—what a person thinks important. It includes the person's moral beliefs, but is not restricted to them. It reflects the person's character and is expressed in the person's conduct, both overtly and in more subtle forms. One's morality is expressed in one's conduct even in cases where it does not determine the conduct; where, for instance, one acts contrary to one's morality. For such conduct gives rise to feelings of guilt or shame or remorse, which are expressions of one's morality. But in distinguishing one's personal morality from the morality of one's society the emphasis is on the standards that

[13] Henry Sidgwick, *Philosophy, Its Scope and Relations* (London: Macmillan, 1902), p. 42.

are part of one's own idea of right and wrong, whether in agreement with one's society's or not. And these standards sometimes do guide our conduct, as they guide our judgements of others and as they guide our judgements of our own society.

Now common sense is intimately connected with morality. 'Common sense' relates as much to common feelings of humanity as it does to common capacities for knowing and to common items of knowledge or belief. Hume, in his epistemology so far from common sense, in his ethics, with its emphasis on the common sentiment of humanity, is much closer to it. And both ethics and common sense relate essentially to practice. It is actually a supposition of common sense that there is such a thing as a common moral sense, noticeable both in cases in which it is manifested and in cases in which it is absent. How a common moral sense can be reconciled with the existence of an individual moral sense, especially one that on occasion departs from the holdings of the common moral sense, is not a question that common sense attempts to answer. It constitutes one of the problems of moral philosophy, and not one of the easiest. But the problem is far from unsolvable; the two are eminently reconcilable.

5. COMMON SENSE ON COMMON SENSE

We have been considering common sense as both a capacity and also as the product of that capacity. When considered as what is called common knowledge, and especially when referred to derogatorily, it is being taken as product, not as capacity. But we must also distinguish between common sense as something local and as something general, something genuinely common. In the local sense it links with public opinion; in the general sense it does not. If we reflect on the necessity of common sense for survival this last point should be apparent. Although he refers explicitly to the rudiments of science, it is really of common sense that Malinowski is speaking when he says:

No art or craft however primitive could have been invented or maintained, no organised form of hunting, fishing, tilling, or search for food could be carried out without the careful observation of natural process and a firm belief in its regularity, without the power of reasoning and without confidence in the power of reason; that is, without the rudiments of science.[14]

---

[14] Bronislaw Malinowski, 'Magic Science and Religion', in Joseph Needham (ed.), *Science, Religion and Reality* (New York: Macmillan, 1925), p. 21; repr. in Malinowski's *Magic, Science and Religion* (Garden City, NY: Doubleday (Anchor Books), 1954), pp. 17–18.

What Malinowski is saying here was foreshadowed, more metaphorically, by Emerson:

The perception of matter is made the common sense, and for cause. This was the cradle, this the go-cart, of the human child. We must learn the homely laws of fire and water; we must feed, wash, plant, build. These are the ends of necessity, and first in the order of nature. Poverty, frost, famine, disease, debt, are the beadles and guardsmen that hold us to common-sense. The intellect, yielded up to itself, cannot supersede this tyrannic necessity . . . The common-sense which does not meddle with the absolute, but takes things at their word . . . is the house of health and life. In spite of all the joys of poets and the joys of saints, the most imaginative and abstracted person never makes with impunity the least mistake in this particular— never tries to kindle his oven with water, nor carries torch into a powder-mill, nor seizes his wild charger by the tail.[15]

The common sense depicted here is not something local or regional, but something genuinely common, thus universal. And it is also something necessary. It is necessary for life and survival, of individuals, of cultures, of the species. And common sense thus understood is an eminently practical faculty or capacity. Although a metaphysics too literally attached to it may be false as metaphysics, no metaphysics that contradicts it in its context and about its proper business can be true. As William James put it:

Common sense appears . . . as a perfectly definite state in our understanding of things . . . satisfies in an extraordinarily successful way the purposes for which we think . . . It suffices for all the necessary practical ends of life.[16]

Though one might demur as to the 'all', it is common sense in this sense that we have to grasp. For in ethics even more than in science and in metaphysics it is essential to stay close to it and not depart too far from it. Common sense can get along without metaphysics; it cannot get along without ethics.

Once we get beyond the boundaries of the practical, the limitations of common sense become apparent. As James, again, puts it: 'The moment you pass beyond the practical use of these [common-sense] categories . . . to a merely curious or speculative way of thinking' trouble begins; something, he says, even common sense must acknowledge. 'The scientific tendency in critical thought . . . has opened an entirely unexpected range of practical utilities to our astonished view . . . The scope of the practical control of nature newly put into our hand by scientific ways of thinking vastly

---

[15] Ralph Waldo Emerson, 'Poetry and Imagination', in *Letters and Social Aims* (Boston: Houghton, Mifflin, 1883), pp. 9–10.

[16] James, *Pragmatism*, pp. 181, 182.

exceeds the scope of the old control grounded on common sense.'[17] But the lesson I derive from this is not the one James himself drew. The lesson I derive is that common sense about its business does not interfere with science, and science about its business does not interfere with common sense. It can modify it, it can improve it, it cannot replace it.

Hobhouse gives us a conception of common sense that repays contemplation. Common sense, he says, 'means the result of thought acting on masses of experience too great to be perfectly articulated'.[18] But if this is what it is, then there is great chance that what is common sense for one is not common sense for another, and common sense would not be common. Something here has to be understood of the idea of common thought acting on masses of *common* experience. But I assume that Hobhouse had something like this in mind, else why speak of *common* sense.

This point is made in Hans Morgenthau's marvellously perspicuous conception of common sense as 'the rational and moral manifestation of a common human nature experiencing a common world'.[19] For there is a common human nature, though it is modified by great differences in culture and education, language and environment, manners and morals, traditions and values. And there is a common world, though there are also many different worlds defined by the different cultures.

And common sense, in the sense of the result, is transmitted by culture, tradition, and education. In the process it can be distorted as it can become ossified. Hence by itself common sense is no substitute for intelligence and enquiry. But enquiry and intelligence presuppose common sense, cannot function without it, at least in some minimal degree, just as they cannot operate without memory.

Common sense distorted by culture and tradition results in folklore, and it is imperative to distinguish common sense from folklore. Folklore consists of traditional beliefs, customs, sayings, and legends preserved unreflectively among a group or population. Though folklore may provide interesting lessons about a given people, there is no reason to think any element of folklore true, yet there is every reason to think many elements of common sense true (as product) and reliable (as capacity). Bergen Evans says that his book *The Natural History of Nonsense* 'is intended as a sort of handbook for young recruits in the gay cause of common sense'.[20] Here

---

[17] Ibid., pp. 186, 187.

[18] L. T. Hobhouse, *The Theory of Knowledge* (London: Methuen, 1896), p. 377.

[19] Hans J. Morgenthau, *The Purpose of American Politics* (New York: Alfred A. Knopf, 1960), p. 224.

[20] Bergen Evans, *The Natural History of Nonsense* (1946) (New York: Vintage, 1958), p. 3.

common sense is regarded as the opposite of nonsense and as at war with it. Yet the book contains delightfully witty accounts of folklore parading as wisdom and demonstrations both of its falsity and of its unfounded character. Folklore is not so much common sense as common nonsense. And this is true even though it is hard to distinguish sharply between them. Common nonsense—folklore—is what results when common sense engages in enterprises not its business, when it deals with matters it is not fitted to deal with. Ortega y Gassett points out, in a celebrated passage, that: 'In the disturbances caused by scarcity of food, the mob goes in search of bread, and the means it employs is generally to wreck the bakeries.'[21] But to wreck the bakeries is stupidity, not common sense, as any member of the mob in isolation would realize, and just the sort of rampant stupidity that is brought on by demagogues and hysteria. It is when persons turn over their common sense to the machinations of another, or temporarily lose it in some other way, that they become members of mobs. Common sense needs room to operate, does not work well in close quarters.

Philosophers delight in telling us such things as:

Common sense is no infallible guide to philosophical truth. There would, indeed, not be much point in the study of philosophy if common sense had already discovered for itself the answers to the problems that we are investigating. That there exist witches and fairies, that the earth is flat and the sun goes around it, that women are incapable of higher education, that it is dangerous to sleep with the bedroom window open, have all been firmly established principles of common sense in their day.[22]

It may be granted that common sense is no infallible guide to philosophical truth, if only because there is no infallible guide to philosophical truth. But the passage supposes that common sense attempts to find answers to philosophical questions. It does not. That, in terms we have used already, is not the business of common sense. The opinions registered may be taken as all false. But are they—were they ever—principles of common sense? This cannot be answered without distinguishing among them. That there exist witches and fairies is an instance of superstition, not common sense; that women are incapable of higher education is an instance of prejudice. That it is dangerous to sleep with the bedroom window open turns out to be true at certain elevations and in certain cities, as true as that in some places it is dangerous to sleep with the front door unlocked. In the sense intended, however, it is not an instance of common sense but of folklore.

---

[21] José Ortega y Gasset, *The Revolt of the Masses* (1930) (New York: W. W. Norton, 1932), p. 65.
[22] C. H. Whitely, *An Introduction to Metaphysics* (London: Methuen, 1950), p. 61.

That the earth is flat and the sun goes around it is, I think, a genuine instance of common sense, and false, and it is an instance that shows that common sense uninstructed unenlightened and by itself is insufficient. Yet for all ordinary practice on earth it suffices. Only when taken out of its proper sphere does it lead to falsity. Whether or not the earth is flat or stationary is a question for astronomical science, not a question of or for common sense. Actually none of the statements listed provides an answer to a *philosophical* question, though someone might easily suppose otherwise and consequently get a distorted view of common sense. It is no more the business of common sense to discover the distance between the sun and the moon than it is to discover the ultimate nature of reality or the status of sense-data. Here as elsewhere we must watch out for common sense appropriated for imperialistic enterprise, for common nonsense under an alias.

This is not to deny that such items have been taken as common sense or presented as what passes for common sense. But this only illustrates all the more the need to distinguish between the reality of common sense and the appearance, between common sense and what passes for it or is presented as having its sanction. I earlier referred to the need to distinguish between the 'local' common sense and the general. The expression 'the local common sense' I take from Hamerton, who identifies it with the local public opinion:

The mental centre of ordinary people is simply the public opinion, the common sense, of the class and locality in which they live, so that to them the common sense of people in another class, another locality, appears irrational and absurd . . . Ordinary people, if bred in the same neighborhood and class, are sure to have a great fund of ideas in common, all those ideas that constitute the local common sense. If you listen attentively to their conversations you will find that they hardly ever go outside of that . . . if there is the least touch of any original talent or genius in one of the parties, it is sure to result in many ideas that will be outside of the local common sense, and then the other party, living in that sense, will consider these ideas peculiar and perhaps deplorable.[23]

So the local common sense, in this sense, is the public opinion—the common beliefs—of the ordinary people of a given class and locality. This is something common sense itself is peculiarly liable to be confused with, as it is liable to be confused with folklore, myths, superstitions, common misconceptions, and widespread fallacies. The beliefs that homing pigeons have an innate capacity to find their way home unerringly from any place

---

[23] Philip Gilbert Hamerton, *Human Intercourse* (London: Macmillan, 1884), pp. 52–3.

at any distance, and that the ostrich buries its head in the sand at the approach of danger, are two more examples of widespread myths or misconceptions, folklore, that are sometimes confused with common sense. Common sense they are not. They are simply instances of conventional false beliefs.[24]

6. COMMON SENSE AND POSITIVE MORALITY

Can we distinguish clearly between common-sense morality and positive morality? It is not easy, but a distinction can be made, even though for a number of purposes they can be treated as congruent. Sidgwick ventured such a definition, albeit in passing, in which each is defined in relation to and in contrast with the other, and this can serve as a starting-point. Sidgwick defined positive morality as 'the *ensemble* of rules imposed by common opinion in any society, which form a kind of unwritten legislation, supplementary to Law proper, and enforced by the penalties of social disfavour and contempt'.[25] He says also that 'Positive Morality' is used to refer to 'the actual moral opinions generally held in a given society at a given time' (IV. 3. 458). There is a shift here between *imposed rules* and *opinions* that is not altogether felicitous. But in the place where Sidgwick draws the distinction in question this vacillation drops from view. Sidgwick says that both common-sense morality and positive morality consist of 'general rules, as to the validity of which there would be apparent agreement at least among moral persons of our age and civilisation, and which would cover with approximate completeness the whole of human conduct'.

Such a collection [Sidgwick adds] regarded as a code imposed on an individual by the public opinion of the community to which he belongs . . . is the Positive Morality of the community: but when regarded as a body of moral truth, warranted to be such by the *consensus* of mankind—or at least that portion of mankind which combines adequate intellectual enlightenment with a serious concern for morality—it is more significantly termed the morality of Common Sense'. (III. 1. 215)

---

[24] Evans, *Natural History of Nonsense*, pp. 52, 54. Other instances of what are called variously folklore, folk belief, vulgar convictions, 'old wives' tales', popular beliefs, superstitions, folk zoology, and vulgar lore are provided on pp. 32, 35, 38, 39, 41, 78, 81. Common sense, in the form of 'a common-sense argument', is appealed to on p. 102 as well as on p. 3.

[25] Sidgwick, *Methods*, bk. IV, ch. 5, p. 480.

According to the distinction drawn by Sidgwick, positive morality is a code imposed by public opinion and enforced by social sanctions, whereas common-sense morality is a body of moral truth, or rules that make a claim to moral truth, thought to be so warranted by the consensus of mankind, not merely the public opinion—or the traditions, usages, and customs—of a given community. The distinction, it is clear, is one that can be made only from the point of view of one who is acquainted with the diversity of different moral codes and the changeability of public opinion. Sidgwick's distinction does not imply that the rules of positive morality and common-sense morality must be identical, only that they merge. So they could contain the same rules, but do not have to. Positive morality relates to public opinion, is determined by it, presumably together with traditions and customs and usages. And the two can often be indistinguishable, though that does not make them identical. They tend to vary together, can vary independently. The latter would tend to happen when the positive morality of a group departs from common sense and is overladen with rules that are encrusted with age and reek of obsolescence, perhaps even have become self-defeating. One complication is that individuals belong to different societies, even different communities. But this shows only that they can be bound by conflicting rules and may owe allegiance to different constituencies of opinion. It is out of such conflicts that personal morality develops and that we can get a glimpse of rational morality. Common sense provides procedures for dealing with such conflicts—though usually not sufficient procedures—; positive morality does not. And it is at this point that we can see a further significant difference between positive morality and the morality of common sense. Positive morality does not leave much room for individual differences on moral matters; common-sense morality does, at least on matters not essential for survival. We can say that positive morality consists of rules, common-sense morality largely of principles or standards. But they are most often congruent.

Another way of looking at Sidgwick's distinction is to stress the reference to how the rules are *regarded*. On this basis, when one regards the positive morality of a society merely as a set of rules sanctioned by public opinion, one claims not that it is true but only that it exists and has such-and-such force in the community. One takes, as it were, an external point of view towards it. However, when one calls it common sense, or common-sense morality, one makes a normative claim, to the effect that it is sensible, justified, true: 'regarded as a *body of moral truth* warranted to be such *by the consensus of mankind*'. When one terms it so one takes an internal point of view with respect to it, regards it as one's own morality and therefore as true or correct.[26] It is easy to see how, on this distinction, one can in certain circumstances regard the morality of one's society and common-sense morality as congruent; and how in others one can regard them as at variance with one another. One who regards them as at variance, and so describes them, might not feel bound by positive morality, though one might feel coerced by it; while one would feel bound by what one regards as common-sense morality, as one would feel bound by what one regards as true morality.

Now the positive morality of a society also has great affinities with its positive law, develops in similar ways. As Cardozo observed: 'The constant assumption runs throughout the law that the natural and spontaneous evolutions of habit fix the limits of right and wrong. A slight extension of custom identifies it with customary morality, the prevailing standard of right conduct, the mores of the time.'[27] All attempts to draw a sharp line between them are doomed to failure. But, though there is overlapping and intermingling between the positive morality and the positive law of a society, they are still distinct. Morality is not law, though they both link with custom and develop along with it. And custom can be contrary to law just as it can be contrary to morality. Of course it cannot be contrary to customary morality—without there being contrary customs—but this shows only that it is a mistake to identify morality with customary or positive morality.

7. COMMON SENSE IN ETHICS

The common sense (in the product sense) of one community is not necessarily the common sense of another. Common sense can vary from one community to another as it varies over time. Common sense develops in a manner something like common law and takes its roots from the same source: custom, common predicaments, and common-sense reasoning. Custom and common predicaments being different, the results will be different, even if the reasoning is the same.

---

[26] The distinction used here between external and internal points of view is akin to but not exactly the same as the one drawn by H. L. A. Hart in *The Concept of Law* (Oxford: Clarendon Press, 1961), at pp. 86–7; cf. pp. 55–6, 99 and *passim*.

[27] Benjamin Nathan Cardozo, *The Nature of the Judicial Process* (New Haven, Conn.: Yale University Press, 1921), p. 63.

The value of common sense is in application, not in the realm of abstract principle. Some of the key developments in morality and in the moral consciousness of the world have not stemmed from common sense, though they have resulted in great changes in common sense. These developments can in large part be characterized as extensions of the boundaries of the moral community, so that it now includes all humanity and is thought by some to include all animal or sentient life. They have resulted from moral insight and moral theory, not from common sense. Common sense is not innovative or creative. It is conservative. Still, common sense changes, though only slowly, at a glacial pace. On many matters it is now in flux, reflecting the confusion and revolution and terror of our time. This affects manners as well as morals, demeanour as well as institutions.

Common-sense morality can be narrow, prejudiced, bigoted, and oppressive, as in the phenomena of racism and anti-Semitism. In such contexts, 'That's just common sense', heard so often, is just a question-begging phrase. But that common sense can be counterfeited is no more a point against it than the fact of counterfeiting is a point against money. Reason can also be counterfeited. The problem is whether an analogue of Gresham's Law (that bad money tends to drive good money out of circulation) operates with common sense as well. I do not think so, but it is a danger, as hysteria is a danger.

To take a well-worn though still useful example, it was once part of common sense and is still a part of common language (so it may still be part of common sense), that the earth is motionless and the sun in motion. This is the view that is impressed upon us and thus pressed upon us by all the features of ordinary experience. We cannot feel the earth moving; it feels as though it is stationary; although its apparent motion is so slow we do not actually have the sensation of seeing the sun move, nonetheless it looks as though the sun is moving. All that is apparent to common sense. And we still speak of 'the sun rising' and 'the sun setting'. Yet in recent centuries people have come to be taught that it is the other way around, and that this is something that has been proved by science. It is testimony to the power of science and education and imitation that so many people have come to accept as part of their view of the world this view which is so contrary to common experience and to the testimony of their senses. This is done almost solely on faith, since the number of people who can cite evidence or argument for what is now the received view is vanishingly small. Most people believe it because they have been taught so. But that the sun is stationary and the earth in motion can hardly be regarded as initially a common-sense belief. Common sense still has its feet on the ground; it does not deal in abstractions though it deals in broad principles. The acceptance of something like a heliocentric theory is a triumph of science and education over common sense; it is also a case of common sense being enlightened.

Nonetheless, common sense is essential to morality. If Common Sense equals native good sense, as in one sense it does, then it is clear that there is no doing without it. But the common sense that equals native good sense is not the common sense that is congruent with positive morality. The rules of positive morality, especially the local rules that vary from culture to culture and from time to time, are often narrow, stupid, vicious, and cruel. They can be the results of ignorance, superstition, prejudice, fear, and folly, can embody taboos and desiccated habits, can be oppressive intolerant and unjust. Positive morality cannot by itself distinguish fundamental moral rules, essential to the survival of the society and the welfare of its members (such as the rules prohibiting murder, assault, rape, robbery, and gross dishonesty), from local rules, which vary across time and space and which constitute the part of morality that is felt as changing, sometimes giving rise to feelings of being adrift.[28] Here again we see the systematic ambiguity of common sense. But there is also no doing without positive morality. It is because we are brought up in a culture that has a morality that we are enabled to acquire a morality of our own and hence the capacity to improve on the morality of our group. Hence there is no doing without the common sense that is involved in positive morality. But positive morality is necessary in a way different from the way in which native good sense is necessary, and for different purposes. Without minimal sense there is no surviving, without good sense there is no possibility of improvement.

If common sense is essential to morality, it is also essential to ethics. For ethics must take its start from common sense, both as method and as substance, and must also take its start from morality. That is where the problems are. Ethics is about morality, attempts to understand it and to enlighten it, and must in the process be constrained by it.[29] This is a paradox only to theorists who have taken leave of common sense, not to common sense.

---

[28] The distinction between local and fundamental rules is developed in *Generalization*, ch. 5, pp. 112–23. The rules relating to sexual conduct and supposed to regulate relations between the sexes, typically regarded by so many as basic to morality, are mostly local rules, where they are not mere matters of mores, custom, and tradition.

[29] On these points, about the relation of ethics to our common moral life, cf. Murphy, *Theory of Practical Reason*, esp. pp. 10–13, 13; also the introd., by A. I. Melden, pp. xi–xii, xvii.

8. LESSONS OF COMMON SENSE IN ETHICS

What then are the distinctive features of common sense in ethics? These virtues are manifested in the ethical works of Aristotle, Reid, and Sidgwick, the most famous and most representative of the common-sense moral philosophers, and it is interesting that this same common-sense tradition extends over vastly different societies and such vast stretches of time.

(1) The first lesson of common sense in ethics is not to demand or expect more precision or certainty than the subject is capable of, and in ethical matters this is not very great. Aristotle's statement on this is well known; one wonders if it is as well understood:

Our discussion will be adequate if it has as much clearness as the subject matter admits of, for precision is not to be sought for alike in all discussions ... fine and just actions ... admit of much variety and fluctuation of opinion, so that they may be thought to exist only by convention, and not by nature. And goods give rise to a similar fluctuation because they bring harm to many people ... We must be content, then, in speaking of such subjects and with such premisses to indicate the truth roughly and in outline ... In the same spirit, therefore, should each type of statement be received; for it is the mark of an educated man to look for precision in each class of things just so far as the nature of the subject admits.[30]

What Aristotle is saying in the last sentence quoted can be better understood, I think, if for 'an educated man' we substitute 'good sense'; it is certainly the mark of good sense to look for precision in each class of things just so far as the nature of the subject admits. It is, indeed, to overlook the basis of this observation to suppose that Aristotle said this only because he was aware of the inexactitude of his own ethical theory, whereas a truly rational and scientific ethics would attain as much precision and certainty as is attainable in logic or anywhere. This is not so. The result of aiming at such absolute rigor is only the rigor of rigor mortis, and ethical theories that aim at this certainly depart from common sense, are out of touch with life and out of touch with morals. This is true even though some philosophies most attuned to common sense occasionally stray from their own moorings.

This is not to say that nothing is certain in ethics or that there is no precision to be attained in it. This is not so. It is rather that on many matters neither certainty nor great precision is attainable, and attempting to foist

---

[30] Aristotle, *Nicomachean Ethics*, 1. 3, 1094ᵇ.

these ideals of precision and certainty on the subject-matter is most likely either to distort the subject-matter or disappoint the theorist. We should beware of supposing that our characteristic defects are some higher form of health. But what is a defect in one setting is not necessarily a defect in another. And it is worth noting that few philosophers of physics have been able to make sense of ethics.

(2) The second lesson of common sense in ethics is an immediate corollary. It is to not expect every ethical and moral question to have a unique and definitive answer that everyone must accept on pain of self-contradiction or irrationality. Moral questions and moral judgements do not universally or characteristically have this character. This is recognized by common sense, though not readily by philosophy.

(3) The third lesson of common sense in ethics is that a view that has been held a long time by a large number of people, especially ordinary decent reasonable people, is not likely to be wrong (though of course it may be), and is most unlikely to be entirely wrong (though there have been instances of this too). Aristotle put a similar point as follows: 'Some of these views have been held by many men and by men of old, others by a few eminent persons; and it is not probable that either of these should be entirely mistaken, but rather that they should be right in at least some one respect or even in most respects' (1098^b28-30). Also: 'We must, as in all other cases, set the observed facts before us and, after first discussing the difficulties, go on to prove, if possible, the truth of all the common opinions about these affections of the mind, or failing this, of the greater number and the most authoritative; for if we both refute the objections and leave the common opinions undisturbed, we shall have proved the case sufficiently' (1145^b2-7).

(4) The fourth main lesson of common sense in ethics is that the truth in practical—ethical—matters is to be discerned in and tested against the facts of life. Aristotle put this as follows: 'the truth in practical matters is discerned from the facts of life; for these are the decisive factor. We must therefore survey what we have already said, bringing it to the test of the facts of life, and if it harmonizes with the facts we must accept it, but if it clashes with them we must suppose it to be mere theory' (1179^a17-23). Of course there can be disagreement, even sharp disagreement, over what the facts of life are, but disagreement over what they are is sensible only because this Aristotelian tenet is both valid and reasonable.

These are all lessons that Aristotle learned and passed on very early in the history of ethical thought, and it is adherence to these lessons, in spirit if not in every point, that distinguishes a common-sense ethics, such as Aristotle's, from one of a Parmenidean type.

(5) The fifth lesson of common sense in ethics is that ethics is to be applied to the facts of life in accordance with the facts of life; that is, in accordance with good sense and good judgement. The opposite of common-sense ethics is provided by fanatical ethics, a priori rationalists, ideologues, and those who cling at all costs to one supreme principle as the bedrock of all moral knowledge and regard it as itself independent of moral judgement. One defender of such a view, who takes it for granted that practically all existing social arrangements are unjust and to be discarded, has said: 'If we have a soundly based moral theory, we ought to be prepared to accept its implications even if they force us to change our moral views on major issues. Once this point is forgotten, moral theory loses its capacity to generate radical criticism of prevailing moral standards, and serves only to preserve the status quo.'[31] But, naturally, *if* we have a *soundly based* moral theory, we ought to be prepared to accept its implications. How do we know, however, that our theory is 'soundly based'? Surely it is not soundly based because it would lead us 'to change our moral views on major issues'. Nor is it soundly based because it would 'generate radical criticism of prevailing moral standards'. To suppose this would be insanity. For, there would then be no ground for accepting the theory or for regarding it as 'soundly based' and a theory can be soundly based and not be true. The idea that one can have a 'soundly based' moral theory that has moral implications and that is not in turn based on moral judgements—that is to say, good sense and good judgement—is chimerical. (I am reminded here of the story of the modal logician who said to another modal logician, 'The contradictory of your theorem is a member of my axiom set.' Is absolute a priori ethics in a different case?) Abstract deduction from abstract principles to supply rules of conduct and precise directives for action must be measured against common sense, especially when these deductions go against common-sense rules, and this for reasons that Russell has so nicely put. For, as Russell observed (even though he was in other respects as guilty of this excess as any), there is greater likelihood of error in very subtle, abstract, and difficult arguments than in the common-sense beliefs and convictions they are often invoked to undermine. Russell said of the Greek philosophers that: 'They would prove . . . that all reality is one, that there is no such thing as change, that the world of sense is a world of mere illusion; and the strangeness of their results gave them no qualms because they believed in the correctness of their reasoning.' It is the part of wisdom—

---

[31] Peter Singer, 'Philosophers are Back on the Job', *New York Times Magazine*, 7 July 1974, pp. 19–20.

and common sense—to be aware that arguments that lead anywhere at all are liable to lead one astray if one does not check their leading tendencies with good judgement and good sense. As Russell further observed: 'Plato . . . adopted from the Eleatics the device of using logic to defeat common sense, and thus to leave the field clear for mysticism.'[32] But the logic that is used to *defeat* common sense is really illogic, and is the illogic that is used to leave the field clear for tyranny and injustice. For, to surrender one's powers of judgement to the elaboration of some abstract principle is on a par with surrendering one's powers of judgement—one's common sense— to the whims and dictates of an absolute ruler. It is because this type of reasoning, or logic-chopping, was so characteristic of Parmenides that I refer to it as Parmenideanism. Parmenideanism in ethics is the opposite of common sense in ethics. It is curious that Moore, who so ably defended common sense elsewhere, should have departed so far from it in his ethics. But the extreme conservatism of Moore's ethics, which maintains that one should always abide by the rules of one's community that are generally recognized and generally observed—which is a wholesale 'justification' of the status quo on a par with that provided by the theological utilitarianism of Paley—is as absurd, and as contrary to reason and common sense, as the self-conscious radicalism that would hold any view correct that would lead to the overturning of all established rules and institutions. One who goes pretty fast in the wrong direction can go pretty far wrong, and there is more than one wrong direction.

(6) The sixth lesson of common sense in ethics is that common sense is not a system and does not pretend to be. What is referred to as the morality of common sense is not a system of ethics. The need to systematize and coordinate and clarify common-sense morality is a demand of philosophical ethics, moral philosophy, not a demand of common sense. Here, curiously, is where Sidgwick, normally so careful and so circumspect, went astray. And here also is where we can notice some deficiencies of common sense, which is by no means a complete or infallible guide to ethics or morality. Common sense, though it is essential to ethics, is not sufficient for it.

---

[32] Bertrand Russell, *Our Knowledge of the External World*, pp. 17–18, 15, 30. Some of the observations here are drawn, from 'Justice, Theory, and a Theory of Justice', *Philosophy of Science*, 44 (December 1977), pp. 608, 615–16.

9. ETHICS IN COMMON SENSE

Something further common sense brings to ethics is a saving grace: common sense in application. Common sense is impatient with regulations, forms, procedures, bureaucracy, and red tape, goes and wants to go straight to the point. The problems Mark Twain ran into with a branch-railroad in Australia illustrate the point of the common-sense attitude. Here is his account of what is said by an impatient resident of the country:

that train from Maryborough will consist of eighteen freight-cars and two-passenger kennels; cheap, poor, shabby, slovenly; no drinking water, no sanitary arrangements, every imaginable inconvenience; and slow?—oh, the gait of cold molasses; no air-brake, no springs, and they'll jolt your head off every time they start or stop. That's where they make their little economies, you see. They spend tons of money to house you palatially while you wait fifteen minutes for a train, then degrade you to six hours' convict-transportation to get the foolish outlay back. What a rational man really needs is discomfort while he's waiting, then his journey in a nice train would be a grateful change. But no, that would be common sense and out of place in a government.[33]

Through the film of whimsy with which Twain was given to embellishing his stories, we can see it, common sense itself. That *would* be common sense. But common sense is hard to arrange on a large scale, or, evidently, on a railroad.

Common sense in ethics, for all its affinity to common law, with its reliance on custom and practice and tradition, is more akin to equity than to law. It has been observed, by Frederick Pollock, that the moral judgement of 'an average right-minded person'—by which, as we shall see, we can understand a reasonable person—'does on the whole follow precedent and is guided by settled principles'.[34] But the precedent and the principles, and especially the procedures, must be those of common sense and hence very unlike those of the common law, just as they are very unlike those of the casuistry said to have been practiced by the Jesuits. And there are laws, at any time and at any place, manifestly inconsistent with common sense, even the common sense of the time and place. Common-sense judgement will go straight to the heart of the matter—or what it takes to be the heart of the matter—to render justice in the individual case, even if that breaches

[33] Mark Twain, *Following the Equator* (New York: Harper, 1899), vol. i, ch. 31, pp. 279–80.
[34] Frederick Pollock, 'The Casuistry of Common Sense', in his *Essays in Jurisprudence and Ethics* (London: Macmillan, 1882), p. 270.

precedent and principle. It tends to regard learned arguments involving subtle distinctions or raising complex questions as a sort of 'trained incapacity to make relevant practical distinctions'.[35] As Pollock says: 'This habit of instinctive moral judgement, acquired by living in society, and analogous to the instinct of the expert in a particular branch of knowledge, is what we specially denote as the moral sense.'[36]

The link with common law is brought out further by the link with legal standards of negligence and due care, which appeal to a community sense of reasonableness, and are not fixed once and for all. Thus the common-law conception of common sense is provided by the common-law standard of due care, which is the degree of care that a reasonably prudent person, a person of ordinary prudence, would exercise under the same or similar circumstances. Common sense as it is understood in the law is 'that degree of intelligence and reason, as exercised upon the relations of persons and things and the ordinary affairs of life, which is possessed by the generality of mankind, and which would suffice to direct the conduct and actions of the individual in a manner to agree with the behavior of ordinary persons'.[37] Ordinary, reasonable, or due care (the law uses these terms interchangeably) is that degree of care 'which reasonably prudent persons exercise in the management of their own affairs'.[38] But ordinary or reasonable care is equivalent to prudence; a prudent person is one who exercises attentiveness, concern, and good judgement—in other words, good sense—in the ordinary affairs of life, in running his or her own life and dealing with other people. Now, reasonable care is that degree of care which a person of ordinary prudence (and a person of ordinary prudence in this context is the same as a reasonable person of ordinary prudence) would exercise in the same circumstances. This is the basis of what is known as 'the standard of the reasonable person'. A *standard* links with a standard way of proceeding—an average, normal, ordinary, common way of proceeding—and this carries the implication that the standard, usual, ordinary, common way is (or is at least, taken to be) the reasonable way, hence the right way.

The interconnectedness of these notions provides insight into the common notions, hence into common sense, common law, and common-sense morality. Reasonable care is the same as ordinary care and the same as prudence, the care that a reasonable person of ordinary prudence would

[35] Murphy, *Practical Reason*, p. 17.
[36] Pollock, 'Casuistry', p. 275.
[37] *Black's Law Dictionary*, 5th edn. (St Paul, Minn.: West, 1979), p. 250.
[38] Ibid., p. 989.

exercise under the same conditions. Note that this refers to ordinary prudence, not exceptional; and to a person of ordinary, not exceptional, intelligence. But a person who is reasonable as so construed is a person who is prudent. Hence in common law and in common sense reasonable equals prudent, and 'prudent' does not import concern only for one's own welfare though it does imply and presuppose a good healthy concern for one's own welfare.

But what is reasonable is what is fit, suitable, proper, fair, just—common sense makes no distinctions among these conceptions. And the reasonable is contrasted with what is immoderate, excessive, or extreme, and in that sense beyond the common (and, in a way, beyond the pale).

There is, consequently, a normative standard built right into the very conception of common sense. A person of common sense is a person of ordinary intelligence who applies this intelligence in the ordinary affairs of life and in relation to other persons in the community. Such a person is prudent, and in being prudent is reasonable and in being reasonable is prudent. In being reasonable such a person considers the interests of others, and is prepared to judge and to act in the light of the interests of others rather than on merely self-interested desires, and this implies some measure of respect for the interests of others, hence for the welfare of others, hence for others. Just so, a reasonable price is a fair price, a moderate price, one not excessive, too far above or below the average; it is a price such as one would be prepared to pay if one were in the position of the buyer. And we thus see that the requirement of reciprocity, or impartiality, is already part of common sense.

Thus we have the answer to the question: Given that there is such a thing as common sense, is there such a thing as a common moral sense? Common sense thinks there is, takes it for granted, has no patience with anyone lacking it or failing to manifest it, regards some whose violations are gross and seemingly inexplicable as monsters and as 'inhuman', and is deeply puzzled about how to deal with them.

In all these ways, common sense is deeply and ineradicably normative. Ethics in the code-of-conduct sense is an essential and deep-seated part of common sense.

I have already made some use of an essay of uncommon sense on these matters, Frederick Pollock's 'The Casuistry of Common Sense', which, though it has been available for some time, seems to be little known. In it we find exhibited very well the casuistry of common sense; that is, the methods used by common sense for dealing with 'new problems in conduct as they arise', 'that art, which we all have to exercise more or less, of applying ethical knowledge to the solution of new ethical problems in practice'—which is not to say that it details the decision in every case or claims to provide a method for so doing. Pollock points out something that moral philosophers as a profession are professionally inclined to overlook, that a person's 'competence to decide on a particular case of conscience is by no means necessarily in proportion to his scientific knowledge of ethics. There are many persons whose judgment on the morality of a proposed course of conduct one might almost implicitly trust, but who know nothing whatever of moral philosophy.'[39] This is what we mean by common sense, which functions well in its proper domain even though not aware of its sources principles or methods. Thus the 'Autocrat of the Breakfast-Table':

> Some of the sharpest men in argument are notoriously unsound in judgment. I should not trust the judgment of a clever debater, any more than that of a good chess-player. Either may of course advise wisely, but not necessarily because he wrangles or plays well.[40]

As I have said, common sense is intrinsically and ineluctably ethical in character, could not function if it weren't. Common sense knows the difference between right and wrong and knows that it knows it, in the common sense of 'know'. And it has no patience with epistemological theories which 'attempt to persuade us that in order to know something which we know quite well, we must also be knowing something which seems actually, and after the most careful inspection, to be very doubtful indeed'.[41] Professional moralists—ethical thinkers—tend to be impatient with this, think that theory is to be elevated above ordinary moral rules and the alleged wisdom of practice and experience—above, that is, common sense. But they often confuse common sense with folklore or with something else masquerading as common sense. And, again, what this indicates is that we must be on our guard to distinguish common sense from that which only passes for common sense. Melden observes that 'what passes for common sense turns out, upon closer inspection, to be a disorderly clutter of opposing judgments that reflect the idiosyncracies of individuals and the variety of traditions to which they subscribe. Moral reflection must inevitably come into conflict with some facets of everyday moral thinking.'[42] Yes,

---

[39] Pollock, 'Casuistry', pp. 265, 266.

[40] Oliver Wendell Holmes, *The Autocrat of the Breakfast Table* (Boston: Houghton, Mifflin, 1858, 1882), P. 14.

[41] Murphy, *Reason and the Common Good*, p. 105.

[42] A. I. Melden, *Rights and Persons* (Berkeley and Los Angeles, Calif.: University of California Press, 1977), p. 26.

emphatically. I will turn shortly to some of the reasons that make such conflict both inevitable and also desirable. But I do not think we have here
been provided with them. Notice that the passage speaks of what '*passes for
common sense*'. I do not think that it intended to emphasize the 'passes
for'; it bears emphasizing nonetheless. We have seen ample reason to bear
that out. Something can pass for common sense, as a counterfeit bill can
pass for genuine, and it will be taken for genuine so long as it so passes. As
it is not always easy to distinguish between what is real and what only
appears to be, there is no reason to think it any easier in the case of common sense, even common-sense moral thinking. It will be an aid in this
process to recur to the distinction between common sense as capacity and
common sense as the product—and possibly the encrusted product—of
that capacity. The product of one time and place may be inapplicable to
another. For the product of that capacity may not be an enlarged and
refined capacity but only an ossified one. It may be only the positive morality of a given society or the quirky personal morality of some individual—
and the latter especially may have little relation to common sense though it
is thought to and may seem to.

I once heard a student say in a classroom debate about capital punishment that 'Common sense dictates that capital punishment does deter
crime' and 'Common sense alone without the benefit of knowledge, wisdom, or experience tells us that no one who would expect to be executed
for it would commit a crime.' Does it? The latter statement may be taken
as true, with some qualifications that need not here be stated, but it does
not entail the former, and this little instance of common-sense reasoning,
as I take it to be, is fallacious. On the death penalty itself common sense
dictates nothing, and the appeal to it as supporting one's preconceived
position is only an appeal to dogma. All that we can say on this score is
that there was a time when common-sense morality did not regard the
death penalty as wrong, any more than it regarded as wrong flogging, the
pillory, or the stocks, or any more than it regarded as wrong the rack or
the thumbscrew or other forms of torture. And on these latter matters the
morality of common sense is now different from what it was.

But the fact that appeals to common sense, in the form 'Common sense
dictates' or 'Common sense shows' or 'It is just a matter of common sense',
can be mistaken and fallacious—especially when by itself such an appeal
is taken as establishing some position on a controversial and complex
matter—shows nothing. People also say such things as 'History shows',
'Experience indicates', 'Reason shows', 'It stands to reason', 'Science has
proved', and often say them fallaciously. It does not follow that appeals to

experience, history, science, or reason are all and always fallacious, or that history, experience, science, and reason establish nothing. Similarly with common sense. The only difference is that on many matters it is so much harder to be sure what the verdict of common sense is.

Melden actually provides, though unwittingly, an example of this elusive character and deceptive appearance in what he says about promises to the dead (by which is meant not a promise made to someone already dead, but a promise made to someone who dies after the promise is made—a qualification needed to ward off deadly wit). Sidgwick judged it to be part of common-sense morality that promises to the dead ought to be kept.[43] Melden takes it to be 'the common sense conviction' that 'a deathbed promise—and in general, any promise that can be kept only after the promisee has died—does not bind the promiser and serves only to comfort or relieve the anxiety or distress of the promisee during his last moments', and he pits against this his own 'conviction that a deathbed promise does bind'.[44] I should not argue with the latter. But I should with the former. How is it ascertained that this is 'the common sense conviction'? What we have here would seem to be simply a case of some people thinking one way and others thinking another. Both convictions seem part of common morality in the sense that different views are held about the matter by reasonable persons of common sense. Hence it can be said that both convictions, incompatible as they are, are part of the morality of common sense. It is thus unlikely that any decisive arguments are going to be found for one or the other. That is one reason why Sidgwick found such confusion in what he took to be the morality of common sense. For he was looking for, and hoped to find, decisive convictions on one side or the other on matters on which common sense does not decide. In the sense of holding specific views such as this it is dubious that common sense has any morality, at least any consistent morality. The morality of common sense is not a moral system, and does not pretend to either consistency or completeness.

This brings us to the deficiencies of common-sense morality.

10. DEFICIENCIES OF COMMON-SENSE MORALITY

One deficiency of common-sense morality is that by itself it can make no advance on the moral standards of the day, is essentially conservative. And

---

[43] *Methods*, p. 295.   [44] Melden, *Rights and Persons*, pp. 48–9.

we do know—nearly everyone takes it for granted, it may even be said to be a matter of common sense—that there has been moral progress, at least on some matters. As Pollock put it, a person 'may be blameless and even punctilious in his life according to the moral standard of the society he lives in, but quite incapable of seeing that the standard itself is faulty'.[45] Pollock instances slavery (p. 296) and the code of duelling (p. 266)—strangely disparate examples—which were both at one time accepted practices of positive morality, hence of common-sense morality (though in different circles), and have since been repudiated by it. Torture, witch burning, and human sacrifice are other matters on which there has been a fundamental change in the morality of common sense. It would be hard to find many even advanced thinkers who would not agree that these practices are wrong and that they used to be engaged in systematically (and in the belief that they were right). But everyone who now takes it for granted that they are wrong—and that is practically everyone—must admit that there has been, on such matters at least, moral progress, which is consistent with moral retrogression on other matters and even with retrogression in practice with regard to these. We live in a world in which torture, for instance, is practically everywhere vehemently condemned even while its incidence is in so many places increasing. But this progress was not initiated by common sense.

A marvellous example of the conservative character of positive morality is provided in Mark Twain's *Huckleberry Finn*, when Huck tells Aunt Sally that he was delayed by an explosion on a river boat:

'It warn't the grounding—that didn't keep us back but a little. We blowed out a cylinder-head.'
'Good gracious! Anybody hurt?'
'No'm. Killed a nigger.'
'Well, it's lucky; because sometimes people do get hurt. Two years ago last Christmas your uncle Silas was coming up from Newrleans on the old *Lally Rook*, and she blowed out a cylinder-head and crippled a man. And I think he died afterwards.'[46]

Dear, gentle, kindly Aunt Sally, who though she was not especially intelligent did not altogether lack common sense, was imbued with a morality

---

[45] Pollock, 'Casuistry', p. 266.
[46] Mark Twain, *The Adventures of Huckleberry Finn* (New York: Harper, 1884), ch. 32, pp. 306–7. Hart comments on this (*The Concept of Law*, p. 254): 'Mark Twain's novel is a profound study of the moral dilemma created by the existence of a social morality which runs counter to the sympathies of an individual and to humanitarianism. It is a valuable corrective of the identification of all morality with the latter.' But it is just as true that it is a valuable corrective of the identification of all morality with the former.

that did not regard 'niggers' as people, but as property—which is presumably what the use of the abusive word 'nigger' now imports. And when people with that outlook came, albeit begrudgingly, to regard 'Negroes' or black people as people, not as property, that was change for the better in the positive morality of that society, consequently in the common sense of that society.

Lionel Trilling has commented on this: 'No one who reads thoughtfully the dialectic of Huck's moral crisis will ever again be wholly able to accept without some question . . . the assumptions of the respectable morality by which he lives, nor will ever again be certain that what he considers the clear dictates of moral reason are not merely the engrained customary beliefs of his time and place.' Another astute comment on this passage is by D. J. Tice: 'Once slavery is accepted as an unremarkable fact of life, as it is by Huck and every other character in the novel, Huck's treatment of Miss Watson does indeed seem shabby, Jim's plan to "steal" his own children does indeed seem shocking. Nowhere else in literature is the power of socially sanctioned untruth to pervert ordinary morality more startlingly and subtly dramatized.'[47] Note that the author is here unashamedly making a moral judgement; by 'ordinary morality' he does not mean the socially sanctioned morality but rather true morality, or the morality of common sense. For the ordinary morality of the time and place was perverted in the respects mentioned. And what makes us so sure that the 'ordinary morality' of our time is not also perverted in respects not mentioned?

There is a valuable lesson here and a warning which *Huckleberry Finn* and these astute comments help drive home. It is very easy to mistake the dictates of the conventional morality of one's society—or the views that seem to one to be sound—for the dictates of common sense or of moral reason. And it is also easy to suppose that because conventional morality can be short-sighted and even cruel—in a word, morally deficient—that therefore it always is and is never to be trusted, and that therefore there is no such thing as a sound morality of common sense or dictate of moral reason. Both inferences are equally absurd, though they go in opposite directions. Each is on a par with the absurdity that what is new and up-to-date is therefore good and right and sound, and that where previous generations differed from us they must obviously and ludicrously be wrong. As we

---

[47] Lionel Trilling, 'Huckleberry Finn', in *The Liberal Imagination* (1948, 1950) (Garden City, NY: Doubleday (Anchor Books, 1953), p. 114; D. J. Tice, 'Huckleberry Finn', *TWA Ambassador* (Sept. 1983), p. 45.

must beware of egocentrism and ethnocentrism, we must also beware of presentism and futurism; both are forms of faddism, of supposing that what is going on now is the standard for all time because up-to-date. 'Hitch your wagon to a trend' is not a maxim worth following, though followed it often is. Moral progress is a possibility and in some cases a fact, but it is not something inevitable. As Tom Paine observed, long ago: 'Those who lived a hundred or a thousand years ago, were then moderns, as we are now. They had *their* ancestors, and those ancients had theirs, and we also shall be ancients in our turn.'

Occasionally such a change for the better in common-sense morality is itself regarded as an instance of common sense. Emerson says: 'Society is always taken by surprise at any new example of common sense and of simple justice, as at a wonderful discovery. Thus . . . at the introduction of gentleness into insane asylums, and of cleanliness and comfort into penitentiaries.'[48] But this may be because in such a statement 'common sense' is being used in the sense of good sense, or else because the reform in question is almost immediately accepted, which means that it is accepted as common sense.

What these instances establish is the need to supplement and reform common-sense morality—the common moral sense—by moral insight, which sometimes can be attained by moral theory. Aristotle, for all his acuity, genius, perception, and wisdom was unable to get beyond the assumptions of his time with respect to slavery—with the exception that he saw that it needed justification. An ethics that is tied too closely to common sense will thus be unable to generate or sustain any moral progress, and can too easily turn into an apologia for the status quo, unable to get beyond the limitations of common-sense morality.

Notwithstanding these limitations of common sense, there are circumstances under which we can be pretty certain of what is common sense and, if we are not blinded by a false theory, that it is sensible. Thus, common sense is in touch with different kinds and degrees of wrong, and on this matter ethics as a discipline has much to learn from it. There are some things which, though wrong, are still permissible, given the world we live in and the exigencies of living. For instance, teenagers often find that in order to get a first job or a summer job, even part-time, they have to shade the truth, or, in a word, to lie about whether they are planning to go back to school or on to college, or they will not be able to earn any money.

---

[48] R. W. Emerson, 'Celebration of Intellect', in *Works*, centenary edn., xii, *Natural History of Intellect* (Boston: Houghton Mifflin, 1921), p. 118.

Common sense regards this, though with some hesitation, as unfortunate; as permissible though wrong; as wrong but not so terrible; on the ground that one who is punctilious in observing every feature of the moral code, no matter how minute, will find it too hard to survive. But there are other things that common sense does not regard as permissible ever, such as murder, mayhem, brutal rape, mutilation, torture, gratuitous injury, vandalism. Common sense regards these one and all as horrible, inhumane, inhuman, monstrous, sick, insane and as never justifiable or even excusable. Though there are 'white lies' allowed by common sense, there is no equivalent allowable murder, mayhem, torture. We live in an imperfect world and sometimes, in order to live in it, have to do such things as lie (in situations of the sort described, though common sense does not itself attempt to describe them or provide a theory for recognizing them). But the imperfection of the world, and the need to live in it as imperfect as it is, is not regarded by common sense as warranting any of these other activities, which are never necessary for just getting along in the world; those who engage in such activities are regarded as enemies of the community, as they are, to be dealt with accordingly—though on the matter of how to deal with them there is great confusion and disagreement.

Ethics as theory and as proclaimed guide to life often at least appears to deny the reality of this distinction, perhaps because it can find no theoretical basis for the category of permissible wrongs, inclines to treat the idea as self-contradictory—which it is not to common sense—hence to regard common sense as confused (which it is not). And that is not sensible. Ethics often attempts to supply imperfect humans with rigid rules for living in an imperfect world, unexceptional and unexceptionable criteria for solving all problems that arise, and thus brings itself into disrepute. For that also is not sensible. It is the idea of common sense that life cannot be lived according to formulas, that common sense must be exercised.

It is clear from this one example that ethics as discipline has much to learn from common sense. There is no substitute, anywhere, for common sense in the form of good sense and good judgement. But just as certainly common sense is not enough. In a paraphrase of a great philosopher who certainly went well beyond common sense but nonetheless understood very well the importance of the common moral understanding, we can say that common sense without ethics is blind, while ethics without common sense is empty. We can also say that common sense without ethics is meaningless, while ethics without common sense is senseless. But common sense without ethics is really inconceivable. Unfortunately, ethics without common sense is not.

CODA

Some afterthoughts, and a brief summary.

Common sense is involved in our common moral life and is essential for there to be any community in and from which our ethical ideas take their origin and to which they refer and which in turn they attempt to enlighten and advance. For common sense is essentially conservative and, crusted over, can get enmeshed with unenlightened and oppressive positive morality, and even confused with it. Common sense also has no patience with close analysis and fine distinctions. Although there are times when these are out of place and not needed, hence justly condemned by common sense, there are also times when they are needed, for breaking through the encrusted shell of a self-satisfied unreflective moral outlook and for the resolution of really difficult moral problems—and for realizing, sometimes, that they exist. Common sense by itself is not proof against corruption, greed, selfishness, sloth, or irresponsibility. This is where ethics is needed, ethics married to common sense—and sometimes an ethical ideal or sense of moral revulsion not married to common sense. The Abolitionists did not operate with common sense—they went well beyond it, and a good thing it is too, for common sense as well as the experiment with freedom that constituted the Republic. Abraham Lincoln, who for many constitutes something of a model of practical wisdom, also went well beyond the common sense of his time in the way in which he clarified the aims of the government he headed, tailored means to those ends, and formulated workable ideals for the country he led; and this required him to repudiate the Abolitionists as well as the defenders of slavery. Thus we see that although common sense can get along without metaphysics, it cannot get along without ethics, and both moral theory and moral inspiration are needed. But if moral theory is applied without the saving grace of common sense what results is the fallacy of delusive exactness, which is an element of the learned ignorance; such a theory, if successful, in action can too easily become only another ideology and be conservative and oppressive in its turn. And if moral inspiration is applied without the saving grace of common sense we are too likely to reap the wind of chaos, fanaticism, anarchy, and terror, as in the French, Russian, and Iranian revolutions.

A standard fallacy, myth, misconception, or prejudice can be enshrined in idiom, hence in common sense, and when this happens is very difficult to dislodge from this privileged position. Some such misconceptions can cause no trouble—at least for common sense—as for instance the standard idea that the sun rises and sets. Some can cause great trouble, as for instance the idea that some races or groups of people, or people who speak a different language or have different customs, are subhuman if human at all, and for that reason are as lacking in rights as they are in the benefits of material culture and the language of the selected people. And here is where moral theory, as well as, sometimes, moral inspiration, and sometimes even the making of a great deal of noise, plays not just an important but an essential role.

And this is the basis of the conclusion that ethics and common sense are essential for each other, that one without the other is immoral and the other without the one is stupid.

ADDITIONAL NOTES AND COMMENTS

A. 'Ethics and Common Sense' was originally published in *Revue Internationale de Philosophie*, 40(3) (1986), pp. 221–58, a special issue on 'common sense'. It was written in 1984–5, when I was at the Royal Institute of Philosophy in London, shortly before I started writing 'The Ideal of a Rational Morality', so repetition here of some ideas expressed there is not completely coincidental. It was the late Professor Chaim Perelman who specifically asked me to contribute an essay on ethics and common sense to that special issue of the *Revue* and I was glad to try to oblige. Here is the result, reprinted here with little change, and with the addition of the Coda.

B. The most valuable discussion I know of on common sense and philosophy is Henry Sidgwick's 'The Philosophy of Common Sense', *Mind*, NS 4(14) (April 1895), pp. 145–58, repr. in *Essays on Ethics and Method*, pp. 139–50. See also Murphy, 'Moore's Defence of Common Sense' in *Reason and the Common Good*, pp. 108–20. Two papers by Edward H. Madden, 'The Metaphilosophy of Commonsense', *American Philosophical Quarterly*, 20(1) (January 1983), pp. 23–36, and 'Victor Cousin and the Commonsense Tradition', *History of Philosophy Quarterly*, 1(1) (January 1984), pp. 93–109, are illuminating on a good part of the history of the philosophy of common sense. A recent entry is Brian Grant, 'The Virtues of Common Sense', *Philosophy*, 76 (April 2001), pp. 191–209, an eccentric though penetrating paper.

C. Charles Peirce developed a view that he called 'critical common-sensism', which he took to be equivalent to pragmaticism. See Peirce, *Collected Papers*, ed. Charles Hartshorne and Paul Weiss (Cambridge, Mass.: Harvard University Press, 1934), v, *Pragmatism and Pragmaticism*, esp. bk. II, ch. 7, 'Issues of Pragmaticism', and bk. III, chs. 2 and 3, 'Pragmaticism and Critical Common-Sensism' and 'Consequences of Critical Common-Sensism'.

D. The following encyclopaedia articles can be illuminating: 'Common Sense', by C. A. J. Coady, in *The Oxford Companion to Philosophy*, p. 142, and 'Common Sense' by S. A. Grave, in *The Encyclopedia of Philosophy*, ii. 155–60. Neither of these pieces discusses the relations between common sense and ethics. But see William Kluback's 'Common Sense and Communicability: Two Sources of Political and Moral Life', in the 'common sense' issue of *Revue Internationale* (see n. A above), pp. 259–75.

In his article Professor Coady says: 'It seems likely that common sense defies definition; certainly no one has succeeded in giving a satisfactory definition, and very few have tried. To define it may be a self-defeating enterprise.' I flatter myself that in this essay I have not only tried, but succeeded. Of course, my account of common sense must not be construed as definition on the traditional model of definition by genus and differentia. No phenomenon as complex as common sense can be defined in this way. There is a useful but not especially penetrating article on definition in the *Oxford Companion to Philosophy*, a much more elaborate one by Raziel Abelson in *The Encyclopedia of Philosophy*, ii. 314–24. The most comprehensive discussion I know of is Richard Robinson's book *Definition* (Oxford: Clarendon Press, 1950). A somewhat more penetrating analysis, which frees the topic from its Aristotelian shackle, was developed by Max Black, in 'The Definition of Scientific Method' and 'Definition, Presupposition, and Assertion', *Problems of Analysis* (Ithaca, NY: Cornell University Press, 1954), pp. 3–45.

E. A somewhat different view of positive morality, under the heading of 'social norms', is taken by Thomas Green in 'Education as Norm Acquisition', in Kenneth R. Westphal (ed.), *Pragmatism, Reason, and Norms* (New York: Fordham University Press, 1998), pp. 145–84, esp. pp. 150–1:

By 'norm' I mean 'social norm', not 'statistical norm' and I do not refer simply to 'the done thing'. A social norm is not simply the modal tendency of behavior within some social group. On the contrary, we may take as a kind of paradigm that a social norm is a rule of conduct . . . It does not describe how persons behave; rather, it prescribes [is this the right word? I should think that 'describes' would fit better here too] how they think they ought to or should behave. It is not merely a statement of what people do, but a rule formulating what they think they ought to do.

Green's paper is an important contribution to the topic of this essay and, more importantly, to the theory of moral education. Its central argument is reproduced as a chapter in his *Voices: The Educational Formation of Conscience* (Notre Dame, Ind.: Notre Dame University Press, 1999). But nothing I have said about the rules of positive morality denies that social norms are normative, as distinct from being merely descriptive or statistical. I would add, however, that the way members of a social group typically behave, and especially what they say in judging the conduct of others, is excellent evidence of the social norms, the positive or conventional morality, of the group.

F. Anyone who still thinks that we cannot detect with certainty instances of common sense is invited to peruse the following:

On July 2, 1993, chambermaid Rosalita Vasquez was finishing her shift at the exclusive Casa Del Sol resort in Cancun when she saw smoke pouring from beneath the door of the hotel's Grand Imperial Suite. A malfunction in the air-conditioning system had started the blaze, and the suite's residents, seventy-five-year-old real-estate mogul Harvey Trestle and his wife, Lenore, were lying unconscious in their beds. As choking soot filled the hallway, Rosalita raced to the hotel's front desk and quit.[49]

Another example is provided by the proposal, promoted in late September 2001 by two members of the Wisconsin State Senate, that the death penalty be reinstituted in Wisconsin as a deterrent to suicide bombers. That should do it, of course.[50]

Surely, even a sceptic can tell what common sense is not. And once we realize what common sense is not, common sense itself is not too far off.

[49] Paul Rudnick, 'Profiles in Common Sense', *New Yorker*, 18 December 2000, p. 52, an instalment in the *New Yorker's* 'Shouts and Murmurs' feature. The one I selected is, in my judgement, the choicest of the lot.

[50] I am not making this up, though it does seem unbelievable. My source is an item in the *Capital Times* (Madison), 26 September 2001, 8A, under the heading 'The Death of Common Sense'.

6

Value Judgements and Normative Claims

A person's values are what that person regards as or thinks important; a society's values are what that society regards as important. A society's values are expressed in laws and legislatively enacted policies, in its mores, social habits, and positive morality. Any body's values—an individual person's or a society's—are subject to change, and in our time especially. An individual manifests his or her values in expressions of approval or disapproval, of admiration or disdain, by seeking or avoidance behaviour, and by his or her characteristic activities. What one values one seeks for or tries to maintain. Sometimes attaining it leads to unexpected enlightenment— that isn't what one wanted after all. But a person's values are discovered most significantly in a reflective way by becoming aware of what one is willing to give up to attain or maintain one's values. This is the price one is willing to pay for it, and values are occasionally, and in the money and stock markets always, expressed in terms of price. This can be significant or it can be misleading; it depends on how it is interpreted. Not everything has a monetary equivalent, despite the attempts of the law to provide recovery for damages in monetary terms, and despite the cynical maxim 'Everyone has his price'.

In addition to value behaviour, one expresses one's values in value judgements. Sometimes these are called evaluations, and an evaluation is either a mental process, a result of that process that remains unexpressed, or a statement expressing it. The latter, an oral or written statement expressing a valuation, is what, for convenience of access, is most often referred to in philosophical discourse as a value judgement.

But our topic is not restricted to value judgements as just described; it is meant to include under one general heading moral judgements as well, and sometimes in philosophical discourse one finds the expression 'ethical statements' being used as an omnibus word, covering all and sundry. There are distinctions that this usage obscures, and I shall get to them presently, must first get our topic sorted out. The omnibus term I propose to use is 'normative claims', and I shall use this to cover both value judgements in the more restricted sense mentioned and also moral judgements. A normative claim is a claim to the effect that some standard ought to prevail, a claim about what ought to be done or would be good if it were. In sociological usage, a normative claim is one about norms, and in this sense a norm is a standard, in the sense of average or usual or normal, that *does* exist among a certain group; in this sense a normative claim is a statistical measure. This is not the philosophical use of 'normative'. A normative claim is one about what standard *ought* to be followed, as distinct from what is normal, standard, or average.

The distinction just presented presupposes a distinction between statements of fact and judgements of value, sometimes called the 'fact/value' distinction, sometimes the 'is/ought' distinction, and to explain this I must say something about other kinds of statements. The account I am about to give is fairly standard if not canonical; we shall later see reason to question some of its claims.

A statement of fact is a statement about what was, is, will, or would be; about what did occur, is now occurring, will occur, or would occur under certain conditions which may or may not be realized; the category also covers generalizations about past, present, or future events or existences. 'I am now in Wisconsin' is such a statement; so is 'In 1988 I was in London to give this lecture'; and so is 'Next week I shall be in Chicago'. The examples just provided happen to be true, but statements of fact, so-called, can be false, do not necessarily state facts. To call them statements of fact is merely to say that they make factual claims, and not to evaluate them as true. This indicates that a statement of fact may not be a fact, and also that statements of fact can themselves be evaluated. But statements of fact are also not 'necessary' statements, though some of them can state physical or natural necessities. Though it is true that I am now in Wisconsin, it could be false. 'I am now in Moscow', though a statement of fact, is false. If I were in Moscow it would be true, but I am not and it is not.

Another standard category of statements, then, is called in accordance with tradition necessary statements or statements of logic. These are what Hume called 'relations of ideas' in distinction from 'matters of fact'. A relation of ideas can be determined to be true or false by reasoning about it, or merely from the meanings of the terms used in its statement. Statements of fact cannot; their truth-value has to be ascertained empirically, by experience, observation, experiment. Some relations of ideas are trivial, such as 'A lecturer who talks too long is one who talks too long', or 'A person who stammers has a stammer'. Others are not, require elaborate and complex reasoning to establish, such as in mathematical proofs. Given the axioms of Euclidean geometry, the Pythagorean theorem, 'the square of the hypotenuse of a right-angled triangle is equal to the sum of the squares of the other two sides', holds necessarily. So does the proposition that '5,876 × 4,321 = 25,390,196' (a result obtained by calculation—I must admit that I used my pocket calculator, and I am not sure that pressing buttons on a calculator is an operation identical with calculating itself; but I took a calculated risk). Another proposition having this a priori character is: 'If there are more trees in the world than there are leaves on any one tree, and there are no trees with no leaves at all, then there are at least two trees with the same number of leaves.' Some people on first hearing are not sure whether this proposition is true or false, but the proof is easy once you get the right idea. If you don't get the right idea right away, it can be frustrating, even deceiving. I shall put the solution in a note, so as not to deprive connoisseurs of the pleasure of figuring it out for themselves; and I add an admonition to readers: Don't look down yet![1]

Now one prime question about value judgements and normative claims is this: Are they capable of being established by empirical means, as are statements of fact: or are they discoverable by the operations of our reason, as are relations of ideas; or are they to be established by other means; or are they incapable of being established at all? If normative claims were deducible from premisses containing statements of fact alone, we should have a ready answer to this question. The standard view of the matter is that no 'ought'-statements—normative claims—can be deduced from 'is'-statements—statements of fact alone. Similarly the standard view is that no value judgements can be deduced from statements of fact alone, that a value judgement must be among the premisses of the deduction. This view, though not uncontroversial, is widely held; and the controversy about it is called 'the is/ought controversy'. Professor Hare calls this principle—namely, 'No "ought" from an "is"'—Hume's Law; others call it Hare's Rule. Still others call it false; these are usually those who call it Hare's Rule.

---

[1] Imagine that there are just five trees in the world. Match up each tree with the number of leaves it has, and name each tree by that number. Then tree one will have 1 leaf, tree two will have 2 leaves, tree three will have 3 leaves, and tree four will have 4 leaves. What about tree number five? By hypothesis it cannot have no leaves, and it cannot have five or more leaves because of the hypothesis that there are more trees in the world than there are leaves on any one tree. It follows, then, that it must have either 1 leaf or 2 leaves or 3 or 4; we don't know which, but it doesn't matter, since no matter which there will be two trees with the same number of leaves. Now nothing in this reasoning depends on our initial assumption that there are just five trees in the world; it holds for any number. Hence if there are *n* trees in the world, on the conditions of the problem no tree will have more than *n*-1 leaves, no matter what *n* is. And there is nothing in the reasoning restricting us to trees and leaves, we could have spoken instead of books and pages, *und so weiter*.

The is/ought problem is the problem of determining how factual and normative claims are related, how facts are related to values; this is in effect the question of how value judgements and normative claims are to be established. If value judgements could be deduced from statements of fact alone, to establish a judgement of value we should need only to establish the statements of fact from which it is deducible. If this route is not open, as Hare's Rule claims, then what route is? How, in other words, are normative claims to be established, justified, proved? Although some can be regarded as tautologous, such as 'Murder is wrong' (since murder is by definition simply wrongful killing), this does not take us very far, and actually takes us nowhere with respect to the interesting and controversial cases. Indeed, it could be argued, and perhaps should be, that 'Murder is wrong' is for this reason not a normative claim at all. Other instances, for example 'Business is business', have the *form* of tautologies, but simply beg the question. This only looks like a tautology, is used under this tautological cover to advance the normatively dubious claim that the rules that apply in the conduct of ordinary life are inapplicable to the affairs of business, so that whatever one does in the conduct of business is justified because it is in the conduct of business. (Of course no one believes this who is in the role of recipient as distinct from agent.) A similar example with no tautological disguise is 'All's fair in love and war'; this is not established by the fact that it is often stated and apparently widely accepted—at least by the winners.

Some philosophers have claimed that normative claims are self-evident or deducible from self-evident truths, or are in general establishable by a priori means. Kantian ethics is a very elaborate form of this view. The alternative view is that normative claims are to be established by establishing some connection to matters of fact, albeit complicated matters of fact. Utilitarianism, in any of its multifarious varieties, maintains this. Rationalism in ethics is the view that certain ethical propositions or principles can be established or proved a priori. Empiricism in ethics denies this, maintains that ethical propositions are establishable as facts or by their connections with facts. And both alternatives are denied by moral sceptics, who deny that normative or value claims can be proved at all; some even deny that there are any. But there are many and manifold varieties of moral or value scepticism. It is not any unitary view, must be defined by disjunction, and this is a topic, or set of topics, in itself.[2]

---

[2] In general, any theory that maintains that there can be no good and sufficient reason for a normative claim, that there are no sound normative or evaluative arguments, that ultimate normative principles cannot be proved, that normative claims cannot be true or false or correct or incorrect, that normative claims have no rational basis, or that the difference between right and

Non-sceptical normative theories take different forms, depending on how they answer this basic question of moral philosophy. One standard distinction is that between teleological and deontological theories. I think it more adequate (though still troublesome) to distinguish between deontological theories on the one hand, and teleological and consequentialist theories the other, and will presently say something about this conventional distinction.

However, first I must go back to draw a distinction between value judgements and moral judgements; this often overlooked distinction is often vital.

I

A value judgement is an opinion, assessment, estimate, or claim about the value, worth, quality, merit, or desirability of something—a thing, a state of affairs, an institution, or an activity. Such judgements are either comparative or non-comparative. In a comparative value judgement one makes a comparison of the relative merits or value of two or more things, for a certain purpose, in a certain context, or from a given point of view. In a non-comparative (or absolute) judgement no such comparison is expressed. It is a nice question of theory whether there is not always some comparison implicit or in the background, but we shall here keep that question in the background.

Moral judgements are made about different sorts of things: actions, kinds of actions, persons, and institutions; and a moral judgement is a judgement about the morality or moral status of an action, a general kind of action, a person, or an institution. Thus an action can be judged right or wrong, as what ought or ought not to be done, as what someone has or has not a right to do; a person may be judged a good or a bad person—as kind or cruel, considerate or inconsiderate, trustworthy or untrustworthy, generous or selfish; and an institution may be judged just or unjust, harmful or beneficial, as monstrous (slavery), difficult (marriage), or essential (language). One proviso should be inserted immediately: we judge an action on the supposition that it is (or was) voluntary, we judge a person on the

wrong, good and bad, better and worse, is merely a matter of custom, convention, taste, feeling, preference, opinion, or tradition, is a form of moral scepticism; but moral scepticism can take still other forms. I have discussed this matter in 'Moral Skepticism', in Curtis L. Carter (ed.), *Skepticism and Moral Principles* (Evanston, Ill.: New University Press, 1973), pp. 77–108 supposition that the person is sane. But the claim that some person is irresponsible is a moral judgement, not a withdrawal of judgement.

I have spoken about what moral judgements are in fact made about. The question 'What *ought* moral judgements to be made about?' is not easy to attach any definite sense to. The following might provide a case: We judge conduct on the supposition that it is voluntary and that the person in question is not insane, and on a showing to the contrary we tend to withdraw the judgement. Now one might claim that we ought not to pass moral judgements on the behaviour of people not responsible for their actions or that we ought not to condemn such people, and some sense can be made of this—certainly enough to generate controversy on the nature reality and limits of responsibility.

A moral judgement, in the primary sense, is an answer to a moral question, a proposed solution to a moral problem. When the question is one of practice, a judgement is a hypothesis to be carried out in conduct.

To understand what a moral judgement is, then, we must understand what a moral problem is. A moral problem arises out of conflicting moral considerations, considerations of what is right or wrong or ought to or may rightfully be done, about what would be equitable, just, fair, decent, or rotten in the way of conduct or the treatment of persons. A moral problem arises in a social context, where one already has some realization of and to some extent accepts the standards of conduct out of which the problem arises. One who has no moral beliefs can have no moral problems, probably could not even grasp the concept; and that is a heavy price to pay for the elimination of perplexity. Something is a practical moral problem if it calls for action of some kind to resolve it, if it substantially affects the interests of others, and if one ought to take those interests into account in deciding what to do. This last provision makes the determination of whether some problem is a moral problem itself in part moral problem, but this circularity, if such it is, is not serious. And it is not necessary that a moral problem involve the interests of others. One can have a moral problem where one feels that one's self-respect or sense of self-worth or self-esteem is somehow at stake, whether the interests of another are involved or not. But even though in some given situation the interests of others may not be materially affected, one can acquire a sense of self-respect or self-esteem only in a social setting in which one has acquired a moral code and developed a moral sense, a sense of right and wrong.[3]

---

[3] I have here used and modified somewhat some ideas presented in Ch. 11 below, 'Moral Issues and Social Problems'. Let me add that there are at least three types of moral problem. Type (a) occurs when two moral beliefs clash, and one then has the problem of determining what or

Nonetheless, the notion of a moral problem is a peculiar one because of the complexities of the notion of 'solving' one. What is it to *solve* a moral problem? One thing is obvious. If the problem is a practical one, and not a theoretical problem about some past happening, it calls for action to resolve it. No practical problem can be solved *merely* by thinking about it, though many call for thought beforehand. If my problem is to determine what to do with a sum of money at my disposal—which fund, say, to invest it in—my problem is not solved if I merely work the thing out on paper, conclude 'There—that's the solution', and leave the money in my current account or under my mattress. I have to *do* the thing I decided ought to be done, and without the doing the problem has not been solved. What may have been solved was some intellectual enterprise, but not a practical problem. Similarly, if my problem is what to do with my elderly, ill, and increasingly senile mother, since having her in the house is causing problems with my marriage and for my children, this will no doubt take careful consideration and consultation. But if after I contemplate and consult and make up my mind about what the best course of action would be, I then do nothing but simply continue as before, although I may have arrived at a correct answer to the question 'What would be the best thing to do?', I certainly have not solved my problem. This would be analogous to W. C. Fields's recipe for curing insomnia: 'Get plenty of sleep!' The last problem mentioned is both a practical and a moral problem. Does it have a *solution* in any ordinary sense? Certainly scientific problems have solutions, as do mathematical and logical problems. And presumably so do social and ecological problems (the latter being a subclass of the former). And some practical problems do, though some may not.

John Dewey once said that 'intellectual progress, usually occurs through sheer abandonment of questions together with . . . the alternatives they assume—an abandonment that results from their decreasing vitality and a change of urgent interest. We do not solve them: we get over them.'[4] Surely something similar occurs with moral problems. Yet this is not altogether accurate. Some we do not get over, and some disappear or simply become less urgent. But in the main the way to solve moral and social problems is

---

which is right in this instance. Type (b) occurs when a moral belief (about which one really has not much doubt) conflicts with a desire or aversion, and the problem then is not—or not so much—to determine what is the right thing to do, as to *do* it—or get oneself to do it. Type (c) occurs when, as sometimes happens, the second type merges into the first, when our desire or aversion is so strong it leads us to question or doubt the original belief; this can sometimes be enlightening; it can also be corrupting.

[4] John Dewey, *The Influence of Darwin on Philosophy* (New York: Holt, 1910), p. 19.

by *dealing with them*, in the light of intelligence and informed thought and an enlightened moral sense and a developed sense of values.

A moral problem may not have a solution in the same sense as a problem of science, mathematics, or logic, or in the same sense as a problem of cookery or a military or chess problem. But a practical moral problem does call for action of some kind, even though the action might go astray. It might be ill-calculated to deal with the problem in question, or unforeseen events might intervene. John Passmore manifests on this matter a curious combination of acuity and absent-mindedness. 'To solve any sort of social problem', he says,

is to describe a satisfactory way of reducing the incidence or the severity of the phenomenon stigmatised as a problem. To solve the problem of alcoholism is to describe a satisfactory way of reducing the number of alcoholics; to solve the problem of traffic accidents is to describe a satisfactory way of reducing the number and the severity of such accidents . . . 'Satisfactory way' is of course, vague. The conclusion that a social problem has been solved . . . involves an evaluation just as much as does the decision that the problem exists.[5]

This last point is a significant one, and applies as well to moral problems. The conclusion that a moral problem has been solved involves evaluation just as much as the judgement that the problem exists. Hence value judgements are involved in the very being of moral problems. However, in saying that 'to solve' such a problem is merely 'to describe' something, Passmore goes curiously off the mark. This may do so far as the work of an expert brought in for consultation goes. It does not for the society or official concerned. Merely 'to describe a satisfactory way of reducing the number of alcoholics', though no doubt a considerable achievement in itself, is not to solve the problem of alcoholism, even if it is thought to do so by some consulting expert. The 'solution' has to be carried out in practice, and here is where it may be discovered that the 'solution', which seemed so reasonable on paper, will not work. This is why I earlier referred to moral judgements as hypotheses to be tested. An 'intellectual solution', though no doubt very important, cannot be regarded as identical with a *solution*; it may even be some distance from it.

II

Now to the distinction between consequentialist and deontological theories. A consequentialist theory maintains that the morality of an action depends

[5] John Passmore, *Man's Responsibility for Nature* (New York: Scribners, 1971), p, 44.

solely on the value of its consequences: if the consequences are good, the act is right; if the consequences are bad, the act is wrong. Utilitarianism is a form of consequentialism, and a fairly rigorous formulation of the principle of utility was first provided by Sidgwick in 1874 (*Methods*, bk. IV, ch. 1, p. 411): 'the conduct which, under any given circumstances, is objectively right, is that which will produce the greatest amount of happiness on the whole . . . taking into account all whose happiness is affected by the conduct'. Mill, in his *Utilitarianism* (1863), provides a looser formulation which nonetheless brings out the point that is of moment here. Mill says that 'actions are right in proportion as they tend to promote happiness, wrong as they tend to pro-duce the reverse of happiness. By happiness is intended pleasure, and the absence of pain; by unhappiness, pain, and the privation of pleasure' (ch. 2, para. 2, Everyman edn., p. 6). And Mill goes on to distinguish from 'this the-ory of morality' what he calls 'the theory of life on which [it] is grounded—namely, that pleasure and freedom from pain are the only things desirable as ends'. What Mill here calls a 'theory of life' is a theory of value, and the the-ory of value Mill is here presenting is hedonism: pleasure is the only thing intrinsically desirable, good in and for itself. Non-hedonistic varieties of utilitarianism have been developed since Mill's and even Sidgwick's time, by Moore (1903) and Rashdall (1907), and later multifarious varieties by numerous writers.[6] But the essential point for our purposes is that on utili-tarianism, and on any form of consequentialism, all moral judgements are taken to rest on value judgements, so that moral theory presupposes value theory, 'axiology' as it is called in Germany and America, in some sort of alliance against English. If pleasure is the good, whatever produces pleasure is good and ought to be done; if pain is bad, whatever produces pain, other things equal, is bad and ought to be avoided. The intramural disputes among utilitarians are not now on our agenda, so I am content to leave the state-ment as it is, even though it is capable of indefinite refinement. If we do not specify what utility is, or take it as something other than pleasure, the prin-ciple will tell us that whatever produces or maximizes utility is right and ought to be done; that whatever fails to produce or maximize utility is bad and ought not to be done. Utility can be measured by the satisfaction of desires, or by the satisfaction of persons, interests, or needs; it is all one. And this is true for all consequentialist theories.

---

[6] G. E. Moore, *Principia Ethica* (Cambridge: Cambridge University Press, 1903) and *Ethics* (London: Oxford University Press, 1912). Hastings Rashdall, *The Theory of Good and Evil*, 2 vols. (London: Oxford University Press, 1907)—see esp. vol. i, ch. VII. entitled 'Ideal Utilitarianism', the name that came to be adopted generally. An excellent account of utilitarian ethics is Anthony Quinton's book of that title—*Utilitarian Ethics* (New York: St. Martin's Press, 1973).

Teleological theories, which emphasize purposes rather than results, do not usually take a maximizing form, place aiming at good ends in paramount position. Aristotle's *Nicomachean Ethics* opens thus:

Every art and every inquiry, and similarly every action and pursuit, is thought to aim at some good; and for this reason the good has rightly been declared to be that at which all things aim. But a certain difference is found among ends; some are activities, others are products apart from the activities that produce them. Where there are ends apart from the actions, it is the nature of the products to be better than the activities.

and continues:

. . . If, then, there is some end of the things we do, which we desire for its own sake (everything else being desired for the sake of this), and if we do not choose everything for the sake of something else (for at that rate the process would go on to infinity, so that our desire would be empty and vain), clearly this must be the good and the chief good.[7]

Although it is not absolutely brought out by these opening passages, Aristotle's ethics, though teleological, is not a form of consequentialism, nor does it require any maximizing formula. The basic idea is that the realization of some good end is the criterion of whether an action is virtuous or not, so that value judgements, judgements of the worth of the end, are prior to the moral judgement of the conduct. But for Aristotle the manner of the action and the disposition of the agent play a role in the evaluation of the action, another reason why teleological theories are not necessarily consequentialist.

In Bentham's version, ethics is thought of as a science. Since the morality of acts, individual, governmental, and legislative, depends solely on the consequences, and since the consequences have their value determined, in

---

[7] *Nicomachean Ethics*, bk 1, chs. 1 and 2, 1904ᵃ. For the sake of comparison, consider Welldon's translation:

Every art and every scientific inquiry, and similarly every action and purpose, may be said to aim at some good. Hence the good has been well defined as that at which all things aim. But it is clear that there is a difference in the ends; for the ends are sometimes activities, and sometimes results beyond the mere activities. Also, where there are certain ends beyond the actions, the results are naturally superior to the activities. [This offhand remark by Aristotle is by no means self-evident, as Aristotle evidently takes it to be.]

. . . If it is true that in the sphere of action there is an end which we wish for its own sake, and for the sake of which we wish everything else, and that we do not desire all things for the sake of something else (for, if that is so, the process will go on *ad infinitum*, and our desire will be idle and futile) it is clear that this will be the good or the supreme good. (*The Nicomachean Ethics of Aristotle*, trans. J. E. C. Welldon (London: Macmillan, 1892), pp. 1, 2)

Bentham's view, by the hedonic calculus for determining the value of 'a lot of pleasure or pain'—which is, at least in principle, a semi-mathematical operation—the question whether some proposed act would be right or wrong is the question of what its consequences are likely to be compared with the consequences of the available alternatives and the value of those compared consequences. On a maximizing interpretation of the principle of utility, that act will be right which maximizes utility (pleasure, happiness, good, satisfaction) and the question whether an act is right or wrong turns out to be a matter of fact, in principle if not always in practice answerable by appeal to scientific procedures for predicting consequences and measuring their value. Value theory—axiology—thus becomes prior to moral theory, which is thus, and not in any mysterious way, amenable to scientific treatment.[8]

Another form of consequentialism that is not a form of utilitarianism has been presented by Dewey. Thus Dewey says:

the moral issue concerns the future. It is prospective. To content ourselves with pronouncing judgments of merit and demerit without reference to the fact that our judgments are themselves facts which have consequences, is complacently to dodge the moral issue . . . The moral problem is that of modifying the facts which now influence future results (*HNC*, p. 19)

Again:

consequences fix the moral quality of an act . . . In the long run but not unqualifiedly, consequences are what they are because of the nature of desire and disposition (*HNC*, pp. 44–5)

And again:

Consequences include effects upon character, upon confirming and weakening habits, as well as tangibly obvious results (*HNC*, p. 46)

And in reporting on one aspect of a view that he ultimately regards as one-sided, Dewey says:

---

[8] The most sophisticated account of this procedure is in a book apparently little known to moral philosophers or to philosophers in Britain, Felix Cohen's *Ethical Systems and Legal Ideals* (New York: Harcourt Brace, 1933), ch. III, sect. 1 and *passim*, esp. pp. 115–26. The idea that was distinctive of Bentham—and, through Bentham, later utilitarianism—is the dictum that each is to count for one, none for more than one. In Hutcheson's prior version of a hedonic calculus, the importance or status of persons could give their pleasures or pains greater or lesser weight (see Francis Hutcheson, *Inquiry Concerning Moral Good and Evil* (1725), sect. III, esp. viii and xi, in Selby-Bigge (ed.), *British Moralists* (Oxford: Clarendon Press, 1897), i. 98–117, esp. pp. 107 & 110.

Morality is found in consequences; and consequences are definite, observable facts which the individual can be made responsible for noting and for employing in the direction of his further behavior. The theory gives morality an objective, a tangible guarantee and sanction. Moreover, results are something objective, common to different individuals because outside them all. (*Ethics*, p. 234)[9]

It is manifest that Dewey is a consequentialist, of a sort that has not been adequately understood because it is so thoroughgoing. Dewey includes under consequences effects on character, habits, dispositions, and even motives, much in the manner of Mill in some passages in *Utilitarianism* (ch. 2, paras. 23–5) that are often overlooked, in which Mill talks about secondary or remote consequences, such as the effects on the character of the agent, on habits, and on social expectations and institutions.

But the theory that morality depends solely on consequences runs into both difficulties and opposition. The opposition is provided by so-called deontological theories which maintain in various forms that the morality of a line of conduct depends either on the motive or disposition or intent of the agent, or on the character of the agent, or on something in the nature of the action—and either not at all or only to some degree on consequences. Theories of this sort tend to emphasize general rules or principles of conduct, which can be applied to an action in virtue of the kind of action it is, and independently of consequences. Such theories range from various forms of intuitionism, to will-of-God theories that make right and wrong depend on divine commands, to will-of-the-state theories that make it depend on the commands or rules of the state or sovereign (Hobbes, Austin), to a theory of the complexity of Kant's.

Kant certainly holds that the morality of an action is not a function of its consequences. Instead. Kant tells us, whether an action has moral worth— a conception that has no parallel with anything mentioned so far— depends on whether it is done from duty; that is, out of the sincere belief that it is morally right and for no other reason. This is the meaning of the famous opening sentence of the *Groundwork of the Metaphysic of Morals*: 'It is impossible to conceive anything at all in the world, or even out of it, which can be taken as good without qualification, except a *good will*.'[10] This

---

[9] John Dewey, *Human Nature and Conduct* (*HNC*) (1922) (New York: Modern Library edn., 1930); John Dewey and James H. Tufts, *Ethics* (New York: Holt, 1908: 2nd edn., 1932, thoroughly rewritten); passage quoted is taken from 1st edn.

[10] Kant, *Grundlegung zur Metaphysik der Sitten* (1785), Prussian Akademy edn., iv. 393, trans. Paton, abbreviated in text as *Gr.*, with page number given thereafter. The German is relatively simple: 'Es ist überall nichts in der Welt, ja überhaupt auch ausser derselben zu denken möglich, was ohne Einschränkung für gut könnte gehalten werden, als allein ein Guter Wille.' It is the next sentences that are hard.

introduces the conception of *moral* value or *moral* worth, and it also introduces the unprecedented concept of being good unconditionally or without qualification, which is not the same as having value as an end. The Good Will does not play the same role for Kant as happiness or utility does for utilitarian theories—it is not the end towards which everything else is to be accounted a means; and Kant does not accept the standard means–end model of action according to which all actions are to be understood as means to ends other than themselves and as deriving their value from the end to which they are subservient. Kant is saying that in order for an action to have moral worth it is not enough for it merely to correspond to what duty requires, it must be done for the sake of duty. One consequence of this famous first proposition is that only a good will, and those persons and actions that manifest a good will, can be *morally* good, have *moral* worth or value. A good will is the settled determination to do what is morally right simply because it is morally right; another word for this is 'conscientiousness'; still another is 'character'. Thus Kant is drawing a distinction between an act's being morally right and its having moral value. Kant is saying that an act has moral worth only if it is right (in accordance with duty) and done for that reason (done from duty).

The principle on which a person of good will acts is called the 'Categorical Imperative', and Kant provides us with a number of statements of it, which, though they are intended to be at bottom one and the same, do not give that appearance. One formulation is: Act only on that maxim you can at the same time will to be universal law. Another is: Act always so as to treat humanity, whether in your own person or in that of another, always as an end in itself, never merely as a means. A third is: Every rational being is subject only to laws that are self-given and are at the same time the same laws for all. This is the principle of autonomy, the basis of Kant's concept that rational beings have dignity, a value beyond price. If something 'has a price', Kant says, 'something else can be put in its place as an *equivalent*; if it is exalted above all price and so admits of no equivalent, then it has a *dignity*' (*Gr.* 434).

Nothing can have a value other than that determined for it by the law. But the law-making which determines all value must for this reason have a dignity—that is, an unconditioned and incomparable worth—for the appreciation of which, as necessarily given by a rational being, the word '*reverence*' [or 'respect'] is the only becoming expression. Autonomy is therefore the ground of the dignity of human nature. (*Gr.* 436).

This clearly is not consequentialism or any form of utilitarianism or teleological theory. For Kant the moral law determines the morality, in the sense of the rightness or wrongness, of an action, and some actions are ruled out as immoral in advance irrespective of any advantage or happiness they may bring to no matter how many people. Kant's theory also provides us with another conception of value, that of *moral* value, which is held to be so far superior to any other form of value (such as economic value, aesthetic value, literary value, scientific value, entertainment value, nutritional value, hedonic value and so on) that no comparison is possible or even permissible. This is I think the origin of the idea, often stated though not well defended, that moral considerations necessarily take priority for a moral person over all other considerations, that *moral* values are pre-eminent.

Not everyone, of course, accepts this estimate. I once heard a television interview with Edward Teller, in which he first responded to some question of the interviewer (whose name and question I do not recall) by saying, 'What? What was that?', and then, when the question had been clarified, said, 'Oh, I see—merely moral objections'. Again, at the time of the Watergate scandal, Warren Burger, then Chief Justice of the United States, is reported to have said: 'Apart from the morality, I can't see what they did wrong.'

Kant defends his principles by arguing that they are presupposed in the common ordinary moral judgements of the ordinary good person, such that one cannot engage in moral thinking or make any moral judgement without presupposing them. Kant also thinks that an 'ought' cannot be derived from an 'is'; but his way of dealing with the is/ought problem is to maintain that these principles of morality and moral worth are presupposed in the moral judgements that all who make moral judgements actually make. This would bypass the need for any such demonstration.[11]

---

[11] Kant's other line of argument on this score is contained in his basic supposition that what a perfectly rational being *would* do, out of necessity, is what an imperfectly rational—therefore a human—being *ought* to do. Cf. pp. 28–9 of Paton's 'Analysis of the Argument' prefixed to his translation of the *Groundwork*, entitled *The Moral Law* (London, Hutchinson's University Library, 1948), and *Gr.* 412–14. I have provided a more detailed account of Kant's ethics in 'Morality and Universality'—ch. 25 in G. H. R. Parkinson (ed.), *An Encyclopedia of Philosophy* (London: Routledge, 1988), pp. 568–86. An excellent account is H. B. Acton's *Kant's Moral Philosophy* (London: Macmillan, 1970). As mentioned, Kant's ethics is not the only form of deontological ethics. It is only (until recently, at any rate) the most difficult and complex. Another main form of deontological ethics is represented by the views of Butler (*Sermons Upon Human Nature*, 1726; 'Of The Nature of Virtue', 1736). Richard Price (*Review of the Principal Questions in Morals*, 1758), Thomas Reid (*Essays on the Active Powers of Man*, 1788), W. D. Ross (*The Right and the Good* (Oxford: Clarendon Press, 1930) and *Foundations of Ethics* (Oxford: Clarendon Press, 1939)), and H. A. Prichard (*Moral Obligation* (Oxford: Clarendon Press, 1949)). More recent versions of note—though with them the notion of 'deontological' begins to get very slippery—are John Rawls, *A Theory of Justice* (see esp. pp. 3–4), and Alan Gewirth, *Reason and Morality* (Chicago: University of Chicago Press, 1978).

There is another difficulty with maintaining that only consequences have moral relevance, and that therefore antecedents have none, which is what consequentialism has been taken, quite properly, as maintaining. Some actions cannot be understood or conceived of apart from the intention of the agent. One example is lying, which involves the intention of deceiving, and otherwise would be indistinguishable from honest error, which is not a moral fault. Sophisticated forms of consequentialism will have ways of getting around or attempting to get around this apparently minor obstacle. But motives, so important in Kant's ethics, are also held important by other thinkers. Thus Bishop Whately held that: 'It is entirely on the motives and dispositions of the mind that the *moral* character of any one's conduct depends.'[12] Another point of consequence is that since only voluntary actions are the objects of moral judgement, this necessarily brings in the matter of intent. Even a cursory survey of human actions and reactions brings out that intent can in some situations make all the difference. Whether one has been tripped accidently or on purpose is of vital import. 'Even a dog distinguishes between being stumbled over and being kicked';[13] and so, of course, do human beings. The purely physical damage may be the same, but the hurt to feelings—and the moral import—is much greater if the hurt was intended, or is felt to be. A theory that ignores the role of intentions in determining what an action is, what actually was done, is in no position to determine or assess the consequences, and consequently in no position to assess the morality of the action.

'Tis a pity that Mill, who so unqualifiedly held that 'the motive has nothing to do with the morality of the action, though much with the worth of the agent' (*Util.*, ch. 2, para. 19, Everyman edn., p. 17), did not face up to this and give greater consideration to the nature of actions in relation to agents. And it is especially surprising, since Mill's forerunner Hume, regarded so widely as a utilitarian, emphasizes the essential importance of character and motives in morality. Thus Hume held that

when we praise any actions, we regard only the motives that produced them, and consider the actions as signs or indications of certain principles in the mind and temper. The external performance has no merit. We must look within to find the moral quality. (*Treatise*, bk. III, pt. II, sect. i, p. 477)

---

[12] Richard Whately, *Paley's Moral Philosophy* (London: Parker, 1859), p. 14. Cf. Jean Piaget: 'All morality consists in a system of rules, and the essence of all morality is to be sought for in the respect which the individual acquires for these rules' (*The Moral Judgment of the Child* (London: Routledge & Kegan Paul, 1932), p. 1).
[13] Oliver Wendell Holmes, jun., *The Common Law* (Boston, Mass.: Little, Brown, 1881), p. 3.

The conflict between consequentialist and deontological views of ethics, though an instance of a perennial dialectic of thought, is not really necessary, and a balanced view would select the meritorious elements in each. Because for each there is a great deal to be said—as one side of the story. Adlai Stevenson was given to saying: 'We judge ourselves by our motives, others by their actions.'[14] As a statement of a perennial human tendency, I have no doubt that this is true, and there would have been no point in the remark—and Stevenson's remarks always had point—if it was something he was advocating. I take the point to be that we *ought* to judge ourselves and others by a consistent standard: if we judge ourselves by our motives, we ought to judge others by theirs; if we judge others by their actions, we ought to judge ourselves by ours. This is but a version of the Golden Rule, so widely accepted but so seldom practiced. And we have here found a point where we can move from an 'is' to an 'ought'. All it requires is a little reverse English.

III

All right, then, how are facts and values related? Can morals or values be derived from facts or otherwise established by them? I cannot do more here than provide a few hints and clues, but provide a few hints and clues I will.

First to the distinction, and the connection, between facts and values. The terms of the problem, in my judgement, have been distorted, partly by a confusion about facts, partly by confusion about values.

The concept of a 'fact' is both elastic and chameleon-like. What is a fact varies with the context and with what it is being compared with. A statement of fact in one context can be in another, or in comparison to something else, a statement of law, of morals, of values, of opinion, of theory, of interpretation, of logic, or of convention. And the term 'fact' has a multiple ambiguity. It can mean: (a) something that exists in reality; (b) a true proposition (as in 'It is a fact that . . .'); (c) a state of affairs; (d) what 'is the case'; or even (e) testimony (in legal usage the testimony of a witness is referred to as fact, with no implication that the 'facts' so related are true; an

---

[14] Quoted in Herbert J. Muller, *Adlai Stevenson: A Study in Values* (New York: Harper & Row, 1967). p. 277.

attorney in summing up might say: 'The facts related by this witness have been shown to be totally false').[15]

In the law a distinction is normally drawn between qustions of fact and questions of law, with questions of law said to be for the judge, questions of fact for the jury. But what is a question of law in one case or context can be settled fact in another. John Lucas, in a brilliant paper, pointed out that what are taken to be and referred to as the facts of some matter are what are not in dispute but are accepted by both sides to a dispute, and I think he is essentially right, though I do not think that that is all there is to facts.[16]

A fact is a fact relative to a given dispute, or relative to two or more persons at a given time arguing about a given point. The points that both sides accept as true, each side will describe by the word 'fact' . . . The word 'fact' is an incomplete symbol; the complete locution being 'facts in respect of such and such a dispute'. (Lucas, p. 146)

And on values as well Lucas makes some very telling points:

A similar variableness appears in value-judgments. Very seldom is the distinction between facts and values either as sharp as [supposed], or drawn where [it is thought] it ought to be drawn. Often the facts which we adduce to support an evaluative conclusion, are not absolutely non-evaluative themselves. In a dispute about a man's moral worth we claim, and it will be conceded to us, that at least *this* action was generous and that just, and it will be claimed against us, and we shall concede, that some other deed was inexcusable and yet another difficult to defend. (p. 147)

---

[15] Consider the famous opening sentences of the *Tractatus*: 'The world is everything that is the case. The world is the totality of facts, not of things' (L. Wittgenstein, *Tractatus Logico-Philosophicus*, trans. Ogden (London: Routledge & Kegan Paul, 1922), p. 31). There is an intriguing account of 'facts' in M. R. Cohen and E. Nagel, *An Introduction to Logic and Scientific Method* (New York: Harcourt, Brace, 1934): 'It denotes at least four distinct things. 1. We sometimes mean by "facts" certain discriminated elements in sense perception . . . 2. "Fact" sometimes denotes the propositions which *interpret* what is given to us in sense perception . . . 3. "Fact" also denotes propositions which truly assert an invariable sequence or conjunction of characters . . . What is *believed* to be a fact in this (or even in the second) sense depends clearly upon the evidence we have been able to accumulate; ultimately, upon facts in the first sense noted, together with certain assumed universal connections between them. Hence, whether a proposition shall be called a fact or a hypothesis depends upon the state of our evidence . . . 4. Finally, "fact" denotes those things existing in space or time, together with the relations between them, in virtue of which a proposition is true. Facts in this sense are neither true nor false, they simply *are* . . . Facts in this fourth sense are distinct from the hypotheses we make about them. A hypothesis is true, and is a fact in the second or third sense, when it does state *what* the fact in this fourth sense is . . . Consequently, the distinction between fact and hypothesis is never sharp when by "fact" is understood a proposition which may indeed be true, but for which the evidence can never be complete' (pp. 217–19).

[16] J. R. Lucas, 'On Not Worshipping Facts', *Philosophical Quarterly*, 8 (April 1958), pp. 144–56.

Two parties may agree that *it is a fact* that one ought not to lie, as a general thing, but disagree on the evaluative or normative judgement to be derived from that 'fact' on some specific occasion. Here what is supposedly a moral matter is taken as a 'fact', and no one has any problems with that. Is the theory of evolution a fact? When then-candidate Ronald Reagan was asked this question back in 1980 he said—and I paraphrase—Well, it's called a theory, isn't it, so it can't be a fact. Brilliant deduction, of course. Is it a fact that the earth revolves around the sun. Well, in one context, yes; in another, it is a theory or hypothesis.

A. E. Murphy more than once observed that every attempt to state the problem of the separation between facts and values 'is at once a distinction and a connection between' them:

> And it is only as the distinction is kept clear that the connection can be understood. If 'fact' is used broadly to cover everything that is discoverably the case, then it is a fact that there are some things we ought, and others we ought not, to do.[17]

A similar variation affects values. What is a value in one situation is a fact in another.

IV

A distinction is sometimes made between 'absolutist versus relativist theories of value'. A relativist theory of value is one that maintains that values are relative to persons or to cultures, that nothing is good for or to everyone or in every setting. There is much sense in this, but generalized into a universal theory it becomes so refined as to evaporate. Milk may be good for you; it is bad for me, since I lack the enzyme required to digest it. This shows no more about the relativity of values than it does about the relativity of enzymes. If I did not lack lactase, milk would be good for me, and there is nothing relative about that, though it may be somewhat speculative.

Sometimes by the relativity of values is meant no more than that whether something is good or bad is relative to the situation in which it is performed. Customs, expectations, and traditions vary from place to place and time to time; therefore, since whether something is right or good depends so much on custom and tradition and the way it is received and interpreted in the place it occurs, it is held that morals and values are rela-

---

[17] Murphy, *Theory of Practical Reason*, p. 265. Cf. p. 267; indeed, the whole of ch. 10.

tive. 'In Rome', we are sagely told, 'do as the Romans do'. But that, though sagely said, is not such sage advice. It depends upon what the Romans are doing. Though Caligula was a Roman that is no reason for doing as Caligula did, in Rome or anywhere else; and if you are in Rome, hard luck—you had better get out before you become someone Caligula does it to.

The sensible interpretation of this idea is that 'the character of every act depends upon the circumstances in which it is done'.[18] Under certain circumstances one may be justified in telling a lie or taking a life, although in general one is not. And it may be right for me to do something, because of certain traits or skills I possess, that would not be right for another. If this were the sole content of relativism there would be nothing wrong with it.

Relativism is usually taken as the polar opposite of absolutism, and if one is ill-defined, so is the other. In one meaning of the term, absolutism is the idea that certain selected moral rules hold absolutely, no matter what the circumstances or consequences. Something akin to this can on occasion be defended. For instance, rape is always wrong, no matter what the circumstances or consequences. But not many act types—indeed, very few—match this description, and, as Mill has pointed out, 'rules of conduct cannot be so framed as to require no exceptions, and . . . hardly any kind of action can safely be laid down as either always obligatory or always condemnable' (*Util.*, ch. 2, para. 25, Everyman edn., p. 23). But it is certainly more comfortable, though not more reasonable, to latch upon some rule that seems agreeably easy, or difficult, to abide by absolutely, and maintain it as holding absolutely. This sometimes takes the form of maintaining that the standards and practices of one's own time or community are inherently right, while others are wrong, simply because they differ. Another term for this is *parochialism*, and it is put out of court by the fact that conflicts occur among the rules and standards so enshrined, and the selection of one over another in a case of conflict is bound to be arbitrary. The opposite of parochialism is another form of relativism, which holds—if 'holds' is the appropriate term—that there are no valid standards, because there are so many. This often leads to the avant-garde view that no one ought ever to make any moral judgements, because it is unfair for one to impose one's values on others. The incoherence of this should be obvious. No doubt it is unfair to impose one's own values on others—though this might depend on the nature of the imposition. But this claim itself presupposes a normative standard. Merely to make a judgement is not to impose anything on

---

[18] Cf. *Generalization*, pp. 13 ff.

anyone. Both these views confuse mores with morality—what is or is thought to be with what ought to be—which of course makes them perennially up-to-date.[19]

V

In a letter to one of his correspondents—Miss Pauline Goldmark—written in September 1901 from Silver Lake, New Hampshire, William James says: 'Dear Pauline,—your kind letter . . ', and then interrupts himself with '(excuse pencil—pen won't write)'. Now what was wrong with that pen of William James's? Was it merely out of ink, with no supply on hand? Or was it broken? Was it a defective pen to begin with? If so, why did James attempt to use it? Indeed, why did he buy it in the first place?

I am not really about to embark on a historical enquiry along these lines, and now that I have introduced my next topic by means of this example, I leave James's letter to Miss Goldmark in midstream, as it were (and to the readers of *The Letters of William James* (Boston: Atlantic Monthly Press, 1920, ii. 162)) and go on to point out that value judgements, at least of certain kinds, are capable of being verified hence established beyond doubt. The judgement that a pen is a good one can be verified by empirical facts. If a pen holds ink without leaking, will write, does not splatter ink all across the page and the writer's hands, holds a plentiful supply so that it does not need refilling too frequently, lets the ink flow in a relatively uniform way, and is a comfortable fit in the hand—all of which can be discovered by trying it out—then it is a good pen. On the other hand, a pen that will not hold ink, or won't write, splatters ink, leaks, or is too heavy to hold is a bad one.[20]

Similarly with evaluations of watches and knives. A watch that won't tell the time or tell it accurately is not a good one, no matter how pretty it is or how much it cost. It might be a nice piece of jewellery; it is not a good watch. A knife that won't cut meat and cannot be sharpened so as to do so,

---

[19] Some of these points have been borrowed from 'Metaetyka a istota etyki', published in Polish in *Etyka*, 11 (1973), p. 121 ff.; translated into Polish by Ija Lazari-Pawlowska.

[20] It is hard to improve on what Kurt Baier has said on this matter in the chapter on 'Value Judgments' in *The Moral Point of View* (Ithaca, NY: Cornell University Press, 1958). Another key work is J. O. Urmson, 'On Grading', *Mind*, 59(234) (April 1950), pp. 145–69. A brief earlier effort of the present writer's appears in a review in *Ethics*, 70(4) (July 1960), pp. 330–2, of Alan Montefiore's *A Modern Introduction to Moral Philosophy* (New York: Frederick A. Praeger, 1959).

or whose handle starts to detach itself from the blade, is not a good knife, no matter what the ads said about it, no matter how much it cost, and no matter how much its diamond and silver handle impresses the dinner guests. Once the meal starts and they try using it to cut their food their 'oohs' and 'ahs' might change to 'uh-ohs', 'ouches', and curses (expressed more silently of course). Similarly with hosts of other things or activities or persons. We need not restrict ourselves to functional or manufactured articles. We have criteria for whether someone is a good tennis player, a good philosopher, a good teacher, or a good student, even though some of these evaluations, such as 'good teacher' and 'good father', involve some measure of moral judgement, are not morally neutral evaluations. There are standards or criteria of evaluation involved in such evaluations, which are what connect the facts with the value judgement. A word or two about these.

First, something about the relations between objectivity and truth. Objectivity is a matter of degree; it is an achievement; not something one starts with but something one aims at. This means that one's personal predilections and prejudices must be kept to a minimum. For we are here talking about evaluation, which is a matter of judgement, not a matter of taste or preference. Objectivity is dependent on reasons and is a function of impersonality; hence it is independent of the person, since it is meant to be the same for all who would use or evaluate the thing or make the judgements in question. However, a judgement can be objective and not be true and can be true without being objective, just as a belief can be probable and not be true and true without being probable.

Second, a value judgement can be made intelligently only on the basis of appropriate and relevant standards or criteria, standards appropriate to the thing being evaluated and also within the range of human possibility. (Someone who says that no human being ever has run a good mile because to run a good mile one would have to travel faster than sound may be drinking good whiskey but is not exercising good judgement.) A value judgement is objective when related to and made consciously and deliberately in the light of criteria or standards of value which are sensibly judged relevant and appropriate to the kind of thing being judged and to the human purposes such a judgement can sensibly be supposed relevant to. In judging the standards relevant and appropriate, and determining and judging the relevant facts in the light of them, one is claiming that the standards are the same for all who would evaluate the thing in question. In this way, then, the standard is supposed to be and is regarded as impersonal, hence objective, and the standard in turn rests on a judgement, not merely a preference.

There can of course be discussion and disagreement, sometimes fruitful, about the standards themselves, whether *these* are the appropriate ones or whether *those* are, or what are the relevant and appropriate standards. Sometimes we simply don't know, or else the topic is inherently controversial, as in at least the more rarified air of aesthetics. But someone who thinks that 'Roses are red | violets are blue | sugar is sweet | and so are you' is a better poem than any of Shakespeare's sonnets, say Sonnet 129, someone who genuinely thinks that is, in Bradley's marvellous phrase, either a fool or an advanced thinker, and in either case is quite wrong. As you can see:

> The expense of spirit in a waste of shame
> Is lust in action; and till action, lust
> Is perjur'd, murd'rous, bloody, full of blame,
> Savage, extreme, rude, cruel, not to trust;
> Enjoy'd no sooner but despised straight;
> Past reason hunted, and no sooner had,
> Past reason hated, as in swallowed bait,
> On purpose laid to make the taker mad—
> Mad in pursuit, and in possession so;
> Had, having, and in quest to have, extreme;
> A bliss in proof, and prov'd, a very woe;
> Before, a joy propos'd; behind, a dream.
> > All this the world well knows; yet none knows well
> > To shun the heaven that leads men to this hell.

When I read such a poem as that and experience its searing beauty, I think that talk of criteria and standards is out of place. We do not grade poems as we grade apples, nor should we. One must read it and reread it and understand it and feel it—and perhaps have had some experience of the sort emblazed in it to appreciate it.

Yet consideration of the quality, the merit, the exquisite beauty of at least some poetry is also part of value theory, and is what is discussed in literary criticism or poetic aesthetics. A theory of value is a theory of the nature and basis of value and value judgements, for distinguishing good from bad and better from worse, and for determining how such judgements can be sustained in difficult or controversial cases. This can get immensely complicated, especially since there are so many different forms of value, moral value being just one type. That is why we should not let ourselves forget the obvious cases. Not everything is controversial here, or there could be no controversy; not everything is doubtful, or doubt could have no meaning.

Instances of manifestly fallacious reasoning to normative claims are not hard to find. I give the following because of its quaintness. You remember the famous 'Checkers' speech in 1952 when then Senator Nixon was running for Vice-President on the ticket with General Eisenhower; he saved his place on the ticket, and in political life, with that speech. Well, 'Mr Clark C. Thompson . . . chairman of the executive committee of the American Spaniel Club'

heard the celebrated Nixon speech over the radio. 'When Nixon mentioned his cocker spaniel, it made me prick up my ears', he said. 'I liked his little touch when he said he was going to keep the dog, regardless. Anybody who feels that way about cocker spaniels must be a good man.' (*New Yorker*, 11 Oct. 1952, p. 26)

With hindsight we can see how accurate Mr Thompson's conclusion was, but the fallaciousness of the reasoning was evident a priori, with hindsight irrelevant to that. Now, if some reasoning to normative claims can be judged poor, as can this, then some can be judged good, and there are standards for such determinations whether we can make them out or not.

VI

Do values exist? What are values? Talk about 'a value', which often goes along with talk about 'creating' or 'discovering' or 'changing' values, is difficult to decipher. Surely there are values, for a person's values are what that person thinks important, but this does not somehow embed value in the universe or give warrant for talking of values as somehow 'there' somewhere independent of us; and such talk, it has always seemed to me, is either nonsense or elliptical for something sensible but much more complex. (This may be why in Anglo-American philosophy the tradition has been more to talk about 'value judgments' than about 'values'.) Values are not objects, and it does no good to talk of them as though they are. Values are relations, albeit complex relations, and are related to persons and purposes. This does not mean that a person's sense or scale of values cannot be objective, that values are ineradicably and essentially subjective. What has already been said about objectivity applies immediately here. What a person thinks important can be actually and objectively and truly so, and a discussion about values is not and need not be merely a trading of prejudices—though of course that is often what in fact it is.

Do we choose values? Can we? People talk this way. Such talk needs interpretation. The Dean of Students at my university has been quoted as saying that students 'have to make choices about careers, ethics and values'.

Certainly they have to make choices about careers. But choices about ethics and values? All this can mean is that they have to make choices of fundamental kinds that will either develop or stunt their ethics and values, that will require them to think in ethical and value terms in ways they never had to think before when they lived in the cocoon of the home. But to talk of literally choosing one's ethics is literally nonsense, as though one can choose one's values as one can choose what shoes to wear or whether to have sex tonight. One's values will be manifested in the latter choice, one's taste in the first. Given that a person's values are what a person thinks important, to choose one's values is to choose what to think, and this is impossible for anyone, no matter how high the degree to which one aspires and no matter how hard one studies.

So we can interpret what the Dean has said and make sense of it, though we cannot interpret it literally and make sense of it. To 'choose values' means to make choices that will reflect one's values and perhaps give one's values a chance to change in a better direction, which is in turn a value judgement about values.

I have seen it said, with great assurance, that 'An individual can espouse any morality he chooses'.[21] This is literally nonsense; not even the most devout believer in free will can believe that. The most it can mean is that an individual can do whatever he or she chooses (and even that is hyperbole). But no one can *choose* a morality. One's choices are guided by the morality one has—just as sometimes they are stimulated by rebellion against it. With morality and values we reach the limits of the commodities available in the marketing or consumer society. They are not for sale or even selection. One can choose to try to change the principles on which one acts, but this means no more than that one can try to change how one acts—it involves no change in the principles themselves, except that what were once one's principles are one's principles no longer. But one can no more choose a morality than one can choose one's beliefs or choose to make one's principles true.

---

[21] By Carll Tucker, in the *Saturday Review*, 26 November 1977, p. 5. For the antidote, G. J. Warnock's 'On Choosing Values' (*Midwest Studies in Philosophy*, 3 (1978), pp. 28–34) can be recommended as choice. On the matter of the existence of values a recent book that has given me pause is Hans Reiner's *Duty and Inclination* (The Hague: Martinus Nijhoff, 1983); my review of it, *Philosophical Review*, 96(2) (April 1987), at pp. 300–1, will provide the requisite references.

VII

Certain confusions which are plentiful in this area can be avoided by taking seriously certain essential distinctions.

(1) First is the distinction between 'I want it' and 'It's in my interest'. The fact that one wants something does not prove that it's in one's interest; we have all had sufficiently painful experiences to make us aware of this. One may want that last drink for the road; that doesn't mean that it's in one's interest to have it, or in anyone else's for that matter. A few years ago in the US there was a television ad that was very clever in bringing this out. A man sitting on edge of the bed, looking ill and awful, says: 'I can't believe I ate the whole thing! Did I eat the whole thing, Alice?' Wife, disgusted resigned look on face, says: 'You ate the whole thing, Ralph.' This (I think) was supposed to be an ad for Alka-seltzer, or maybe it was Bromo-seltzer. You see why as an ad it might not have been so good. But in bringing out the difference between what one wanted and what was in one's interest it was superb, though of course that was hardly its object.

Just recognizing this distinction is sufficient to establish a basis for certain judgements of value; namely, judgements of prudence. One can recognize 'I want that, but it wouldn't be good for me. I shouldn't have it'. This brings out the distinction we all must in sanity recognize between what we want and what is good, at least good for us. This in turn establishes a basis for some value judgements, judgements of prudence, which rest on a conception of what is one's own best interest on the whole. It is not easy to recognize, in particular situations or in general, what is in one's own best interest or for one's own good. It is in fact one of the hardest yet one of the most important tasks of life. Yet the simple distinction mentioned is sufficient to bring out that there is such a conception, that we all recognize it, and that there are occasions on which in practice we can make it out. Just how one's good on the whole is related to what one wants is a philosophical question of great difficulty, but the difficulty of the question is no reason for denying the reality of the distinction.[22]

(2) Closely related to this first distinction is that between preference (aversion, liking, disliking) and opinion or judgement. To like something or prefer one thing over another is a matter of taste. In the gustatory, which is the primary, sense of taste this is manifestly an individual matter about

---

[22] There is considerable wisdom on this matter in Murphy's *Uses of Reason* pt. II, ch. I, 'The Context of Moral Judgment'.

which disputes are silly (though they do go on). If something tastes salty to me, it is salty to me, even if it is 'just right' for you. Salt tastes salty, sugar tastes sweet, lemons taste sour, pepper tastes sharp. These are facts about taste about which few would disagree. But preferences—in that sense, tastes—vary, and there is really no occasion for argument (though they do go on). Where there are differences they are not, usually, over whether something in being sugared tastes sweet, or in being salted tastes salty, but over whether, as salty, or sweet, or sour, it tastes *good*. This is a matter of preference in the primary sense, over which there can be no sensible disputing, though there can be discussions and proposed trials that might lead to a change in taste. (I here put to one side the question whether something salty or sweet is good for one, in some medical sense, as irrelevant to the present point. I put to another side the sort of tasting engaged in by professional wine tasters, as too recherché.)

One can have a preference without having an opinion, and one can have an opinion without having a preference; further, where one has both they do not have to coincide. Plenty of people have been of opinion that sex was a bad thing and still enjoyed it. Newspaper item: 'What is your favorite Christmas song? You can call in your opinion [it says] between 6 tonight and 2 p.m. tomorrow'. Actually, that is not so; you cannot call in your opinion on what is your *favourite*, since you cannot have an opinion on which is your favourite. 'Opinion' is here out of place. The item illustrates how the two are often confused. Another newspaper item: 'We are interested in your opinion of which columnist would be of more help to you before we make our decision. So who would you prefer?' But the one I prefer might not be the one who in my opinion would be of most help to me. What am I being asked? No doubt those who bothered to phone in their—what was it, their preferences or their opinions?'—were not bothered by the nicety of usage that I have here singled out an abuse of. It is nonetheless abuse and confusion.

An opinion is something that is capable of being true or false, correct or incorrect. It contrasts on the one side with preference, which cannot be correct or incorrect, and on the other side with fact. Another word for opinion in this context is 'judgement'; a matter of judgement is not a matter of preference, taste, or liking, though someone's judgement can be corrupted by preference, taste, liking or aversion.

(3) The third distinction is between approving of something and liking it. To approve of something or someone is to make a favourable judgement of it or him or her; to disapprove is to make an unfavourable judgement. Approval and disapproval rest on reasons, though one may not always be able to make one's reasons explicit. Liking or disliking need not rest on

reasons. I can dislike someone without being aware of my reasons for doing so, and I can like someone even though I disapprove of him; that is to say, take an unfavourable view of his behaviour, judge it bad or wicked or indecent or scandalous. To disapprove is to make a moral judgement, to regard as wrong, and a judgement must rest on reasons; if it does not, it is only a disguised expression of liking or disliking. Now one may have reasons for liking something or someone, but one need not; and on some matters, such as liking the taste of chocolate, it would make no sense to ask for one's reasons.

(4) Related to these others, though subsidiary to them, is the distinction between a matter of opinion and a *mere* matter of opinion. A matter of opinion is a matter on which all the evidence is not in (or perhaps cannot be in) and different people can hold different views, in the light of different interpretations of the evidence and different weights placed on them. God is incapable of having opinions; God knows. Sometimes a second physician is called in for another opinion, sometimes a third, though the process must end sometime. When judges disagree they issue conflicting opinions. But none of these people, if they are genuinely professionals, can think that the opinions issued are *mere* opinion; that is to say, not something capable of being correct or incorrect. The way in which a medical opinion is shown to be correct or incorrect differs from the way in which a legal opinion is; nonetheless, neither party to the dispute believes for a moment that neither opinion has any claim to correctness. Justice Holmes held a sceptical meta-ethics. 'Our system of morality', he held, 'is a body of imperfect social generalizations expressed in terms of emotion.'[23] Nonetheless, when he was not expressing a meta-ethical view but was making moral judgements for himself—when, in other words, he was in the context of moral judgement, as he often was in his position on the Supreme Court—he took a different view, and necessarily so. This is brought out by the concluding words of his dissent in *Abrams* v. *United States* (250 US (1919) 616, 624): 'I regret that I cannot put into more impressive words my belief that in their conviction upon this indictment the defendants were deprived of their rights under the Constitution of the United States.' The words are pretty impressive; they simply failed to convince the majority. And the fact that Holmes speaks of his 'belief', not his 'opinion', solidifies the point.

A *mere* matter of opinion would be one on which no evidence one way or the other is available, no arguments, no reasons except spurious ones; but then the alleged opinions put forward are preferences under an alias.

---

[23] *Collected Legal Papers* (New York: Harcourt, Brace, 1921), p. 306.

VIII

One use of the term 'ethics' is to speak of a person's character, as honest, reliable, trustworthy, kind, generous, just and their opposites, either absolutely or in various degrees, and in sum good or bad. An ethical person, in this sense, is one who has in noticeable degree a good moral character, and who (usually) has this not accidentally but deliberately, because concerned with the moral character of contemplated behaviour. Thus an ethical person is one who, completely by instinct or training and without reflection on the consequences of his or her actions, does the right thing, or else one whose conduct is governed by the concern to do what is right. An unethical person, on the other hand—and there are many about—is either one who pays no attention whatever to the ethical ramifications of his conduct, or else one who, knowing the moral dimension of his conduct, is not moved by it. Thus an unethical person is one who is prepared to lie, to cheat, to steal, to cause pain to others, on the slightest provocation or simply because he feels like it.

Character and conduct are by no means independent of each other. A person's conduct is informed, influenced, determined, by that person's character, and a person's character is formed, affected, modified by, can on certain occasions even be drastically changed by, the felt and observed nature and consequences of his conduct.

A person's values also enter into this equation. A person's values—what that person thinks important—are those standards, principles, ends, aims, and ideals that affect that person's conduct. They are consequently part of and enter into the composition of that person's character.

By reflection and the experience of life, either first- or second-hand, one can modify one's values, come to think that what was before thought important no longer is or perhaps never was, or that what was before not valued should be or should have been. In this process one's character is modified, for better or worse, and this has effects on the person's conduct, sense of self-respect, and relations with others.

Thus one who by such reflection comes to think it a horrible and unacceptable thing that there are people in the community—or in the world at large—who are starving or suffering or homeless through no fault of their own but by the action of thoughtless or heartless or careless social agencies, may set out on a course of social reform and realign his or her values accordingly. Things that seemed important before no longer seem so, but seem rather trivial or worse, while things that were never thought of before—the sufferings of people three blocks away or across the world—loom large as top priorities for action and for changes in social policy. The psychology of character studies the psychological mechanisms by which this process works. Ethics concerns itself with the standards by which it can itself be appraised as good or bad, wise or foolish, right or wrong. And one's own ethical philosophy, so far as one has one or has snatches or glimpses of one read about or studied in school, also plays a role in this process. This gives an especially prominent role to the teaching of ethics and morals and values. It is itself a moral responsibility, not just another academic subject.

ADDITIONAL NOTES AND COMMENTS

A. 'Value Judgements and Normative Claims' was originally a lecture delivered to the Royal Institute of Philosophy, London, on 8 January 1988, published in A. Phillips Griffiths (ed.), *Key Themes in Philosophy* (Cambridge: Cambridge University Press, 1989), pp. 145–72, reprinted here with some slight verbal changes.

B. A strikingly different conception of *value* has been developed by Thomas F. Green, in 'The Value of "Values"', *Career Development Quarterly*, 38 (March 1990), pp. 208–11, and in his book (cited *supra*) *Voices*, ch. 5, 'Teaching Values: The Grand Delusion'. The gist of Green's criticism is that the notion of 'having values' is a deviant usage, departing from the historical use and etymology of 'value'. Put more precisely, Green says: 'I believe that most talk about teaching values and about people having values is more an obstacle than a help . . . The main reason we talk about "values people have" is to avoid talking about anything serious.' Again: 'No longer do we speak of the value that *things* have, their worth. Instead, we can speak only of the values that people have, not of what is desirable, but of what is desired, not of what things have worth, but only of what people prefer, only of their values' ('The Value of "Values"', pp. 208, 210). Something is out of joint here. First, when we talk of someone's values or what some person values, we are not talking of what that person *desires* or *prefers*, but of what that person *judges* important, or valuable, or desirable, and there is an enormous difference between what a person desires or likes or prefers, and what that person *judges important*—or worthwhile or worth having or worth doing. Second, it is flatly false that in the locution in question, we can no longer 'speak of the value that *things* have . . . not of what is desirable . . . not of what things have worth'. Of course we can, and do.

7

Moral Worth and Fundamental Rights

In what follows I state a number of large theses of consequence in largely a summary way, and for lack of time must leave out some essential interconnections and supporting arguments. I think it better, in the time available, to present an overall view, even at the risk of seeming unduly asseverative, than to deal with a narrow and limited problem. This, of course, is a value judgement but instead of arguing for it, which would be here unseemly, I proceed instead to act on it.

I start from the premiss that a person's values are what that person deems important, a society's values what that society deems important. This is not a matter of preference or liking, but a matter of judgement; for what a person deems important is what that person regards as, thinks, or judges important. Though there may be some relation to preferences and aversions, that relation is certainly not one of identity. We can change our preferences and aversions; we cannot change what we think, as distinct from what we think about. What we think, what we believe, what we judge is not within the area of choice. For what we believe we believe to be true, and we could have no conception of truth and falsity if we conceived of it as something in turn dependent on what we think.

But, though a person's values are what that person deems important, these values are not necessarily subjective or incapable of being defended. And a person's values are to be distinguished from the value of the person and of other persons or things, and also from the soundness of those values. For we express our values in our conduct and our attitudes and also in our value judgements, and value judgements, as distinct from preferences and aversions, can be true or false. Our values are themselves implicit judgements—not mere preferences.

Values are of different kinds, which can be briefly listed though not briefly described, relating to different contexts and purposes. Thus we speak of dramatic value, monetary value, literary value, poetic value, scientific value, educational value, medical value, news value, entertainment value, nutritional value, political value, and comic value—and much much more. In each case, when we talk about the value of something we are making an estimate of the degree to which it possesses qualities of a certain kind or of its capacity to contribute to the success of the enterprise at hand. When we speak of moral value, however, we are not making that kind of estimate; success is not a criterion. That does not mean that capacity to contribute to failure is a mark of moral merit. Nor is moral value something extrinsic to the person. Objects can have no moral value.

What has moral value is character and the conduct that embodies it. What has moral value, furthermore, is what contributes to the development of character and to the development of institutions that help mould character. Moral value, in short, relates to character, volition, the will, the motives from which we act, and the actions that are within our control; consequently to the control we exert on the actions we perform, and, consequently to responsibility. For when we speak of *moral* value we speak of what we can be held responsible for, what we can control, and therefore what is within the control of the will. The expression 'moral worth' is used most often for the moral value of character and it is the expression that, following Kant, I shall use here. 'Value' and 'worth' are close synonyms in many contexts, though not in all. 'Worth' fits the moral case better because of its use in 'worthy', which links with 'worthy of' and 'deserving of'; there is no similar form for 'value'.[1]

I think Kant is right in his claim that the only thing that can be conceived of as good without qualification—that is, good unconditionally—is a good will, understood as the settled determination, tending to develop into a habit, to do what is morally right simply because it is morally right. And I do not think that in saying this Kant was as far from tradition as has been thought. This striking first proposition of Kant's *Groundwork of the Metaphysics of Morals* ('There is nothing in the world, or even out of it, that can be conceived of as good without qualification, except a good will') has a number of implications, among them that a good will is necessarily good and that only a good will or what manifests a good will can be *morally* good. By a good will, then, Kant means—and he makes this quite

---

[1] Two philosophers who have made a point of emphasizing the difference between value and worth, hence between moral value and moral worth, are Felix Adler, in *An Ethical Philosophy of Life* (New York and London: D. Appleton, 1919), esp. p. 117 n., and *passim*; and Kurt Baier, in 'Moral Value and Moral Worth', *Monist*, 54 (1970), esp. pp. 24–9. I found the work of Baier of inestimable value in preparing this paper. Two other significant papers by Baier on this topic are 'What is Value? An Analysis of the Concept', in Kurt Baier and Nicholas Rescher (eds.), *Values and the Future* (New York: Free Press, 1969), pp. 33–67, and 'Value and Fact', in Howard Kiefer and Kilton K. Minitz (eds.), *Contemporary Philosophic Thought, iv. Ethical and Social Justice* (Albany: State University of New York Press, 1968, repr. 1970).

explicit—character. And what is morally good, or has moral worth, is not just a good will, but also actions and persons that manifest a good will, sentiments and attitudes that facilitate its operation, and institutions that help develop and protect this human trait of pre-eminent worth.

The concept of the moral worth of an action can be summed up in the following formula, which though it goes beyond the Kantian text, nonetheless brings out what is implicit in it: 'A's doing of x has moral worth if and only if (i) x is morally right, or else (ii) A believes x is right and (iii) A's belief is reasonable or justified; and (iv) A does x because x is right, or because A has a reasonable belief that it is; and (v) (though this is more problematic) A had to overcome obstacles to do x'. This last condition, that A had to overcome obstacles to do x, is not only debatable but dispensable. It is not necessary to moral worth as primarily understood, but we can understand by it that the moral worth of an action increases with the effort required to overcome obstacles, either external or internal. And the formula itself is only a hypothesis to be explored in another context. What I shall do here is say a bit about the setting of this conception and trace out its implications for fundamental rights and social policy.

The germ of the idea is in Aristotle's distinction between moral and intellectual virtue. By moral virtue Aristotle meant virtues of character eventuating in conduct and developed by habit, and, except for the Aristotelian emphasis on habit, this is not too far from the Kantian conception. The idea that morality relates primarily to character is also, to be sure, in Hume, and is one feature of Hume's ethics that Kant did not dispute. Thus Hume held that:

when we praise any actions, we regard only the motives that produced them, and consider the actions as signs or indications of certain principles in the mind and temper. The external performance has no merit. We must look within to find the moral quality.[2]

Whately, a moral-sense theorist, held that 'It is entirely on the motives and dispositions of the mind that the *moral* character of any one's conduct depends'. I take this to mean not that one's motives, if good, make one's conduct, no matter what it is, morally right, but that it is one's motives that give one's conduct, and one's character, its moral worth, and that this is the central locus of morality. But whether Whately or Kant or anyone else held it I take it as manifest that morals, morality, and moral worth primarily and fundamentally refer, relate to, and depend upon what is within the control

---

[2] David Hume, *A Treatise of Human Nature*, bk. III, pt. II, sect. I, p. 477; cf. pt. III, sect. I, p. 575.

of the will, what we can be responsible for, and that they relate primarily to character.[3]

Given that the pre-eminent value that we call moral is the value of character, of the will, it follows that what has fundamental value and therefore should be given top priority in the arrangement of human affairs is the unfettered operation of human thought and the human conscience. This brings us to fundamental rights. It might be thought that asserting a right is nothing more than expressing a wish in emotively enticing language, in accordance with some now-exploded meta-ethical theories, or in virtue of a current tendency to claim a right to something simply because one wants it or demands it. This is not so. Saying 'I have a right to X' is different from saying 'I want X', and *claiming* a right to something does not prove that one *has* that right, any more than claiming to know proves that one knows. When we use such locutions ourselves we are conscious of meaning something different and something more, just as when we hear them used by others. And we must recognize that when someone else asserts a right to something, what is being asserted is, apart from the validity of the claim, different from demanding it or asserting a desire to have it, because we recognize that that is true of ourselves when we assert or claim a right. Nor is there any contradiction in saying 'I have a right to X, but I don't want it'. Thus the concept of moral rights is ineliminable in favour of wants or interests. Therefore, on the basis of the generalization principle ('what is right for any one person must be right for any similar person in similar circumstances'), it follows that rights talk is significant, and consequently that there are rights.

Ronald Dworkin has claimed that the fundamental right is the right to equal concern and treatment. This is surely an important right, but it is not the fundamental right. The fundamental right is derived from the fundamental moral value, moral worth, and is such that without its exercise there could be no moral worth or moral value. The only thing that meets this description is the right to freedom of thought and conscience, the right to think the thought that one is led to think through the unfettered operation of one's own mind. What makes this fundamental is that it cannot be violated without destroying the individual person's capacity to think, to feel,

---

[3] Richard Whately, *Paley's Moral Philosophy: With Annotations* (London: John W. Parker, 1859), p. 14. For an interesting dissent see P. H. Nowell-Smith, *Ethics* (Harmondsworth: Penguin Books, 1954), p. 259. And for an interesting perspective on this matter see Friedrich A. Hayek, *The Road to Serfdom* (Chicago, Ill.: University of Chicago Press, 1944), pp. 211–12; also W. D. Ross, *The Right and the Good* (Oxford: Clarendon Press, 1930), pp. 155–6. I am of course sliding over differences not essential in the present context.

to be aware as a distinct autonomous person as distinct from a heteronomous automaton, and this is to destroy the person. This right is closely linked with, may be equivalent to, the right to be oneself, and links closely with the right of autonomy, which also has fundamental moral value. It is also a *natural* right, in the sense defined by Dworkin; that is, it is 'an objective moral reality . . . not . . . created [or constructed] by [people] or societies but rather discovered by them', and either recognized and respected or ignored and violated.[4] The right to freedom of thought and conscience is essential to personality, self-identity, and self-respect.

Although the fundamental character of the right of freedom of thought has been remarked on before, it has been thought of little value by itself. Thus Bury, in his *History of Freedom of Thought*, says: 'thought is free. A man can never be hindered from thinking whatever he chooses so long as he conceals what he thinks. The working of his mind is limited only by the bounds of his experience and the power of his imagination. But this natural liberty of private thinking is of little value.'[5] There are a number of instructive errors here. It is false that thought is naturally free, that no one's thought processes can ever be interfered with. Perhaps this mistake arose because Bury was writing before the advent of the concentration camp and the development of modern techniques of indoctrination and brainwashing. Secondly, what one thinks is not a matter of choice. One does not think what one chooses. One's thoughts are chosen for one, by processes of which we are only dimly aware and over which we have little control. We may choose what to think about, but not *what to think* about what we think about. And it is, finally, false that 'this natural liberty of private thinking is of little value'. Considered as the right to freedom of thought and conscience it is of immense value, because it is the basis of all other rights. Bury, following John Stuart Mill in *On Liberty*, thinks that 'freedom of thought, in any valuable sense, includes freedom of speech' (ibid, p. 8). No doubt to be accorded freedom of thought but not freedom of speech is frustrating, and thought tends to bubble over into speech—at least with some among us—but freedom of thought does not '*include* freedom of speech', though it might call for it as its suitable accompaniment. The justification of the right to freedom of thought is one thing, and has already been supplied. The justification of the right to freedom of speech or discussion, though not hard to come by, is yet something else, because to exercise freedom of speech is to do something, perform an act, which nec-

[4] Ronald Dworkin, *Taking Rights Seriously* (Cambridge, Mass.: Harvard University Press, 1977), pp. 180–3, 272–8, 160.
[5] J. B. Bury, *A History of Freedom of Thought* (London: Oxford University Press, 1913), p. 7.

essarily affects others, and there are all sorts of circumstances where this may be legitimately restricted. And this right can be restricted, circumscribed, abridged without destroying the person. The right to freedom of thought and conscience cannot.[6]

Another right that in society is fundamental is, in the words of Hobhouse, 'the right to be dealt with in accordance with law'. The 'first condition of free government', Hobhouse observed, 'is government not by the arbitrary determination of the ruler, but by fixed rules of law, to which the ruler himself is subject'.[7] This is an excellent statement of the prime condition, not of free government, but of *just* government, since it flows from the prime source of justice, the Golden Rule—'Do unto others as you would have them do unto you'—and the principle of justice or generalization principle ('What is right for one person must be right for every similar person in similar circumstances'). Hobhouse has here given us an essential minimal statement of the ideal of the rule of law, which must be the aspiration of every state that aspires to a condition other than mere domination and control, in which the subjects are autonomous beings, subject to laws to which they can rationally consent and which are the same for all.

It follows that the right to life, often taken as fundamental on the ground that it is essential to having any other rights, is not fundamental but derived. For it is not the *right* to life that is essential to having any other rights; it is simply being alive and capable of functioning. Given that there is a fundamental right to freedom of thought, and that one must be alive to exercise this right, it follows that everyone has a right to life; and this is the

---

[6] On this point I directly contradict a prime point in Mill's *Liberty*. I have the greatest admiration for this work, think it works in contexts where others don't, don't think it works in this. What Mill says on this matter is: 'the appropriate region of human liberty . . . comprises, first, the inward domain of consciousness; demanding liberty of conscience in the most comprehensive sense; liberty of thought and feeling; absolute freedom of opinion and sentiment on all subjects, practical or speculative, scientific, moral, or theological. The liberty of expressing and publishing opinions may seem to fall under a different principle, since it belongs to that part of the conduct of the individual which concerns other people; but, *being almost of as much importance as the liberty of thought itself, and resting in great part on the same reasons, is practically inseparable from it*' (1859, ch. I, para. 12; Oxford World's Classics edn., p. 18; Everyman edn., p. 75; emphasis added). The word 'almost' is significant here. Mill adds (para. 16; WC edn., p. 20; Everyman edn., p. 77) that 'it is impossible to separate the cognate liberty of speaking and writing . . . from . . . the Liberty of Thought'. It has been my argument not that it is desirable but that it is possible to separate them, both in theory and in practice, and that the two rights or liberties rest on different reasons. My argument makes no appeal to utility, whereas Mill thinks his does, and this may help explain the discrepancy. It is worth noting that Mill's second chapter is entitled 'Of the Liberty of Thought and Discussion' and is about the two taken together.

[7] L. T. Hobhouse, *Liberalism* (London: Oxford University Press, 1911), pp. 21, 23.

derivation. There are other conditions that are in fact necessary for the exercise of this right, such as adequate food and shelter and a minimum of other factors, such as health care, that enable one to lead a minimally decent life without scrounging like a jungle beast for the minimum means of subsistence. It thus becomes a vital political and social responsibility to secure the conditions under which everyone can be assured a certain minimum welfare, so far as this is attainable by the efforts of human beings, and nothing less can be sanctioned by the principle of justice. (Perhaps I should add, given some current confusions about this matter, that I am not advocating a situation of rights but no duties. A moral agent is a person who has, and must have, both rights and duties.)

To what extent does this fundamental moral right to freedom of thought and conscience generate a right to freedom of expression, speech, and discussion, and of the press (although 'the press' is now an inordinately vague concept)? This depends on social and political conditions. It is nonetheless something at which morality, as the expression of the unfettered human conscience and sense of responsibility, naturally aims, and therefore the right to freedom of expression, speech, and discussion is something that can justly be restricted only with special and strong justification. It follows that restrictions on freedom of speech and expression always require justification, of a moral not a political nature; for there is a moral presumption in their favour, and the absence of such restrictions, except those required to assure a like freedom for others, does not require justification. A good society, therefore, is one in which this right is encouraged to develop and be exercised, and in which people exercise it responsibly, with respect for the equal moral rights of others. It follows, further, that from a fundamental thesis about moral worth and values we can derive conclusions of consequence about fundamental human rights and about what political and social arrangements ought morally to prevail and therefore ought morally to be striven for. The ideal of bringing about a social structure in which moral values can flourish therefore constitutes a prime moral and political obligation, as well as a fundamental moral ideal.

ADDITIONAL NOTES AND COMMENTS

A. 'Moral Worth and Fundamental Rights' was presented as an invited paper to the 18th World Congress of Philosophy, Brighton, UK, on 23 August 1988. Originally published in *Wisconsin Academy Review*, 37(1) (winter 1990–1), pp. 23–5; published here with some slight changes and with the original notes.

8

On Race and Racism

1. The Word 'Racism'
2. The Term 'Race'
3. Boxall on Race
4. Barzun on Race
5. Montagu on 'Race'
6. Benedict on Race
7. Montesquieu's Parody
8. Ardrey on Race
9. Cultural Generalizations and National Character
10. Racism and Race
11. The Tawneyesque Conception of Racism

One may wonder whether there is anything more to be said about racism except to deplore it, or anything more to be done about it except to eradicate it. And the answer immediately presents itself: yes, we can understand it. Marx to the contrary, the task of philosophy is not to change the world but to understand it. There is always change. Understanding is the precondition of intelligent change.

In what follows however, I present no general theory, as would be required for an adequate understanding; only some thoughts on the matter, on the way to understanding.

1. THE WORD 'RACISM'

Let us first consider the word. The term 'racism' is a relative newcomer to the language, entering it not much more than half a century ago. Its forerunner, now rarely used, is 'racialism'. Thus if we look at *Webster's Fifth Collegiate Dictionary* (1936), we find the term 'racialism' defined in it—as 'racial prejudice; race hatred'—but we do not find the term 'racism'. It does appear, however, along with 'racist', in the 'New Words Section' (1941), where it is defined as 'assumption of inherent racial superiority or the purity and superiority of certain races, and consequent discrimination against other races; also, any doctrine or program of racial domination and discrimination based on such an assumption' (p. xxxii).

Similarly if we turn to the second edition of the *Shorter Oxford English Dictionary* (also 1936) we find that 'racism' does not appear in it, although 'racialism' does, as an undefined appendage to 'racial'. 'Racism', however, does appear in the 'Addenda' to the third edition (of 1944; p. 2506), where both it and 'racialism' are defined. 'Racialism' is said to date from 1907 (we are here, remember, talking about the word), and to be 'used esp. of antagonistic or provocative emphasis on race', while 'racism' is said to date from 1942 (again, we are talking about the word) and is defined as 'the theory that fundamental characteristics of race are preserved by an unchanging tradition'.

I cannot give this high marks as a dictionary definition. But if this is all that was meant, in England in 1942, by 'racism'—merely a certain sort of theory about race—then the term would seem to have shifted in meaning a bit since then, perhaps because those advocating racism (racists) tended also to be racialists and vice versa.

'Racism' also does not appear in *Webster's Second New International Dictionary* (1934), though, not surprisingly, 'racialism' does. But 'racism' is defined in the 'Addenda' section (either from 1939 or 1945), as 'assumption of inherent racial superiority, and consequent discrimination against, or attempted domination over, other races; a doctrine or program based on this assumption; broadly, race hatred or discrimination' (p. cxxv). 'Racialism' is defined, in the body of the work (p. 2049), as 'racial characteristics, tendencies, prejudices, or the like; spec., race hatred'. And 'racialist' is defined as 'one promoting or animated by racialism [presumably in the meaning of racial prejudice or race hatred]; esp. one who maintains that some races are inherently superior to others'.

These dictionary findings are confirmed by comparing the two editions of Jacques Barzun's *Race: A Study in Superstition*. Although 'racialism' is used abundantly in the first edition of 1937, the term 'racism' does not appear in it at all. And, curiously, in the second edition of 1965, 'racialism' is replaced by 'racism' in practically every occurrence.

Finally, in Ruth Benedict's *Race: Science and Politics*, which appeared in 1940, the term 'racism' seems to have taken over. 'Racism' appears abundantly (in the first chapter racism is called the 'ism' of the modern world), while 'racialism' puts in only a few final appearances, and the terms do not appear to be used with different meanings.

It seems evident, from these rather few out-of-the-way indications, as well as from innumerable other manifestations that are, unfortunately, too familiar and too odious to bear reciting here, that the phenomenon of racism, or racialism, was one of those special phenomena which in the 1930s and 1940s was being talked about—as it was occurring and being fought against—with greater and greater frequency and vehemence and horror. This could well account for the change in usage and the replacement of the more theoretical and pedantic term 'racialist' by the more vehement term 'racist', which comes more rapidly and expressively off the tongue. 'Racism' came into use, as did the term 'genocide' at about the same time, as a label for practices that were felt to be unprecedented, and unprecedented in their enormity, monstrosity, and evil.

And so they were, beyond a doubt. But since these are the feelings that accompanied and generated the early use of the term, it has come to be highly emotive, and is now, I have come to think, one of the most overworked and most highly emotive terms in the language. It is not, of course, solely emotive (like 'boo' or 'hurray'). It is more like a four-letter obscenity for some such bodily function as defecating or copulating. But it is not just like these either. This aspect of 'racism' will bear looking at.

2. THE TERM 'RACE'

It turns out that the term 'race' also presents difficulties. The anthropologists, biologists, and geneticists, as well as other scholars who write on this matter, are not themselves agreed on what the concept is, or on whether and what it denotes. Some say that there are races, others say that there are not; some say that there are three races of mankind, others say that there are five, still others say that there are a very great many; some say that the concept is fairly precise or can be made so, others that it is 'arbitrary' and unscientific; and so on.

The term 'race', in the sense appropriate to this discussion, is to be taken as referring to *distinguishing* characteristics of human beings that are (1) *inherited*, or believed to be inherited, (2) shared by fairly large numbers of people (but not by all), and (3) readily *apparent* to ordinary sense perception, especially the sense of sight.

Thus purely scientific definitions of 'race', as by reference to gene frequencies or gene pools, or classification of human beings by reference to blood groups (which, though real, are not readily apparent), do not here concern us. As has been remarked: 'There are no prejudices against genes'.[1] Of course; genes are not apparent to ordinary sense perception. And one can have the concept of a race, and make distinctions along 'racial' lines, without having a concept of a gene. But racism is not concerned with genes either.

The definition as stated so far is relatively uncontroversial. It is when it is asked whether there is anything to which the term applies, or how many races there are, that controversy first enters—though on these matters it is relatively benign controversy. Controversy of a rather more serious nature arises from (4) the idea that these visible characteristics determine or accompany other less apparent physical, mental, emotional, or cultural traits, and (5) the idea that these inherited physical—so-called racial—traits are therefore relevant to how a person or a group should be treated or regarded—to status in the society.

A racist, in one appropriate meaning of the term, is one who regards race as a fact about persons that is always relevant to how they should be treated—for determining social status and standing and opportunities and in the assignment of rights and duties, privileges and responsibilities, benefits and burdens. But in *this sense* of the term a racist could be simply someone who holds a certain abstract theory about the meaning and significance of racial traits, or what are taken to be 'racial' traits. A racist, in the sense in which racists are rightly condemned and racism is rightly deplored, is (speaking loosely) someone who practices or engages in or encourages or incites race prejudice, hostility, enmity, or warfare. One who holds such a theory is usually, though not necessarily, one who engages in the practices and activities that are rightly condemned as 'racist'. One might believe that one's own race (or ethnic stock) is superior to others and entitled to greater privileges for that reason, without engaging in activities that I have called 'racist'. Holding such a theory or set of beliefs does not always or necessarily lead to the practices that are rightly to be deplored and eradicated. There seems to be some confusion about this.

3. BOXALL ON RACE

Someone like George E. Boxall, for example, is a 'racist' in the sense—and only in the sense—that he thinks there are innate and inherited differences,

---

[1] William C. Boyd, *Genetics and the Races of Man* (Boston: Little, Brown, 1950), p. 274. See also pp. 263, 252, 207.

between races, of intelligence, aptitude, capacities, and propensities.[2] But he is not thereby a racist in the sense of someone who 'discriminates against a person on account of that person's race—or against a group on account of theirs'.

It is Boxall's belief that 'Anglo-Saxon' is the name of a race, and that 'the Anglo-Saxon is a cross between two well-defined races ["the Xanthochroi" and "the Melanochroi"] which differ considerably from each other, both mentally and physically. In order to understand him, therefore', says Mr Boxall, 'it is necessary that we should know something of each of the two races from which he has been derived'. It is also his belief that 'the Anglo-Saxon' is 'superior . . . both physically and mentally, to his conqueror the Latin'. Further, Boxall 'assumes' that

the union of two or more races is necessary to produce a new race, because, if we take a survey of the races of man now existing, we find that in Australia, Tasmania, New Guinea, and other isolated countries, where there has been but little or no admixture of races, there has been no new race produced during immense periods of time, and no advance has been made in civilization.

It is not, I must confess, altogether clear to me what Mr Boxall means by 'a race', and puzzlement is especially acute when he says things like:

the antipathy of the Slav to the Teuton is racial, and indicates that these people belong to different races; but at present our knowledge on this branch of the subject is so slight, that it is impossible to distinguish between racial and mere national antipathy or jealousy.

That he is not a racist, however, in the modern and vehemently derogatory sense of the term, is clear from the title of one of his chapters, 'The Unity of the Human Family', and from such observations as that 'we . . . have to divest our minds of the belief that there is or ever has been a "favoured race"'. It is also said, in a section headed 'Race Hatred Inexcusable', that:

The man who accepts the theory of evolution has no . . . excuse for racial antipathy. To him the older races represent stages in the evolution of his own race. It is because he has inherited all that is best in these older races that he is superior to them, and not on account of his own efforts. He owes a debt of gratitude to them which he is incapable of repaying in full, and he can only show a sense of his indebtedness by treating the remnants of these races with kindness and consideration.

It is true that racists tend to stereotype, and those who stereotype tend to be racists. All the more reason, then, for being wary of stereotyping as

[2] George E. Boxall, *The Anglo-Saxon: A Study in Evolution* (London: T. Fisher Unwin, 1906). The passages cited and quoted are from pp. 12, 13, 20, 26–7, 42, 430, 329, and 183 respectively.

racists those who speak of race or have race theories. And this suggests that perhaps we should re-examine our stereotype of a racist.

Mr Boxall moves even farther away from our stereotype of a racist when he says that:

There is no evidence to support the popular belief as to the hereditariness of crime. All the evidence with which I am acquainted tends to prove that crime is not hereditary, but is propagated by education or training . . . I am not prepared to say that all crime . . . is due to a revolt against unjust or oppressive laws, but I am convinced that this is very largely the cause of crime, and until the racial characteristics are much better understood than they are at present, I shall continue to believe that the criminal is rather to be pitied than condemned in the majority of cases.

Not all who say 'race', or speak of races, are racists, and if they are, then a lot of persons who have dedicated their lives to combatting racial prejudice and enmity would be racists, and we should have more racists among us than we can hope to deal with. But there is some evidence that this stereotyping tendency has been at work among some who have most vehemently deplored and condemned 'racism' and 'racialists'. This becomes apparent if we look carefully at the work of a few such writers.

4. BARZUN ON RACE

One of them, I am afraid, is Jacques Barzun, whose book on the subject was referred to just before (sect. I).

Barzun maintains that 'a satisfactory definition of race is not to be had':

The formulas in common use do not really define or do not accord with the facts, so that a prudent man will suspend judgment until genetics can offer a more complete body of knowledge. But to expect prudence in thinking about subjects charged with political emotion is folly too; and so we find the racists of the past 150 years leaping over the initial obstacle to race-theorizing, making assumptions to suit their object and failing to define their terms, just like the man in the street who borrows their language without questioning its validity.[3]

We have already seen that there are difficulties with the concept or definition of race, just as there are disputes among reputable scientists over how many races there are and the defining traits of different races. But Barzun

---

[3] Jacques Barzun, *Race: A Study in Superstition*, 2nd edn. (New York: Harper & Row, 1965), p. 16. The 1st edn. was subtitled *A Study in Modern Superstition* (New York: Harcourt, Brace, 1937).

seems to be inferring from the difficulty over definition that there are no races or race differences amongst peoples, which is a gross *non sequitur*.

In an appendix entitled 'Race-Thinking: A Brief Anthology', Barzun provides a number of quotations 'chosen to illustrate the extremes and the common-places of race-thinking' (p. 221). In this section there appears a quotation from Darwin, the very presence of which is a suggestion that Darwin is to be regarded as a racist. Now, what Darwin is quoted as saying is this:

There is . . . no doubt that the various races, when carefully compared and measured, differ much from each other—as in the texture of the hair, the relative proportions of all parts of the body, the capacity of the lungs, the form and capacity of the skull and even in the convolutions of the brain.[4]

Apparently because Darwin thinks that there are such things as races, he is to be judged as guilty of 'race-thinking', and therefore as a racist. Thus, by this descent to 'entertaining a vulgar error' (p. 221), Darwin is allied with those who, by the quotations given, are represented as believers in racial superiority or supremacy—racists (as I have no doubt they are) in a more obvious and direct and brutal sense. These include Emile Faguet, who is quoted (pp. 226, 233) as saying:

The barbarian is, after all, of the same race as the Roman and the Greek. He is our cousin. The Yellow man, the Black man, is not in the least our cousin . . .

The yellow and black perils will smother our race and destroy our civilization.

And this collection also includes choice quotations from Cecil Rhodes, Galton, LeBon, Gaillaird, and Sir John Squire—and apparently anyone else who ever used the term 'race' to signify anything other than a contest of speed.

Barzun insists that: 'Race-thinking is bad thinking and that is all' (p. xiv), but what is labelled 'race-thinking' can range all the way from the

---

[4] This is quoted (on p. 222) from *The Descent of Man*, ch. VII, 'The Races of Man', para. 3 (New York: Modern Library, p. 530). Judging from the two citations Darwin gives in just one sentence, it is evident that he was going by the scientific evidence of the time (1871). Darwin also says (para. 21, p. 539): 'Although the existing races of man differ in many respects, as in colour, hair, shape of skull, proportions of the body, etc., yet if their whole structure be taken into consideration they are found to resemble each other closely in a multitude of points. Many of these are of so unimportant or of so singular a nature, that it is extremely improbable that they should have been independently acquired by aboriginally distinct species or races. The same remark holds good with equal or greater force with respect to the numerous points of mental similarity between the most distinct races of man.' Is this race-thinking? The point of the chapter was to show that human beings are all members of the same species, and Darwin argues in it that, from the evolutionary point of view, the similarities among human beings are more significant than the differences.

malignant, such as the thinking (if that is what it was) of a Hitler or a Dr Rosenberg, to the assumption or belief, which is neither obviously false nor obviously mischievous, that there are different races of human beings, as there are different breeds of cats. We are warned against 'the folly of thinking that groups are made up of identically hateful or identically lovable people' (p. xiv), and there is some suggestion that this is 'race-thinking'—if not identical with it then a close relative of it—and it is certainly true that that sort of thinking is fallacious and foolish and ignorant, but it does not follow that all who think that there are different races share in *this* thinking. It is observed that 'there are established ways of coping with the conflicts of political and economic groups, and there are none for racial strife'.[5] But this presupposes, if there can be such a thing as racial strife (and who can deny that there have been 'race riots'?), that there are different races and race differences—whether real or only thought to be is irrelevant to the phenomenon.

The term 'race' is obscure, elastic, and slippery, like 'time', and is also controversial and emotive, like 'democracy', 'law', 'freedom', 'equality', 'happiness', 'right', 'justified', 'good', 'real', 'true', and 'beautiful'. But because people dispute about whether something is really true, right, good, or beautiful, it does not follow that these terms are meaningless or that nothing can be true, right, good, or beautiful. And the problems of racism are not about to disappear with the disappearance of a word.

5. MONTAGU ON 'RACE'

A somewhat similar idea of 'race', which Barzun regards as a superstition, is presented by Ashley Montagu, a physical anthropologist, who has written voluminously on the subject, who approaches it with a good deal of fervour, and who regards 'race' as 'a myth' and 'a fallacy'. Montagu defines what he calls 'the myth of "race"' as:

the belief that physical and mental traits are linked, that the physical differences are associated with rather pronounced differences in mental capacities, and that these differences are measurable by IQ tests and the cultural achievements of these populations.

---

[5] Barzun, *Race*, p. xix. Barzun does define 'race-thinking' more precisely in ch. I, sect. iii, pp. 12–14. I do not think, however, that in his zeal to expose it he is always consistent with this more restrained account.

But 'the myth of "race"' does not refer, he says,

> to the fact that physically distinguishable populations of man exist. Such populations are often called races. Distinctive populations of this kind are not myths, but neither are they races in the sense in which that term is usually employed.[6]

There is a message here, but just what it is is crucially imprecise. For Montagu goes right on to put in the same boat, with respect to this matter of 'race', 'most of the older and some modern physical anthropologists, race classifiers, and racists' (p. 25). Now of course a physical anthropologist may be a racist, but a physical anthropologist, even one who studies the classification of races and propounds theories of racial differences, does not have to be. And one need not be a scholastic in the making of distinctions to see that some distinctions here would be of some help in separating the true from the false. One can analyse and dissect and give a rational basis for condemning racism without dealing with the question whether there is a scientific conception of race, and it might be better to do so, since racism (as we shall see) does not really depend on the existence of different races in any scientific sense.

Yet Montagu feels constrained to proclaim that, as he puts it in one place, 'the term "race" itself, as it is *generally applied* to man, is scientifically without justification, and . . . *as commonly used* the term corresponds to nothing in reality . . . The word is predominantly an emotionally loaded one.'[7]

But compare this passage with one where Montagu tells us why he always writes the term 'race' in 'quotation marks'. It is because, he says, 'I do not believe that what this term is used to mean by those who *habitually use it* corresponds to anything in reality'.[8]

In the previous passage our anthropologist had referred not to 'those who habitually use' the term, but to how 'the term is commonly used', and he appears not to see that these notions are quite distinct. Let it be granted that those who 'habitually use' the term are racists, who, in Barzun's words, 'think race night and day, see it everywhere'.[9] Nothing follows about how the term is 'commonly used' or 'generally applied'. And in condemning the one usage as mischievous and empty, Montagu seems to think that he is condemning the 'common usage' as mischievous and empty. He is not. Thus he says that:

---

[6] Ashley Montagu, *Man's Most Dangerous Myth: The Fallacy of Race*, 4th edn. (Cleveland, Ohio: World Publishing 1965), p. 24.

[7] Montagu, *Myth*, p. 351, emphasis added.

[8] Montagu, *Race, Science and Humanity* (New York: Van Nostrand Reinhold, 1963), p. iii, italics added.

[9] Barzun, *Race*, p. 132.

when the intellectual history of our time comes to be written, the idea of 'race', both the popular and the taxonomic, will be viewed for what it is: a confused and dangerous idea which happened to fit the requirements of a thoroughly exploitative period in the development of Western man. The idea of 'race' was developed as a direct response to the exploitation of other peoples, to provide both a pretext and a justification for the most unjustifiable conduct, the enslavement, murder, and degradation of millions of human beings.[10]

We have here a lot of loose emotion, but not much clear thought. I regard this as nonsense, and as harmful nonsense, because such emotive nonsense. Hitler's idea of race meets this description, but not '*the* idea of "race"'. There are too many ideas of race.

Consistent with this confused idea, however, Professor Montagu goes on to recommend, quite seriously, that the term 'race' be replaced by the expression 'ethnic group':

The layman's conception of 'race' is so confused and emotionally muddled that any attempt to modify it would seem to be met by the greatest obstacle of all, the term 'race' itself. This is another reason why the attempt to retain the term 'race' in popular parlance must fail. The term is a trigger word; utter it and a whole series of emotionally triggered responses follow. The term 'ethnic group' suffers from no such defect. If we are to clarify the minds of those who think in terms of 'race' we must cease using the word primarily because in the layman's mind the term defines conditions which do not in fact exist. There is no such thing as the kind of 'race' in which the layman believes.[11]

But no investigation has been initiated as to 'the kind of "race" in which the layman believes'. We have been told only about what certain scientists, would-be scientists, race theorizers, and professional racists believe, not about 'race', but about race. The recommendation to replace the term 'race' by 'ethnic group' is then, curiously, stunted by the claim that 'the phrase "ethnic group" is not a substitute for the term "race"'.[12] The point of this odd claim is to ward off the natural objection that if 'race' is replaced by 'ethnic group', then race prejudice would simply be replaced by ethnic-group prejudice.[13] The reply to this, apart from some vehement denial and

---

[10] Montagu, *Race, Science and Humanity*, p. vi, emphasis added.

[11] Montagu, *Race, Science, and Humanity*, p. 64; see also *Myth*, p. 375.

[12] *Myth*, pp. 376 ff.

[13] The point is obvious, but it is worth noting that it is also made, and very nicely too, by L. C. Dunn and T. B. Dobzhansky, in their book *Heredity, Race, and Society* (New York: Penguin Books, 1946), pp. 94–5: 'Some have used "ethnic group" in place of race; but unfortunately "ethnic group prejudice" is easily exchangeable for "race prejudice"; and one can hate "ethnic groups" just as venomously as real or imaginary races.' To be sure, it is not the *words* that are easily exhangeable. Another point that is made in this book (which may help explain some of

the citation of others regarded as authorities who are taken to agree with the point, is summed up in the claim that: 'If what the phrase "ethnic group" means is clearly understood and accepted, "ethnic group prejudice" would hardly require to be taken seriously.'[14] One can agree that the *expression* 'ethnic-group prejudice' would hardly require to be taken seriously, but the phenomenon it signifies obviously already exists, so this claim is not only false but silly, as an instance of word magic, and I note that it is not supported by reasons. Of course, 'ethnic group', as normally understood, is not a 'substitute for "race"'. The terms have different meanings and refer to different things. The members of a given ethnic group may be of the same race or they may not. And those of the same race may be members of different ethnic groups.

Montagu's main reason for liquidating the term 'race' may be simply this: 'The term "race" is used both by biologists and by laymen alike in so many different senses that it would serve the interests of clear thinking very considerably if that term were to be dropped altogether.'[15] But this is hardly clear thinking; for on this line of reasoning there would be hardly any terms left in the language, certainly no abstract ones.

The point that Montagu, it may fairly be supposed, has all along been leading up to is embraced in the following proclamation:

We are, each of us, members of a single human family, the family of humanity, and like the members of a family, each with his physical and behavioral uniqueness, each of not less worth because of those differences than the other.[16]

That the word 'family' is used metaphorically here, and thus in a question-begging way, seems not to have occurred to him. It may be true, as we are also told, that 'the "race" problem is a problem of ethics', but from such reasoning as this we will never be able to determine what this 'problem of ethics' is.

I am not one of those who maintain that all inferences from 'is' to 'ought' are necessarily fallacious. But I am certain that there is this much truth in

Montagu's evident animosity towards it) is: 'Do not conclude . . . that because the dividing lines between races are frequently arbitrary races are imaginary entities. By looking at a suburban landscape one can not always be sure where the city begins and the country ends, but it does not follow from this that the city exists only in imagination. Races exist regardless of whether we can easily define them or not' (p. 110).

[14] Montagu, *Myth*, p. 376. Elsewhere in the book (p. 311) it is pointed out that 'body odor varies from individual to individual within the same ethnic group and . . . members of different ethnic groups, and even classes, find the odor of members of other ethnic groups and classes distinctly different and frequently objectionable'. It is almost self-evident that here 'ethnic group' is being used as just a substitute for 'race'.

[15] Montagu, *Race, Science, and Humanity*, p. 61.

[16] Montagu, *The Idea of Race* (Lincoln, Nebr.: University of Nebraska Press, 1965), pp. 79–80.

the doctrine, that each such inference needs to he examined carefully before being accepted, and this instance of the naturalistic fallacy is no exception. Professor Montagu may not be aware of the point, but the scientific facts about race (or 'race') he has been presenting do not, even if they are facts, alone and without further argument, support this normative conclusion, which is largely sentimental and almost wholly metaphorical. Kant said, in a pronouncement of considerable moral importance: 'What I *ought* to do that I *can* do'. This may be difficult to sustain, but it is neither a moral nor a scientific absurdity. Our anthropologist says (at the end of a section on 'What is the Solution?'): 'What I can do I ought to do; and, by the grace of God, I *will*.'[17] One would need the grace of God to act on such a maxim as this, because it is a moral, metaphysical, and physical absurdity.

What Montagu has been mainly arguing is that it is race-classifying, hence racism, hence bad, even to suppose that there are different races of mankind, and also that, since racism is a bad thing, we should quit using the term 'race'.[18] Neither point has any cogency. This sort of logic has a familiar ring in philosophical discussion. 'Races do not exist' has its parallels to 'Material things do not exist', 'Consciousness does not exist', 'Other minds do not exist', 'Relations do not exist', 'Propositions do not exist', 'Universals do not exist', 'Truth does not exist', and so on, interminably and indefinitely. None of these is a scientific claim, and none can be supported by either the facts of science or the authority of scientists. And to go on as though they have some scientific status is no service either to science or to society.

6. BENEDICT ON RACE

But this sort of reasoning, in which a moralistic conclusion about how human beings ought to treat one another is fallaciously inferred from a presumably scientific discussion of the facts of race (or 'race'), is not peculiar to Montagu. We find such reasoning elsewhere. For instance, we find it in an influential work by Ruth Benedict, whose work on this subject is in so many other respects so sound and so sensible.[19]

---

[17] Montagu, *Myth*, p. 359.   [18] See Montagu, *The Idea of Race*, pp. 6ff. and 98ff.

[19] Ruth Benedict, *Race: Science and Politics* (New York: Modern Age, 1940). I also quote from the revised edn. of 1947 (New York: Viking), which contains 'The Races of Mankind', by Benedict and Gene Weltfish, a pamphlet that had enormous circulation during World War II.

In what seems an obvious allusion to Barzun, Benedict says that: 'Race is not "the modern superstition" as some amateur egalitarians have said. It is a fact ... Race ... is not the modern superstition ... Racism is.'[20] Benedict is very clear on the distinction, which is, of course, not surprising, since her book was written to explain it. Thus, in a foreword to the first edition (unfortunately omitted in the later editions), she says: '*to recognize Race does not mean to recognize Racism*':

Race is a matter for careful scientific study; Racism is an unproved assumption of the biological and perpetual superiority of one human group over another. *The confusion between race and racism is not confined to the man on the street* ... Confusion between the facts of race and the claims of racism is almost universal in the modern world, and this volume is arranged to show that they are poles apart.[21]

What Benedict does, then, is take questions about race and race differences seriously, as they ought to be taken, but what she says is such that in Montagu's use of the term she would have to be counted as a racist, which merely shows how loose this use is.

Thus Benedict says:

The study of [race] has already told culture-historians much, and further invest-igations, for which as yet science has not the necessary basic knowledge or tests, may even show that some ethnic groups have identifiable emotional or intellectual peculiarities which are biological and not merely learned behavior.[22]

This question is left open, as one for further enquiry, and not as something to be settled or foreclosed by ideological reaction for, as she is acutely aware, racism, as she understands and explains it, does not follow from and is in no way supported (except emotionally, of course) by any answers that might be established to these questions. In other words, to recognize dif-ferences between persons or groups, even inherited or genetic differences, is not by itself to determine anything about superiority or inferiority or about what ought or ought not to be done.

But, though Benedict in this way so effectively and so accurately points up the confusion between (the facts of) race and (the ideology of) racism, she is nonetheless impelled, or so it appears, to go on to draw normative conclusions from her discussion of the facts of race. Thus we are told that: 'The fact of the unity of the human race is proved, therefore, in its

---

[20] It does seem odd for Barzun to be referred to as an 'amateur egalitarian'. Perhaps what was meant was 'amateur anthropologist'.

[21] Benedict, *Race*, 1st edn., pp. v–vi, italics added.

[22] Benedict, *Race*, 2nd edn., p. 98 (ch. 7, para. 2).

anatomy.'[23] But here 'unity' is being used metaphorically, and implies a recommendation. All that the facts establish is that all human beings are members of the same species. Nothing follows from this about what ought to be done or how human beings ought to treat one another. If this is all that is meant by 'the unity of the human race' (which is not obviously unified in any other way), well and good, but there is evidence that it is not.

This is shown by the very next paragraph, where it is said that: 'The races of mankind are what the Bible says they are—brothers. In their bodies is the record of their brotherhood.' This is just like Montagu's 'All humans are members of the same family'. They are equally metaphorical, equally sentimental, equally unfounded.

One must skate carefully here. I trust that no one with any capacity for thought will suppose me to be recommending race war or race enmity or race hatred or even any doctrine about race superiority. I regard all such ideas as vicious nonsense. But the temper of the times is such—as Benedict pointed out well over thirty years ago—that such confusion is common.

The point I am making is simply that we have here, in these two examples, an instance of a scientific fact being used, with no further elaboration or explanation, to support a normative conclusion, which is itself metaphorical, and one that tends to cover up and obscure all sorts of immensely important human problems. This, in my considered judgement, is sentimentalism in the worst sense, and amounts to unscientific preaching, and this, in my view, is to play into the hands of the genuine racists, for it tends to discredit science and reason and intelligence.

7. MONTESQUIEU'S PARODY

Not only is '*race*' a trigger word (as Montagu observes), so is 'racist' (as he does not observe) and even more so. But 'racist' is not just a highly emotive term. It is a bludgeon word. Thus, when Daniel Patrick Moynihan, then United States Ambassador to the United Nations, called Idi Amin a 'racist murderer', this was a much more powerful, effective, and expressive expletive than the mere expletive 'murderer' would have been. Yet, though we have excellent evidence that Idi Amin was a murderer, so far as I know we have no such evidence that he was a racist. He seems to have murdered whites and blacks alike, without discrimination.

---

[23] Benedict, *Race*, 2nd edn., p. 171. This quotation and the next are from 'The Races of Mankind'.

And at the same time some people who have come to concern themselves with this matter seem to come equipped with built-in amplifiers, high in volume but low in fidelity, with an inverse signal-to-noise ratio. Race is an area where even irony must proceed with caution. An example *par excellence* is Montesquieu's ironic parody of racialist arguments in support of slavery:

Were I to vindicate our right to make slaves of the negroes, these should be my arguments:

The Europeans, having extirpated the Americans, were obliged to make slaves of the Africans, for clearing such vast tracts of land.

Sugar would be too dear if the plants which produce it were cultivated by any other than slaves.

These creatures are all over black, and with such a flat nose that they can scarcely be pitied.

It is hardly to be believed that God, who is a wise Being, should place a soul, especially a good soul, in such a black ugly body.

It is so natural to look upon color as the criterion of human nature, that the Asiatics, among whom eunechs are employed, always deprive the blacks of their resemblance to us by a more opprobrious distinction.

The color of the skin may be determined by that of the hair, which, among the Egyptians, the best philosophers in the world, was of such importance that they put to death all the red-haired men who fell into their hands.

The negroes prefer a glass necklace to that gold which polite nations so highly value. Can there be a greater proof of their wanting common sense?

It is impossible for us to suppose these creatures to be men, because, allowing them to be men, a suspicion would follow that we ourselves are not Christians.[24]

At this point the editor of the edition from which I am quoting feels obliged to interject a comment: 'The above arguments form a striking instance of the prejudice under which even a liberal mind can labor'. This, in my estimation, is priceless. If the editor of this translation, who had presumably made a special study of the work, could go so far wrong, in 1899, in his understanding of what Montesquieu was about, think how it would fare today.

This is a matter, to be sure, on which there is great sensitivity, and understandably so. Perhaps Montesquieu's parody was misplaced or in poor taste. Yet how could anyone fail to feel the force of his final point: 'Weak minds exaggerate too much the wrong done to the Africans. For were the case as they state it, would the European powers, who make so many needless conventions among themselves, have failed to enter into a general one, in behalf of humanity and compassion'?

[24] Charles de Montesquieu, *The Spirit of the Laws* (New York: Colonial Press, 1899), bk. xv, pp. 238–9.

But perhaps we should remember that Montesquieu's work was published in 1748.

8. ARDREY ON RACE

One writer who takes the idea of racial differences seriously, as he takes the whole matter of biology and biological determination seriously, is Robert Ardrey. But some realization of the motive force and the emotive use of 'racist'—and its use to restrict freedom of thought and enquiry—obviously informs his first hesitant, then bold, treatment of the matter. It is Ardrey's view that there are racial—that is, biological, inheritable, genetic—differences among people and populations that lead to different kinds of performances, aptitudes, and abilities, and even to hostility, enmity, and conflict. Thus he said, not all that many years ago, that 'Israel's problem is race', and he speaks of the 'Zionist fallacy', which is explained as the fallacy of supposing that 'the Jew is a Jew', no matter what his racial or cultural or national background:

That the racial reality of the Jew did not exist did not enter [the Zionist's] calculation, nor that out of the conglomeration of background would come two entirely different peoples, the Jew of the East and the Jew of the West . . . The attitude toward education differs as does the eagerness to work. While the Western Jew, renouncing the ghetto, has accomplished the agricultural miracle, the Eastern Jew, creating a new ghetto, has crowded over half his numbers into the Tel-Aviv area. There is little intermarriage . . . The Oriental Jew is today in a 55-percent majority. He makes bitter charges of racial discrimination. Israeli leadership recoils at a phrase that for any Jew is a blow to memory's solar plexus. Yet discrimination exists.[25]

It is obviously Ardrey's view that 'the Oriental Jew' is genetically, hence racially, different from 'the Western Jew'. Now I do not know whether this is so or not, or whether or not the situation Ardrey describes exists or ever existed, since my travels have not yet taken me to Israel, where I could see for myself. But one thing I am sure I could never see for myself is whether the differences in the Jews from the East and the Jews from the West are *racial* or not. This can be determined only in the light of a theory, and I am not satisfied that Ardrey has not let his own theory of biological determinism determine him to see all sorts of differences as genetic and racial that

[25] Robert Ardrey, *The Territorial Imperative* (New York: Atheneum, 1966), pp. 311–12.

could just as simply and plausibly be ascribed to culture and background and heritage. But, of course, Ardrey does have such a theory, and he does see that its working out requires him to say just such things as this. At any rate, in this, his first shot at racial matters, Ardrey does claim that it is false that 'the Jew' is a race, and that there are racial, therefore vital and possibly ineradicable, differences amongst Jews. Whether any of this is so or not need not concern us here.

Four years later, in *The Social Contract*, we find Ardrey speaking of 'entering the lethal area of race. Yet', he says, 'little will come of this most fateful of entrances but the spectacle of the sciences bearing a white flag. Despite all claims, we know almost nothing'—and he then goes on in the space of a few pages to explain the 'almost nothing' we know, as though he has it all within him. He says that, though we may be 'tempted . . . to dismiss races as non-existent, still we cannot'.[26] The reason we may be tempted is that the problem is so complex, since races are so unhomogeneous: 'A race, or subspecies, is a mosaic of populations which has followed its own line of evolution through many generations separated from other mosaics by natural barriers.' And the reason we cannot is that there are such differences. He concludes that because black people, who make up 'no more than seven percent of the human species', have lately been running off with most of the Olympic medals, therefore race and genetic racial differences *must* exist, which is a great example for a logician's holiday:

Despite all hybridization, all cultural disparity, all environmental divergence, such common traits as superb teeth and the capacity to run forever or to jump over the moon or knock a baseball from San Francisco to Los Angeles must find an explanation in some dominant genetic complex inherited from common West African ancestors.

Yet there really is no 'must' about it (though there is plenty of mist). All we are entitled to say is that it could be, and this 'could be' then presents a hypothesis to be explored. If the rest of Ardrey's theories of evolution and biological determinism and the animal nature of man rest on conjectures as shaky as this, then they are material more for the playwright than the scientist. But nonetheless Ardrey's biological and genetic orientation does not make him, in any intelligent, reasonable, and honest sense of the term, a racist. As he says: 'We do not know about race' (p. 65), and one reason we do not know is that the area is so lethal. Making reference to the notorious Jensen Case, Ardrey says:

[26] Robert Ardrey, *The Social Contract* (New York: Atheneum, 1970), pp. 56, 59.

Until the scientist, without threat to his life, is free to explore in all candor racial differences, and to prove or disprove systematic inequalities of intelligence, an observer of the sciences has little to offer. But then, neither racist nor egalitarian has much to offer, either, beyond emotion.[27]

9. CULTURAL GENERALIZATIONS AND NATIONAL CHARACTER

The term 'race' has actually done much more than double duty as a term covering multitudes of differences among groups of human beings, and the paramount feature of racial differences being hereditary has seeped over, so that all such differences between different populations come to be thought of as somehow genetic or inherited. This is in part what writers like Barzun and Montagu are upset by in recommending that the term 'race' be dropped. But the differences will remain, no matter what language is employed, and people will continue to remark on and be interested in them.

Leaf through practically any book on travelling or living abroad, and you are sure to run across statements of the following sort:

A Spaniard is very much an individual; never try to force him in any direction; never humiliate him; he can be extremely touchy . . . On the whole one can think of Spaniards as being fiery, intense, often cruel, but also extremely polite and courteous, graceful, friendly, and vivid—but ornery . . . All nations have their prides, but the Spanish 'pride of race' is something special. You can see it in the way they carry their heads, in the way they stamp with an arrogant flourish in their dances, in the flashing shine of their incredibly polished shoes . . . You would do well to take this pride into account in your dealings with Spaniards . . .

. . . There is . . . a definitely Swiss personality . . . They are first and foremost *thorough* . . . their skilled and patient dexterity is world famous . . . They hate waste. They save every penny possible, so all lights go out the moment a room is left empty . . . The Swiss are passionately fond of outdoor sports and move up and down their mountain paths like agile goats, despite their heavy boots. These are some of the characteristic traits that bind them together despite regional differences . . .

Germans are a thorough people who do not like to see time wasted. The preliminary courtesies and flourishes that are required with Spanish, French, or Italians are wasted with Germans . . .

---

[27] Robert Ardrey, *The Social Contract* (New York: Atheneum, 1970), p. 65. For an account of the Jensen Case see 'The Jensen Uproar', by Antony Flew, *Philosophy*, 48 (January 1973), pp. 63–9, which received an expectable number of replies in later issues.

Virtually no one in the Netherlands will ever short-change or overcharge you. They are rigorously honest . . .

. . . Italy is . . . the most popular tourist country in Europe. Surely this must be in large measure because of the people . . . They are a warm, excitable people; when they talk, their hands fly. What may at first sight appear to be a street fight turns out on closer inspection to be two men explaining something to a third.[28]

In another such book, picked up at random, I find the following:

A Scotsman . . . is a genius with his hands, a stickler for thrift, a conscientious workman who thinks like a Frenchman. An Irishman is mercurial, whimsical, stubborn, mystical. A Welshman is shrewd, deep, intense, music-prone, hewn from his native granite . . .

If you are able to understand the age-old, mercurial, Gallic temperament, you'll find that this national group can be highly stimulating companions and wonderfully loyal, durable friends, with warmth and hospitality which will overwhelm you . . .

You can't push a Spaniard around; you can flog him, cajole him . . . and he'll still go his own way, in his own sweet time. Personal pride and dignity reach their zeniths here.[29]

Statements of this sort: 'The Ruritanians are *x*, *y*, and *z*', or 'Fredonians are characteristically *t*, *u*, and *v*', or 'Such and such is a typically Brondigmalian trait', which may be called cultural generalizations, are exceedingly common. Human beings, especially those who have travelled or have contemplated travelling abroad, tend to make them constantly or else to be especially interested in them when made by someone else. There is no use in complaining that they oversimplify. Of course they oversimplify. They are meant to. They are intended to provide rough-and-ready guides to 'national character' or national or regional characteristics of people, and that there is something in the genus, as distinct from random specimens of the kind, is shown by the fact that, by and large, they work—they provide the sort of guide that is wanted—and by the fact that, by and large, you can get general agreement on them. It sometimes seems as though one travel book is copying another, but that is extremely unlikely. It is much more likely that there is something in such generalizations, at least those made by people with large, broad experience of travel and foreign lands, who have had considerable experience in dealing with and observing people in many

---

[28] Alison Raymond Lanier, *Living in Europe* (New York: Charles Scribner's Sons, 1973), pp. 330–1, 361, 383, 290, 253.

[29] Temple Fielding, *Fielding's Guide to Europe*, 1975 edn. (New York: Fielding, 1974), pp. 231, 377, 1075.

different lands, and who have to make such observations carefully and responsibly, because their reputations and their livelihoods are at stake. Thus the agreement on the character of Spaniards in the two sets of statements just reproduced is neither coincidence nor collusion; it is, rather, evidence that there is 'something in it'.

But what? This is the question that is so difficult to answer; because it is evident right away that not all the Ruritanians are and x, y, and z, that not all the Fredonians are t, u, and v. Still, cultural generalizations do not make this claim. They are, it is evident, unlike ordinary factual generalizations. They do not maintain that *all* the F's are x, etc. Nor are they simply statistical generalizations, saying something about *most* Fredonians, etc. Such observations are made and recorded and confirmed without any statistical surveys and the use of questionnaires. If we try to insert such a quantifying term as 'all' or 'most' or 'some' in such a statement as 'The Fredonians are typically t, u, and v', or 'The Ruritanians are characteristically x, y, and z', we get nonsense. Though it may be false, still it makes sense to say that Americans are characteristically energetic; but it makes no sense to say that *most* Americans are characteristically energetic. Similarly, and typically, it makes sense to say that Swiss people typically hate waste; but it makes no sense to say that *all* Swiss people typically hate waste. The presence, either actual or implied, of such terms as 'typical' and 'characteristically' indicates that such generalizations are of a different order.[30]

Nor does it do any good to object to such statements on moral grounds, on the principle that human beings should be considered and treated as individuals. Of course they should. But one who makes cultural generalizations, or learns from the cultural generalizations of others, is not violating anyone's rights. For certain purposes, such as computing the national income or the gross national product or the incidence of disease, we are all considered merely as members of a collection, and as long as our consideration in this way is restricted to purposes of this sort, our rights are not violated. Indeed, it is difficult to see how they could be protected if governments were always forsworn, on moral grounds, to refrain from applying statistics and considering their citizens merely as units in a collection.

Such cultural generalizations as these lead to the view that there is such a thing as national character, that nations or members of different nations differ from one another in character or personality or dominant traits, as they differ in language, or dialect, or accent, and to the further view that

---

[30] There is a brief discussion of the logic of cultural generalizations in a review of Morris Cohen's *American Thought*, in *Philosophical Review*, 65 (April 1956), at pp. 258–9.

these characteristic (or typical) national (or cultural) traits can be investigated and known.

To speak of a nation bears some affinity to speaking of race, and to speak of national character bears some affinity to speaking of racial characteristics, and to the supposition that hereditary physical traits determine mental or emotional traits. Some affinity, but not an identity. We should not let our national consciousness of race stop us from investigating the concept of national character. It is a subject that is both interesting and important. As Mill observed, the study of national character may well be the most important area of social enquiry.

The character which is formed by any state of social circumstances is in itself the most interesting phenomenon which that state of society can possibly present . . . It is also a fact which enters largely into the production of all the other phenomena . . . Above all, the character . . . that is the opinions, feelings, and habits of the people, though greatly the results of the state of society which precedes them, are also greatly the causes of the state of society which follows them.[31]

Mill also observes that:

The causes of national character are scarcely at all understood and the effect of institutions or social arrangements upon the character of the people is generally that portion of their effects which is least attended to, and least comprehended.

This state of affairs, it may truly be said, still prevails today.

Now what relation does national character have to race? The question is difficult, for the terms are both so obscure and so vague. In order to deal with it we should have to ask whether any of the features of the character of a group (assuming that character can be described in a determinate way) have any relation to the race of its members (assuming that can be determined also), either by way of cause and effect or a relation of some other kind. And here we come to territory Ardrey, for one, branded as lethal. For there is current an ideology that would brand such enquiry as racist, if not in origin or intent or motive, then in effect, and this has a tendency to prevent such enquiry from proceeding beyond the asking point.

Thus, if a racist is someone who believes in 'race' as a belief in 'race' is characterized in one of his more fervent ideological moments by Ashley Montagu, then one who believes in national character is practically a 'racist'. For Montagu's characterization, if I may add further to the set of

---

[31] J. S. Mill, *A System of Logic* (1843) (8th edn. 1872) (London: Longmans, Green, 1949), bk. vi, ch. ix, sect. 4, pp. 590–1.

quotations I have already provided from his work, runs this way. He first tells us that 'the belief in "race"' (that is, what he calls 'the popular belief in "race"') is (let us call this set of characteristics set Q):

the belief that 'race' is a something about the individual and the group of which he is a member that is characterized by a peculiar and indissoluble union of physical and behavioral traits. These traits are inherited, it is popularly believed, and account for the differences in individual and cultural achievement between the 'races'.

So far, it should be noticed, there is nothing about this 'belief' that is in any way morally objectionable. I say nothing about its intellectual pedigree, though it is worth remarking that there is nothing about the belief, as so far characterized, that is a priori absurd or preposterous. From here on, though, the dice begin to be loaded. For Montagu says further (let us call this set P):

The 'races' that have achieved most are obviously biologically 'superior', so it is reasoned, to those who have achieved less. There is, therefore, so the argument runs, a natural hierarchy of 'races'. *Racists*—that is to say—*persons who believe or subscribe to such ideas*—feel that certain discriminations are necessary in order to protect themselves from the contaminating effects of social or biological admixture with members of 'inferior races.'

At this point the emotional loading of 'racist' peaks sharply in intensity. For at this point we have a passing reference to Adolf Hitler, who, we are told, 'did not believe in "race", but found it politically expedient to pretend to'; from which it necessarily follows, though Montagu, in his zeal, is blissfully unaware of this, that Hitler was not a racist—which is as preposterous as anything can be.

Montagu goes on to explain that:

Racists will not be changed by anything that is said in these pages ... We are concerned here with the racist only insofar as he is the source of pathological ideas ... And ... we are concerned with the demonstration of some of his techniques and methods for perpetuating ideas that he often knows to be false.

And I interrupt again to point out that, if taken literally, this last remark cannot apply to 'racists', as just defined. For a 'racist' was before defined by reference to a certain set of beliefs, and one does not believe what one 'often knows to be false'. The implication of this, speaking strictly, is that 'racists' are not racists, and it becomes more difficult than ever to determine unequivocally and unemotionally just exactly what Montagu is talking about.

The upshot of this characterization is reached in the claim that:

Racists are often viciously unscrupulous persons who will, literally, stop at nothing to further their sick ideas. Because they are sick they are dangerous, for they carry infection with them wherever they go.[32]

This is the sort of characterization that would typically serve as a preamble to the order to 'Shoot to kill!'. And if one is going to say such a thing as this one should be doubly sure that the target has been identified unequivocally. One of the characteristics of racism in practice is paranoid emotionalism, and this is something that *is* contagious.

As I said before, on the characterization given, one who believes in the reality of national character would be practically—that is, tantamount to—a 'racist'. For one who believes in the reality of national character could have beliefs that correspond to or are equivalent to those in set Q. And it should be plain enough that one can 'subscribe to such ideas' as those in set Q without advocating or recommending or subscribing to anything remotely resembling the propositions of set P. But the logical gap between P and Q is, apparently, not apparent to everyone who has set up as an authority on this subject.

An example of someone who accepts ideas very like those in set Q without accepting anything like those in set P would be the historian John Lukacs, who says (and when he says it makes a certain amount of sense):

Consider a 'typical' Russian baby who was brought to France, brought up in France, who acquired French habits, tastes, expressions, marries a Frenchwoman at thirty and returns to Russia at the age of forty: has he not become something different not only from other 'typical' Russians but from the kind of person he would have become had he stayed in Russia all his life? I came to the United States in 1946, I married my wife in 1953, our son was born in 1956. I believe that, had I remained in Hungary and met and married my American wife there, our son would have had certain characteristics different from his present ones—by which I mean *physical* as well as nonphysical ones—not only because of another environment, but also because his father would have been a different person at the time when the mother was fertilized by his seed.[33]

The question here is not whether this is true, but whether believing such propositions as these makes one a 'viciously unscrupulous person who will stop at nothing to further his sick ideas'. It ought to be obvious that this is

---

[32] Montagu, *Race, Science, and Humanity*, pp. iii–iv for all these passages quoted (all italics added).

[33] John Lukacs, *Historical Consciousness* (New York: Harper & Row, 1968), pp. 255–6.

false, and that whether or not such propositions as these are true or false they are not obviously unreasonable.

There is no need to multiply examples from the literature on national character, though it would be easy to do.

10. RACISM AND RACE

Racism, we must recognize, is really independent of race. Race is not essential to it, though of course it often goes with it. Benedict comes close to seeing this point, but not quite clearly. Yet it is evident from her discussion of racism, which ranges over such phenomena as class warfare, ethnic conflict, and nationalism. She points out that: 'Racism was first formulated in conflicts between classes. It was directed by the aristocrats against the populace', and 'the history of national racism, wherever one looks, is the history of chauvinism'. Yet she still thinks, for some reason, that racism must be tied to race. For on one page she speaks of 'racial anti-Semitism' and on the next she says: 'The more clearly one studies European anti-Semitism in its *modern racial guise* the less it appears that the conflict is racial; it is the old problem of unequal citizenship rights.' Further, she remarks that Houston Chamberlain, 'the most frank of the prewar racists . . . disavows race completely and boasts that it is irrelevant to the racist position. In the interval between two world wars racists have repeated Chamberlain's self-contradiction whenever it was to their advantage to do so.'[34]

That the theory of racism, especially as represented in such rantings as the writings of Houston Chamberlain, is self-contradictory as well as confused I would not deny. But I do not think there is any contradiction *here*. As Benedict has just made us aware, the phenomenon known as racism is logically independent of race, and race, as such, is not essential to it. Either other differences between the opposing parties will come to be thought of as 'racial', or else the traits objected to are thought of as resulting from or causing racial differences.

Barzun points out, I think with justice, that: 'Not merely Marxist propaganda but Marxist doctrine at its purest is in form and effect racist thought.

---

[34] Benedict, *Race*, cit. *supra*, pp. 112, 137, 152, 153, and 133 (italics added). Chamberlain's book is *Die Grundlagen des Neunzehnten Jahrhunderts* (Munich, 1899) (which was translated into English in 1911, and went into its 28th edn. in 1942—in Munich).

Indeed, the class struggle is but the old race antagonism of French nobles and commoners writ large and made ruthless. Marx's bourgeois is not a human being with individual traits, but a social abstraction, a creature devoid of virtue or free will and without the right to live.'[35] This is, I think, an acute observation. But the dogma referred to has not generally been regarded as racist in character because race itself has not been regarded as a difference between economic classes. Yet one can inherit wealth and position and status, and these can come to be thought of as part of one's (racial) heritage.

One who maintains that Greeks are better than Turks and who hates Turks accordingly (or vice versa) would not normally be called an 'ethnicist', if only because that word (or non-word) has, for what seem like obvious reasons, not come into use. But he could be called a 'racist', because that word is in use, even though the differences our hater of Turks (or Greeks) relies on may be ethnic rather than racial, and even though he may *think* that they are ethnic (or cultural or national) rather than racial— learned rather than inherited.

Other writers have, of course, seen and commented on this independence of racism from race. Desmond Morris, for example, regards racial conflicts, or what appear to be racial conflicts, as instances of in-group/out-group conflicts:

The key error of assuming that a member of another group must possess certain special *inherited* character traits typical of his group, is constantly arising. If he wears a different uniform, speaks a different language, or follows a different religion, it is illogically assumed that he also has a *biologically* different personality.[36]

And, of course, this tendency is exacerbated if the other person has a different skin colour, something which, for some reason, has generated some of the most violent and long-lasting prejudices and hostilities.

Another observation of Morris's that is worth noting is:

Thoughtful white Americans struggle desperately to overcome their prejudice, but the cruel indoctrinations of childhood are difficult to forget. A new kind of prejudice creeps in, an insidious one of over-compensation. Guilt produces an over-friendliness, an over-helpfulness that creates a relationship as false as the one it replaces. It still fails to treat Negroes as individuals. It still persists in looking at them as members of an out-group.

---

[35] Barzun, *Race*, p. xi.
[36] Desmond Morris, *The Human Zoo* (London: Jonathan Cape, 1969), ch. 4. I am quoting from the edn. published by Bantam Books in 1970, pp. 110, 127, 126, and 128.

He further observes that human beings have a tendency to react to 'skin colour as if it were being deliberately worn as the badge of a hostile out-group', and that one of 'the fundamental similarities between any one man and any other man . . . paradoxically, is the tendency to form distinct in-groups and to feel that you are somehow different, really deep-down different, from members of other groups'.

These observations are acute, but Morris has for some reason not realized that it is his task, given what he set out to do, to *explain* these traits, not just to observe and record them, and there is some question whether they can be explained on the biological base he, along with Ardrey, takes as fundamental. If the tendency to form 'distinct in-groups' is 'paradoxical', how could it have originated from solely natural or biological causes? Only minds can generate a paradox, as only minds can conceive one: 'The key error of assuming that a member of another group must possess some special inherited character traits typical of his group, is constantly arising.' True, but how then can it be biologically determined, or a result of natural selection? If it is to be regarded solely and simply as a natural phenomenon, determined by factors beyond human control, then it cannot also be *error*. And if it is something that human beings, by taking thought, can govern and control, then it is not something biologically determined. In pointing out our combative nature, writers like Morris and Ardrey have performed a useful service, but they overstate the point when they allege that such characteristics are not only natural but determined by evolutionary and biological forces beyond the control of the beings thus determined. Their whole point in attempting to teach us the lessons of the new biology is undermined by the theory they present, which is the curious fate of all forms of determinism and cultural relativism.

11. THE TAWNEYESQUE CONCEPTION OF RACISM

There is an interesting word buried within the thick covers of *Webster's Second International Unabridged* that could well be put to work in our present situation. This is the verb 'to racialize', which means 'to imbue with a consciousness of race distinctions'. This is not a term of much currency today, but it does denote a widespread tendency, on the part of both racial oppressors and the racially oppressed, and also, unfortunately, on the part of defenders of the oppressed. So racializing is very much with us, regardless of the racist or racialist proclivities of those who practice it.

For, as with 'politicize' and unlike 'nationalize', one with a tendency to hurl the terms 'racism' and 'racist' about is doing something 'to imbue' both himself (or herself) and others 'with a consciousness [whether true or false is here irrelevant] of race distinctions', and consequently to racialize. Whether this is good or bad, necessary or unnecessary, justified or unjustified, is something else again, but this is, nonetheless, the epitome and the paradox of racism. Without a consciousness of race distinctions, there would be none made, and there would be no race prejudice, animosity, hatred, or warfare.

This reflection suggests a way in which, in our present predicament, this phenomenon can be understood. R. H. Tawney, in *The Acquisitive Society*, has presented a distinctive account of certain 'isms', or 'ism-words', that is especially enlightening. It will, clearly, not apply to all ism-words, for there is no unitary category, but it may extend far enough.

The 'isms' Tawney was especially interested in were individualism and industrialism, and the perspective in which he puts them is provided by his account of militarism, nationalism, and imperialism. Here is what he says about militarism:

The possibility that one aspect of human life may be so exaggerated as to overshadow, and in time to atrophy, every other, has been made familiar to Englishmen by the example of 'Prussian militarism.' Militarism is the characteristic, not of an army, but of a society. Its essence is not any particular quality or scale of military preparation, but a state of mind, which, in its concentration on one particular element in social life, ends finally by exalting it until it becomes the arbiter of all the rest.[37]

I shall call the sort of account here given of militarism (or 'militarism') the Tawneyesque account of ism-words. Notice how, in the following passage, this type of account is applied to industrialism:

The essence of industrialism . . . is not any particular method of industry, but a particular estimate of the importance of industry, which results in its being thought the only thing that is important at all, so that it is elevated from the subordinate place which it should occupy among all human interests and activities into being the standard by which all other interests and activities are judged.

It would be an interesting exercise to determine how far the Tawneyesque account applies to other isms, or ism-words. It would, one would think, not apply (or not clearly apply) to heroism, or patriotism, or altruism, or rationalism, for none of these is a quality of a society. But even here I am

---

[37] R. H. Tawney, *The Acquisitive Society*, ch. 4, pp. 46–7, 48. (In the US edn. pp. 43–4, 45.)

not prepared to swear that there could never be states of society in which these attributes, ideals, theories, or governing tendencies would take over and become dominant. One can conceive of patriotism, for instance, becoming as predominant in a society as militarism (though this is likely then to be rather a perversion of 'true' patriotism). Still, there are others, more closely related to militarism and industrialism, to which the Tawneyesque account applies immediately and without question. Commercialism, for example.

Commercialism, on this account, is the characteristic, not of a commercial activity or a commercial enterprise, but of a society that has erected the ends and values and ideals of commerce into the overriding standard for judging and determining all the other activities and enterprises of the society. Thus when Calvin Coolidge said 'The business of America is business', he gave expression to commercialism in this sense, and to the extent that this expressed the operative ideals and standards of American life, American life was (and is) a manifestation of commercialism: the values of commerce—business and advertising—took over, like a cancer, and became predominant (as they still are).

Now when we think of racism (as well as racialism) on the lines of the Tawneyesque account, it may open up new perspectives. For on this account the essence of racism—meaning, in this context, the most important thing about it—is the erecting of what may have some importance in some limited sphere of activity—race—into the standard for determining the importance and value of everything else. As Tawney points out: 'Industrialism is no more the necessary characteristic of an economically developed society than militarism is a necessary characteristic of a nation which maintains military forces . . . and the idea that it is something inevitable in a community which uses coal and iron and machinery, so far from being the truth, is itself a product of the perversion of mind which industrialism produces.' No more is racism the necessary characteristic of a society made up of different races, and the idea that racism is something inevitable in a society made up of different races and racial groups is itself a product of the perversion of mind that racism induces.

Whatever tends to increase our consciousness of race and race differences in the active affairs of human beings, and to lead us to erect the consciousness of race and race differences to a status of paramount importance—no matter what its motives (even, one must admit, scholarly or would-be-scholarly discussions of it)—is a form of racializing, and hence, in this sense, a form of racism. This does not make it necessarily bad. There may be some good and sufficient reason for it. But let that reason be given. For, given what racism has done and led to, there is a presumption against it.

Barzun, in a felicitous phrase I had occasion to call attention to before, speaks of those who 'think race night and day, see it everywhere'.[38] This incessant preoccupation with race on the part of race-intoxicated people—who think race all the time, see it everywhere—is racemania, and when it becomes not the preoccupation of this person or that person, this group or that group, but a preoccupation of the society, it is racism. When race and questions about race and race distinctions and race origins and race differences—along with, we should note, too quick and easy allegations of 'racism'—become the be-all and end-all, the characteristic cast of a society, then we have racism incarnate, and it is as debilitating to the life of society and the life of reason as militarism, industrialism, commercialism, vicious bigotry, and rampant racial enmity itself.

ADDITIONAL NOTES AND COMMENTS

A. 'On Race and Racism' was originally published in *Philosophia*, 8 (2–3) (November 1978), pp. 153–83, in a special issue on racism; reprinted here with only slight verbal changes.

B. I considered the matter of cultural generalizations in a bit more depth in 'The Context of American Philosophy', in M. G. Singer (ed.), *American Philosophy* (Cambridge: Cambridge University Press, 1985), at pp. 12–16. The subject has still to be dealt with on its own.

C. I came across the book by George Boxall by chance, had never heard of it before, have no knowledge of who Mr Boxall was, what he did, or what else he wrote. Does it matter? No.

D. There is a view, which seems to be gaining ground in some quarters, that *race* is only an artificial 'social construct', corresponding to nothing in reality—in other words, that there really are no different races or differences between races. There are some differences among peoples that are, to be sure, merely social constructs with no correspondence to anything in nature, such as differences between people who live on one side of town and people who live on the other, rich people and poor people, people who have jobs and those who don't, or the fairly standard (and silly) in-group/out-group rivalries. But races, and physical differences among races, are found in nature, and the definition of race provided in this chapter should make that clear. As I said, this is like maintaining that there are no different breeds of cats or of dogs, so that there are no innate differences between, say,

---

[38] Barzun, *Race*, p. 132 (ch. 7, last para.)

an Irish setter and a pit bull, or a dachshund and a Labrador, which is absurd on its face. Racism cannot be understood or dealt with by denying manifest truths or by claiming that there are no races of mankind. As I also argued, the phenomenon of racism, which unquestionably does exist, does not depend on race. Anti-Semitism is a form of racism, even though Jews do not constitute a distinct race of people or even a distinct ethnic group, and there are racial differences among Jews.

This idea, that race is only a social construct, with no counterpart in nature or reality, may be thought to derive some support from the more general idea that all concepts are social constructs. But this is trivial. I wonder if people who talk this way—usually well-meaning people, anxious to eradicate racism—realize that in so talking they are talking metaphysics. They are, and it is particularly bad metaphysics. Whatever the best way of dealing with racism may be, it is certainly not in playing with words and concepts.[39]

E. *The Burden of Race: A Documentary History of Negro–White Relations in America* (New York: Harper & Row, 1967), by Gilbert Osofsky, contains a useful collection of materials on this subject. In a somewhat different way, so does Studs Terkel's *Race: How Blacks and Whites Think and Feel About the American Obsession* (New York: New Press, 1992).

F. Consider the following remark by Lucy Mair, in *Introduction to Social Anthropology* (1965) (2nd edn., Oxford: Clarendon Press, 1972): 'When one turns to the actual situations of racial conflict that present us with problems today, there is not in fact anything about them that is peculiar to the confrontation of people with different physical characteristics. They are all manifestations of group exclusiveness on the one hand and reactions of the excluded on the other.' Though this is provocative, I very much doubt that it is true, at least in the United States and in other countries with a history of apartheid. It may be that Dr Mair is simply reflecting the British experience—up to that time. Racial conflicts—and that includes ethnic-group conflicts—may be *sui generis*. This may complicate the subject of group conflict unduly, but that possibility has to be faced.

Yet the in-group/out-group phenomenon has unquestionably played a role, and it is interesting to compare this observation by Lucy Mair with the account of the genesis of racism provided by Bernard Lewis in 'The Historical Roots of Racism', *American Scholar* (winter 1998) pp. 17–25, a brief yet very informative account. Professor Lewis speaks of racism indifferently as 'a disease' and a 'great social evil'. At the end of the article he observes that:

[39] In 'Race Counts', *The Sciences* (September/October 2000), David Berreby says: 'to say race is a social construction is not to say it doesn't exist, any more than telling people that their chronic pain is psychosomatic makes it go away. Race and ethnicity are facts of people's lives' (p. 41). Interesting, but then what does it mean to say that 'race is a social construction'? Despite denials, to say that 'race is a social construction' is to imply contextually that it has no objective reality, does not exist in nature. And telling people that their pain is psychosomatic or all in their heads is in effect to pooh-pooh it. On anti-Semitism as a form of racism, see Carey McWilliams, *A Mask for Privilege: Anti-Semitism in America* (Boston: Little, Brown, 1949).

The primitive, one might even say, animal mistrust of the Other is part of our deepest instincts, and it has required centuries of civilization to tame and control it. In the longer perspective of history, the struggle to advance from primitive hostility through tolerance to the ultimate aim of coexistence with mutual respect has achieved some remarkable successes. It has also suffered some catastrophic failures, notably in our century, when primitive hatreds have been used—aroused, increased, and systematized—by theorists and practitioners from some of the most advanced of civilized societies, and what used to be a European disease has infected other continents.

G. Another statement by Lucy Mair of some interest is that 'before the Second World War the term "race prejudice" . . . suggested anti-Semitism, whereas today it would be more likely to suggest attitudes towards dark-skinned persons' (p. 309). This may well have been true in Britain, but I am not sure it was true, even prior to the Second World War, in the United States.

H. Another item of interest: an article by Hilton Als about the black novelist Chester Himes, entitled 'In Black and White: Chester Himes Takes a Walk on the Noir Side', *New Yorker* (4 June 2001) pp. 90–6. Thus Als says: '[Himes's book] "The Night's for Cryin'"' is . . . partly about the prison of race that Himes learned from his mother, the color scale by which blacks judge other blacks: yellow-skinned people are elitists; brown-skinned people are strivers; and anything darker is unspeakable. Even free, Himes implies, the black man is living in a jail that his own people have helped to build' (p. 94). Consider further what Himes said in a speech in 1948:

If this plumbing for the truth reveals within the Negro personality homicidal mania, lust for white women, a pathetic sense of inferiority, paradoxical anti-Semitism, arrogance, Uncle-Tomism, hate and fear of self-hate, this then is the effect of oppression on the human personality. These are the daily horrors, the daily realities, the daily experiences of an oppressed minority. (p. 96)

To be sure, some advanced thinkers maintain that 'race is just a social construct'. Evidently some social constructs can be very damaging.

I. Over a large part of its history, in the United States and elsewhere, as slavery has been an *institution,* so has racism—and it still is—in the sense (or one of the senses) delineated in chapter 10, even though 'racism' is a term of fairly recent coinage, and even though racism—along with prejudice and bigotry and their allies—is currently under fire in a way it had not been for too long.

9

Judicial Decisions and Judicial Opinions

1. Politics, Government, and Law
2. The Functions of Courts
3. Judicial Opinions
4. The Importance of Opinions
5. The Aims of a Legal System
6. The Direction of Guilt and the Direction of Innocence
7. Law and Morality
8. Rational Morality and Law

A perennial question in the philosophy of law is that of the relations between law and morality. Is law passed by a legislature, or laid down by a superior court, still law, having some sort of binding power, irrespective of whether it is good or bad, just or unjust? Or is it essential to a legal system that it have some intrinsic relation to justice or morality, lacking which it would not genuinely be a system of law at all, but something usurping the name of a legal system? The former position has come to be called *legal positivism*, in accordance with the view of John Austin (*The Province of Jurisprudence Determined* (1832), chs. 1 and 5) that positive law, or 'law properly so-called', is what it is in virtue of the positive facts of specific enactment and superior force—the power the state has to enforce compliance. The opposing view, which takes many forms, is often called *natural-law theory*, since it reflects the view of the ancient Stoics that there is a natural law, independent of the conventional law of the state, which is discoverable by right reason (as the Stoics put it), and which provides a standard for determining whether conventional law is genuine law.

The liveliest controversy on the matter in the past few decades is that between defenders of the position presented by H. L. A. Hart in *The Concept of Law*—a modified form of legal positivism—and critics of Hart, such as Lon Fuller and Ronald Dworkin. Both Fuller and Dworkin develop a sort of natural-law theory, though each is decidedly different from the other. Fuller appeals to what he calls 'the internal morality of law', lacking which, he argues, nothing can genuinely be law. Dworkin appeals to certain legal principles, as he calls them (often called maxims of the common law), which are incapable of being changed by judicial decision or even by legislative enactment, and which are or seem very like moral principles, to make the point that such principles are at the heart of the law and consequently beyond the reach of courts or legislative bodies.[1]

One example Dworkin gives of such a principle is that invoked by the New York Court of Appeals in *Riggs* v. *Palmer*, a case of 1889 in which the defendant, who stood to inherit under the will of his grandfather, and having some reason to fear that he would be disinherited, killed his grandfather before his grandfather could change his will. He was convicted of murder, but then claimed the right as testamentary legatee to inherit under the will. The court decided against him, stating as its main ground that:

All laws as well as contracts may be controlled in their operation and effect by general, fundamental maxims of the common law. No one shall be permitted to profit by his own fraud, or to take advantage of his own wrong, or to found any claim upon his own iniquity, or to acquire property by his own crime.[2]

This 'fundamental maxim of the common law', clearly a moral principle, is taken by Dworkin as a legal principle, at the heart of the legal system, not subject to legislative change or judicial overruling.

However, I am not about to intervene in this area of controversy. In what follows I shall be looking at the matter in a somewhat different light. First, I want to consider the relation between judicial decisions and judicial opinions—more specifically, the question whether opinions are necessary or dispensable and what light that question throws on the question of the relations between law and justice; and, second, I want to consider anew, and, I think, from a somewhat different angle, the relations between law and morality.

1. POLITICS, GOVERNMENT, AND LAW

Consider, at the outset, the relations between political philosophy and philosophy of law. In political philosophy there are very few references to

---

[1] H. L. A. Hart, *The Concept of Law* (Oxford: Clarendon Press, 1961); Lon Fuller, *The Morality of Law*, rev. edn. (New Haven: Yale University Press, 1969), pp. 41–4 and *passim*; Ronald Dworkin, *Taking Rights Seriously* (Cambridge, Mass.: Harvard University Press, 1977), pp. 22–8.
[2] *Riggs* v. *Palmer*, 115 NY 506 (1889) at 511; 22 NE 188 at 190.

courts, court decisions, and law as it is understood by lawyers. Political philosophy emphasizes politics and government and moves from that to considering questions of legislation and legislative policy. In philosophy of law, especially Anglo-American philosophy of law, the emphasis is on courts and the judging of cases and the interpretation of statutes and precedents.

A curious dichotomy has thus been set up within political philosophy. One way to understand this dichotomy is to think of government as more closely related to legislation than to adjudication; government, in the sense in which the government can be changed by election or succession or by usurpation of power, is not closely related to adjudication. There is typically a closer relationship between the government and the legislative body of a country than there is between the government and the courts (though of course that was not so in such a place as Hitler's Germany, and there are still some countries like that in existence). That is why courts are often thought of in connection with if not as identical with the legal system—or the legal system is thought of as a system of courts of law[3]—and why it is so easily taken for granted that the government and the legal system can be treated of and thought of independently of one another; and hence why, in philosophical discussions, politics and law are ordinarily thought of as in isolation from one another. A government often takes office with a legislative programme, and rarely takes office with a judicial programme; although noises are often made about taming or restraining the courts, that is actually part of a legislative programme and an appointment policy. So governments can enact or propose legislation affecting the size, composition, jurisdiction, and powers of the courts, but it is legislation affecting judicial *bodies* that is thus enacted or proposed, not *judicial decisions themselves*. Hence matters relating to legislation are normally dealt with in political philosophy, or philosophy of government, while matters relating to courts and judicial decisions are thought to be and have been, at least within Anglo-American jurisprudence of the last two hundred years, the peculiar province of philosophy of law.

---

[3] It is that in part, but only in part. A lot more than a system of judges and courts of law is required to have a legal system. For one thing, police are required to enforce the judgements of courts. But this is by the way. There is an excellent account of what is entailed in the existence of a legal system in Hart's *Concept of Law*, pp. 107–14.

2. THE FUNCTIONS OF COURTS

What are the basic functions of courts of law? The first, and most important, is to decide cases that arise under the law. Indeed, this is a necessary
part of the conception of a court of law—a 'court of law' that never decided
cases and made no attempt to would not be a court of law at all but could
be at most a superannuated relic of one. But courts have other functions as
well.

A second function of courts is to interpret the law (that is, to determine
its meaning for the decision of cases), where this is necessary for the decision of cases and in the process of deciding cases. A third function of courts
is to fill in the gaps—'interstices'—in the law where this is necessary for the
decision of cases. And fourth, in the United States at any rate, courts have
the power of judicial review; that is, the power to determine the legal validity (constitutionality) of statutes and other measures, such as executive
orders, having the force of law, though only if a case is brought raising that
question. But this last is not a necessary part of the function of courts of
law. Furthermore, it is conceivable that even the function of interpreting
the law could be assigned to another body—some supercourt, say; the system could be so arranged that a court seeking to decide a case and having
some problem about how some statute should be interpreted would have
to appeal the matter to 'the court of interpretation', which would not itself
have the power to decide the case directly but only the power to issue an
authoritative interpretation. That would no doubt be inefficient but it
would not be impossible. The same is the case with the power of filling in
interstices in the law. This too could be assigned to some other body, some
quasi-legislative-judicial body, and need not be restricted to the body with
the power to decide cases.

Oliver Wendell Holmes, in his famous paper 'The Path of the Law', refers
to a case brought before a Vermont justice of the peace by a farmer against
another farmer for 'breaking a churn'.[4] The justice, after taking some time
to consider the matter, said that he had looked through all the statutes and
could find no mention of churns, and consequently found for the defendant. Not too long ago, in a small town in Wisconsin, it was discovered that
the mayor, who had built a new house the preceding year, had disconnected
the water meter, and it was estimated that the mayor had received 100,000

---

[4] Oliver Wendell Holmes, jun., 'The Path of the Law', 10 *Harvard Law Review* (1897), 474–5;
repr. in Holmes's *Collected Legal Papers* (New York: Harcourt, Brace, 1921), p. 196.

gallons of free water. The upshot was that he was forced to resign as mayor, but no criminal charges were brought against him because, it was said, there was no ordinance in the town specifically prohibiting disconnecting a water meter; the upshot of that, presumably, was that such an ordinance was very soon passed. Clearly, there was what was called a gap in the law, and in that case it was decided, for who knows what reason, not to fill it in by judicial decision, though that certainly could have been done. In the Vermont case, the justice of the peace may have had some other reason for deciding the way he did, or he might have been literally a literalist—'nothing is said about *churns*'. But normally courts are not that reluctant to fill in the interstices; they do it in the process of deciding cases, and the absence in the statutes of a specific word for a specific thing is not normally by itself a bar to finding for the plaintiff. After all, a churn is a piece of property and, though I have not checked the Vermont statutes of the period on this point, I have no genuine doubt that there was some general rubric under which churns would fall.

Of course the gaps can also be filled in by legislation, and occasionally courts have suggested that the appropriate route for the solution of such problems is the legislative route, though that is almost inevitably a slower process, and one that is of no avail in deciding the instant case. But what is the basic function of legislative bodies? First and foremost, to enact laws. But merely to say this sounds strange, because tautological: a legislative body simply is a body that has the power to make laws; and presumably it does so for some purpose other than that of simply enacting laws. So a better way to put it is, I suggest, this: A legislative body lays down rules (laws) for the ordering and governance of the society and for dealing in advance, and in general terms, so far as foresight allows, with the problems government is established to deal with. Another way of expressing this point (though perhaps this is a different point) is that legislatures seek to remedy, in general terms, problems in the society that law is fit to deal with, and legislatures thus use law as a vehicle of national policy. Given these facts, it is not surprising that legislative bodies and legislation fit more clearly into a pattern of governmental policy than do judicial bodies and adjudication.

3. JUDICIAL OPINIONS

Appellate courts characteristically hand down opinions in connection with their decisions, explaining and justifying them; this is especially prominent in but not restricted to cases of split decisions. What is the significance of judicial opinions?

It has been claimed, and is actually a tenet of a whole school of jurisprudence, that the opinions handed down are merely *ex post facto* rationalizations that have nothing to do with determining the decisions arrived at. The idea appears to be that the judge decides the case first on some basis or other, possibly some hunch or intuition or feeling, and then afterwards looks for some propositions of law that can be used as premises for an argument to provide a sort of justification, though the judge's argument is really a rationalization, since it literally had nothing to do with determining the decision arrived at. The decision is determined by other factors, not by anything in the opinion. Furthermore, the argument goes, the really important thing for the litigants, and therefore for the study of law, is the decision, not the opinion. The operative slogan for this school of thought is 'Look at what the judges *do* (that is, the decisions they hand down), not at what they say (that is, the opinions they render)'.

One of the writers who most vigorously maintained this position is Jerome Frank, who was prominent both as an appellate judge and as a writer on jurisprudence. Frank defined law from the point of view of the average person:

For any particular lay person, the law, with respect to any particular set of facts, is a decision of a court with respect to those facts so far as that decision affects that particular person. Until a court has passed on those facts no law on that subject is yet in existence. Prior to such a decision, the only law available is the opinion of lawyers as to the law relating to that person and to those facts. Such opinion is not actually law but only a guess as to what a court will decide.[5]

Thus Frank maintains that, from the point of view of a particular individual, law simply *is* the decision with respect to a particular case, and until the case is decided there is no law at all with respect to that case. 'Clients want those concrete determinations rather than generalizations', he says: 'Judges are called on not to make rules, but to decide which side of some immediate controversy is to win. The rules are incidental, the decisions are the thing' (p. 126).

Frank goes on to argue that:

Whenever a judge decides a case he is making law: the law of that case, not the law of future cases not yet before him. What the judge does and what he says may somewhat influence what other judges will do or say in other cases. But what the

---

[5] Jerome Frank, *Law and the Modern Mind* (New York: Tudor, 1930), p. 46.

other judges decide in those other cases, as a result of whatever influences, will be the law in those other cases. The law of any case is what the judge decides. (ibid.)

What Frank has to say about opinions, then, readily follows:

Often when a judge decides a case he simultaneously publishes an essay, called an opinion, explaining that he had used an old rule or invented a new rule to justify his judgment. But no matter what he says, it is his decision which fixes the legal positions of the litigants. If Judge Brilliant decides that Mr Evasion must pay the federal government $50,000 for back taxes or that Mrs Goneril is entitled to nothing under the will of her father, Mr Lear, the contents of the judge's literary effusion makes not one iota of practical difference to Mr Evasion or Mrs Goneril.

Frank then claims that the judge's 'decision is primary, the rules he may happen to refer to are incidental . . . The law, therefore, consists of *decisions*, not of rules' (p. 128), and, as he is no doubt ready to add, the law does not consist of opinions. For, he says:

Many a case is decided without the writing of an opinion. The trial judge usually does not bother to tell why he thinks John Doe should lose to Richard Roe. But does he any the less make the law of the case because he has not tried to tell the story of his reactions to the evidence in the shape of legal formulas? Surely law does not come into being only in those cases that are appealed to an upper court which will write an opinion reciting some rules (pp. 128–9)

This last is an exceedingly weak argument. Frank is saying that because there can be decisions without opinions, therefore the law cannot be found in opinions where there are opinions, but must be found solely in the decisions; this simply does not follow.

Although Frank's other arguments have somewhat more to be said for them, I do not intend to attack Frank's arguments directly. I want first to contrast Frank's opinion on the matter of opinions with the opinions of some others, and if I appeal to the opinion of someone higher than Frank in the judicial hierarchy—a justice of the Supreme Court of the United States—it is not because in these matters philosophical authority goes along with legal authority. It does not.

At the very end of his opinion in the case of *Douglas* v. *Jeanette*, concurring in the result but not on the reasons, Justice Jackson says:

Civil liberties had their origin and must find their ultimate guarantee in the faith of the people. If that faith should be lost, five or nine men in Washington could not long supply its want. Therefore we must do our utmost to make clear and easily understandable the reasons for deciding these cases as we do. Forthright observance of rights presupposes their forthright definition.[6]

Now that is the sort of thing Frank would refer to as a 'literary effusion'. Justice Jackson is concurring in the decision, and is, according to Judge Frank, 'simultaneously publish[ing] an essay, called an opinion, explaining that he . . . used an old rule or invented a new rule to justify his judgment'. However, we have here a claim made by Jackson that the opinions issued by courts are of enormous importance. Obviously he thought so, or he wouldn't have bothered to say so nor would he have bothered to write an opinion. And his very next sentence, after the paragraph just quoted, is: 'I think that the majority has failed in this duty'. (In what duty? Did Jackson mean that the majority failed in its duty to 'make clear and easily understandable the reasons for deciding' the case as it did? Or did Jackson mean that the majority had failed in its duty of supplying 'forthright definition' of these rights? Perhaps both. He didn't say.) The opinion of the Court was written by Chief Justice Stone, and the decision was unanimous. Yet Justice Jackson concurred only in the result, not in the opinion and not on the reasons given by the Court; and his opinion in *Douglas* v. *Jeanette* was in the curious position of concurring in the result in Douglas but expressing his reasons for dissenting in a whole series of other cases, involving the same general questions of law, decided on the same day. I do not stop here to explain the issue, since I have brought this matter in only in illustration. So *are* opinions important, and what importance do they have?

As a way of getting somewhat closer to an answer, consider a brief passage by Henry M. Hart, jun., Professor of Law at Harvard Law School, who, in an essay entitled 'Holmes's Positivism', strongly disagrees with the legal positivists' position on the matter of opinions, on the ground that it leads simply 'to behaviorism'. As he puts the position he is arguing against:

It is not what the judges say which is important but what they do. It is not the reasons for decision which the judges think they follow to which we should look but the behavior patterns which, willy-nilly, they do follow. And so we seem to arrive, if we take this path, at the monstrous conclusion that reason and argument, the conscious search for justice, are vain. Man's most elaborately contrived instrument for the application of thought to human affairs we seem to have transformed into a gesture of futility.

That, of course, is an expression of strong feeling, highly emotive, hardly itself an argument. Yet it might suggest an argument. And Hart does provide one, as follows:

[6] *Douglas* v. *Jeanette*, 319 US 137 (1943), at p. 182.

Exactly why is it important to know what the officials do? The cynical but plausible answer that this is the thing that matters to the litigants does not really help. It states at most no more than a fact of human experience; it is only a half-truth, and a dangerous half-truth. The reasons that officials give for what they do often matter to people also; and we ought to remember everlastingly that this is so. A solid answer to the question, and the only solid answer, is that we need to test the correspondence between official action and our formulations of what official action ought to be in order to see whether one or the other needs to be changed.[7]

This is promising, but there is a slight problem with it, and that is that the vast majority of people never read these opinions. Thus, when Justice Jackson says that the Court must do its utmost to make clear and readily understandable the reasons for its decisions, where the reasons are contained in the opinion, and when Professor Hart says that the reasons officials give for what they do often matter to people also, that is all well and good, but how many people ever pay any attention to them apart from theorists and students of the subject? Very very few. In fact, hardly any. Accounts of Supreme Court opinions in the press are usually severely abbreviated, are often wrong, and are typically written with an eye to current events rather than their legal significance. Most people, it is safe to say, are not in a position to pay any attention to the opinions of courts, even when they hear about the courts' decisions. The legal news most likely to be reported in the press concerns local trials, especially criminal trials; and accounts of appellate decisions and opinions are given very little play. So even if it is true that the reasons officials give for their official acts are important to people, it is rare for people to go out of their way to find out what they are.

4. THE IMPORTANCE OF OPINIONS

To be sure, there are cases of such interest that when they are decided the opinions of the court, and of dissenting judges, do receive considerable coverage in the press. The Bakke Case of 1978 is an example.[8] When it was decided many newspapers not noted for their coverage of judicial decisions devoted considerable space to the matter. This reflected the great interest

---

[7] Henry M. Hart, jun., 'Holmes's Positivism—An Addendum', 64 *Harvard Law Review* (1951) 929 at 933, 933–4.

[8] *Regents of the University of California* v. *Bakke*, 438 US 265 (1978).

the case had for large numbers of people, and perhaps also the complicated nature of the decision the Court rendered. It would really be impossible to determine merely from the specific holding (ruling) just what the Court had decided. It is true that Bakke won, in the sense that it was decided that he had been unconstitutionally denied a place in medical school, but it was not this alone that prompted people's interest in the case. What was of general interest was not the specific dispute between Bakke and the Board of Regents of the University of California (though that may have been all that was of interest to Bakke). What was of widespread public interest was the general question whether race can constitutionally be used to accord or deny someone some special treatment (in the instant case, admission to medical school, but the question went way beyond that specific issue in the case). And whenever some general issue of that kind becomes of general interest and is discussed outside the confines of the courtroom and the law school, a case in which it is dealt with will get wider notice than others. In such cases as these the points made by Justice Jackson and Henry Hart take on some greater plausibility.

I do not wish to underplay the value of the considerations advanced by Justice Jackson and Henry Hart. Opinions expressed in concurrence or dissent have often later changed the path of the law. A line of reasoning expressed some time ago can, on occasion, take on more force and moment than a whole line of precedents. And on occasion, at least, the reasons given can matter even to the litigants, even to the one who lost. Is it not better if you have lost a dispute to have the feeling that your claim has at least been heard? Surely that is better than feeling that it has been totally ignored. An opinion can bring out this factor, unreachable by mere decision. And here we come across the wisdom, which ought not to be forgotten, that it is not the results only that matter to human beings—at least civilized and reasonable human beings—but also intentions, motives, feelings, and reasons. To quote Holmes again: 'even a dog distinguishes between being stumbled over and being kicked'.[9] An intentional harm is felt, at least by reasonable people, as more grievous than an unintentional one, an accident, especially where an apology is forthcoming.

Such considerations, however, though they bear on the matter, are not sufficient to settle the question of the importance of opinions in connection with decisions. So let us try a thought-experiment. Imagine a legal system in which cases are decided but in which no reasons are ever given for the decisions, and let us suppose that the cases are decided by flipping

---

[9] Oliver Wendell Holmes, jun., *The Common Law* (Boston: Little, Brown, 1881), p. 3.

coins. That certainly would be an efficient arrangement, one in which courts would be very unlikely to have crowded dockets, though it would likely lead to more crowded prisons. But it is not evident that such an arrangement would for long be found acceptable by the bulk of the population or by people who would otherwise want to take a case to court. The important thing is to figure out why.

I have used this example for some time in my course in philosophy of law, and some years ago a student came in with a clipping, datelined New Orleans, stating that a municipal judge in Baton Rouge had been flipping coins to determine verdicts, and that the Supreme Court of Louisiana had upheld the vote of a judiciary commission to censure him. 'The censure', the article continued, 'will have no practical effect on Judge William H. (Hawk) Daniels, who will continue hearing cases in Municipal Court in Baton Rouge'.[10] Now I have not researched the matter to find out what happened to Judge Hawk Daniels, apart from the censure, or whether he continued or gave up the practice of flipping coins to determine verdicts. I am sure that such a practice could not be tolerated if it were widespread and public, even though an isolated exception or eccentric might be. Many judges have indicated that they would like to be able to decide cases in this way, and some have written learned articles extolling the virtues of the hunch or of guessing as a method of getting a just decision as often as discursive argument. But such judicial effusions in the law journals do not settle anything either. Judges who write this way about the practice of deciding cases and issuing opinions do not noticeably write fewer opinions than those who hold an opposite view, and such a view has not had any appreciable effect on their actual practice, which is something to marvel at.

But let it be known—widely known—that judges regularly decide cases by flipping coins, and what will happen to the legal system? To answer this, we have to consider again the functions of courts of law, in the context of considering the aims of a legal system and why a legal system has courts of law. It is not enough for a legal system merely to decide cases. If it were, there would be nothing that could be said against deciding them by flipping coins. The second, third, and fourth functions I mentioned—to interpret the law, to fill in the interstices in the law, and to determine legal validity— can be put aside in the present context as not essential to the functions of a court of law, though the second and the third clearly are essential in a legal system considered as a whole. But it is not enough, as I have just said, simply to decide cases. It is also necessary, fifth, to decide cases *in accordance*

[10] This was a UPI dispatch from New Orleans, 10 November 1976.

with justice, and, sixth, in such a way as to *satisfy the public sense of justice*—
that is, so that it will be generally believed, and for good reason, that cases
are being decided in accordance with justice, or at least that a genuine sincere and honest attempt is being made to settle cases in accordance with justice. But this means that it is being taken for granted, as an item of public
faith in the society, that an honest attempt is being made to settle cases *on
their merits*, and this presupposes that there are merits, and that these merits can be ascertained. A legal system in which cases are known to be decided
by such methods as flipping coins could not long meet the condition of satisfying the public sense of justice, because it could not meet the condition
of deciding cases in accordance with justice, and it would be known that it
could not meet that condition. It is possible, of course, as a matter of
abstract logic, that such a method of deciding cases would always result in
the just decision, but there could be no possible reason to believe this. And
why pay a lawyer to argue your case for you if the outcome is not to depend
in any way on the briefs or the testimony or the arguments, but simply on
the flip of a coin? Knowledge of the practice would be a signal that judges
either did not believe that cases had merits, or did not believe they could
ascertain them if they did, or did not believe that it was worth the trouble to
ascertain them if they could. But people who want their day in court do
believe, and very strongly, that their cases do have merits. The net result
would be a crashing loss of confidence in the legal system.[11]

5. THE AIMS OF A LEGAL SYSTEM

Consider the matter now in the context of the aims and functions of a legal
system as a whole. Can we describe in general terms what a legal system
aims at? I think so. What we must notice is that the aims and functions of
a legal system are many and manifold; there is never just one. A legal system aims at:

(a) providing a forum for resolving disputes and conflicts, so as to keep
     the society in which it functions from falling apart in internal dis-
     cord; and

---

[11] I am here bypassing the point that cases are supposed to be decided in accordance with the
law, and the law itself is not always in accordance with justice. This would simply bring in a consideration not germane to the topic, a complication that need not be dealt with in the present
context.

(b) resolving these disputes (i.e. deciding cases that arise under the law—the first function of courts of law).

But a legal system also aims (as I just said) at:

(c) resolving disputes *in accordance with justice*; and
(d) resolving them *in such as way as to satisfy the public sense of justice*, so that people are satisfied that in general justice is achieved or achievable in or under the legal system.

One problem in the administration of a legal system arises because aims (c) and (d) can come into conflict. The public sense of justice may be distorted (or the public might be ill informed) so that a case decided in accordance with justice does not satisfy the public sense of justice—that is, the case is not perceived by the public as having been decided in accordance with justice. And a case decided in such a way as to satisfy the public sense of justice may not be decided in accordance with justice. (I see no need to dwell here on the possibility that the sense of justice of the judges might be distorted. That, of course, is possible as well—I have seen it happen, and so have you—just as it is possible that there may be conflicts between deciding cases in accordance with justice and deciding them according to law. But such problems cannot be resolved wholesale and all at once.)

A conflict can also arise between aims (b) and (c): the aim of resolving disputes in accordance with justice can conflict with the aim of resolving disputes. The pressure to decide cases quickly may be such as to prevent them from being decided in accordance with justice, or the attempt to take the time to decide cases in accordance with justice may make it impossible to decide others at all. For every case decided there is another waiting to be, and the apparatus of appeals, essential to justice, certainly works against the efficiency of the system—where efficiency is measured in terms of speed, at any rate—leading to more and more crowded dockets. I take it that the saying 'Hard cases make bad law' reflects this phenomenon. It was Justice Holmes, I believe (or was it Justice Brandeis?), who said that it is better to decide a case in any way that seems plausible and get on with the next than to agonize over some one decision with the effect of increasing the backlog of cases to be decided. When this happens to an appreciable extent, the system is failing in its aim of providing a forum for resolving disputes. Thus the first aim can also conflict with that of deciding cases in accordance with justice. And, *a fortiori*, the aim of deciding cases can conflict with that of deciding them in such a way as to satisfy the public sense of justice, and, to spell it out, so can the aim of providing a forum for resolving disputes. We have all heard the slogan 'Justice delayed is justice denied', and 'the law's delay' has been a problem at least since the time of Shakespeare's *Hamlet* along with 'The insolence of office, and the spurns | That patient merit of the unworthy takes'.[12] Yet the standing possibility of conflict between these aims and functions does not mean that they are not essential or any the less aims. The potential for inner tension is only an indication of the complexity of the subject (and, incidentally, helps explain the persistence of philosophical differences about what a legal system is and ought to do and how it can best do it).

The aims (a)–(d) just mentioned are largely judicial in character, though conciliation and mediation and arbitration can often serve the function of resolving disputes without involving formal litigation, so courts are not the only agencies the legal system provides for settling disputes. Also, the aims of deciding cases in accordance with justice and in such a way as to satisfy the public sense of justice can lead to attempts at legislative reform of the judicial system, so, with aims (c) and (d) we can begin to get an admixture of legislative aims. But the aims already mentioned do not exhaust by any means the aims of a legal system as a whole. A legal system also aims:

(e) at providing elementary precautions against assault, theft, murder, rape, etc.—that is, to provide basic protection of the person and personalty;

(f) to provide rules to govern the behaviour of members of the society, to facilitate plans and projects, so that expectations may be ordered, conduct may be regulated, and legitimate interests not unduly frustrated; and

(g) to provide rules to govern behaviour in economic activities, where conflict is likely and competition may or may not be regarded as desirable but is to some extent inevitable, and where some cooperation is necessary—since, in a civilized society, competition must always occur in a context of cooperation and under regulation.

Although these latter aims are largely legislative in character, part of deciding cases in accordance with justice and in such a way as to satisfy the public sense of justice is to keep these larger aims of the legal system in mind. They are always relevant, though their application to any individual case is not always determinate. And that the rules for achieving these aims are often vague and themselves conflicting is—or should be by this time—self-evident.

---

[12] *Hamlet*, III. i. 72–4.

Finally, the basic aims of the legal system are moulded, certainly affected, by the political structure and goals, the mores, traditions, and customs, and by the constitution and the positive morality of the society. These also are subject to vagueness, to different interpretations, and to change over time, sometimes in incompatible directions. Nor can we afford to overlook the important, sometimes overriding, influence of different political outlooks and ideologies, which can at times distort the basic aims of the legal system as a whole. We have seen this happen too.

6. THE DIRECTION OF GUILT AND THE DIRECTION OF INNOCENCE

I have been considering the question whether opinions are necessary in a legal system and have thus necessarily been talking about appellate courts, not trial courts or courts of first instance, where the primary aim is to arrive at a verdict. I have suggested that the role opinions play is to bring out the reasons for decisions, not so that members of the general public will always know what they are, but so that the public can sense that a genuine sincere and honest attempt is being made to decide cases in accordance with justice. I should like now to provide another argument in support of this idea by taking a general example from an area of law where we must be understood as talking in the first instance about trial courts (though what is said can easily be extended to appellate courts). The example will, however, bring out how cases can be decided on their merits and what it means for one not to be.

The basic principle of a system of criminal justice, in so far as it genuinely aims at justice and is not a system of repression, is that a person (accused and on trial) should be judged legally guilty if and only if that person is *in fact* guilty. However, it is impossible to meet this condition perfectly. A perfect system of criminal justice would be one in which this principle is satisfied in all cases. But, given human error and fallibility, it is impossible to set up a system of criminal justice in such a way as to guarantee that everyone who is innocent (and who is for some reason on trial) will be found innocent and that everyone who is actually guilty will be found guilty. This means that any actual system of criminal justice must necessarily be weighted in one way or the other, and the way in which it is weighted will normally be that which is in accordance with the dominant moral ideas of the society in which it is embedded.

By *actually guilty* I mean only that the person in question actually did the act in question, which I take to be a matter of fact purely, and by *legally guilty* I mean that a judgement of guilt has been entered by a court of competent jurisdiction. I am not here including in the idea of guilt the notion of responsibility or competence or sanity, which tends to make our actual conception of 'guilty', as embedded in our present legal system, so complex and obscure. (The concept of responsibility or sanity is not a matter of fact purely, but is as obscure and contested as anything in the area of morality.) So, given these four concepts—*actually guilty, legally guilty, actually innocent* (meaning 'this person did not do it'), and *legally innocent*—a perfect system of criminal justice is, by definition, one in which these factors would match perfectly. Whoever is actually guilty would be legally guilty, and whoever is actually innocent would be legally innocent.

Now in any criminal case there are merits which are, at least in principle, ascertainable. It is possible, therefore, for a case to be decided on its merits as well as not. But, given that it is not possible to ensure this perfect matching in all cases, every system is in practice weighted in one direction or the other. It can be weighted in the direction of guilt—that is, of finding actually guilty persons to be legally guilty. This, however, would be at the cost of finding an increased percentage of actually innocent persons to be legally guilty. Or the system can be weighted in the direction of innocence—of finding actually innocent persons to be legally innocent, which would be at the cost of finding an increased percentage of actually guilty persons legally innocent. So the question arises: How ought the legal system to be weighted? Which way is better? Since, in an imperfect world, it is impossible for perfect justice to be achieved, only an approximation to it can be achieved, and the approximation will be in the direction determined by some moral judgement or other as to the direction in which it is best to err. For error there must be. (Of course it is possible for a legal system to have been so constructed, willy-nilly, that weighting in one of these directions by some factors is cancelled out by weighting in the other direction by other factors. But this indicates either inconsistent ideas or inconsistent execution of them in the construction of the legal system, and is not worth further attention in the present context. In the present context, such randomness simply confirms that there is and must be weighting in either the direction of innocence or the direction of guilt.)

The question, then, is whether it is better for a legal system to be weighted in the direction of guilt or in the direction of innocence, since one of these goals can be achieved only at the cost of failing, to some extent at least, to achieve the other. The question is inescapable, and how the legal system should be weighted is a question of morality or social policy, not one that can be determined solely on legal grounds.

The tendency, where there is presumption of innocence that is actually operative and not a false front, is to operate on some such principle as: 'It is better that ten guilty persons should go free than that one innocent person should be punished for a crime he or she did not commit.' The opposite of this idea would be: 'It is better that ten innocent persons should be found guilty than that one guilty person should go free.' Our legal system, accordingly, is weighted in the direction of innocence. But that it is better for a legal system to be weighted in this direction rather than in the direction of guilt is not self-evident; it is in need of argument, and the argument would have to be a moral argument. It has been disputed, and in an interesting way, by William Paley, who, in his once widely influential *Principles of Moral and Political Philosophy*, criticized the maxim that favours freeing ten guilty persons in order to prevent the imposition of punishment on one innocent person. Paley was a utilitarian, and took the view that the proper and only object of the criminal justice system is the prevention of crimes. From this utilitarian point of view, then, when it is said that 'it is *better*' for the legal system to be weighted in the direction of innocence, what is meant is that it would be more 'for the public advantage', and, Paley argued, this 'cannot be maintained. The security of civil life', he claimed, 'which is essential to the value and enjoyment of every blessing it contains . . . is protected chiefly by the dread of punishment. The misfortune of an individual . . . cannot be placed in competition with this object.'[13] On Paley's view, clearly, it would be better for an actually innocent person occasionally to be legally guilty than for ten guilty persons to go free; for that would be more conducive to the prevention of crime and therefore to the public advantage. (It might even be better, on this view, that ten actually innocent persons be found guilty than for one guilty person to go free, but this is not clear.) That is quite right as a matter of fact, I should think, but it would also be conducive to quite a number of other things as well, and it does not even reach the question of justice involved. We should take pains to note that Paley did not contend that, even for the object of preventing crimes, the life or safety of an innocent person ought 'to be knowingly sacrificed; no principle of judicature, no end of punishment', he says, 'can ever require *that*', though he did not explain how this *obiter dictum* is in accordance with his utilitarian theory of punishment. And Paley did not explain why, from

---

[13] William Paley, *The Principles of Moral and Political Philosophy* (1785) 7th edn. (London: 1790), vol. ii, bk. VI, chap. IX, p. 301.

the utilitarian point of view to which he tries to adhere, it is still a necessary condition of justice that the person actually guilty should legally be found to be so by a fair process. Paley was in favour of taking the risk of 'confounding the innocent with the guilty', because, as he put it, 'certain rules of adjudication must be pursued . . . certain degrees of credibility must be accepted, in order to reach the crimes with which the public are infested', and consequently he rejected the maxim of protecting the innocent and advocated that the maxim of punishing the guilty be adopted instead (*Principles*, pp. 301–2).

I do not here want to go further down the road of criticizing a utilitarian theory of criminal justice. I have only wanted to point out that the legal system has to be weighted in one direction or the other, and that how it ought to be weighted is a matter for moral judgement. The legal system cannot by itself determine how it ought to be weighted. This is not a judgment of law; the weights that are built into the system do not result from merely legal judgements. This then brings out one way in which law is essentially related to morality. And similar considerations indicate that it is impossible for courts of law to decide cases simply and solely on their merits without some extra-legal aids for determining those merits; there must be rules of social policy for determining how these merits are to be ascertained. Thus there are rules of procedure and rules of evidence for determining admissibility and for determining which presumptions are to have legal weight. With respect to such matters of judicial decision, some moral judgement that determines a matter of social policy must either have been settled on beforehand or be presupposed.

I have now illustrated a way in which courts of law relate to justice, and the answer I have provided to the question of the importance of judicial opinions is, in short, this: Unless opinions are issued, opinions that explain the reasons for decisions, there is no reason for anyone to think that cases are being decided in accordance with justice, and the cases therefore could not be decided in such a way as to induce general confidence that an attempt has been made to decide them on their merits. If it were known that cases were being decided by flipping coins, it would be known that no effort was being made to decide them on their merits. A legal system that followed the practice of deciding cases in such a way would, in effect, be saying that there are no merits, or else that it is not worth the trouble of legal officials, who are presumably sworn to uphold the law, to try to determine what the merits are. And that would bring the whole legal system into disrepute. Because, as any fool knows, any fool can flip a coin.

7. LAW AND MORALITY

I turn now more directly though more briefly to the question of how law is related to morality. The question of the relations between law and morality can become very complicated; for it does not yield to simple analysis, though it is often the subject of hasty generalization. Some light can be thrown on the question by bringing in the distinctions, already discussed in previous essays (Chs. 1 and 5), between different senses or kinds of morality. Although I shall not so much be answering the question as analysing it, the analysis, it will become apparent, can itself yield some answers.

Let us notice, at the outset, that when we ask how law and morality are related, we may be asking whether one of these factors *does* affect the other, or, alternatively, whether it *ought to*, and the influence can, in principle, go in either direction. Thus the initial question divides into four subordinate ones: How does law affect morality? How should law affect morality? How does morality affect law? How should morality affect law? These questions are all distinct.

There are some obvious ways in which law does affect morality. This was pointed out by Whewell in his *Elements of Morality*.[14] That stealing is wrong presupposes the concept of property, and property is defined by the law; also changes in moral ideas can lead to changes in the scope of property rights. Again, that adultery is wrong presupposes the institution of marriage, which is defined by the law. Thus the law affects morality by specifying institutional frameworks relevant to a judgement that an act is right or wrong.

But this does not get at the question of how law *should* affect morality. And what sense or kind of morality do we have in mind? As I argued in the first chapter, the concept of morality is systematically ambiguous between positive morality, personal morality, and ideal or rational morality. There is no point in my repeating here what has already been said about this distinction earlier in this book. What should be evident is that the original four questions about the relations between morality and law now divide into twelve, depending on which sense of morality we are considering. And

---

[14] William Whewell, *The Elements of Morality, Including Polity* (1841) (3rd edn., London: 1854), vol. ii, suppl., ch. 2, sect. 3, pp. 305–6. See bk. 2, ch. 19, arts. 364–5, and bk. 4, ch. 6, arts. 760–3, which contain some (unfortunately almost forgotten) good sense on the relations between law and morality.

we can take it for granted, on the basis so conveniently supplied by Whewell and some other writers quoted earlier, that there is in fact inter-action, both between law and positive morality and law and personal morality—the personal morality of the judge or legislator, for instance, can affect law—and that there ought to be, though no doubt this process has its proper limits, which remain to be specified, and it also goes in both direc-tions. Can morality be legislated? Yes, and occasionally it has been, both positive morality and personal morality, though we must recognize that often the change takes time and may spread over several generations, since long-standing habits do not die easily.[15]

Does morality affect law? Yes, the law by and large reflects the conven-tional morality of the society, and if there is to be reasonable congruence between the two by and large it needs to. In somewhat the same way the strongly held moral views of certain people, who develop considerable influence, can change the law, and in a number of instances ought to, just as in a number of instances they ought not to. The moral outlook of Martin Luther King, jun., has had an effect on the law in a number of jurisdictions, and there is no doubt that that is by and large a good thing. By a similar token, the moral ideas of, say, the Ku Klux Klan had a long-standing effect on the laws of a number of states, now, happily (slowly) receding. But both the *de facto* and the *de jure* relations between law and morality in these first two senses have been rehearsed for some time by others, and need no fur-ther review from me here and now.

8. RATIONAL MORALITY AND LAW

We cannot sensibly ask how rational morality affects law, but we can sensi-bly ask how *the idea of it* does, and also how the idea *should* affect law. Here we have a different sort of question altogether, and what I shall do now is

---

[15] During the civil-rights struggles of the 1950s and 1960s one often heard the slogan 'you can't legislate morality' repeated as a kind of mantra. People who are given to uttering this non-platitude are ignoring, or perhaps they are ignorant of, certain obvious facts of history; and perhaps what such persons are afraid of is that some legislation will be passed that will force them to change their customary ways. Yet the latter does happen, from time to time. And we should note that the law that attempts to 'legislate morality', to use the vulgar expression, almost invari-ably proceeds from deeply felt moral beliefs and moral motives. So the situation is more accur-ately depicted as one where the personal morality of some, usually moral reformers, operating through the legal system, changes the positive morality of certain segments of the population. (See the next para.)

bring out something of the distinction and the complication of the matter. In doing so, I shall, almost necessarily, be repeating some of the points made earlier, in Chapter 1.

Some examples should illustrate how the conception of rational morality is involved in our ordinary thinking. Consider slavery. No one today claims (at least in public) that slavery is justified, even though slavery still exists in parts of the world, yet two hundred years ago, or even less, such claims were quite common; for slavery was quite commonly and openly practiced. Even people who were defensive about the ownership of slaves (and some were) did not deny that they had them. We have now reached the point in the development of the moral conscience of the world where no one—or hardly any one—would admit to having slaves or even to approving of slavery. For no one (or almost no one) would admit to having a conscience that would approve of having people as property. Slavery was once, and for a long time, an accepted and unquestioned institution, and then was, for not so long a time, a controversial matter. It is now no longer controversial. There is no question about the immorality of slavery. Capital punishment, on the other hand, is a controversial matter. There are numbers of people (especially in countries in western Europe) who think it horribly unjustified, but there are also large numbers of people who do not think that it is unjustified at all where the crime is horrendous enough, and if the convicted party is actually guilty. And public opinion on the matter, if public opinion polls are to be trusted, is in a state of flux.

Consider now torture. We know and the revelations of Solzhenitsyn and Jacobo Timerman have brought the realization home to us[16]—that torture has come back into existence as an instrument of national policy—as it has remained in some places a tool of police interrogation—in an astonishing and disturbing number of places in the world, that there are people in those places who are encouraged and taught to torture others and to get pleasure out of it, and that this trend is not just the isolated aberration of a few sadists. At the same time we know that no one will admit to using it. Yet for centuries torture was practiced as an instrument of political or religious policy all over what was then regarded—and regarded itself—as the civilized world. In that period, to say 'They practice torture there' would not automatically have been taken as condemnation. People had all sorts of 'justifications' for torture, and there was a time when no attempt at justification

---

[16] Alexander Solzhenitsyn, *The Gulag Archipelago, 1918–1956*, 3 vols. (New York: Harper & Row, 1974, 1975, 1978); Jacobo Timerman, *Prisoner Without a Name, Cell Without a Number* (New York: Alfred A. Knopf, 1981).

was thought necessary, when torture was an accepted institution. At the present time, the vast majority of civilized people do not think that torture is justified even to get the truth out of a condemned criminal, much less as a form of punishment or of penance, and today no one will admit, at least in a public forum, to practicing torture.[17] Allegations of its existence as an institution are vehemently and indignantly denied; where it is admitted that torture was once engaged in, it is claimed that the practitioners acted illegally, on their own, and are being sought and will be punished, but it is not admitted that any such thing is allowed to go on now.

Such examples illustrate, and in the process demonstrate, how one can distinguish between personal (that is, one's own) morality and the ideal of rational (that is, correct or true) morality. As I said in the first chapter, the distinction is recognized every time one recognizes that one has changed one's mind and believes that the change is a change for the better, in the direction of a more enlightened view.

This is all I was attempting to bring out on the present occasion about the relations between law and morality. To deal adequately with the subject, we must distinguish these three senses of morality, and we must determine what we are asking when we ask how law and morality are related or how one can affect the other. In any event, in the mere existence of a criminal-justice system—that is, a system of criminal law that aims or claims to aim at justice—some relationship between law and justice must be recognized as not merely important but *essential*. The argument I have presented is meant to show that there is a necessary connection between law and justice, not a merely contingent one, and to give some indication of the nature of that connection. In particular, the demand that no one who is innocent be punished for a crime he is known not to have committed is a basic demand of justice and of rational morality, and a basic component of the public sense of justice. Violations of it must be kept dark—or denied—or else the system in which it is violated will no longer be regarded as a system of criminal justice but as a system of repression and terror—as we might say, a criminal system of justice. This demand is therefore one of the many

---

[17] Yet even today there are those who torture women or children, but these people are either psychologically disturbed or morally beyond the pale. To put it another way, they are evil. The practice of sex slavery, in which women who wanted only to emigrate from a country in which they had known only oppression to find some measure of freedom and comfort elsewhere find that they have been sold into slavery or traduced into being sex slaves, required to keep working at prostitution in order to pay off a 'debt' that everlastingly recedes, is a combination of slavery and torture. As such this practice, or quasi-institution, is not just wicked, it is evil—where 'evil', used precisely, is the worst possible term of opprobrium imaginable—as are the perpetrators of the practice.

important features of justice that courts must reckon with in their attempts to decide cases and that legislatures must abide by in their attempts to devise general remedies for social problems and to advance social goals. The demand that no one be punished for a crime he (or she) is known not to have committed is at the intersection of law and morality. And the demand that no innocent person be executed amounts to a moral necessity—a necessity of rational morality—placing a categorical and absolute moral demand on the legal system of every state.

ADDITIONAL NOTES AND COMMENTS

A. 'Judicial Decisions and Judicial Opinions' was originally published in *Criminal Justice Ethics*, 2(1) (winter/spring 1983), pp. 17–30; revised, in part rewritten, for its appearance here.

B. As I was informed some time ago by a law student in one of my philosophy of law classes, there are some judicial districts which do not publish all of their opinions ('depublished' is the expression often employed), and consequently prohibit lawyers and lower courts from citing them. Fairly recently, my friend Michael Reiter informed me that the Eighth Circuit Court,

like many appellate courts, had a rule that provided that certain opinions of the court are to be unpublished and not to be cited by lawyers in briefs or in arguments in later cases. I always thought that rule was unconstitutional on First Amendment grounds. Recently, the Eighth Circuit declared its own rule about unpublished opinions unconstitutional on other grounds.

The grounds advanced by the court are much like those argued here—the essential importance of opinions in determining the meaning and basis of the decision, i.e. the holding (ruling). *Anastasoff* v. *United States of America*, US Eighth Circuit, 223 F. 3d 898 (2000). The opinion is very interesting. Of course, cases that are decided *per curiam* are (often) decided without the issuance of an opinion. But if all decisions were *per curiam*, handed down with no explanatory text (= opinion), no decision could serve as a precedent, and violations of the principle of justice, which is really equivalent to the rule of law, would be rampant, much more so than they are now. A legal system that, as a general rule, allowed or required such a practice would not be a rational legal system.

C. More recently, Dr Reiter has informed me of a decision by the Ninth Circuit Court of Appeal in *Hart* v. *Massanari*, 9th Cir. No. 99–56472, (24/9/01), which rejected the opinion of the Eighth Circuit Court as holding in the Ninth Circuit. The gist of its reasoning was that:

Writing a published opinion is an 'exacting and extremely time-consuming task' . . . because the judge 'must envision the countless permutations of facts that might arise in the universe of future cases' and draft the ruling so that it 'sweeps neither too broadly nor too narrowly' and avoids colliding with other binding precedent bearing on the issue. For that reason [the court said] federal appellate courts publish opinions in only about one-fifth the cases that they decide.

If parties could cite unpublished opinions as precedent, courts would be forced to treat those dispositions as 'mini-opinions', and much of the time saved under the current regime of published and unpublished opinions would be lost [the court said].[18]

Thus the gist of the reasoning is that the depublication of certain opinions is a matter of efficiency and pressure of time. As so described, this reasoning does not apply to all opinions, and I have no immediate quarrel with it. Though how a decision in a case where the opinion is depublished can serve as precedent is not explained, nor is it explained how this practice conforms to the ideal of the rule of law, which requires compliance with the principle that similar cases are to be decided similarly.

D. Some plausible explanation for this practice of depublishing opinions is provided by Alan M. Dershowitz in *The Best Defense* (1982) (New York: Vintage Books, 1983). Thus: 'The judge was so incensed by Morvillo's actions that he went out of his way never to mention him by name in the course of his fifty-page opinion. He referred to him only by his title 'the Chief'. But in order to avoid any public criticism of Morvillo, the judge refrained from publishing his opinion' (p. 378). This explanation is plausible, but the statement is nonetheless distinctly odd. The judge writes a 'fifty-page opinion', which is seen and read by Mr Dershowitz (for the defence), and by the prosecution (therefore Mr Morvillo), and by other court officials and aids, but 'refrained from publishing his opinion'. In one sense of 'published', once a piece of writing has been made available to others and is not explicitly said to be a draft but is available in final form, it can be said to be published. Still, saying that the judge did not publish his opinion means something more than this. Dershowitz goes on to say:

Rosner appealed—for the fifth time—to the court of appeals. In December 1980 a unanimous court of appeals affirmed the district court in an order relying 'on the opinion below' ... Attached to the court of appeals' order was a stamped form warning that its statement 'shall not be reported, cited or otherwise used *in unrelated cases* before this or any other court'. The decision would mean that 'Rosner loses', but the reasoning could not be used as precedent in any other case. (p. 380, emphasis added)

Here the 'depublication' of an opinion does not mean that it is not released to be read by the parties and their attorneys, but that it may not be cited or quoted in other cases. Note that the stamped warning says 'in unrelated cases', which would not appear to prohibit its use in related cases. The catch is that we are not told how to determine what a 'related case' would be.

---

[18] To (12) *US Law Week* (2001), p. 1183.

10

Institutional Ethics

My title may generate some perplexity. It is certainly not a familiar one. So I should make it plain at the outset that I shall not be discussing the ethics of organizations or associations or groups. I want to direct attention to the ethical and valuational questions associated with social institutions, and I distinguish institutions from associations and organizations. One question I am aiming at is whether the principles and standards applicable to moral judgements of actions (either tokens or types) and of persons—call them individual principles—are also applicable, or applicable with only minor changes, to the judgement and critique and evaluation of institutions and practices. This is not the sole question of institutional ethics, but it is a main one.

I

Consider the following statement by R. H. Tawney:

An appeal to principles is the condition of any considerable reconstruction of society, because social institutions are the visible expression of the scale of moral values which rules the minds of individuals, and it is impossible to alter institutions without altering that valuation.[1]

Tawney's statement may seem unduly optimistic. We have seen institutions altered, valuations changed, societies reconstructed—at least fundamentally changed—without any appeal to principles whatever, certainly not any appeal to rational considerations, although there may have been the illusion of such an appeal. It is, nonetheless, worth taking as a point of reference. For it is a good account, in my judgement, of the basis on which critiques and evaluations of societies and social institutions ought to rest.

[1] R. H. Tawney, *The Acquisitive Society*, ch. 1, para. 4, p. 3.

Consider now the following example from an ethics text of some years back:

As I make out the grades for a logic class, I am tolerably sure of the following facts. Student No. 1 will not get into law school next fall unless he receives a *B*. He has earned a *C*. To miss entering in the fall means having to wait another entire year. Student No. 2 will be dropped from college by the dean if he fails to get a *C* in each of his courses. He has earned a *D*. The logic course was not in any sense necessary to him in his future work; he registered for it because he had heard that it was interesting and not too difficult. Student No. 3 will be able to graduate if he receives merely a *D*. If he receives an *F*, he will not. He has earned an *F*. His low mark was probably due to a combination of laziness and indifference. What ought I to do in each case?[2]

I could add further examples with individual variations, to sharpen and further refine the moral judgement that needs to be made, but there is really in this context no need. As it stands, each question, and even the general question, is a question of individual ethics, not of institutional ethics. Should all of these students be treated in the same way? That is to say, should the grade be changed in each case, in accordance with the specified need of the student? Or should the grade rather be determined in each case by the instructor's judgement of what grade the student has earned? If we are to distinguish one case from another, and determine that the grade should be raised in some cases and not in others, on what standard should the distinction be made? At this point we come up against what I have called the generalization principle,[3] but we still do not have a question of institutional ethics.

Such questions as these are perfectly familiar; many teachers as well as others are called upon, more or less often, to make such judgements and evaluations as are called for in the grading of examinations and papers and of candidates for prizes and positions and degrees. But what is of special interest about this particular problem is the way it tends almost inexorably

---

[2] Albury Castell, *An Elementary Ethics* (Englewood Cliffs, NJ: Prentice-Hall, 1954), p. 5.

[3] 'What is right (or wrong) for one person must be right (or wrong) for any (relevantly) similar person in (relevantly) similar circumstances'. This corresponds in a number of respects, though not in all, with what R. M. Hare and others have called 'universalizability'. I have explained these differences and attempted to dispel some confusions about the generalization principle in 'Universalizability and the Generalization Principle', in Nelson Potter and Mark Timmons (eds.), *Morality and Universality: Essays on Ethical Universalizability*, (Dordrecht: D. Reidel, 1985), pp. 47–73; 'Imperfect Duty Situations, Moral Freedom, and Universalizability', in William Starr and Richard C. Taylor (eds.), *Moral Philosophy: Historical and Contemporary Essays* (Milwaukee, Wisc.: Marquette University Press, 1989), pp. 145–69; and 'Universalizability', in *Cambridge Dictionary of Philosophy*, 822–3; 2nd edn., pp. 940–1.

to raise questions about the relevant or related institution, in this case the institution of grading. In a system—an institution in another sense—in which the institution of grading did not exist, no such problems could arise. Where the institution operates under radically different rules—where, for example, there is only a pass/fail option—the only question that can arise is about student No. 3. Is this a reason for changing or abolishing the institution of grading? Someone who, confronted with a grading problem such as has been described, asks such questions as 'What are grades for, anyhow? What does a grade mean? How are grades used?' is raising questions about the institution of grading, not about a particular case—even if one is impelled to raise such questions as a consequence of considering a particular case. This may be perfectly sensible and appropriate. Then again it may not. For if one is operating within the confines of the institution of grading as it is determined in a particular institutional setting—that is, in a particular school or college—it may not be open to one, in those circumstances, to raise the question about the appropriateness, fairness, or reasonableness of the institution of grading. One might of course decide to subvert the institution—or 'the system', as it is so quaintly called— by giving everyone As, or most of them As and the rest Bs. Such a person would not, and could not, have any of the particular problems detailed. For one who does not accept or is in rebellion against the institution as it exists, there can be no moral problems arising *within* the institution. But another question arises, though our subversive grader might not recognize it, and that is whether anyone has the right to subvert the institution of grading in this way (especially given the network of institutions in which grading operates). Does the power to grade convey the right to grade in any way one pleases? Is this right or even sensible?

These last questions are institutional questions, and they arise for anyone with a moral sense in a setting in which the institution exists or is in operation, and who therefore comes within the scope of the institution, whether that person is predisposed to accept the rules of the institution or not—because others accept the rules and act on them and expect others to act on them; otherwise there could be no such institution.[4]

---

[4] The institution of grading has been to a considerable extent subverted in the US by the phenomenon of grade inflation, which started in the middle 1960s as a protest against the Vietnam War and as a way of subverting the draft, and has since taken wing in many if not most US colleges and universities, and, I am given to understand, even in high schools. The consequences of this are and have been serious. To put it another way, the 'impact' has been severe. A teacher of philosophy who hands out easy As and Bs is conveying the message that in philosophy no distinction can be made between work of quality and work of no or low quality, and this is a crime against philosophy itself.

Contrast the grading example with one taken from baseball, suggested by John Rawls. Though good reasons might be given for changing any rule of the game, such as the rule that three strikes are out, it is not open to a player in a particular game to argue that he ought to be allowed four strikes, even though it may be—supposing omniscience for a moment—that his having four strikes would have best results. Somehow, we feel, there is a difference, that it is absurd even to imagine the player pleading for another chance to hit, even though he has had three strikes already, whereas it is not absurd, or not as absurd, to imagine a student pleading to have his grade raised on the ground that this would get him something he needs or wants very badly, or even on the ground that this would have best results. What, if there is this difference, explains it?

In his earlier writings on this theme Rawls used the term 'practice' as a surrogate for 'institution', and defined 'practice' as 'a sort of technical term meaning any form of activity specified by a system of rules which define offices, roles, moves, penalties, defenses, and so on', and he gave 'as examples . . . games and rituals, trials and parliaments . . . markets and systems of property'.[5] In this sense, a technical sense, the existence of a practice implies the existence of rights and duties and of rules for determining them. But one ordinary sense of 'practice' that is worth noting is 'a regular, habitual, or customary doing', as in 'the practice of law', 'the practice of medicine', or 'the practice of one's religion', or even 'practicing the piano' or 'practicing swimming'. In this sense of 'practice' the existence of a practice does not imply the existence of rights and duties. There is no question that there are practices in this sense, in which practices are regular, habitual, or customary activities. There is also no doubt that this is not a primary sense; three of the examples I just used actually presuppose institutions—law, medicine, and religion.

What, then, is an institution? And what is the relevance of institutions to morals and moral philosophy? The latter question is more easily answered than the first.

---

[5] John Rawls, 'Two Concepts of Rules', *Philosophical Review*, 44 (1955), p. 3n., and 'Justice as Fairness', ibid. 47 (1958), p. 164n.; in *Papers*, pp. 20, 47. In *The Rationale of Legal Punishment* (New York: Humanities Press, 1966), ch. 3, sect. 2, pp. 53–6, Edmund L. Pincoffs provides an especially intriguing analysis of the distinction between practices and institutions. Although I was not persuaded by Pincoffs's arguments to shift my use of the term 'institution'—indeed, I am convinced that 'institution' is the right word for my purpose, while 'practice' would not be—these arguments are certainly worth considering. One reason for regarding 'institution' as preferable is this: Rawls defines a practice as 'any form of *activity*'; but property is not itself a form of activity, nor is marriage (as distinct from marrying), and neither is money; so they are not practices, yet they are all institutions. Again, the practice of law is one thing, and not what we want here; the institution of law is; and 'the practice of the Supreme Court' implies something quite different from 'the institution of the Supreme Court'.

Their relevance is twofold. First, in virtue of the existence of an institution in a given society, an action can have a moral quality that it otherwise might not, would not, or could not have. Some actions could not exist, could not be performed, could not be what they essentially are apart from some appropriate institution that defines them, that constitutes them as being what they are. I shall call an action 'defined by' or 'falling under' an institution (to use some expressions commonly used in this context) an 'institution-constituted action'. No action could be the breaking of a promise unless there were the institution of promising. There could be no theft without (the institution of) property, no adultery without (the institution of) marriage, no divorce either, though there could be murder, assault, viciousness, and kindness apart from any specific institutions. To understand better the character of the moral judgements that can be made about such institution-constituted actions, one must have an understanding of the presupposed institution.

Second, the character and quality of a society—of a culture, if you will—is determined by the character and quality of its characteristic institutions, which also play a role in moulding the character of the people of the society. Some institutions are common to all societies—are universal—some are common to most, some exist only in some societies and not in others. Criticism and evaluation of a society is criticism and evaluation of its characteristic institutions, as well as of the character and characteristic behaviour of its inhabitants. How can institutions themselves, as distinct from individual actions or kinds of actions, be judged and evaluated?

This is one basic question of institutional ethics, but it cannot be answered or even approached without getting straight on what institutions are, their essential nature and character. Hence this task is fundamental.

An institution is not the same as an organization, nor is it the same as an association, though a number of organizations and associations are also institutions. 'Cricket, five-o'clock tea, the House of Lords, Eton, the Workhouse, a hospital, the National Gallery, marriage, capital punishment, the Law Courts', to cite a list presented by Fowler, 'are all institutions'.[6] So they are, but they are, many of them, institutions of quite different kinds, and in many different senses of the term, and the fact that most of the ones listed exist only in Britain should help bring this out. The term 'institution' is one of those special terms whose importance is matched only by its ambiguity and the complexity of its conception.

---

[6] H. W. Fowler, *A Dictionary of Modern English Usage* (Oxford: Clarendon Press, 1926), p. 278.

I now set forth two definitions of 'institution', two alternative accounts of what is intended to be the same concept, not two different concepts. I am not altogether satisfied with either, and put them forward only as an aid in organizing the subject, as hypotheses to be tested.

An *institution* can be thought of as (1) a relatively permanent system of social relations organized around (that is, for the protection or attainment of) some social need or value; or as (2) a recognized and organized way of meeting a social need or desire or of satisfying a social purpose.

What both these definitions do is bring out the conception of an institution as an abstraction, as a complex of rules defining rights and duties, roles, functions, privileges, immunities, responsibilities, and services, and this is the main subject of institutional ethics, though it is not the sense of 'institution' that is at the forefront of ordinary, or even ordinary sociological, discourse about institutions. Neither the University of Wisconsin nor the First National Bank nor the *New York Times* is an institution in the sense intended. They are all, to be sure, institutions, but in some other sense of the term or on some other conception of an institution. They are what I call *concrete embodiments* of the institutions of the university, banking (or finance), and the press. Similar things can be said about the House of Lords, the National Gallery, Eton, and the Law Courts, even though it may not always be possible to specify the abstract institution that some more concrete institution is a concrete embodiment of—and I am actually not certain that there need be an abstract institution corresponding to every more concrete one (though naturally there would have to be for every one that is a concrete embodiment).

Thus the sense of 'social institution' primarily relevant to this subject is the sense in which law, property, punishment, marriage, the family, industry, money, advertising, religion, contract, and promising are institutions. Even here, there are differences among the institutions listed that may or may not correspond to differences of meaning and may or may not correspond to differences in the relevant and appropriate criteria of evaluation. For example, though the family—more precisely, a family—is an association of persons, property is not, even though it necessarily involves relations among persons. A stockbroker who handles institutional accounts may handle accounts for universities, corporations, unions, foundations, and other organizations, all of which are institutions in a perfectly proper and legitimate sense of this elusive term, but does not thereby handle accounts for the university, *the* corporation, *the* union, which are of necessity incapable of buying or selling or having accounts though they are nonetheless still institutions.

There are four or five different conceptions of an institution to be distinguished. There is, first, the sense in which marriage, property, money, and the press are institutions. This is the *abstraction* sense. Second, there is the sense in which corporate bodies, organizations, groups, or associations, such as Harvard University, the *Washington Post*, Leavenworth, the Mayo Clinic, and the Philadelphia Orchestra are institutions. This is the *concrete embodiment* sense. Third, there is a sense related to the influence and relative permanence or importance of the institution in the society. In this sense, only institutions in the concrete sense that are regarded as somehow more permanent, important, or influential are called institutions, and in this sense the *New York Times* is an institution while the local 'Daily Bugle' is not, and Carnegie Hall is an institution while the hall in which the local civic orchestra plays is not. I shall call this the *importance* sense. Fourth, there is a metaphorical sense in which some person of considerable fame, influence, importance, or reverence comes to be regarded as an institution; for example, Bernard Baruch, Bertrand Russell, Sol Hurok, Casey Stengel, Eleanor Roosevelt, Arturo Toscanini, and possibly John Wayne, at least while they were alive.[7] Fifth, certain buildings or complexes of buildings are sometimes referred to as institutions. The Flat Iron Building, the Empire State Building, the Eiffel Tower, and the Tower of London will serve as examples.[8] But this, I think, is not a separate sense of 'institution'. It seems to be some combination of the third, the importance sense, with the fourth, or *person* sense, and seems also to involve often a confusion of *institution* with *institute*. On this, Fowler has another interesting observation:

institution has seized, as abstract words will, on so many concrete senses that neatness is past praying for . . . An *institute* is deliberately founded; an *institution* may be so, or may have established itself or grown. A man leaves his fortune to institutions, but perhaps founds a parish or a mechanics' institute, i.e. an institution designed to give instruction or amusement to a special class of people. Whether a

---

[7] Consider the following remark: 'Arthur Fiedler is an established American institution, like baseball and politics, and like most such institutions can easily be taken for granted' (Michael Mark, *American Record Guide*, 47(1) (November 1977), p. 14). Arthur Fiedler was alive in 1977, is not now. Is he *now* an 'established American institution'? Of course, Arthur Fiedler was not at all like baseball and politics, and baseball and politics, as institutions, are very unlike each other, more unlike than baseball and cricket. Here is another instance. Harold C. Schonberg in an obituary notice said of Sol Hurok: 'He lived long enough to become an institution. He not only made news, through his activities in music; he himself was news' (*New York Times*, Sunday Arts and Leisure section, 10 March 1974).

[8] And so, until September 11th, were the twin towers of the World Trade Center in New York City.

particular institution founded for a definite purpose shall have *institute* or *institution* in its title is a matter of chance or fashion.[9]

I am inclined to think that all institutions in the importance sense (sense 3) are institutions in the concrete-embodiment sense (sense 2). But only the first two conceptions have special relevance to ethics, and the first, the abstraction sense, is primary. I proceed to give further examples, repeating some from before, of the sense or kind of institutions I have in mind. It should be evident that this set of institutions, far from complete, comprises an intersecting and overlapping network.

II

Examples of institutions (with concrete embodiments bracketed):

(1) Government, The State [The Presidency, The Legislature, Congress are concrete embodiments] [but 'the Presidency' is still an abstraction];

(2) Elections, The Constitution [The Constitution of the United States is a concrete embodiment of the institution of the constitution];

(3) Law, The Legal System, Courts of Law, The Decision, The Opinion [The Supreme Court, District Courts, Appellate Courts];

(4) Punishment, Capital Punishment, Imprisonment [The Electric Chair, Leavenworth];

(5) Property, Money, Private Property [The Dollar, The Pound, The Yen, The Euro are not concrete embodiments, only less abstract];

(6) Business, Industry, Finance, The Credit System, Debt, Money, Stocks, Bonds, The Stock Market, The Bond Market, The Market;

(7) Advertising, Public Relations, Propaganda, Persuasion;

(8) Education, The School, The University, Scholarship, Science;

(9) Marriage, The Family, Monogamy, Divorce, Annulment, Adoption;

(10) Religion, The Church, Monotheism [The Church in a concrete-embodiment sense];

(11) The Press, The Media, 'The Free Press';

(12) 'Freedom of Speech';

(13) Promises, Contracts, Covenants, Treaties;

[9] Fowler, *English Usage*, p. 27. Cf. the following remark: 'When the exile returns to Oxford, he visits his College—and Blackwell's. It is more than a great bookshop; it is an institution' (Ved Mehta, *John is Easy to Please* (New York: Farrar, Straus & Giroux, 1971), pp. 80–1, quoting an article in the *Observer*).

(14) Language, Writing, The Book, The Dictionary, The Encyclopaedia;
(15) The Internet, etc.;
(16) War, Conflict, The Strike;
(17) Negotiation, Bargaining, Arbitration, Mediation, Conciliation, Litigation, Legislation.

III

Note the following. First, promises (and promising) and language seem to have a special status, that of being necessary institutions, institutions necessary for there to be any society at all. This does not seem true of property or punishment. Second, institutions overlap: some are included in others, as sub-institutions. Thus monogamy is included in marriage, as a form of marriage. Others are not included as subsets, but are presupposed, as divorce presupposes marriage but is not a form of marriage.

In addition to overlappings and intersectings, and different senses and levels of institutions, we should notice that institutions are of different kinds: legal, political, economic, cultural, civic, aesthetic, religious, educational, military, and sporting, and still more. But *social* is not a species of institution; it is the genus. There is plenty of overlapping here as well. Thus property is both an economic and a legal institution; marriage is a religious, cultural, and legal institution. The museum can be both a cultural and a civic institution. War is a political and, obviously, a military institution, but also an educational and civic and technological one. Money is an economic and also a political and legal institution. Here again, though, there is no need to multiply examples.

We should notice two different senses of '*legal* institution'. In one sense, it is an institution defined or determined by the law, such as property, marriage, contract, torts, misdemeanour, and felony. In another sense, it is an institution necessary for the law to operate, such as courts, the trial, legislature, adjudication, etc. In still a third sense, on which I do not dwell, it can mean a lawful institution, and in this sense conforms to the systematic ambiguity of the expression 'legal rule', which can mean either a rule of law or a lawful—that is, not unlawful—rule. One question that arises in the study of institutions is this: if an institution, say property, is an instance of different kinds of institution—in this case, legal and economic, perhaps also political—does it take on different import or meaning when viewed separately as an instance of these different kinds? If so, how can it be determined which kind is predominant, and what difference would it make? (But I shall not stay for an answer.)

Even though a number of the examples I have supplied may ambiguously fall either into the abstraction sense or the concrete-embodiment sense, there is nonetheless a precise ground of distinction between the two categories. In the abstraction sense, an institution cannot act; it does not and cannot *do* anything; in the concrete-embodiment sense, an institution can act. Concrete embodiments are always associations, organizations, groups, or corporations, all of which, as we know, are capable of acting (though not necessarily of taking responsibility).[10] But it makes no sense to speak of property doing something, or the family, or law, or government (as distinct from *the* Government). And it is in the abstraction sense that actions are or can be institution-constituted (that is, fall under or presuppose an institution). Yet it should be noted, if only in passing, that institutions in the abstract sense can in a complicated way be said to have effects—or what we would think of as effects. Thus power can corrupt, as can money; property can demean, and convey power; and so forth. But the complicated way in which institutions can have effects, and hence serve as causal agents, needs analysis. There is certainly no mechanical cause-and-effect relationship operating. It is not power as such that corrupts, but the power possessed by some particular person in some particular position that tends to corrupt that specific person.

IV

I suggested before two definitions of institution: (1) a relatively permanent system of social relations organized around some social need or value; or (2) a recognized and organized way of meeting a social need or desire or of satisfying a social purpose. Although I am not altogether satisfied with these accounts, they seem to me to bring out the abstraction sense I am after and to do a better job than some others I have seen. Consider, for instance, the following alternative accounts:

---

[10] The law, especially the common law, often has trouble determining, especially in the case of a corporation, how or on whom sanctions are to be imposed, a problem on which some progress could be made by statutory means, though a further problem is that drafting the appropriate statutes precisely and fairly is a task that is notoriously difficult (and would no doubt be endlessly hampered by lobbyists with lots of money at their disposal).

[i] An institution is a pattern or framework of personal relationships within which a number of people cooperate, over a period of time and subject to certain rules, to satisfy a need, fulfil a purpose, or realize a value.[11]

There are some interesting points here, and I have learned a lot from contemplating this account, but it fails to fit property or law, seems modelled on the family or an organization of some sort.

[ii] 'Institution'... stands... for a form of social union... for the modes or organs through which forms of Society operate... An institution is a special society... It is an organization, created and sustained by individual wills, and equally creating and sustaining them ... *A* family, *a* church, *a* trade union, *a* University, *a* social club, *a* State—each of these is an institution.

Again, this is instructive, but on this account law and government, property and punishment, would not be institutions. Furthermore, it has the somewhat awkward consequence that each and every family is a distinct institution; thus my family is an institution, your family is another, her family is a third, his is a fourth, and so on. Although the number of institutions is probably beyond counting, this conception does seem to multiply institutions well beyond necessity.

One other alternative account is worth a brief look:

[iii] One general characteristic of complex societies is the development of a number of *institutions*— relatively self-contained social groups within which a number of different social careers are organized into a system. The term 'institution' ... here ... refers to actual social groups (such as governments, churches, and military organizations) which play important parts in the structure of large-scale societies. Institutions (in this sense) tend to be at least semipermanent; they are quite formally organized, often in a hierarchical manner. Within the institution is found a large variety of social roles which are linked into careers and authority relationships.

Although this is a perfectly legitimate conception of *institution*, and certainly an important one, it involves the sense of 'institution' in which it means a group or organization or corporation, a concrete embodiment of an institution in the abstraction sense. And again, such major institutions as punishment, property, and money would not count, on this account, as institutions, since none is a 'social group', actual or potential. And, while

---

[11] A. MacBeath, *Experiments in Living* (London: Macmillan , 1952), p. 73. Account (ii) is from H. J. W. Hetherington and J. H. Muirhead, *Social Purpose* (London: George Allen & Unwin, 1918), pp. 119–20; and account (iii) is from Philip K. Bock, *Modern Cultural Anthropology* (New York: Alfred A. Knopf, 1969), p. 157.

social groups can act, institutions, in the abstract sense, cannot. Their role is much more subtle. I do not disparage any of these other accounts. Each has merits for certain purposes. I have highlighted them here to bring out the conception of institutions on which I want to concentrate, which I regard as more central to ethics, and also incidentally to illustrate some of the fascinating complexity of the subject.

V

Money is certainly an institution. Here is an especially intriguing account of money:

> The money illusion is ancient and universal, present in every transaction and absolutely necessary to every exchange. Money is worthless unless everyone believes in it. A buyer could not possibly offer a piece of paper in exchange for real goods—food or clothing or tools—if the seller did not think the paper was really worth something. This shared illusion is as old as stone coins and wampum—is a power universally conferred by every society in history on any object that has ever been regarded as money: clamshells, dogs' teeth, tobacco, whiskey, cattle, the shiny metals called silver and gold, even paper, even numbers in an account book.
>
> Modern money . . . requires the same leap of faith, the same social consent the primitive societies gave to their money. Modern money, in fact, is even more distant from concrete reality. Over the centuries, the evolution of money has been a long and halting progression in which human societies have hesitantly transferred their money faith from one object to another, at each step moving farther away from real value and closer to pure abstraction.[12]

What I am interested in here is not the specific account given of money—as fascinating as it is—but the idea that 'money is an illusion', that 'money is worthless unless everyone [more accurately, I should think, *nearly* everyone] believes in it', that it is a 'shared illusion' and 'requires . . . [a] leap of faith'. (The idea of 'real value' that occurs in the passage, and its contrast with 'pure abstraction', and the attendant implication that money has no

---

[12] William Greider, *New Yorker*, 16 November 1987, p. 68, published since as *Secrets of the Temple: How the Federal Reserve Runs the Country* (New York: Simon & Schuster, 1987); the ideas in the quoted passage may be found on pp. 226–9. It is interesting that Greider does not adhere consistently to the idea of money as illusion (cf. pp. 242, 265, 453, 620, 673, 685, 688, and 714). Discussion of the consistency of Greider's ideas, however, is more appropriately reserved for a discourse explicitly on money. I have quoted his striking account of money because it is an observation on an especially interesting, unquestionably important, nearly universal, and certainly abstract institution, which may have application to other institutions as well.

'real value' and that 'pure abstractions' are not real, are ideas that in another context I should take issue with, but I here bypass them.) The question for us here is whether all institutions are 'shared illusions' (assuming that money is) or whether money is special or distinctive or unusual in this respect. But this characteristic of money, so dramatically described in this passage, is not shared by such institutions as the legal system, the injunction, imprisonment, or advertising. Advertising comes close, though it is not so much shared illusion as something that generates illusion. But it appears true of property—unless property is identified with land, yet that is obviously error. I do not think it true of marriage, or of promising, which marriage presupposes. It may be taken in some degree as applying to punishment, especially legal punishment such as imprisonment, in so far as in the so-called civilized world the system of punishment tends to operate largely with threats, which are often illusory.[13] The central characteristic of institutions that this account points to is the characteristic of shared beliefs and values and social purposes. And the concept of social relations, necessarily involved in the concept of an institution, though not an illusion by any means, is something very difficult to characterize exactly.[14]

VI

The question to be faced now is whether there really is a distinct branch of ethics to be called institutional ethics, which is what I am claiming. If the same principles that apply to actions (which I am calling individual principles) can apply to institutions, even in the most abstract sense, one incentive to the project at hand would seem to be removed. So is this so?

It is in some instances. Consider slavery, certainly an example of an institution even if not one that is current, approved of, or legal in this society (though it has unfortunately not been altogether eradicated from the world). Surely the ground—or a ground—for condemning slavery can be found in the Categorical Imperative, in either its Universality form or its

[13] I owe the thought behind this point to my colleague Claudia Card. If it is wrong, it is her error, not mine—a point I bring in to illustrate (in a somewhat twisty way, to be sure) something about the institution of responsibility, and also the academic institution of acknowledging intellectual debts.

[14] An interesting discussion, almost the first word on the topic, is provided by Peter Winch in *The Idea of a Social Science* (London: Routledge & Kegan Paul, 1958). But of course there are valuable discussions by Durkheim and Weber and others.

Humanity form.[15] Slavery is to be condemned (1) because its maxim could not be willed to be universal law, and also (2) because it involves treating human beings merely as means to ends in which they cannot share and to which they cannot (rationally) consent, and therefore not as ends in themselves. So even though slavery is an institution, and not either an action or a kind of action, it looks as though this individual principle of action more than suffices in application to it. No doubt a similar argument could work in application to a number of similar institutions.

However, it seems clear that it would not work for all. I do not see any parallel argument either for or against or even with respect to advertising, industry, property, or legal punishment. Punishment, of course, is an old figure in this game, since it has been the favourite institution exercising the ingenuity of moral philosophers for decades. What we need to look for are principles, or simply considerations, that apply to, throw light on, and serve as a basis for criticism and improvement of an institution—say education or the university or marriage or law—and not simply as a basis for a judgement that it ought or ought not to exist, be practised, or be tolerated. This sort of search will bring us into somewhat closer contact with our subject. The application of a moral principle is not an automatic matter in any case.

Consequently, even if individual principles, whatever they are, could be applied as they stand or with a minimum of modification to institutions, they would not meet the requirements of the problem. Intelligent appraisal and evaluation and critique and modification of an institution—of the sort exemplified by Tawney's work, whatever one thinks of his conclusions—requires more than merely applying an external standard to it, on a sort of litmus-paper model. It requires understanding the institution on its own terms.

VII

Let us consider now the criteria or standards for evaluation of institutions. These standards—the first three at least—will on the surface appear similar to if not identical with some standard principles of individual ethics. I mention four.

---

[15] 'Act only on that maxim that you can at the same time will to be a universal law', that is, a maxim that everyone can act on; and 'Treat everyone in every case always as an end in itself, never merely as means'.

1. *A utilitarian or consequentialist type.* This involves considering the consequences of an institution and its various alternative arrangements—including the alternative of not having anything like it at all—and judging which alternative has results that are best on the whole. This is an important consideration and I do not depreciate it. Indeed, I think utilitarianism understood this way makes better sense in application to institutions or practices than it does in application to actions. It is, however, terribly difficult to apply, if only because we lack the requisite knowledge, and because of the fairly external view it takes of the workings of an institution. By itself I should not think it would be anywhere near adequate.

2. *A functional evaluation* relates to the institution's end or purpose or function. This requires dealing with a number of questions. Does it meet its purpose? Does it meet it efficiently? What other consequences does it have—that is, what are its side effects? This involves something like a cost-benefit analysis, only it involves in addition the difficult task of figuring out what benefits and costs are, and this itself requires normative evaluation and can be done effectively only in the light of a knowledge of sensible alternatives and standards. Further questions present themselves. Just what is the function or purpose of the institution? Is this function itself good or worthwhile? We must, moreover, distinguish between what the function or purpose *is* and what it *ought to be*. With an institution this is neither easy nor obvious. Indeed, it may be that when we consider the purpose or function or ends of institutions the distinction between *is* and *ought* begins to break down, since they so readily merge into each other. Tawney says that

the purpose of industry is obvious. It is to supply man with things which are necessary, useful, or beautiful, and thus to bring life to body or spirit. In so far as it is governed by this end, it is among the most important of human activities. In so far as it is diverted from it . . . it possesses no more social significance than the orderly business of ants and bees, the strutting of peacocks, or the struggles of carnivorous animals over carrion.[16]

But this sounds to me, especially given Tawney's target in *The Acquisitive Society*, more an account of what the purpose of industry *ought to be*, or would be in a better arranged or functional society, than what it *is* in fact in the 'acquisitive society' Tawney was castigating, and in which we still in great measure live. Tawney also says that it 'is patent' that 'the purpose of industry is to provide the material foundation of a good social life', so that, consequently, 'any measure which makes that provision more effective, so long as it does not conflict with some still more important purpose, is wise,

[16] Tawney, *The Acquisitive Society*, p. 9.

and any institution which thwarts or encumbers it is foolish', and he goes on to say that 'It is foolish . . . to cripple education . . . for the sake of industry; for one of the uses of industry is to provide the wealth which may make possible better education' (pp. 96, 97; cf. p. 179). But *is* it patent or obvious? In 'the acquisitive society' the purpose of industry *is* to increase the monetary returns to shareholders; that is precisely Tawney's complaint against it.[17]

So the functional or Tawneyesque criterion is more complicated than it at first appears. In addition, given the definition of an institution as a recognized and organized way of meeting a social need or desire, with respect to any institution the question arises what social needs or desires it meets and whether these are worth meeting. What needs does it organize and satisfy, and do these needs deserve satisfaction? It is better not to try to finesse this question by definition or by the acclamation of something as obvious.

3. This teleological or functional standard actually merges with *a deontological standard* based on considerations of equity, justice, or fairness. Is the institution fair? Does it treat people fairly? Given that fairness can be a matter of degree, how fair, and how unfair? Even if needs are satisfied efficiently, are they being satisfied fairly? Some such principle as the Principle of Humanity comes into play here. The main objection to slavery is not that it is inefficient—that it may or may not be, and efficiency is not an altogether useless test in appraising institutions. But the major, and sufficient, objection to slavery is it is unjust, on grounds that this principle makes manifest.

This point is brought out in a striking way in a passage at the very beginning of Rawls's *Theory of Justice*:

Justice is the first virtue of social institutions, as truth is of systems of thought. A theory however elegant and economical must be rejected or revised if it is untrue; likewise laws and institutions no matter how efficient or well-arranged must be reformed or abolished if they are unjust. Each person possesses an inviolability founded on justice that even the welfare of society as a whole cannot override. For this reason justice denies that the loss of freedom for some is made right by a greater good shared by others.[18]

---

[17] The following statement aptly illustrates the complexity of these terms: 'The function of the press in society is to inform, but its role is to make money' (A. J. Liebling, *The Press* (New York: Ballantine, 1964), foreword, p. 7, para. 22). Suppose 'role' and 'function' were interchanged, to give: 'The role of the press in society is to inform, but its function is to make money.' This doesn't fit as well, and certainly would not say what Liebling wanted to say. Why not, and how are 'role' and 'function' to be defined?

[18] Rawls, *A Theory of Justice*, pp. 3–4. I have discussed this passage in some detail in 'Justice, Theory, and a Theory of Justice', *Philosophy of Science*, 44 (December 1977), pp. 594–618, at pp. 595–8.

4. Rawls's two *principles of justice* should be mentioned at this point, since they emphasize justness as fairness. In their first approximation they state:

First: each person is to have an equal right to the most extensive basic liberty compatible with a similar liberty for others. Second: social and economic inequalities are to be arranged so that they are both (a) reasonably expected to be to everyone's advantage, and (b) attached to positions and offices open to all. (p. 60)

Rawls emphasizes that these principles apply 'to the basic structure of society' (p. 61), 'to institutions' (p. 63), and insists that 'The principles of justice for institutions must not be confused with the principles which apply to individuals and their actions in particular circumstances' (p. 54). One might say that Rawls's theory of justice is an institutional ethics, except that it is much more than that, and also that there are questions of institutional ethics it does not touch on.

The relations among these various modes of institutional critique and evaluation need to be studied. In the tradition they are usually taken to be competing and at odds and irreconcilable. I think the tradition is mistaken. A society is a network of interrelated interlocking and interacting institutions and institutional arrangements, and responsible appraisal must consider the relation of this set of interrelations to institutional criticism. A change in one institution in a society—much like a change in one feature of a legal system—will almost inevitably bring about a change in others, and so on, indefinitely; these institutional consequences need to be taken into account and evaluated on sensible standards of evaluation; for in dealing with something as complex as a society or a social system what we face is *interaction*, not just cause and effect, even social cause and effect. And just as the distinction between *is* and *ought* tends to break down or merge when considering the functions of institutions, so too do the distinctions and supposedly sharp divisions between (or among) teleological, consequentialist, and deontological theories.

VIII

We come now to the problem of the inference gap, a central though certainly not the only problem of institutional ethics. The inference-gap thesis states that no moral judgement of an institution-constituted action follows from a moral judgement of the related institution. The converse thesis is that no moral judgement of an institution follows from a moral judgement of a related institution-constituted action. Is this thesis sound, and is it sound in all its multifarious forms?

Let us put to one side a question about a 'moral judgement following from' something. If something is genuinely a moral *judgement*, then, although inference enters into it—for where there is judgement there is always inference—it cannot strictly speaking be a deduction from anything; for if it is a deduction it is not a matter of judgement. But, as I said, let us put this to one side—and leave it there.

Example 1. Consider the institutional judgements (a) that slavery is unjust, or (b) that slavery ought to be abolished, and imagine we are living in a place where slavery is legal and in operation. Suppose you come to agree with one of these institutional judgements, yet find that you are the owner of slaves, perhaps by inheritance. What ought you to do? In particular, what ought you to do with your slaves? The inference-gap thesis states that no answer to this individual question can be deduced or derived or even inferred from the judgement of the institution. You might think, at first, that you ought to free them. But whether this is what you ought to do depends on a number of factors, including the other laws of the society in which you live—which may not make provision for freeing slaves, for instance—on the disposition of other 'free' people in your society—you might free your slaves only to have them in turn enslaved by Simon Legree; and on the condition, including the educational condition, of your slaves.

It might be thought that there is a difference between the judgement (a) that slavery is unjust and the judgement (b) that slavery ought to be abolished, on the ground that the second judgement implies that there is something that ought to be done, namely abolish slavery, whereas the first judgement, that slavery is unjust, does not imply that there is anything that ought to be done. I agree that there is a prima-facie difference. But this difference in this context is illusory and amounts to nothing. Normally the judgement that some arrangement is unjust implies, everything else being equal, that it ought to be either changed or abolished. But it should be especially noticed that slavery cannot be so changed as not to be unjust, so that with respect to slavery there is no point—no moral point—in talking about changing it though not abolishing it, though this is almost certainly a special case, not applicable to all institutions. So the institutional judgement that slavery is unjust, *tout court*, all things considered, implies that slavery ought to be abolished, and judgement (b), therefore, has no implications not possessed by judgement (a), since judgement (b) is implied by judgement (a). (The logical principle here is that whatever implies a given proposition implies everything implied by that proposition, an implication of the transitivity of implication.)

It is, I think, manifest that no answer to the individual question follows from the adverse judgement of the institution. All that follows is that one has a problem, of the form: What ought I to do, given that I have slaves and have arrived at the opinion that slavery is unjust (or that slavery ought to be abolished)? It does not even follow that you ought to work against or vote against slavery. If your society does not have the institution of voting, you cannot vote against it; if it lacks the institution of free speech, you might be endangering yourself as well as your slaves by working or speaking against slavery. Something ought to be done—that is plain. But *what* ought to be done is a problem, one not solvable by deduction or inference from the negative premiss about the institution. This serves only to generate the problem, not to solve it.

Example 2. Consider again the grading case. Suppose you conclude that grading is unjust or is an inefficient and not very useful educational device. Does that determine what you should do if you are called upon to turn in grades? No, it does not. For it does not follow that you ought not to turn in any grades at all. That would, in any educational institution with a grading requirement, be equivalent to turning in an F for all. And that would be to grade, in an especially harsh manner.

Similarly, to take the positive rather than the negative case, if you judge that the institution of grading, despite its defects, is in general fair and useful—depending of course on how it is administered—that by itself does not determine how you ought to act with respect to any of the supplicants in the grading case earlier presented. You still have the original problem. However, reflection on the purpose and function of grading might enable you to arrive at a more enlightened way of dealing with the matter than you could arrive at without such reflection.

Example 3. From (1) Boxing ought to be abolished it does not follow that (2) Michael Spinks and Mike Tyson ought not to have boxed.[19] In general, no statement like (2) follows from any statement like (1). A statement like

---

[19] This takes us back some years to the heavyweight title fight between then champion Mike Tyson and challenger Michael Spinks. The fight ended early in the first round with Tyson knocking out Spinks in nearly record time, and sports critics afterwards criticized the match as a mismatch which ought not to have been held, especially given the description by sports writers of Spinks as manifesting from the beginning a fear of getting into the ring with Tyson. Consequently my example '(2), Michael Spinks and Mike Tyson ought not to have boxed'. Of course, the names used here are only place-holders, and you are free to substitute any others, such as Ali and Frazier, who put on what boxing *aficionados* regarded as an outstanding fight.

(2) can follow only from some such statement as (3) No one ought to engage in or participate in boxing. But (3) is not an institutional judgement simply because an institution is mentioned in it. It is a general or universal individual judgement. And (3) No one ought to engage in or participate in boxing does not follow from (1) Boxing ought to be abolished.

Example 4. Let us go back a few years, to the period before the so-called 'Tax Reform Act' of 1986. Let us suppose that I am of opinion that the lower capital-gains-tax rate ought to be eliminated and that capital gains ought to be taxed at the same rate as ordinary income. Yet it would be foolish of me, if I have capital gains, not to declare them as such and take the lower tax rate on them. In any case, that I ought not to take the lower tax rate does not *follow* from, is in no way supported by, the adverse judgement of the institution.

Example 5. Consider the judgement (a) This is a bad law and ought to be repealed. Does it follow that (b) The judge ought not to apply this law in deciding this case? It seems plain that it does not. (a) might provide a reason for (b), but it certainly does not entail it. Nor, obviously, does (b) imply (a). Consider now (c) No judge ought to apply this law in deciding *any* case. (c) also does not follow from (a). Now consider (d) No judge ought to apply *any* law in deciding *any* case. (d) is incoherent. Yet (d) implies (c) No judge ought to apply this law in deciding any case, which in turn implies (b) The judge ought not to apply this law in deciding this case, so (d) implies (b). But this does not breach the inference-gap thesis. For (a) (This is a bad law) does not imply (b) (The judge ought not to apply this law in this case), and (b) does not imply (a). From 'The judge ought not to apply this law in deciding this case' it does not follow that this is a bad law and ought to be repealed.

Example 6 (which I provide at the risk of breaching Ockham's razor and multiplying examples beyond necessity). In the United States in recent years a movement has arisen for imposing term limits on occupants of certain elected offices, such as terms in Congress. Now imagine a Senator Whatsina who is in favour of instituting term limits by having a law passed that would limit members of the Senate to no more than two consecutive terms, has sponsored a bill to this effect which hasn't passed, and who has now served two terms and is running for a third. Does the judgement that term limits should be mandated by law imply that Senator Whatsina ought not to run (in the United States one cannot *stand* for office, or one would be bowled over by those running) for a third term? No, it does not. To be in favour of the institutional change, which, if it were in effect, would preclude Senator Whatsina from running for a third term, in no way implies that in the absence of such a law, which would apply to all senators alike, Senator Whatsina is bound by an individual judgement that precludes running again. For Senator Whatsina's original judgement was about an institution, and was not the self-referring individual judgement 'I ought not to serve more than two consecutive terms'. That Senator Whatsina ought to be limited to two terms because there ought to be a law limiting all senators to two terms as senator is not in any way a necessary statement, nor does it generate any presumption. The institutional judgement, however, is often confused with a general or universal judgement—in this case, 'No Senator ought to serve more than two consecutive terms'. This is not an institutional judgement; it is a universal moral judgement that applies to all individuals within its scope. The fact that it makes reference to an institution in no way implies that it is a judgement about an institution, an institutional judgement. Those who fallaciously infer individual judgements from institutional judgements are confusing a general moral judgement with an institutional one, a move that may be called 'the institutional fallacy' (a form of the fallacy of misplaced concreteness).

Example 7. I add one more example, because it illustrates the institutional fallacy so aptly. In a letter to the editor, a reader of *The New Republic* says:

> Michael Kinsley . . . wrote that he didn't support the federal tax deduction for mortgage interest, but nonetheless he took the deduction. Judging himself, Kinsley did not find his action . . . 'hypocritical'.[20]

Nor is there any reason why he should have; there is nothing hypocritical about it. The tax deduction is legally available, so why not take it? No one is under a legal or moral obligation not to, whatever his views on the institution are—though if one were running for office on a platform of repealing that deduction it would be politically impolitic to take it, so there might be a 'political', that is to say, prudential, obligation not to take it. Mr Kinsley did not advance the judgement that no one ought to take the federal tax deduction for mortgage interest; what he held was that the federal exemption ought to be repealed. The example speaks for itself as an example of the institutional fallacy, and is an instance of a widespread kind, infecting the world of politics and journalism. Yet there is not necessarily any moral or logical inconsistency, or even any incoherence, in condemning an institution and at the same time acting under it.[21]

---

[20] *New Republic,* 208, 1 March 1993, p. 5.

[21] Nor is there any redundancy in this sentence. Incoherence and inconsistency are not the same, and one can exist without the other. I argued this in 'Incoherence, Inconsistency, and Moral Theory', *Southern Journal of Philosophy*, 20 (Fall 1982), pp. 389–405.

There can be, in certain cases. For example, one who would condemn as immoral or unjust such an institution as slavery, while at the same time engaging in the slave trade or becoming a slave owner—not by inheritance but by purchase—would be a hypocrite, and is of course involved in an inconsistency. But this is a different sort of case.

Let us determine now what these examples illustrate and in the process demonstrate. Example (5), the judge example, illustrates both the inference-gap thesis and its converse. And on the basis of such examples as these I am convinced that its breach is a recurrent source of fallacious moral reasoning. So we are now in a position to state the inference-gap thesis more generally and precisely (which shows, incidentally, that generality is not always tied to vagueness):

(A) *Negative version*: From the 'fact' or judgement that some institution is immoral, unjust, or wrong nothing follows about what one should do in connection with it or even about whether one should or should not perform an act constituted by the institution.

(B) *Positive version*: From the truth or judgement that some institution is moral, just, or justified nothing follows about whether one should or should not perform an act constituted by the institution.

(C) *Converse negative version*: From the judgement that one ought not to act in a certain way that is constituted by an institution, it does not follow that there is anything wrong or immoral about the institution. Take an example from baseball: from the specific judgement that the player on first base ought not to steal second it does not follow that base-stealing—a technical term from the game of baseball—is wrong or that a rule should be adopted prohibiting it. Again, from the judgement that the judge ought not to sentence this defendant, who has been proved guilty, to death, it does not follow that the death penalty is wrong, odious, or immoral, or that it ought to be abolished.

(D) *Converse positive version*: From the judgement that the judge ought to sentence to death a defendant who has been duly found guilty it by no means follows that the death penalty is a good thing, that it is just, morally justified, or admirable.

These examples alone seem to me to show that the inference-gap thesis holds in its converse versions, so I will say no more about them. They do not, in any case, occur with any great frequency. The positive, non-converse, version, version (B), also seems almost self-evident, as illustrated by the grading example (Example 2). The first—negative non-converse—version is the one that generates the greatest difficulties, so I shall add this about it .

One plausible response to version (A) of the inference-gap thesis is that the premiss that, say, slavery is unjust or ought to be abolished generates a presumptive or prima-facie reason—not a conclusive reason—to conclude that one ought to do one thing or another, depending on the circumstances: free one's slaves if one has some, or work to eliminate slavery, speak or write against it, vote against it if voting is an option, and so on.[22] In general, on this view, an adverse judgement of an institution would provide a presumptive but not a conclusive reason for or against performing any one of a number of actions constituted by or defined by the institution—just which, would depend on the filling in of the concrete details. On this view, such a premiss would have the same relation to a practical conclusion that any consideration would have in practical or concrete moral reasoning. And, on this view, the inference-gap thesis would have no special relevance to institutional ethics, since a similar gap—if it is a gap—prevails in all or nearly all reasoning to a practical moral conclusion.

I conclude with the observation that the inference-gap thesis, if sound, is the first principle of institutional ethics. By this I mean, not that it is a supreme normative principle, but that it is the principle or condition on which the subject is founded. However, as I hope to have brought out, it is not the only principle of institutional ethics and the problem of determining its soundness is not the only problem connected with this topic. I am pleased to commend the subject to students of moral philosophy as a rewarding object of study.

APPENDIX

As mentioned above (Section IV), there are a number of competing accounts and conceptions of institutions. Two others, not heretofore listed, are worth mentioning.

One is *How Institutions Think*, by Mary Douglas (Syracuse, NY: Syracuse University Press, 1986). From the title alone it is clear that Mary Douglas's conception of institution is quite different from mine. I mention the work because it is very astute and important in further enquiry on this matter (see esp. pp. 46–7, 124–5).

The other is *The Institutions of Society*, by James K. Feibleman (1956) (New York: Humanities Press, 1968). This book contains a number of interesting ideas. 'Institution' is defined as

---

[22] This idea came out in discussion at Colgate University in March 1991. Unfortunately I cannot recall who brought it up. I suppose it does not in the end matter so much whose idea it was as that it is a very good point.

that subdivision of society which consists in human beings in groups established together with their customs, laws and material tools, and organized around a central aim or purpose. More briefly, an institution is an established social group working in customary ways with material tools on a common task.

Feibleman comes close to an important part of the conception advanced herein in part of the above definition and also when he goes on to recognize

as institutions two levels of social organization, the level in which 'education' is an institution, and the level in which 'Oxford University' is an institution. The family is an institution, and the Medici in Renaissance Italy may be said to have been one as well. Thus we are ordaining that the genus and the species of institutions shall share the classification (pp. 20–1; also p. 23)

There is much to be gained from each of the works just mentioned.

ADDITIONAL NOTES AND COMMENTS

A. 'Institutional Ethics' was a lecture given at the Royal Institute of Philosophy, 23 February 1993. Published in A. Phillips Griffiths (ed.), *Ethics* (Cambridge: Cambridge University Press, 1993), pp. 223–45, slightly revised for its appearance here. An earlier version, presented at the Inter-American Congress of Philosophy in Buenos Aires, 28 July 1989, was published in Spanish, under the title 'Etica Institucional', in *Analisis Filosofico*, 10 (November 1990), pp. 123–38.

B. John Watkins, who opened the discussion at the Royal Institute, raised a question about my statement that the inference-gap thesis is the first principle of institutional ethics. He said that this sounds odd, something like saying that the naturalistic fallacy is the first principle of ethics. I had to agree that it sounds odd, and added that this principle (if sound) establishes institutional ethics as a distinct branch of ethics, to be dealt with on its own and in its own right. But of course it is not itself a normative principle; it is a condition, and only in that sense a principle.

C. I said that 'there is [no] moral or logical inconsistency, or even incoherence, in condemning an institution and at the same time acting under it.' This may need some further elaboration. There is moral inconsistency, as well as hypocrisy, in condemning abortion, for example, and at the same time acting under it; that is, either having an abortion oneself or encouraging someone to have one. If abortion is conceived of as a type of action or activity rather than an institution, the objection would hold in an even more pronounced way. So take something that is unquestionably an institution—slavery, or capital punishment. There is some inconsistency in, on the one hand, condemning slavery, or capital punishment, and at the same time acting under it, as one would be doing if one were to advocate the death penalty for a convicted criminal (even such a one as Timothy

McVeigh), or to be engaged in the slave trade. On the other hand, there is no obvious inconsistency in condemning the institution of slavery while at the same time being the owner of slaves. I used this example deliberately because of its provocative character. As I mentioned in the text, there are all sorts of reasons why one might be in this predicament.

D. As I mentioned above, racism has been and in many places still is an institution of society, though it is hardly a constructive, just, or moral one. It is one of the legacies of slavery and, considering the prevalence of anti-Semitism and anti-Catholicism, of religious bigotry and superstition.

11

Moral Issues and Social Problems

1. Philosophy and Culture
2. Problems and Issues
3. The Moral Philosopher and the Moral Life
4. Settlements and Solutions

At the beginning of one of his inimitable discourses William James once said: 'I am only a philosopher, and there is only one thing that a philosopher can be relied on to do, and that is, to contradict other philosophers.'[1] In his succeeding discourse James himself departed from this theme. And so shall I. I shall not be contradicting other philosophers—at least not very often. What I aim to do is to take a fresh look at one of the main traditions in American philosophy for insight and illumination on a way of dealing with some of the most serious issues of our time. But before I turn to that, my main theme, I want to pursue for a bit some variations on another, the cultural relevance of philosophy; for, as I view the matter, they are related.

My main reason for pursuing this secondary theme arises from the occasion that called forth this essay, which was originally prepared for the Cowling Centennial Conference at Carleton College and was addressed to a general theme suggested by Bruce Kuklick's book *The Rise of American Philosophy*, which is about what has come to be called the Golden Age of American Philosophy, when James, Royce, and Santayana and other famous philosophers were at Harvard and helped make Harvard famous. Kuklick claims that these classical philosophers aimed to be, and actually were, culturally relevant, and he deplores the change to the professionalism of the present day. The theme suggested, then, was that of the cultural relevance of philosophy, what it is, was, and ought to be, and related matters. I shall deal partly with these, mostly with related matters.

---

[1] William James, 'Remarks at the Peace Banquet', *Memories and Studies* (New York: Longmans, Green, 1911), p. 299.

1. PHILOSOPHY AND CULTURE

How can a philosophy relate to a culture? There seem to be just four possibilities: (1) it can express the culture, (2) it can affect it, (3) it can both express it and affect it, so that there is interaction between them, or (4) it can be independent of it. And it can do any of the four in greater or less degree.

On the hypothesis that a philosophy relates to a culture in one of these ways we can go on to ask whether that is (a) a good thing, (b) a bad thing, or (c) mixed, or (d) indifferent. We can also ask whether the relations of a philosophy to a culture have anything to do with its truth or validity or fruitfulness or intrinsic value—these being intrinsic ways of evaluating a philosophy. We can ask further whether if a philosophy relates to a culture in any of the four ways mentioned, that is a good, bad, mixed, or indifferent thing *about the culture*. A culture, just like a philosophy, can be a subject of criticism, though it must be in different terms and on different grounds.

But we can also ask not what relation a philosophy *does* have to a culture, but what relations it *ought* to have. Thus it can be maintained that a philosophy *ought* to (5) express a culture, or (6) influence it, or (7) do both, or (8) be independent of it. Kuklick, however, seems simply to take it for granted that philosophy ought to be culturally relevant and that there is something wrong with a philosophy that is not. He seems never to consider that there may be something wrong with a culture that is uninterested in the problems of philosophy.

Philosophy does not *need* to be culturally relevant. It has its value in itself, and the idea that philosophy has to justify itself by contributing somehow to something else is itself a philosophy, and one that needs refuting. But philosophy surely *can* be culturally relevant, and there is one branch of it that ought to be—and that is moral philosophy. Even this is not to say that every moral philosopher must be concerned with the particular problems of the time. There can be never-ending fascination with the problems of morally neutral meta-ethics, assuming there is such a thing and that it is not in the end a dead end. (But if it is, that is something to be found out, and it is something that can be found out only through philosophical enquiry.) Philosophers are too much inclined to worry about accusations of fiddling while Rome burns, and thus to be defensive about their subject. But it is time philosophers quit being disturbed by this burned-out metaphor, and it is certainly time they quit using it themselves. The objection to Nero is not that he fiddled while Rome burned; he was not, after all, a member of the fire department. The objection to Nero is that he started the fire in the first place and then would not allow the fire department to put it out. The picture of Nero fiddling while Rome burns is a picture of Nero revelling in a holocaust for which he himself was responsible, and to suppose that such a charge could be applicable to philosophical enquiry is simply ludicrous.

Kuklick deplores what he calls the professionalization of philosophy, and correctly, I think, identifies 'one crucial dilemma of professional philosophy—its inability to communicate with a non-professional readership'.[2] But this is true in varying degrees of all disciplines in this increasingly specialized world. The professors of literature, though they write of works familiar to and of interest to educated persons and lovers of literature, do not themselves normally write works that fit that category. And one may wonder if Kuklick is altogether consistent in his attitude on this matter. For he complains that 'philosophers examined politics in light of their philosophical biases, and their emphases varied' (p. 441); one would think that if they were to examine politics as philosophers it *would* be in the light of their philosophies. If philosophy is automatically to be accounted biased, then how would it be a good thing for philosophy to be 'culturally relevant'? The remark just quoted is not just one of a kind. 'Their interpretations of the causes of world conflict reflected their metaphysical prejudices', we are told. What else would they reflect? (And why prejudices?) And it is hard to know what the complaint is when Kuklick says, of the philosophers of the World War I period—which is after the 'Golden Age' he has been celebrating—that their 'metaphysical positions . . . shaped their response to the war' (p. 445). How is a philosopher's philosophy to be 'culturally relevant' if it is not to determine that philosopher's response to war and peace and social problems and moral issues in general? If the complaint is that one's metaphysical and philosophical views generally *should not* shape one's response to social issues, then that is to say that philosophy should not attempt to be culturally relevant; for it can only be biased and prejudiced. Such a position is, if not unintelligible, certainly confused and hardly coherent.

But that is by the way. Given that a philosophy can relate to a culture as expressing or influencing it, the question arises whether a philosophy can have a distinctive national character. Is there such a thing as a distinctive national character? Relatively few philosophers have considered this matter, and their reports are mixed.

[2] Bruce Kuklick, *The Rise of American Philosophy: Cambridge Massachusetts, 1860–1930* (New Haven, Conn.: Yale University Press, 1977), p. xxvi.

John Dewey, for instance, after pointing out that 'It is easy to be foolish about the connection of thought with national life', said: 'But I do not see how anyone can question the distinctive national colour of English, or French, or German philosophies', and he went on to say:

Philosophy in America will be lost between apologetics for lost causes . . . or a scholastic, schematic formalism, unless it can somehow bring to consciousness America's own needs and its own implicit principle of successful action.

This was written in 1917, at a time when it was not uncommon for thinkers to regard the war then going on as a war not just between nations but between national philosophies. But Dewey was also thinking of what American philosophy must do in its own environment. He was emphasizing the need for philosophy to recover from—get over—the false and illusory problems, as he viewed them, on which it had been wasting its substance, and to 'identify itself with questions which actually arise in the vicissitudes of life'. 'Philosophy recovers itself', he said, 'when it ceases to be a device for dealing with problems of philosophers, and becomes a method, cultivated by philosophers, for dealing with the problems of men,'[3] and this was of the essence of his philosophy.

On the other hand, it seems also important that philosophy not entangle itself with the ephemeral problems of local time and place. William T. Harris, who founded the *Journal of Speculative Philosophy* in 1867, and who served for years as United States Commissioner of Education, said in the very first volume of that journal:

It is not 'American *thought*' so much as American *thinkers* that we want. To *think*, in the highest sense, is to transcend all *natural* limits—such as national peculiarities . . . to be *universal*, so that one can dissolve away the external hull and seize the substance itself.[4]

However, Harris went on, 'the peculiarities stand in the way'. They are, therefore, presumably to be surmounted. But this implies that there are such things as national peculiarities, even if it is not the office of philosophy to express them.

I may be missing some irreconcilable contradiction between these views of Dewey and Harris, but I do not think so. Taken together they illustrate the distinctive character of philosophy, which is at one and the same time both personal and impersonal. As Iris Murdoch has so sagely put it: 'To do

---

[3] John Dewey, 'The Need for a Recovery of Philosophy', in *Creative Intelligence: Essays in the Pragmatic Attitude* (New York: Holt, 1917), pp. 67, 65.
[4] W. T. Harris, *Journal of Speculative Philosophy* 1(4) (1867), Preface.

philosophy is to explore one's own temperament, and yet at the same time to attempt to discover the truth.'[5] And is not one's temperament to some extent determined, affected, influenced by one's cultural milieu, one's nationality, one's environment? Surely it must be. Though we are not products of our environment, we are surely products of our interaction with it. Hence it is more than possible for one's philosophy to be personal, national, and impersonal all at once.

Josiah Royce is one who had no doubts on the matter. For him William James was, as he put it, 'our national philosopher'. For, Royce held that a 'representative' philosopher is 'one who thinks for himself, fruitfully, with true independence, and with successful inventiveness, about problems of philosophy', and who 'gives utterance to philosophical ideas . . . characteristic of some stage and of some aspect of the spiritual life of his own people'. And Royce also held that James 'invented effectively and richly' and that 'in him certain characteristic aspects of our national civilization . . . found their voice'. 'James', said Royce, 'understood . . . shared, and . . . also transcended the American spirit. And just that is what most marks him as our national philosopher. If you want to estimate his philosophy of life in its best form', Royce went on, 'you must read or re-read, not the "Pragmatism", but the essays contained in the volume entitled "The Will to Believe".'[6] This last remark I think is profoundly true, and I will shortly show why.

Royce is not the only philosopher who has accorded James this exalted position. To take just one example, Paul Henle forty years later said that 'More than anyone else, William James stands in the eyes of the world as the representative American philosopher. His life (1842–1910) marks the period in which American academic thought ceased to follow European philosophy and displayed a marked originality. James himself contributed greatly to this development. His philosophy was distinctively American in its formulation and phraseology.'[7]

Although I myself have some questions about the meaning of such cultural generalizations as are involved in the notion of distinctive national traits and about how such generalizations are to be established, I do not propose to raise them here, but basically to accept this idea. In either its Jamesian or its Deweyan form, pragmatism is not unreasonably regarded as typically American in at least four respects: its inherent optimism; its

---

[5] Iris Murdoch, *The Sovereignty of Good* (New York: Schocken, 1971), p. 46.

[6] Josiah Royce, *William James and Other Essays on the Philosophy of Life* (New York: Macmillan, 1911), pp. 3–4, 7, 36.

[7] Paul Henle, 'William James', in Max Fisch (ed.), *Classic American Philosophers* (New York: Appleton-Century-Crofts, 1951), p. 115.

emphasis on action being necessary for the solution of problems; its allowing the values of a situation to be determined by the outcome of a working ongoing process rather than by fixed unalterable standards handed down from above; and in its looking forward to a changeable future rather than back to an unchangeable past. We find this unconscious pragmatism of American life given expression in an address in 1932 by Franklin Delano Roosevelt:

The country needs and, unless I mistake its temper, the country demands bold, persistent experimentation. It is common sense to take a method and try it; if it fails, admit it frankly and try another. But above all, try something. The millions who are in want will not stand by silently forever while the things to satisfy their needs are within easy reach.[8]

That is certainly an expression of the pragmatism that moves a large part of American civilization. And it has its own characteristic problems, to be sure. You cannot just 'try *something*'. You have to try something that has some reasonable chance of working and that will not have side-effects that will stultify its working. But this is something else.

2. PROBLEMS AND ISSUES

Throughout the history of moral philosophy the dominant view of its role has been that the moral philosopher is charged with helping to solve the moral problems of his society, that an interest in ethics is an interest in how one should live one's life, and that ethics aims at making life better, either by making people better or by making the world a better place in which to live or by some appropriate combination. This view has by no means been

---

[8] Franklin D. Roosevelt, *Looking Forward* (New York: John Day, p. 1933), 51. This was a commencement address delivered at Oglethorpe University, 22 May 1932. According to Raymond Moley (*After Seven Years* (New York and London: Harper, 1939), p. 24) the speech was drafted by Ernest Lindley; this does not make it any the less Roosevelt's. How much it represents Roosevelt's thinking is brought out by William E. Leuchtenburg in *Franklin D. Roosevelt and the New Deal* (New York and London: Harper & Row, 1963), pp. 344–45. Roosevelt was the William James of American politics. This assessment is borne out by Moley's narrative and assessments on pp. 385–97, and is not gainsaid by the fact that at the time he wrote this book Mr Moley was no longer a friend of Mr Roosevelt's. The connection between James and Roosevelt is more than coincidence. Though he was not a student of philosophy, Roosevelt was a pupil of James's at Harvard (cf. Moley, p. 174). Arthur Schlesinger, jun., has said of Roosevelt that 'he had the larger wisdom to resist consistency' (*The Crisis of the Old Order* (Boston: Houghton Mifflin, 1957), p. 420), and this was true of James as well. There are still other parallels.

universally accepted, which is of course not surprising—what philosophical view has been? But this is still my conception of it, and I want now in the light of this conception to develop a distinction between a moral *problem* and a moral *issue*, and to explore how moral issues link with *social* problems. I will then go on to consider some ideas for solving or settling moral issues originated by William James and developed by a few—but only a few—others. The theme is moral conflict and how to resolve it or how to live with it. The idea is basically the idea of negotiation as a means of settling conflicts of moral values and ideals, and not merely conflicts of interest.

A problem always arises out of conflicting considerations, and a moral problem is one that arises out of conflicting moral considerations, considerations about what is right or wrong or what ought to or may rightfully be done. The exact nature of a moral problem or question is not easy to determine, for there are philosophical and even moral differences about them. But let me say tentatively that something is a moral problem if (1) it calls for action of some kind to resolve it, (2) it substantially or materially affects the interests of others, and (3) one ought to take those interests into account in deciding what to do. This last provision, notice, makes the question of whether a problem is a moral one itself in part a moral question. This can be disputed, and in any case the provisions given are inexact and even involve some ambiguity. Must a moral problem involve the interests of others? Some would say so, and I have some inclination to think this way myself, but it can nonetheless be maintained that one has a moral problem where one feels that one's self-respect or sense of self-worth or self-esteem—in brief, one's character—is somehow at stake, whether the interests of another are involved or not.

A further question is whether a moral problem must necessarily involve or call for action or conduct. Can we not have or consider moral problems with reference to the past, where no action is called for or even possible? Of course. There is an ambiguity here, which can be resolved by an appropriate distinction. On the one hand, it seems clear that even though one can consider and even answer questions about the morality of some action that occurred in the past, nonetheless one can hardly *solve a moral problem—* that is, a moral problem—by merely uttering or forming a judgement. Action is required for the actual solution, and this is why moral problems are thought of as a species of practical problem rather than theoretical problem. A moral problem, in this usage, is a problem that occurs in actual living, and it is only by some modification of living—of one's situation or of oneself or one's relations to others—that the problem can be *solved* if it can be solved at all. If one merely *thinks* about what ought to be done or arrives at a conclusion about what ought to be done but does not *do* it, there is a perfectly clear sense in which one has not *solved* the problem—has not dealt with it—even though one may have been right about what the solution would have been.

But there are different levels and kinds of moral problem or question. At one level a problem is particular and personal and practical; it is the problem of this particular person in this particular situation, and this exact combination of circumstances is almost certain never to occur again. Here one asks 'What should I do?' or 'Would it be all right for me to do this, or am I obligated to do that?' The answer one arrives at will usually determine what one actually does, and it is the actual doing that constitutes solving the problem, not merely the answer one arrives at in one's head. But at another extreme one can consider some abstract and impersonal question about social policy or about something that has been done in the past, or the hypothetical question 'What should I do if I were in What's-his-name's place?', and here the answer one arrives at need not have any effect on conduct. Though these questions are certainly moral questions, they are not practical questions in the sense of requiring action for their solution; they are more like a species of theoretical questions. For the sake of keeping the distinction straight, we could call these latter moral *questions* instead of moral problems, and the ones that require action moral problems. But it would be equally useful to think of two species of moral problem, theoretical and practical; it makes no difference either way, as long as we have the difference in mind. In any case, between these two kinds of moral problem or question there is subtle gradation and variation, and moral problems can be raised at different levels of generality: one can ask about a particular action, or about a kind of action, or about what social policy should be with respect to a certain activity or practice.

It is a different matter, however, when different persons have made up their minds about what ought to be done and each tries to persuade the other to adopt his point of view or tries to affect law or public policy. Where there exist strong differences of opinion on opposing sides of some moral matter we have a moral *issue*, as I shall call it, rather than a moral *problem*, for there is something at *issue*. The discussions that are resorted to as means of settling them often turn into disputes, controversies, or conflicts, some of which, owing to the failure of other mutually agreed-on means of resolving them, may be resolved only by threats, intimidation, terrorism, or warfare—at least this is what the parties may resort to. Some of the most difficult problems of our time as of any time involve moral issues that have got out of hand in this way. For every issue on which opinion is inflamed, in which the controversy gets worse and degenerates into conflict—and every strongly felt difference of opinion on a moral matter has this tendency—the *society* has a problem, the problem of how best to resolve the issue. Thus every serious, strongly felt, and long-standing moral issue in a society constitutes a social problem, which in turn is itself a moral problem—a second-order moral problem—of how best and most effectively to settle the issue. The still unresolved controversy about abortion is but one example among many. The controversy over preferential hiring or reverse discrimination—describe it as you will—is another. In *ante-bellum* America the great issue was over the moral acceptability of slavery. This was *settled*—there is no longer any issue about the moral acceptability of slavery—but only by a terrible war.

From the point of view of the settlement of moral issues, arguments for the proposition that, say, abortion is or is not morally acceptable are not to the point. They do nothing to help settle the issue. To deal with the issue one must consider not the first-order question whether abortion is or is not morally permissible, but the second-order problem of how best to settle the controversy. With respect to such issues the task of moral philosophy is to devise hypotheses for settling them and procedures for testing these hypotheses. The decision in *Roe* v. *Wade*,[9] the landmark abortion case of 1973, looked for a time as though it might work in dampening controversy by effecting some sort of compromise among dangerously conflicting interests and philosophies. It turns out that it has not, and the abortion issue is with us still, in worse condition than it was before. So the job is still to be done. This aspect, this role, of ethics is often overlooked in debates on fundamental philosophical matters and practical discussions of first-order moral problems themselves. I am not suggesting that fundamental philosophical matters not be considered or that the consideration of the morality of some practice be put aside. But it is important to get straight on the exact nature of the problem one is dealing with. Considerations relevant to one level or type of problem may be irrelevant to another and may also be altogether irrelevant to the moral *issue* involved.

Consider again the different levels at which problems arise. I take abortion again as my example, because it fits the schematism very nicely. There is, first, the personal and most particular level, in which the question takes the form 'Should I have an abortion, or is it wrong to?' (At much the same level the question can take a hypothetical form 'If I were pregnant right

---

[9] *Roe* v. *Wade*, 410 US 113 (1973).

now, would I think it allowable to have an abortion?') Second, there is the general question, 'Is abortion wrong?' Third, there is the social-policy question 'Should there be a law prohibiting abortion?' or 'What should social policy be with respect to abortion?' Fourth, there is the issue, controversy, or dispute with respect to abortion. And fifth, there is the second-order problem with respect to abortion, of how this issue can best be settled. From the *issue* point of view the problem is: 'Given that there is this issue, this long-standing, deep-seated, and highly emotional and inflammatory issue in the society, what ought to be done about it?' This is a moral issue and at the same time a social problem, a problem for the society. Not all moral problems are in this sense social problems, nor are all moral issues necessarily social problems. A moral issue becomes a social problem when opinions on the matter get inflamed and the controversy degenerates into social conflict. The issue over slavery in the nineteenth century is an example of an issue reaching this extreme, but a society can be torn apart by measures short of civil war, as witness the conflict over American involvement in Vietnam. Some moral issues have a perennial character, others are transitory—though of course at the time they seem everlasting and dominant. Some get settled, and some get handled in a different way. To quote Dewey again: 'Intellectual progress usually occurs through sheer abandonment of questions together with . . . the alternatives they assume—an abandonment that results from their decreasing vitality and a change of urgent interest. We do not solve them: we get over them.'[10] Surely something similar occurs with moral issues and social problems, though some may never get solved and some may get over us. In the 1950s it was an issue in the United States whether communists should be permitted to teach, and a very emotional one it was too. It does not appear to be an issue now. We may have got over it.

Consider the following passage:

It is symptomatic of the breakdown of genuine party government that neither party has yet dared to take a strong stand on what is unquestionably the most discussed issue of the time . . . the parties have come to dodge the real issues which may be counted on to divide public opinion, instead of seeking for them.

This sounds familiar, might have been written yesterday, might be written tomorrow. But the book from which I am quoting was published in 1931, in the middle of the Hoover administration and the depression, and the writer was speaking of 'the moral, legal, and other difficulties into which Prohibition has plunged us'. Consider another passage from it:

[10] John Dewey, *The Influence of Darwin on Philosophy* (New York: Holt, 1910), p. 19.

We are not split in America today solely on the morality of taking a drink which contains alcohol. Mixed with that are questions of social welfare, of economics, of entrenched interests, of class distinction in legislation ... of personal liberty, of the real function of a Federal constitution ... of the conflict of different outlooks on life, of different ways of life.[11]

It is evident that we can get considerable insight into the nature of moral issues by examining how issues now dead but once alive were conceived by contemporaries, before the outcome—the issue in another sense—was known or could be known. And the elements mentioned are the elements involved in varying degrees in every moral issue or conflict. There is a split on the morality of some practice, that is, on some first-order matter, and this conflict goes along with conflicts of philosophy and often of interest. And very often when some such issue is settled by getting over it, as happened with Prohibition, the social problems that generated the original issue are not themselves solved, but remain, sometimes in a worse state. We now know what evils the Prohibition Amendment—'that experiment noble in purpose', as Herbert Hoover called it—led to. But we do not know what American life would be like today if Prohibition had not been tried and were still a live option with vehement advocates breaking saloon windows and setting fire to liquor stores because they opposed with great moral fervour the ready availability of alcohol to drivers, minors, wage earners, and incipient alcoholics. We should not forget that there were social problems that Prohibition was intended as a solution for, that though Prohibition was a nightmare it was not *ab initio* a piece of lunacy. At the end of World War I, thirty states out of forty-eight were legally 'dry'; the Constitutional amendment though it went nowhere did not come from nowhere. It was an attempt to solve a social problem; it failed, and in the process made things worse (which is at least one argument against the philosophy of taking a method and trying it and if it does not work putting it aside and trying something else). And in any case it never came near to addressing the original question of the morality of drinking or of the ready availability of alcoholic beverages.

How are moral issues, understood in this way, to be resolved or settled? One way, which has been used in different places with varying degrees of effectiveness, is illustrated in the story of the mid-nineteenth-century South American dictator who, on his deathbed, was asked to forgive his enemies. 'But, Father,' he said to the priest, 'I have no enemies. I have had them all killed.'[12]

---

[11] James Truslow Adams, *The Epic of America* (Boston: Little, Brown, 1931), pp. 394, 250.

[12] C. L. Sulzberger, *Go Gentle into the Night* (Englewood Cliffs, NJ: Prentice-Hall, 1976), p. 37.

We cannot expect always to be able to get over these things; the method of extermination just mentioned is not always available, and it is also of course not morally available. One of the conditions of the problem is to effect a resolution of it by bringing about a *settlement*, or a way of living with it and getting on if it is not settled, and this condition is not met by the liquidation of the opposition, which has other consequences as well. Thus we must consider further the conditions for the sensible resolution or settlement of moral issues.

3. THE MORAL PHILOSOPHER AND THE MORAL LIFE

I turn now to consider what we can learn about the resolution of moral issues from James's essay 'The Moral Philosopher and the Moral Life'. Originally presented as an address to the Yale Philosophical Club in 1891, the essay was first published that year and reprinted in 1897 in James's collection *The Will to Believe and Other Essays in Popular Philosophy*. The essay is rarely discussed and has had little to do in determining the subsequent course of moral philosophy, though it has played a key role in the development of pragmatic ethics. It is James's 'only published discussion of theoretical ethics', and James 'was disappointed at its reception'. In a letter to his brother Henry, James said: 'I gave the address last Monday to an audience of about a hundred, absolutely mute. Professor Ladd, who was my host, did not by a single syllable allude to the address after it was delivered, either on our walk home or the following morn. Apparently it was unmentionable.'[13] 'All intellectual work is the same—the artist feeds the public on his bleeding insides' was James's lament on this. I do not know how to account for the fact that the public at Yale were absolutely mute. Perhaps that was the custom there at the time. Or perhaps, more plausibly, it was because the essay is profoundly original and can easily be baffling and seem merely naive. It is pretty easy to read it as just another rendering of utilitarianism, and I must confess that for many years that was the way I understood it. But it is not.

Even Kuklick, normally so reliable, pays it no attention whatever, mentions it nowhere. Thus, although he alludes to the book *The Will to Believe*

---

[13] William James, *The Will to Believe and Other Essays in Popular Philosophy* (New York and London: Longmans, Green, 1897), pp. 184–215. Ralph Barton Perry, *The Thought and Character of William James*, ii (Boston, Mass.: Little, Brown, 1935), pp. 262, 274–5.

and Other Essays, he regards it as merely an assemblage of 'various addresses in which James ... made his philosophical attitude ... relevant to human life', and says, curiously, that 'A more substantial attempt was his 1902 *The Varieties of Religious Experience*' (p. 291). Kuklick also says that 'If we look to James as a pragmatist concerned with American life, our expectations ... go unfulfilled' (p. 309), which makes me, for one, wonder what those expectations could be. 'James', he says, 'did not even develop a reasoned account of moral judgment, and his social and political philosophy was negligible.... "The Moral Equivalent of War"', he thinks, 'is ... James's only statement on society ... the only hint we have of how he might have applied his concrete theorizing to the affairs of the polis.' All this is, in my estimation, quite wrong. Let us see why.

James sets out 'to show that there is no such thing possible as an ethical philosophy dogmatically made up in advance', that 'there can be no final truth in ethics any more than in physics' p. 184). James here is actually thinking not of moral philosophy as a whole but of what he calls 'the casuistic question' (p. 185). For he himself says that the upshot of his essay is that 'so far as the casuistic question goes, ethical science is just like physical science, and instead of being deducible all at once from abstract principles, must ... be ready to revise its conclusions from day to day' (p. 208). This is true enough. So far as casuistic questions go, of course they cannot be decided in advance of the facts of the circumstances and the consequences; very often it is just these facts that are the main source of uncertainty. What James is contending is that '*concrete ethics* cannot be final' (p. 210). Again—to be sure. Who would contend that we can settle tomorrow's questions today, before we even know what the questions are? But surely the moral philosophy James is advancing in his essay on moral philosophy is intended to be decided 'in advance', though he does not I suppose mean it to be decided dogmatically.

James points to 'a specific and independent sort of emotion' which makes us feel that something is 'hideous'. Philosophers in another clime and tradition would call this a moral sense. James speaks of 'subtilities of the moral sensibility'. This emotion appears in the famous lost-soul example, in which the hypothesis is offered us of a world that outdoes in bliss and good fortune all the schemes of Utopia that have ever been dreamt, 'and millions kept permanently happy on the one simple condition that a certain lost soul on the far-off edge of things should lead a life of lonely torture'. James claims that some 'specific and independent sort of emotion ... would make us immediately feel, even though an impulse arose in us to clutch at the happiness so offered', that 'its enjoyment when deliberately accepted as the fruit of such a bargain' would be *hideous* (p. 188). We *feel* it would be hideous, and for us then who so feel it is. This is a moral feeling which makes a moral claim, and the recognition of this is altogether independent of utilitarian calculation.

James claims that every claim creates an obligation and that there is no such thing as the 'validity' of a claim that 'gives it its obligatory character', certainly no validity 'outside of the claim's mere existence as a matter of fact':

Take any demand, however slight, which any creature, however weak, may make. Ought it not, for its own sole sake, to be satisfied? If not, prove why not. The only possible kind of proof you could adduce would be the exhibition of another creature who should make a demand that ran the other way. The only possible reason there can be why any phenomenon ought to exist is that such a phenomenon actually is desired. (p. 195)

I must say that on this point I part company with James. James is determined to be radically empiricist, and this metaphysical conception—or preconception—seems to him to preclude any independent standard of validity. I do not know what is supposed to establish this, apart from some rhetorical questions, and in any case James is himself (as we shall see in a moment) not consistent with it. Still, though I have chosen to express some disagreement on this matter, this matter is only preliminary and not essential to what I find of most importance in James's essay. And there is still further preliminary matter, such as his claim that all demands as such are 'prima facie respectable', no matter whose demands they are and no matter what they are demands for, and therefore have a claim and create an obligation to be gratified, and 'the best simply imaginary world would be one in which *every* demand was gratified as soon as made'. But that world is simply imaginary, and our world is clearly not that world, since in our world desires not only conflict, but for every end of desire there is some other end of desire in conflict with it, 'and the casuistic question here is most tragically practical' (p. 202).

We are now close to the heart of what it is in James's view to which I want to draw attention. James says that 'the guiding principle for ethical philosophy' is 'simply to satisfy at all times as many demands as we can'. And here we must have James's exact though inexact language:

That act must be the best act, accordingly, which makes for the *best whole in the sense of awakening the least sum* of *dissatisfactions*. In the casuistic scale, therefore, those ideals must be written highest which *prevail at the least cost*, or *by whose realization the least possible number of other ideals are destroyed*. Since victory and defeat there must be, the victory to be philosophically prayed for is that of the *more inclusive side*—of the side which even in the hour of triumph will to some degree do justice to the ideals in which the vanquished party's interests lay ... *Invent some manner of realizing your own ideals which will also satisfy the alien demands*—that and that only is the path of peace. (p. 205)

Now, as before, though this sounds like utilitarianism, it is not. 'Satisfy as many demands as we can' is not the same as 'maximize satisfactions', though it sounds it. The 'best whole', for James, is not the one in which happiness or utility is maximized, no matter who suffers thereby, but the one in which there is along with satisfaction the least dissatisfaction. James says '*by whose realization the least possible number of other ideals are destroyed*'. This is *inclusiveness*, an ideal of an inclusive harmony, and it is the ideal (or the demand) of inclusiveness that is violated in the lost-soul example. Utilitarianism can accept the lost soul at the far-off edge of things, so long as this condition maximizes utility, as it can accept slavery so long as this maximizes utility. But a 'specifically moral sensibility' intervenes and pronounces this condition 'hideous ... when deliberately accepted as the fruit of such a bargain'.

The distinctive feature of James's account is his idea that what we must do is '*invent* some manner of realizing our own ideals which will also satisfy the alien demands'. James thinks that 'that and that only is the path of peace', but that is an exaggeration. The tyrant who had no enemies because he had had them all killed had found a path to peace, both inner and outer. But he lacked the 'specific and independent sort of emotion', the 'subtilities of the moral sensibility'. And James's point is that this moral sensibility makes its own demands which must be satisfied on 'the path of peace', that any settlement that excludes it is not 'the more inclusive side'. '*Invent some manner*', James says. That is, find some way, come up with some idea, develop and try some hypothesis about what will work to attain this aim of satisfying all demands, including the specifically moral demand, at the least cost now and hereafter. But the hypothesis must then be tested by being tried, and all this is an empirical process, not one that can be deduced from axioms postulated in advance of the process itself.

In application to moral issues, then, one is enjoined by this pragmatic method to think of and to try some way of settling the issue that will answer to all the interests involved—one of the interests involved always being the interest in this sort of settlement itself. James of course talks at times as though any demand whatever is entitled to satisfaction, simply because there is, he thinks, no basis for entitlement independent of this process. But he is not consistent with this anarchic idea, nor do I think he can be. For one thing, some demands would strike us as hideous, monstrous, vicious, and mean, and therefore as not entitled to satisfaction. For another, James himself recognizes that there are formal conditions that a moral settlement must meet. Thus he says that 'every ethical principle must be treated . . . as a rule good for all men alike' (p. 99), and he says of some rule which he proceeds to reject on this basis that 'if it be treated as every ethical principle must be treated—namely, as a rule good for all men alike—its general observance would lead to its practical refutation by bringing about a general deadlock' (p. 99). This is, of course, the well-known generalization test, and I am happy—I in particular am happy—to see James acknowledging it as a moral condition imposed on experience and not as one derived from it. But it is inconsistent with the anarchic empiricist idea that 'everything which is demanded is by that fact a good', with the idea that 'the guiding principle . . . must . . . be simply to satisfy at all times as many demands as we can', and with the idea that there is no adequate basis on which any demand can be judged morally invalid.

But this is something else, and what we are to consider here is this: Given the existence of moral issues, of moral strife and controversies, how can they best be settled? James's explicit suggestion is that we must look for some hypothesis, some proposal, some basis on which the parties to the conflict can agree, and of course there is no guarantee in advance that such a way can be found. Some people do not prefer peace, would rather fight. On this we have much testimony, of which I give only this one instance:

The greatest joy a man can know is to conquer his enemies and drive them before him. To ride their horses and take away their possessions. To see the faces of those who were dear to them bedewed in tears, and to clasp their wives and daughters in his arms.[14]

The name of this gay philosopher was Genghis Khan. If your conflict is with a Genghis Khan no peaceful settlement is available, and here, at least, if nowhere else, 'winning isn't everything, it's the only thing'.

James's implicit suggestion is that what is morally right or wrong—the rights and duties of the various parties, to an actual controversy or conflict—can be determined, and morally ought to be determined, by a process of negotiation, bargaining, or compromise. For the alternative to this process—abstract discussion of right and wrong being of no avail—is war. And war is itself a means—sometimes a very effective means—of settling disputes. Of course it does not always, and very often war itself has to

---

[14] Sulzberger, loc. cit.

be terminated by some form of negotiation process. But war still does work on occasion, and very often after a war or a series of wars the relative positions of the parties, their rights and duties with respect to one another, are drastically changed, sometimes irreversibly. Given that there are situations where this is *the* alternative to negotiation (or other devices that are occasionally brought in when direct negotiation fails, such as mediation and arbitration) there is often no rational alternative to negotiation.

James's implicit suggestion was picked up and made explicit by Sidney Hook in an address called 'Pragmatism and the Tragic Sense of Life'. Hook is considering methods of resolving moral conflicts and he discusses what he calls (following Dewey) 'the method of creative intelligence', which

tries to make it possible for men to live with the tragic conflict of goods and rights and duties, to mediate not by arbitrary fiat but through informed and responsible decision. Whoever uses this method must find his way among all the conflicting claims . . . The hope is that as much as possible of each claim may be incorporated in some inclusive or shared interest which is accepted because the alternatives are less satisfactory . . . Every mediation entails some sacrifice . . . Faced by a momentous conflict of values in which some value must give way if the situation is to be resolved, the rational approach is to find some encompassing value on the basis of some shared interest. This . . . involves willingness to negotiate.[15]

Hook goes on to note that there are occasions on which, and parties with which, negotiation is not available. Genghis Khan will serve as one example. Adolf Hitler would be another. But if we consider the moral issues and conflicts between opposing groups in the same culture or society, it must, I should think, always be at least postulated that negotiation is available, that it may be the only means available for solving the social problem set by the inflamed moral issue. Of course, sometimes this is not so. Occasionally legislation works this way. But this is rare, and depends on how the legislation was enacted and how the process is perceived. More often some judicial decision, which threads its way among and between the competing claims and interests and accords some validity and some vindication to each, has this effect. I earlier mentioned the decision in *Roe* v. *Wade*, with respect to abortion. A somewhat later one was the decision in the famous *Bakke Case* in 1978,[16] which was so complicated as to seem more an act of God than a deliberate judicial decision, and which in fact did more to calm

---

[15] Sidney Hook, 'Pragmatism and the Tragic Sense of Life', *Proceedings and Addresses of the American Philosophical Association, 1959–1960*, xxxiii (Yellow Springs, Ohio: Antioch Press, 1960), pp. 19–20, 23.

[16] *Regents of the University of California* v. *Bakke*, 438 US 265 (1978).

the atmosphere over preferential treatment or reverse discrimination than anything else that had been proposed or applied. It may be thought that this is not the function of a court, that the function of a court is simply to settle disputes and not so to arrange things that all parties to disputes come away feeling somewhat vindicated and at least partially satisfied with the decision. It is very true that the function of courts of law is to decide cases—settle disputes—and that very often the outcome of a trial is victory for one party, defeat for the other. But an appellate court, and especially the Supreme Court, is not a trial court. It deals with large issues, of national interest, not *merely* the dispute between the two particular parties before it. In adjudicating the dispute between the two parties, the court is often negotiating a complicated route between wider conflicting interests and ideals. This is what was attempted in *Roe* v. *Wade*, and this in part is what was accomplished—so it appears at the moment—in *Bakke*.

James's essay had considerable influence on Ralph Barton Perry's *General Theory of Value*, and in this work (though not in Perry's general theory of value itself) we can find further illumination on the matter with which we are dealing. Perry amplifies James's contention that there is a 'species of conscience possessed of moral insight' at work in the lost-soul example. When he imagines the situation he experiences 'the firm conviction that the happiness of a million somehow fails utterly to compensate or even to mitigate the torture of one', and this conviction 'involves the rejection of a plausible alternative', which I take to be the utilitarian alternative. For:

It would seem that the happiness of the millions ought so far to outweigh the torture of the lost soul as to reduce the latter to a negligible quantity. One *ought* to comment favourably on the thrifty expedient by which so much good is purchased at so small a price. But no such judgment occurs . . . The claims of the lost soul and the happy millions are incommensurable . . . [and] the situation is not affected by adding persons to either side of the equation . . . The evil of the lost soul is pure, stark, unmitigated and unrelieved.[17]

What then should be done? Perry says the solution of the problem is provided by the 'postulate of concurrence', which is suggested by 'the sentiment . . . James describes': 'We are compelled to go out to that lonely sufferer and *bring him in*', make him part of the community that had been thriving through his suffering. And we do this, we are told, by appealing 'to

---

[17] Ralph Barton Perry, *General Theory of Value* (Cambridge, Mass.: Harvard University Press, 1926), pp. 670–2.

the fortunate so to alter or moderate their claims as to make them consistent with those of the unfortunate'. Exactly how this is to be accomplished
is not something for which we are treated to a blueprint, and it would seem
as though in even postulating the possibility of such a harmonious resolution Perry is departing from the specifications of the lost-soul example. For
what would happen to the happiness the millions are enjoying solely on
condition that one poor lost soul on the edge of existence—and therefore
not noticeable—shall suffer a life of lonely torture? The condition no
longer met, it would seem that the bliss would cease, or else that the one
lonely sufferer is simply replaced by another. Perry does not consider how
to apply the example to the actual conditions of life, which are themselves
mysterious enough, but after all the whole point of the example was to
determine if it would elicit the 'specifical and independent' moral emotion,
the moral sensibility, independent of considerations of bargaining or utility, and that it does, at least in those possessed of moral sensibility. So I see
no need to pursue it further. What is of special interest here is Perry's claim
that we have found a solution to moral conflict 'when, and only when, the
wills of all are so attuned that each is content with a situation in which provision is made for all' (p. 672).

This principle or postulate of concurrence, then, suggests an idea of the
conditions under which a moral conflict or issue *is solved*. Using a phrase
made famous by Woodrow Wilson, Perry says that 'Whatever may be true
of the decision of war, a *solution* of conflict is to be found only in a "peace
without victory"; that is, when those who formerly protested now concur
. . . A conflict of interest can be *solved* only when the conflicting parties are
brought into agreement' (pp. 672–3). Three observations are here in order.

First, James's lost-soul example may be taken as a metaphor for human
society, though of course in human society the enjoyment of the many is not
usually '*deliberately* accepted as the fruit of such a bargain'. But in every society there are people who lead lives of pain and suffering and want that others
may have their fill and more. The problem of poverty in the midst of plenty
has not yet been solved, and is an affront to the sense of justice. Yet, as Max
Beerbohm observed: 'Somehow, our sense of justice never turns in its sleep
till long after the sense of injustice in others has been thoroughly aroused; nor
is it ever up and doing till those others have begun to make themselves thoroughly disagreeable.'[18] This, as should be obvious, generates conflict.

Second, though consent or concurrence may be a necessary condition
for the solution of moral conflicts, it clearly is not sufficient. It depends on

---

[18] Max Beerbohm, *And Even Now* (New York: Dutton, 1921), p. 172.

how the agreement or concurrence is obtained. Was it attained by reasoned methods, or by the methods of the huckster, promoter, trickster, confidence man or propagandist? Is the consent informed and free, or is it sicklied o'er with the hard cake of custom? Concurrence may suffice to settle an issue in the sense of making it go away. It can terminate a dispute, certainly, and often of course that is very important and may be all-important. But does it *solve* it? Not if the consent is not free and informed—two very difficult conceptions to be sure, and conceptions that very probably embody a moral idea. If they do, then whether a conflict has been solved, as distinct from being brought to an end, is not a simple matter of fact.

Third, if a moral conflict 'can be solved only when the conflicting parties are brought into agreement', then not all moral conflicts can be solved. Settled, perhaps, in the sense of terminated; some we might get over, if we are lucky; but some we may have to live with. We may then hope at least to learn from them. But that is not to solve them.

I cannot leave this subject without some brief reference to Kuklick's curious attitude towards Perry. Evidently Perry for him is a transitional figure, an establishment type, a professionalizer, and someone who supported the United States's entry into World War I and is therefore to be castigated. Thus, though he has a fairly reliable account of Perry's book, he says of it: '*General Theory of Value* was a dreary book . . . Its seven hundred pages of small type were closely reasoned' (p. 508). (Philosophers take note!) And Perry, he says, 'was not pretending to deal with actual moral conflict' (p. 513). It is hard to know what to make of this. Surely what Perry was saying, the philosophy he was developing, is *relevant* to 'actual moral conflict'. What more is wanted?

4. SETTLEMENTS AND SOLUTIONS

I want now to say something, but only something, about the conditions that must be met in the solution or settlement of a moral issue. The following are among them, though I should not put this list forward as complete. The question is just now being raised, and I cannot suppose that it can so easily be settled.

(1) The matter at issue must be considered in its context and in the light of its history and development.

(2) It must also be considered in comparison with alternatives—not ideal alternatives but ones actually available. It does no good, for example,

merely to argue against capital punishment, without specifying what the alternative is to be; and if it is to be imprisonment for some definite or indefinite term of years, it is irresponsible not to consider what imprisonment is actually like, given the actual state of the prisons, and what it does, and whether that is actually a more desirable alternative than the death penalty. The point is that if one is dealing with actual moral issues instead of make-believe ones, one must consider them in actuality and not in imagination. This calls for the determination of difficult facts, but there is no real alternative.

(3) Along with considering alternatives one must also consider consequences. The danger now is that all these matters will get thought of in terms of rights only, and that consequences will be neglected altogether. This is happening with such issues as abortion and preferential treatment. We should not allow the acknowledged defects of utilitarianism to blind us to the merits of considering consequences. There is something refreshing and right about asking 'What would happen if it did—or if it didn't?'. The trouble is, of course, that very often consequences cannot be known or even reliably estimated. This is the situation with the issue of nuclear energy and with the problem of world hunger. We just don't know what the consequences in fact would be of going nuclear, say, or of cutting out nuclear power altogether. The partisans, of course, claim to know, very often at the tops of their voices. That is part of the problem.

(4) The issue at hand should be considered not in isolation, as if it were the only issue and social problem there is, but systematically, in connection with other issues on which it may have bearing. This is one reason why there is need for an adequate taxonomy of issues and problems.

(5) The issue at hand must also be considered in relation to the interests affected and at stake. Merely to consider the interests affected is not sufficient by itself. But it is necessary if there is to be a *resolution* of the issue as distinct from merely disposing of it for a time.

(6) It must also, if it is to deserve the name of resolution, be in accordance with fundamental moral principles, though presumably if it is an issue capable of resolution by means other than warfare or threats of war the parties already accept some fundamental moral principles.

To consider moral issues in their context and in relation to one another is to consider them philosophically, and this is the distinctive sort of enlightenment philosophy can bring to these matters, not the idle arguments for one side or the other in partisan spirit divorced from context and alternatives—though to be sure enlightenment often comes out of debating contexts—and not the furious and spurious moralizing that so often takes the place even of debate. In other words, the issue must be considered in the light of a theory, and this is the role of the moral philosopher, and the moral relevance of moral philosophy.

ADDITIONAL NOTES AND COMMENTS

A. 'Moral Issues and Social Problems' was presented as a lead symposium paper at the Cowling Centennial Conference, Carleton College, Northfield, Minnesota, on 19 September 1980. Originally published in *Philosophy*, 60 (January 1985), pp. 5–26.

B. My commentators at Carleton College, J. M. Hinton and George Mavrodes, helped generate a good discussion. The latter kept misconstruing the title of the paper as 'Moral Problems and Social Issues', which helped make me aware of the various ways in which the word 'issue' is used, overused, and misused. Someone might say, for example, 'I have an issue with my health', which doesn't mean that she is having a dispute with her health; or, to take another example, 'I don't have any issues with my car any more', which does not mean that she no longer has disagreements with her car. 'Issues' has come to be used as a surrogate for ideas, points, policies, or programmes, as in 'These are Republican issues', and so on. There is really no point in arguing with the use, or misuse, of a term. One might as well argue with the tides. But that does not mean it is not worth pointing out.

C. Mr Hinton did discuss, in an illuminating way, another use of 'issues'. He said (here I paraphrase from his unpublished paper) that, although there was nothing wrong with my use of 'issue', there is another use of the term 'issue', its use to mean 'the point in question', so that in this use 'settling the issue' would mean deciding the question, answering the question rightly, in a sense that has nothing to do with whether a controversy has been settled or terminated. For, as we all know, some issues can be decided or settled conclusively even though controversy about them continues. This is quite right, and is a very good point. It is just not the sense of 'issue' in which I was primarily interested. To mark off this sense of 'issue', in which an issue is practically identical with a problem, I should prefer to speak of a 'question', leaving the question open whether what is at issue, or in question, is an issue or a problem.

D. It was not my intention to make abortion the central topic of discussion, though perhaps I should have anticipated that it might become so. I merely used it as a convenient example for laying out the different levels of problems. Unfortunately it may not have been so convenient, for a good deal of the discussion at Carleton focused on abortion, perhaps a sign of how inflamed the issue has become. Still, my aim is to distinguish between moral issues and social problems, not to deal with any one problem or issue. This illustrates how the social problems that arise out of moral issues that get inflamed are also moral problems, moral problems for the society. But we must develop the capacity of dealing with inflamed issues dispassionately.

E. With respect to the distinction of different levels of problems, where I used abortion as my example, it was once suggested by one of my students that there is a level or type of problem I had overlooked, namely, 'Whose choice is it?' or 'Who should (have the right to) decide whether someone should have an abortion?' This is the position of those who say they are 'pro-choice' though not necessarily pro-abortion. This is interesting, but one problem with putting the matter in this way is that it is in danger of begging the question of the morality of abortion. If abortion were morally only presumptively wrong, this question could have unquestioned right of entry. But *if* abortion is morally wrong, wrong in every instance (except perhaps in such possibly excusing conditions as rape or incest), no one by *choosing* to have an abortion can make it right, nor can someone make it right by advising someone to have one. The *if* here is all-important. And this point, as should be evident, is perfectly general, does not apply solely to abortion, as inflammatory as that issue is. No one by choosing or merely exercising the power of choice can make right what is wrong. Still, this is an interesting point to consider, which a discussion devoted primarily to abortion must take account of.

On the other hand (in these matters there is always another hand—sometimes even more than one), it is possible that abortion is a special case. This is suggested by the following statement by Ann Jordan of the International Human Rights Law Group: 'We don't support a woman's right to choose because we think abortion is a great thing, but because we believe fundamentally that women should have control over their own reproductive capacity' (quoted by Leah Platt in *American Prospect*, 12(2), [July 2–16, 2001], special insert on 'The Face of Globalism', p. 14). The implication is that abortion is a special case, involving control by women 'over their own reproductive capacity'. If so—and this requires further investigation—then the principle that if an action or a kind of action is wrong, then one cannot make it right by choosing to perform it—which one would think would hold universally if at all—would require some qualification.

F. Consider the latest controversy generated by scientific developments, one which has certain connections to the debate over abortion. This is the issue over embryonic stem-cell research, whether it should receive government funding or even whether it should be allowed to be carried on at all, which may well be with us for some time to come. Now, *if* it is morally wrong to engage in or encourage research on embryonic stem cells—and I emphasize the 'if'—then it would make no sense to ask who would have the right to engage in such research. If it is wrong, choosing to do it could not make it right. I bring this in only as an illustration, will not attempt even to define the issue here. Unfortunately in the United States the issue, as new as it is, has already become politicized, largely because of its connection with the controversy over abortion, but, regardless of what political solution is arrived at in the United States, it is bound to be unstable for a considerable period of time, and in any event the 'political solution' is unlikely to have any relevance to a moral solution—assuming there can be a moral solution.

G. My conception of *moral issues* has been criticized in an instructive way by A. Pablo Iannone, in *Philosophy as Diplomacy* (Atlantic Highlands, NJ: Humanities Press, 1994, pp. 1–12). His basic contention is that my 'conception has four limitations that make it too narrow and unclear for dealing with the entire range of moral problems related to policy- and decision-making about issues', and Iannone places 'the fact of social conflict . . . at the center of issues' (p. 2). His claim, in brief, is that my 'characterization of issues restricts them to differences of opinion. It excludes conflicts . . . that appear to be dominantly . . . conflicts of demands'. Or, in other words, conflicts of interest, not necessarily opinions.

I find this particular point very puzzling, because it appears to commit an elementary logical error. It is false that my 'characterization of issues *restricts them to differences of opinion*'; this is to confuse a sufficient with a necessary condition. I said '*Where* there exist strong differences of opinion on opposing sides of some moral matter we have a moral *issue* . . . rather than a moral *problem*, for there is something at *issue* (p. 246 *supra*). I did not say '*only where* we have strong differences of opinion [do] we have a moral issue'. Only if the latter had been said would there be any warrant for supposing that I was restricting moral issues to differences of opinion, and not including as well conflicts of interests or demands or desires.

The point mentioned is the only one on which Iannone claims that my characterization is unsound; the other criticisms are that the characterization is too limited, and that these 'limitations make it inadequate for dealing with problems posed by issues in all their variety'. This point, which he develops very well, does not call for any response from me. I think we are coming at these matters from different perspectives and with different purposes. In any event, Iannone's contributions to this subject are profound and penetrating.

H. Another essay of note on this topic is 'Minimizing Social Conflicts' (1939), by Morris Cohen, in *The Faith of a Liberal* (New York: Holt, 1946), pp. 119–36. In another essay in the same book Cohen says:

Reflection on human good is not worthy to be called philosophical unless it is scientifically neutral about the various ethical or moral issues [I am not sure whether Cohen means *issues* or *problems*]—i.e., unless it regards its own thoroughly logical procedure as more important than any of the results of such critical study. Unless we are willing to examine critically all the logically possible alternatives to the various accepted moral judgments with the same detachment with which the mathematician studies non-Euclidean geometries, the physicist non-Newtonian mechanics, or the biologist new theories of pathology, we are advocates, not genuine philosophers. (p. 387)

There is something in this, but the point must be taken with extreme caution. On certain practices or institutions, about the wrongness or injustice of which there can be no reasonable doubt, moral neutrality is itself reprehensible. There are a number of '*logically possible* alternatives' to the accepted, and the sound, moral judgements on slavery, racism, rape, oppression, wanton cruelty, wanton torture, etc. Logically possible, but morally impossible. To be willing to examine them, if this implies a readiness to accept the alternative judgement that these are not wrong or unjust (or not wrong if practiced by the favoured few or by 'the master race') is already to evidence a corrupt mind. On doubtful or controversial matters, such as affirmative action, preferential treatment, abortion, capital punishment, and 'the drug wars' and the status of addictive presently illegal drugs, the recommendation is sound. On such matters as these one must be and remain detached, and try to think of ways of resolving the conflicts—unless one is already a partisan on one side of the issue or the other, in which case one is playing a different game. As Cohen knew very well, one of the tasks of the moral philosopher is to help to solve the moral problems of his time; genuine philosophy is not required to stay neutral on these problems, and cannot remain neutral on the nature of good and evil.

12

The Golden Rule

'How do you prove it?' said Mr Escot.
'It requires no proof,' said Doctor Gaster: 'it is a point of doctrine. It
is written, therefore it is so.'
'Nothing can be more logical', said Mr Jenkinson.

Headlong Hall

The Golden Rule has received remarkably little philosophical discussion.
No book has ever been written on it, and articles devoted to it have been
exceedingly few and usually not very searching. It is usually mentioned,
where it is mentioned at all, only in passing, and most of these passing
remarks have either been false, trite, or misleading, though some of them,
as we shall see, have certainly been interesting enough. Considering its
obvious importance and its almost universal acceptance, this dearth of
philosophical discussion is unfortunate, and also somewhat surprising.
One of the things I hope to show about it, though only incidentally, is that
there are problems connected with it of the utmost subtlety, worthy of the
attention of even the most minute philosophers.

One of the earliest formulations of the Golden Rule is the biblical one:
'All things whatsoever ye would that men should do unto you, do ye even
so unto them.' One of its commonest formulations today is: 'Do unto others as you would have them do unto you.' Notice that this last formulation
of the Rule is a positive one. It is very commonly supposed that there are
significant differences between the positive formulation of the Golden Rule
and its negative formulation: 'Do not do unto others what you would not
have them do unto you.' It has often been thought significant, for example,
that Hobbes, in presenting the Golden Rule as the 'sum . . . of the Lawes of
Nature', states it negatively: 'Do not that to another, which thou wouldest
not have done to thy selfe.' Those who regard this as significant, however,
have somehow overlooked the fact that Hobbes, in connection with some
remarks he makes about his second Law of Nature, does state the Golden
Rule positively, when he says: 'This is that Law of the Gospell: *Whatsoever*

you require that others should do to you, that do ye to them.[1] But we need not stop to consider this question of Hobbesian exegesis. I have mentioned it only to indicate that one of the questions that will have to be considered is how the positive formulation of the Golden Rule is related to its negative formulation. I shall argue that they are equivalent.

The negative formulation of the Golden Rule is to be distinguished from its denial: 'Do *not* do unto others as you would have them do unto you.' This is intended to be the outright rejection of the Golden Rule, and not another formulation of it. Another distinction that should be made at the outset is between the Golden Rule and what I shall call its 'Inversion': 'Do unto others as *they* would have you do unto them.' For another question that arises here is how the Golden Rule is related to its inversion, and which of them is a sounder precept. One other precept that should be distinguished is: 'Do unto others as they would do unto you,' or 'Do as you are done by'. This is actually a form of the *Lex Talionis*, and is not likely to be confused with the Golden Rule, though many people have claimed that it ought to be substituted for it. It is not clear to me how this latter claim can consistently be a moral one, if taken as applying universally, but perhaps this is because I am already taking it for granted that the Golden Rule somehow, in some submerged manner, formulates a fundamental moral truth. I can see certain situations in which the *Lex Talionis*, as just formulated, would have a justifiable application, since I am not an adherent of what might be called a 'turn-the-other-cheek morality'. I think that, for example, it would be justifiable to act on it in certain state-of-nature situations, but this is an *obiter dictum*, and I do not intend to pursue this matter further.

One further point should be made clear at the outset. Despite its name, the Golden Rule has to be understood as a moral principle, and not as a moral rule. That is to say, it does not, as does a moral rule, state of some specifically determined kind of action that it is right or wrong, or that it ought or ought not to be done. It rather sets forth, or has to be understood as setting forth, in abstract fashion, a method or procedure for determining the morality of a line of action, and thus is intended to provide a principle from which, or in accordance with which, if it is valid, more specific or concrete moral rules can be derived. It seems to me that one of the mistakes that has often been made in connection with the Golden Rule is

---

[1] Thomas Hobbes, *Leviathan* (1651) (Everyman's Library edn., London: J. M. Dent 1914), ch. xv, para. 35, p. 82; ch. xiv, para. 4, p. 67. See also ch. xvii, para. 2, p. 87: 'For the Lawes of Nature (as *Justice, Equity, Modesty, Mercy*, and (in summe) *doing to others, as wee would be done to,*)'.

to treat it as though it were a specific directive, having a readily determined application.

I

With these preliminary distinctions out of the way—but not, it may be hoped, out of mind—we can now embark on our examination of the meaning and moral validity of the Golden Rule. The method I propose to follow, for the most part, is to consider a number of statements that have been made about it, with the hope that through this consequent sifting of views we may arrive at some closer approximation to the truth about it.

The first statement that I wish to consider is one made just a few years ago by the general counsel of the American Rocket Society. One reason I think it worth considering is that it is so nearly out of this world, and provides, in what it says about the Golden Rule, a neat contrast with its biblical origins:

It's one thing to imagine laws suitable for human beings in space—laws regulating the colonizing of other planets, the mining of meteors, and the like. It's something else to imagine laws suitable for beings that are themselves scarcely imaginable. The word I've coined for such a body of laws is 'metalaw', which I define as 'the law governing the rights of intelligent beings of different natures and existing in an indefinite number of different frameworks of natural laws'. The earth is part of a tiny solar system in a galaxy that contains at least forty billion stars, and there are over forty billion such galaxies in the universe as a whole; the number of planets in the universe capable of sustaining what we would recognise as intelligent life must be enormous. Now, our earthly laws are based roughly on the golden rule and suit us fine, but it would be silly to assume that they would suit any other creatures. I argue that the golden rule would be thoroughly inappropriate to metalaw. Not 'Do unto others as you would have them do unto you' but 'Do unto others as they would have you do unto them.'[2]

This statement, is fantastic in at least two ways. One of them is obvious. The other is that it involves an elementary logical error. From absolute ignorance absolutely nothing follows, yet this statement supposes that something does. If the beings mentioned are really 'scarcely imaginable', then the laws that should regulate our dealings with them should be

---

[2] From an interview with Andrew G. Haley, general counsel of the American Rocket Society, in *New Yorker*, 29 December 1956, p. 19.

'scarcely imaginable' as well, and there is no warrant for supposing that the Golden Rule, in so far as it serves as a basis for 'earthly laws', would not serve equally well as a basis for 'unearthly laws', unless there is some other reason for supposing it defective. There is certainly no warrant for supposing that the Inversion of the Golden Rule ('Do unto others as they would have you do unto them') would serve as a better basis for such 'metalaws', unless there is some other argument to show what its advantages would be, and no such arguments are herein provided. The assumption behind this is that the Golden Rule presupposes some similarity or identity of nature in the beings whose relations it is intended to govern, so that some other rule must serve as the basis for governing the relations among beings whose natures are fundamentally dissimilar. This is an assumption to which I shall return in due course, but first I want to consider why it should be supposed that the Inversion of the Golden Rule has any advantages over it. If we consider its implications, it would certainly not appear so.

Let us suppose that we should do unto others as they would have us do unto them. What sort of conduct would this require of us? Well, for one thing, if you want me to assign to you all of my property, then this rule implies that I should do so; for it requires me to do unto you as *you* would have me do unto you, and in this case you would have me sign over to you all of my property. If your demands should be increased, and you want me to be your slave for life and do your every bidding, the rule would require me to do this. Such requirements are absurd, and the rule that leads to them can be no better. Under such a rule, no woman's 'virtue' would be safe from the desires of any importuning male. Indeed, rape would be morally impossible, since no one would have a right to resist. This reasoning leads irresistibly to the conclusion that this 'rule' leads to consequences that are absurd and morally wrong. But let us now reverse the application of the rule. The rule actually applies to both parties to the transaction, and not just to me. It applies to everyone alike; for it requires everyone to do unto others as they would have him do unto them. So if I should want you to assign to me all your property, or be my slave for life, then you are required to do so. If *A* wants you to do *x*, and *B* wants you to do *y*, and *x* and *y* are incompatible with each other, the rule still requires you to do both. The rule therefore leads to impossible results, and is actually impossible to apply. It is tantamount to: 'Always do what anyone else wants you to do', which in turn is equivalent to a universal requirement of perfect or absolute altruism, the absurdity of which is so manifest as not to require detailing. Perhaps this is what Kant had in mind when he said: 'That one should sacrifice his own happiness, his true wants, in order to promote that of others, would be a self-contradictory maxim if made a universal law'.[3] It may be worth noting that Kant concluded from this that what he regarded as the duty to promote the happiness of others is 'therefore . . . only indeterminate; it has a certain latitude within which one may be able to do more or less without our being able to assign its limits definitely'. Perhaps the Inversion of the Golden Rule is meant to be applied only with certain qualifications, such as 'so far as it is not unreasonable or inconvenient or absurd or immoral or impossible'. But this would not leave us with much of a principle, or even much of a rule.

The arguments just given show pretty conclusively that the idea that the Inversion of the Golden Rule has certain advantages over the Golden Rule, or should be substituted for it, must be given up, and results only from failure to trace out its implications. But it has still to be determined whether the Golden Rule has itself any great merit. Perhaps it is open to similar criticism. The passage that follows conveys a hint that the Inversion has certain merits lacking in the Golden Rule itself, but I want to examine it mainly for other reasons:

Consider the Golden Rule, in its positive form which bids us behave in relation to other people in the ways in which we should wish them to behave in relation to us in the same circumstances. It is clear that this rule is not satisfactory as an explicit guide to conduct, as it stands. It is useful as a protest against a line of conduct which simply moves toward a goal regardless of the consequences to other people, but even here it has its limitations. If I am acting not in a private capacity but as a representative (for example as an engine driver or a postman or an army officer or an employee of any kind) my action has to be determined primarily by the conditions of my employment. A person running for a train would naturally wish the engine driver to hold the train back, but the driver has his prescribed duties. Again, even in the sphere of private activities the rule is insufficient. It works well enough in a society where interests are relatively homogeneous and simple. But in a complex society, where there are wide differences of point of view and taste and need, it suggests too strongly that the individual has only to consult his own tastes and needs to discover how be ought to behave toward other people. What I should wish others to do to me is often quite different from what they would wish me to do to them; and the latter is often much more important than the former. At the same time the rule to behave toward others as they would wish you to behave would be equally inadequate, though it does have the merit of stressing the need for an understanding of other people as a basis of our behaviour toward them. Further the rule as it stands gives no hint of the kind of person it is desirable you

[3] Immanuel Kant, preface to the *Metaphysical Elements of Ethics*, trans. T. K. Abbott, in *Kant's Theory of Ethics*, 6th edn. (London: Longmans, Green, 1909), p. 304.

should be, if you are to be trusted to carry it out. It authorises the quarrelsome person who loves to be provoked, to go about provoking others, and the person who hates friendliness and sympathy, to be cold and unsympathetic in his dealings with others; it authorises the man who loves to find himself in a network of intrigue and sharp dealing, to deal with others habitually in this way.[4]

This passage contains a number of the fairly standard criticisms of the Golden Rule, which will have to be examined very shortly. 'It authorises the quarrelsome person who loves to be provoked, to go about provoking others', and so on. But the really important point here is the claim that 'in a complex society, where there are wide differences of point of view and taste and need, it suggests too strongly that the individual has only to consult his own tastes and needs to discover how he ought to behave toward other people'. Here again we have the implication that the Golden Rule presupposes a certain uniformity or similarity of nature. It is quite true that 'what I should wish others to do to me is often quite different from what they would wish me to do to them'; it is also quite true that 'the latter is often much more important than the former'. But this is no argument against the Golden Rule. It is only an argument against the restricted and faulty interpretation of it represented in this passage. It is asserted that the Inversion of the Golden Rule has the 'merit of stressing the need for an understanding of other people as a basis of our behaviour toward them'. The implication here is that the Golden Rule itself does not; and I shall argue that, when it is properly and sensibly interpreted, it does.

To put the point into focus, let us consider the claim made in the following statement by Mr Walter Lippmann:

The rule that you should do unto others as you would have them do unto you rests on the belief that human nature is uniform. Mr Bernard Shaw's statement that you should not do unto others what you would have them do unto you, because their tastes may be different, rests on the belief that human nature is not uniform.[5]

Here the presupposition that I have mentioned becomes quite explicit, and leads to the claim that the Golden Rule should be rejected outright. And this claim would be quite reasonable if the Golden Rule did involve this presupposition, because the assumption that human nature is uniform, in the sense that everyone's tastes, interests, needs, and desires are the same, is absurdly and grotesquely false. But it is just because this assumption is so absurdly and grotesquely and obviously false that it ought to be quite obvious that the

---

[4] L. J. Russell, 'Ideals and Practice', *Philosophy*, 17 (1942), pp. 109–10.
[5] Walter Lippmann, *Public Opinion* (New York: Macmillan, 1922), pp. 121–2.

Golden Rule does not involve or presuppose it. The Golden Rule does not rest on the belief that human nature is uniform, or, in other words, on the belief that human tastes, desires, interests, and needs are all the same; and that this is so is fairly easily shown.

If I am a quarrelsome person who loves to be provoked, does the Golden Rule authorize or require me to go around provoking others, on the ground that I should do unto others as I would have them do unto me? If I love to hear the sound of tom-toms for several hours at a time in the middle of the night, does the Golden Rule enjoin me to inflict this enjoyment on my neighbours? If I am a masochist who would have others torture me, does the Golden Rule require me to do as I would be done by by torturing others? If the Rule did have these consequences, it would certainly be ruled out as an adequate or even as a sane moral principle, since it would require conduct that is obviously immoral, as involving the violation of the rights of others. However, to suppose that the Golden Rule does have these implications is to overlook the distinction, of vital importance in this context, between the words '*what*' and '*as*', and seriously and quite foolishly to misinterpret its intent. It may be admitted that what others 'would wish me to do to', or for, them is often much more important, as a moral basis for determining how I should act in relation to other people, than 'what I should wish others to do' to, or for, me. But the Golden Rule does not deny this.

Let us distinguish between two different statements, and two correspondingly different interpretations, of the Golden Rule: (a) Do unto others *what* you would have them do unto you; and (b) Do unto others *as* you would have them do unto you. I shall call the first of these the *particular* interpretation of the Golden Rule, and the second the *general* interpretation. Now the particular interpretation is open to the various objections that have been made against the Golden Rule, of the sort that I have indicated. The general interpretation, however, is not.

The particular interpretation implies that whatever in particular I would have others do to or for me I should do to or for them. It is in this particular interpretation that the Rule 'authorises the quarrelsome person who loves to be provoked, to go about provoking others, and the person who hates friendliness and sympathy to be cold and unsympathetic in his dealings with others', and so on, and it is evident that there is nothing to be said for it.

The general interpretation, on the other hand, has no such implications. Here what I have to consider is not what in particular I would have others do to or for me, or what particular desires of mine I would have them satisfy.

Here what I have to consider is the general ways in which I would have others behave in their treatment of me. And what I would have them do, in abstraction from any of my particular desires, and all that I am entitled to expect them to do, is to take account of my interests, desires, needs, and wishes—which may well be different from theirs—and either satisfy them or else not wilfully frustrate them. If I would have others take account of my interests and wishes in their treatment of me, even though my interests and wishes may differ considerably from their own, then what the Golden Rule in this interpretation requires of me is that I should take account of the interests and wishes of others in my treatment of them. I am to treat others as I would have them treat me; that is, on the same principle or standard *as* I would have them apply in their treatment of me. And the same principle or standard in application to differing circumstances or interests can lead to widely divergent particular results. The Golden Rule, then, is clearly compatible with differences in tastes, interests, wishes, needs, and desires, and does not 'rest on the belief that human nature is uniform'. Nor does it imply that 'the individual has only to consult his own tastes and needs to discover how he ought to behave toward other people'. Thus the Rule does not 'authorise the quarrelsome person who loves to be provoked, to go about provoking others'— though it may not be easy to get a quarrelsome person to see this. On the contrary, if he is to do as he would be done by, he must take account of and (not ignore but) respect the wishes of people who do not like to be provoked or to engage in quarrels, and restrict his quarrels to those who, like him, enjoy them. Similarly the person who enjoys hearing the beat of tom-toms in the middle of the night should reflect that the satisfaction of this esoteric desire of his is extremely likely to annoy others, and just as he would not want others to do things that are annoying to him (surely there is something that fits this category—perhaps the blowing of reveille on a bugle after he has fallen asleep), so he ought not to do things that are manifestly annoying to them.

Objections, then, that are conclusive against the particular interpretation of the Golden Rule are not even so much as relevant to its general interpretation. Of course, the use of the particular word 'as' has no great importance by itself, and the principle can be and has been stated with the use of this word without the point I am making having been recognized. Moreover, this particular word need not be used in the statement of the Rule. The important point is to understand the distinction, and to recognize that the statement 'Do unto others as you would have them do unto you' is intended to be equivalent to the principle: One should act in relation to others *on the same principles or standards* that one would have them apply in their treatment of oneself.

Consider the following passage:

So far are business men from being without moral standards that the majority of them, like the majority of other people, have three. There is first the standard which John Smith applies to his treatment of other people—his competitors, his customers, his employees, and those from whom he purchases his supplies. There is, second, the standard which be expects them to apply to him. Finally there is the standard which he applies to other people's treatment of each other.[6]

The reference here to business men is of course completely immaterial. It occurs only because the book from which the passage is taken is a book on business ethics (written, appropriately enough, by two authors named Sharp and Fox). But the point is made that the 'majority of other people', and not just business men, operate with these three different moral standards, and though it may be intended facetiously, it may also be true. It may in fact be the case that the majority of people operate with (or tend to operate with) three different standards. The standard that one uses in judging his own conduct in relation to other people—his treatment of others—will then be different from the standard he uses in judging the conduct of others in relation to himself—their treatment of him—and undoubtedly in both cases the standard is designed to give the advantage to himself, by making his own interest paramount. So presumably one operating on this basis would judge an action right if done by himself or if it is to his advantage which he would judge wrong if done by someone else or if it is to his disadvantage. It is just this which is condemned by the Golden Rule, which requires that the same standard be applied to an action, no matter who performs it and no matter who benefits by it. It requires not only that the standard used in judging one's treatment of others be the same as the standard one uses in judging other people's treatment of oneself, but that this same standard also be used in judging other people's treatment of each other, in cases where one's own interests are presumed not to be affected. For whether one's own interests are involved or not makes no moral difference, though it may make a considerable psychological difference or a difference to oneself, and there is no one whose interests are in *general* entitled to a privileged moral position. This is what has been intended by those theories that have maintained that one should judge everyone's conduct, including one's own, from the point of view of an 'impartial rational spectator'. In other words, to judge an action in which one, or one's own interest, is involved, either as the agent performing the action or as the 'patient'

---

[6] Frank Chapman Sharp and Philip G. Fox, *Business Ethics* (New York: Appleton-Century-Crofts, 1937), p. 3.

affected by the action, one should abstract oneself from the situation and consider how one would judge it then. Anyone incapable of making the requisite abstraction is incapable of making a genuine moral judgement—his judgements will all be biased by the pressure of his own concerns. There is no doubt that there are times when all of us are in this way morally incapacitated. But there is also no doubt that not all of us are morally incapacitated all the time.

Thus, even though the situation depicted in the foregoing passage may be widely prevalent, it is condemned by the Golden Rule as immoral, and anyone who applies to another a standard of which he would complain if it were applied to himself has no moral grounds for his complaint. He is being both immoral and illogical. It follows, then, that the Golden Rule formulates a fundamental requirement of justice, that everyone's conduct must be judged by the same standards, and that no one has, in general, any warranted claim to a special or privileged position. It is therefore at the basis of the Principle of Justice, that what is right or wrong for one person must be right or wrong for any similar person in similar circumstances. Stated differently but equivalently: What is right for one person cannot be wrong for another, unless there is some relevant difference in their natures or circumstances. I have elsewhere discussed this principle, the generalization principle, at some length, and I have no intention of repeating here, any more than necessary, what I have said there.[7] My object here is to consider the Golden Rule, and not the Generalization Principle or the Principle of Justice, and though the two are connected in an important way, it is not thereby impossible to isolate a discussion of one from a discussion of the other.

I have just stated that the Golden Rule requires that one apply the same standard in judging the actions of others in relation to oneself as one applies in judging one's own actions, and that this same standard be used in judging the actions of other people in cases where one's own interests are presumably not affected. But now suppose that someone applies to his own conduct a higher and more rigorous standard than he applies to the conduct of others, that instead of demanding more of others than he demands of himself, he demands more of himself than he demands of others. Would this be unjust and ruled out by the Golden Rule? Clearly this is not the sort of case that the Golden Rule is intended to rule out. The sort of case condemned by the Golden Rule is one in which one claims a privilege for himself that he is not willing to grant to others, and not one in which one

---

[7] *Generalization in Ethics*, chs. 2 and 3 and *passim*.

imposes a burden on himself that he is not willing to impose on others. Such cases are fairly common. There are people who, at least in certain lines of endeavour, are harder on themselves than they are on others. It would clearly be ludicrous to condemn this as immoral. But how should this affect our statement and interpretation of the Golden Rule? As I see it, this way. The sorts of action that the Golden Rule condemns are those in which one is being unfair to others, by claiming a privilege for himself that he would not be willing to grant to them, without there being any good reason to justify this discrepancy. But the sort of case envisaged here is not one in which one is being unfair to others. We might say that such a person is being 'unfair to himself', but this could only be a metaphor. For to be unfair, in the sense in which this implies that one's action is wrong, is literally only to be unfair to others. What this would mean is only that such a person is being foolish, since there is no real need for him to be so hard on himself. But at the same time his actions, and his voluntary assumption of a special burden or sacrifice, may be highly commendable. Only it is not obligatory, and it would not be wrong for anyone not to impose higher standards on himself than he imposes on others—unless these standards are required by the demands of the circumstances or position in which he is placed; but that is another matter. So one in this situation is not violating the Golden Rule as I have stated it. He is not applying a different standard to himself than he applies to the actions of others. He is applying the same standards, only in addition to the common standards that he applies to the actions of everyone, including himself, he applies a higher and more rigorous standard to his own actions, and condemns himself for failures or omissions that he would not condemn others for. This does not violate the requirements of justice or of the Golden Rule, and I see no need to expand or revise my statement of the Rule so as to take explicit account of this situation. The Golden Rule condemns injustice, not heroism; and if there should be competition for the role of hero, then it would be regarded not as a burden but as a privilege. In demanding this role for oneself, one might be unjust, but since this rarely causes any special moral problems, I see no need to consider it.

II

As remarked earlier, it is very commonly supposed that there are significant differences between the positive formulation of the Golden Rule, 'Do unto others as you would have them do unto you,' and its negative formulation, 'Do not do unto others what (or as) you would not have them do unto you.' It is easy to suppose that the negative Rule merely imposes upon us a certain prohibition not to treat others in certain ways in which we would not want to be treated ourselves, and does not impose any duties of a positive nature, duties actually to do certain things as opposed to duties to refrain from doing certain things. If this were so, then the Rule in its negative form would not imply that one who would be helped by others when he is in need of help has a corresponding obligation to help others when they are in need of help, and it would be subject to other limitations along similar lines. I think that this idea is an illusion. There is undoubtedly a difference in emphasis between these two statements of the Golden Rule, and therefore a rhetorical and psychological difference, but there is no logical or moral difference.

Consider an analogous case: the negative rule 'One ought not to lie', or simply 'Don't tell lies', and the positive rule 'One ought to tell the truth', or simply 'Tell the truth'. There is a way in which these two rules can be said to correspond to each other, analogous to the way in which the negative version of the Golden Rule may be said to correspond to its positive formulation; yet these two rules do not seem to be equivalent. For instance, the rule 'Don't tell lies' simply tells us not to tell lies, and does not tell us what we positively should do. One can conform to the rule merely by remaining silent. However, the positive rule 'Tell the truth' does tell us what we positively should do, and does not seem to leave it open to us to be silent. But this is only what seems. If we were to take the positive rule literally as enjoining that we should always tell the truth, and as implying that silence is a violation of it, we get a result that is absolutely absurd. For this would imply that whenever someone says nothing he is violating the rule and therefore doing something wrong. But this would imply that one must constantly be uttering true statements, no matter how inappropriate they may be to the occasion, and is not allowed time in which to sleep, eat, listen, or contemplate; for whenever one does any of these things he is being silent and consequently violating the rule. To interpret the rule as requiring everyone to be constantly talking, with the consequence that no one would ever be able to listen to what anyone else was talking about, is hardly a sensible interpretation. It is evident, then, that the positive rule, 'Tell the truth', must be interpreted as subject to certain unstated but generally understood conditions, just as it is subject to certain unstated but generally understood exceptions. With these conditions made explicit, the rule would take something like the form, 'If you say something, tell the truth.'

This makes it clear that this rule in its positive form also leaves it open to us to be silent, and does not enjoin the constant utterance of platitudes and that everyone be a chatterbox. It follows that the positive rule that one ought to tell the truth is equivalent to the negative rule that one ought not to lie, when the positive rule is sensibly interpreted.

Now somewhat analogous reasoning is applicable to the question of the relation between the positive and the negative formulations of the Golden Rule. In application to the case just considered, it is perhaps clear enough how the Negative Golden Rule shows lying to be wrong: if you would not have others lie to you, then you ought not to lie to them. In the light of the argument just given, it follows that the Negative Golden Rule establishes the positive duty to tell the truth. (But suppose there is someone who wants others to lie to him. Does he therefore have the duty to lie to them? No, for reasons already suggested, but I am not dealing with this sort of case at the moment.) Moreover, if we examine the Golden Rule directly, we can arrive at the same result. What is the difference between a negative desire, a desire not to have certain things done to oneself, and a positive desire, a desire to have certain things done to oneself? In application to a particular thing, there is all the difference in the world between the desire to have it done to oneself and the desire not to have it done to oneself. But in the abstract there is only a difference in formulation, and a want or desire formulated in negative terms can always be reformulated in positive terms. There is no difference between not wanting others to lie to oneself and wanting them not to lie to oneself, wanting them to tell one the truth and wanting them not to fail to tell one the truth. In general, 'A does not want x to happen' is equivalent to 'A wants x not to happen', and 'A wants x to happen' is equivalent to 'A does not want x not to happen'. Given these equivalences, every desire formulated negatively, which would come within the scope of the Negative Golden Rule, can be reformulated positively, and will then come within the scope of the Positive Golden Rule. In particular, the duty to help others who are in need of help is established just as readily by the Negative Rule as it is by the Positive. 'If you want others to help you when you are in need of help, then you ought to help others when they are in need of help.' But by the same token, 'If you do not want others to fail or refuse to help you when you are in need of help, then you ought not to fail or refuse to help others when they are in need of help.' In general, the negative principle 'If you do not want to be treated in a certain way, then you ought not to treat others in that way, unless there is good reason to the contrary,' is equivalent to the positive principle 'If you want others to treat you in certain ways, then you ought to treat others in those ways, unless there is good reason to the contrary.' Consequently the negative and the positive formulations of the Golden Rule are logically and morally equivalent, though they are no doubt not psychologically or rhetorically equivalent. But the only difference is one of emphasis.

III

There are some interesting connections between the Golden Rule and what Kurt Baier calls the condition or principle of 'reversibility':

> Doing evil is doing to another person what it would be contrary to reason for him to do to himself. Harming another, hurting another, doing to another what he dislikes having done to him are the specific forms this takes. Killing, cruelty, inflicting pain, maiming, torturing, deceiving, cheating, rape, adultery are instances of this sort of behavior. They all violate the condition of 'reversibility', that is, that the behavior in question must be acceptable to a person whether he is at the 'giving' or 'receiving' end of it.
>
> Anyone is doing wrong who engages in nonreversible behavior ... Such behavior is 'wrong in itself', irrespective of individual or social recognition, irrespective of the consequences it has. Moreover, every single act of such behavior is wrong ... All nonreversible behavior is morally wrong ... We need not consider whether this sort of behavior has harmful consequences ...
>
> The principle of reversibility does not merely impose certain prohibitions on a moral agent, but also certain positive injunctions. It is, for instance, wrong ... not to help another person when he is in need and when we are in a position to help him.[8]

I am not prepared to go along with all of the instances on Baier's list. One can kill, inflict pain on, and maim another, and one can also do these things to oneself. Adultery, however, is not something that one can do either *to* another or *to* oneself. Adultery may be wrong, but if so, it is not wrong 'in itself', but in virtue of its consequences or the consequences of the general sort of behaviour of which it is a species. This, however, is a mere matter of detail, and not a difference of principle. A more important question is: What is meant by certain behaviour being 'acceptable' to a person? Does this not depend on the specific desires that one has? Suppose one wants to have pain inflicted on himself, and is indifferent whether it is inflicted on him by another or whether he inflicts it on himself? This would then seem

---

[8] Kurt Baier, *The Moral Point of View* (Ithaca, NY: Cornell University Press, 1958), pp. 202–3. Cf. pp. 208–9, 211, and 228. On 'contrary to reason', see pp. 315–17, 89–92.

to be 'acceptable' to him whether he is at the 'giving' or the 'receiving' end of it. Does this principle then justify him in inflicting pain on another? No, not if it is not 'acceptable' to the other. (If it is, then that is their business.) But this point is not brought out by Baier's statement of the principle of reversibility. Behaviour is said to be reversible if it is 'acceptable to a person whether he is at the "giving" or "receiving" end of it'. But the infliction of pain is 'acceptable' to a masochist 'whether he is at the giving or receiving end of it'. Baier's principle is therefore inadequate as it stands, and I do not see any easy way to emend it. We might say that the behaviour must be acceptable *both* to the person who is engaged in it and to the person who is affected by it, where these are different persons, but this has further defects. There will usually be more than one person affected by a given act, and when this is the case we are automatically involved in the weighing of consequences, and have left this particular principle behind. Furthermore, a specific punishment for an offence may not be 'acceptable' to the person who is at the 'receiving' end of it, that is to the person punished (the attitude of the person on the 'giving' end is clearly irrelevant here), but it does not follow that the punishment is unjustified.

These considerations would indicate that we cannot say that reversible behaviour is automatically right nor that non-reversible behaviour is automatically wrong. But a way out may be provided by Baier's concept of what is 'contrary to reason'. 'Doing evil', he says, 'is doing to another person what it would be contrary to reason for him to do to himself.' Now, though it is not impossible, it is nevertheless contrary to reason for a person wantonly to inflict pain on himself (Baier is careful to point out that this does not mean that it is wrong). Consequently, it is wrong for one person to inflict pain on another (unless justified by other factors)—even if the person on whom it is inflicted has no complaint to make about it. For it is contrary to reason for a person to torture or inflict pain on himself (for its own sake, and apart from some other reason one might have for doing so). But the conclusion I am led to by these considerations is that the principle of reversibility requires the same sort of interpretation, involving a distinction between the particular and the general interpretation, as the Golden Rule. The Golden Rule, properly understood, would justify the principle of reversibility, in its proper interpretation, and not vice versa.

These remarks may now be applied to some of the ingenious criticisms of the Golden Rule presented in the following passage by Bishop Whately:

Supposing . . . one . . . had let his land to a farmer, he might consider that the farmer would be glad to be excused paying any rent for it, since he would himself, if he were the farmer, prefer having the land rent-free; and that, therefore, the rule of doing as he would be done by requires him to give up all his property. So also a shop-keeper might, on the same principle, think that the rule required him to part with his goods under prime cost, or to give them away, and thus to ruin himself. Now such a procedure would be absurd.

Again, supposing a jailer who was intrusted with the safe custody of a prisoner should think himself bound to let the man escape, because he himself, if he were a prisoner, would be glad to obtain freedom, he would be guilty of a breach of trust. Such an application of the rule, therefore, would be morally wrong.

And again, if you had to decide between two parties who were pleading their cause before you, you might consider that each of them wished for a decision in his own favor. And how, then, you might ask, would it be possible to apply the rule? since in deciding for the one party you could not but decide against the other. A literal compliance with the rule, therefore, would be, in such a case, impossible.[9]

Whately's own answer to these difficulties is that

if you were to put such cases as these before any sensible man, he would at once say that you are to consider, not what you might wish in each case, but what you would regard as fair, right, just, reasonable, if you were in another person's place. If you were a farmer, although you might feel that you would be very glad to have the land rent-free—that is, to become the owner of it, you would not consider that you had any just claim to it, and that you could fairly expect the landlord to make you a present of his property. But you would think it reasonable that if you suffered some great and unexpected loss, from an inundation or any such calamity, he should make an abatement of the rent. And this is what a good landlord generally thinks it right to do, in compliance with the golden rule.

So also, if you had a cause to be tried, though of course you would wish the decision to be in your favor, you would be sensible that all you could reasonably expect of the judge would be that he should lay aside all prejudice, and attend impartially and carefully to the evidence, and decide according to the best of his ability. And this—which is what each part may fairly claim—is what an upright judge will do. And the like holds good in all the other cases.

The conclusion he draws about the Golden Rule is that it was 'far from being designed to impart to men the first notions of justice. On the contrary, it presupposes that knowledge; and if we had no such notions, we could not properly apply the rule.'

This conclusion would appear to conflict with the one I arrived at before, that the Golden Rule is the source or the basis of the Principle of Justice, and would bear examining for this reason alone, apart from the intrinsic interest of the examples used to support it. But disputes about the origin of the sense of justice are futile, and I do not propose to get involved in one.

---

[9] Richard Whately, *Lessons on Morals* (Cambridge, Mass.: John Bartlett, 1857), ch. IV.

Whately is operating with a moral-sense theory, according to which our judgements of what is right and wrong or just and unjust are guided and determined by our moral sense or sense of justice. This is hardly the place to go into this whole matter in the detail required, so I shall simply say this. I should not deny for a moment the existence of such a thing as a moral sense, that it is an important thing to have, and that it is an important thing to develop. Too many people unfortunately have no moral sense, and too many others have an undeveloped moral sense. (Just as many people lack a sense of humour, but this is rarely of any importance, and in any case is hardly an objective matter.) But it does not follow that one's moral sense or sense of justice is any infallible or even reliable guide to the morality or the justice of an action. On the contrary, principles of justice are required to guide and develop it, and occasionally to correct it. For moral judgements, or judgements of what is just or unjust, must be supported by reasons, and an appeal to one's sense of justice does not provide any reasons. What it provides is a motive to-search for and consider moral reasons, a predisposition to acknowledge them, something that one who lacks all moral sense will not and cannot do. Moral-sense theories, then, are not and cannot be theories about the nature of the moral standard or of the criteria for distinguishing right from wrong; they are theories about the nature or predisposing basis of moral motivation. Let us not confuse the two.

What I am contending then is that the sense of justice does not itself provide moral guidance, but itself requires moral guidance by a principle or principles of justice. Yet I am not contending that the Golden Rule is by itself sufficient for this. But, before going further, let us take just a look at what Whately says is 'the real design' of the Golden Rule. He says it is

to put us on our guard against the danger of being blinded by self-interest. A person who has a good general notion of what is just may often be tempted to act unfairly or unkindly towards his neighbors, when his own interest or gratification is concerned, and to overlook the rightful claims of others.

Therefore 'if we will make a practice of applying the golden rule' we

may have a kind of prophet always at hand, to remind us how, and when, to act on our principles of right. We have only to consider, 'What should I think were I in the other's place, and he were to do so and so to me? How should I require him to treat me? What could I in fairness claim from him?'

But if this is the sort of question we are to consider, the Golden Rule must be more than just a reminder—it must also be something of a guide. The Golden Rule, in fact, is an instrument of moral education, and the most effective one that I know of. If this is so, it must be more than a mere reminder. It must also be something of a teacher.[10]

I propose now, as a possible way out of the dilemma raised here, to go back and examine the examples with which Whately started. *A*, we will suppose, has 'let his land to a farmer', *B*. It is claimed that if *A* were to operate on the basis of the Golden Rule then 'he might consider that the farmer would be glad to be excused paying any rent for it, since he would himself, if he were the farmer, prefer having the land rent-free; and . . . therefore the rule of doing as he would be done by requires him to give up all his property'. Now 'such a procedure would be absurd'. But is it the procedure called for by the Golden Rule? I think not. The catch, I think, lies in the phrase: 'he himself would, *if he were the farmer*, prefer having the land rent-free'. The Golden Rule tells me that I ought to do unto others as I would have them do unto me. It does not tell me that I must imagine myself to *be* another, or that I must imagine myself as constantly shifting back and forth from one role to another. The supposition 'if I were he' is not one from which any definite inferences can be drawn, because the supposition itself is so indeterminate. The Golden Rule requires *A* to do unto *B as* he would have *B* do unto him. That is to say, it requires *A* to act towards *B* on the same standard or principle that he would have *B* apply in his treatment of him. No matter what in particular in this situation *B* may actually want— even if *B* should not just want the land rent-free but should also want to be paid for using it—the Golden Rule does not enjoin *A* to let *B* have the land rent-free, or pay him for using it, because the Golden Rule, when sensibly interpreted, does not require anyone to do for anyone else just those particular things that the other wants to have done. It is only on the particular interpretation of the Golden Rule, which we have already disposed of, that this conclusion can be arrived at, and this would be tantamount to identifying the Golden Rule with its Inversion. The identification, and the result, are both absurd. The rule that we should do unto others as we would have them do unto us does not require us to do unto others *what they* would have us do unto them. Now in its general, sensible, interpretation, the Rule does not require *A* to let *B* have the land rent-free, because, as I have just indicated, it only requires him, in his dealings with *B*, to treat *B* on the same standard as he would have *B* apply in his treatment of him. Such a standard would require only that he charge *B* a reasonable rent, and not that he give

---

[10] Cf. Baier, *Moral Point of View,* p. 202: 'When we teach children the moral point of view, we try to explain it to them by getting them to put themselves in another person's place: "How would you like to have that done to you!"'

up all his property; a conclusion, of course, at which Whately also arrives, but for different reasons.

This conclusion can be reinforced by noticing that the Golden Rule applies not just to *A*, but also to *B*, and if it would require *A* to let *B* have the land rent-free, it would also require *B* to pay a rent that is double or more what he is actually paying, since *B*, if he were the landowner, might reflect that he would want to receive at least twice as much rent for it as was actually asked. Such a conclusion is more than absurd; it is impossible. But it illustrates the consequences of the 'if I were he' sort of thinking, shows that this sort of hypothesis is not called for in the application of the Golden Rule, and brings out the necessity of what I have called the general inter-pretation of the Golden Rule.

This argument has been considerably complicated, and I do not pretend that it is transparently clear. It might help to clarify it if we consider crit-ically Whately's second example, that of the 'jailer who was intrusted with the safe custody of a prisoner' and might 'think himself bound to let the man escape, because he himself, if he were a prisoner, would be glad to obtain freedom'. Let us go directly here to the point of view of the prisoner, who is equally bound by the Golden Rule, and applies similar reasoning by placing himself in the position of the jailer. The prisoner might reflect that he ought not to try to escape, because if he were the jailer, he would want his prisoners to remain in his custody. Of course, thinking of himself now in the position of the jailer, he might apply the Rule further and reflect on what he would want and should consider if he were, as he is, the prisoner. He would probably then arrive at the conclusion the jailer was supposed to have arrived at. But then suppose he reverses roles again? What then? Also the jailer, after thinking of himself in the position of the prisoner, should then apply the Rule to himself in this position, and reflect that he, if he were the prisoner, should not try to escape, because if he were the jailer he would not want the prisoner to escape, and that therefore, since he is actually the jailer, he should not let the prisoner escape. And each of them could go on and on through further convolutions, but there can be only an arbitrary stopping-point. It follows that this way of applying the Golden Rule is ille-gitimate, since it leads to contradictory results, and can terminate only at the end of an infinite series.

The difficulty of applying the Golden Rule in its particular interpreta-tion is brought out further in Whately's third example, that of the judge: 'if you had to decide between two parties who were pleading their cause before you, you might consider that each of them wished for a decision in his own favor. And how, then, you might ask, would it be possible to apply the rule? since in deciding for the one party you could not but decide against the other.' This is true, but it does not follow that it is impossible to apply the Rule. It only follows that it is impossible to apply the Rule in its particular interpretation. Let us refer to the judge as A, and to the contending parties as B and C. Now let us look at this situation from the point of view of B; for, as I have already remarked, it is not only the judge who is supposed to apply the Rule to his conduct, but everyone else as well. On this method of interpretation, B would reflect that if he were the judge he would not want the parties contending before him to place impossible demands upon him, and that he could not possibly decide for both parties. Consequently, he can demand not that A decide in his favour, but only, as Whately goes on to say, that A decide the case impartially and without bias and in accordance with the relevant law and evidence. The same goes for C. Now we could carry this on into further convolutions, and have B place himself in the role of A and then back again in the role of B, and so on. We could also have B place himself in the position of C, and C place himself in the role of B, as, according to this interpretation of the Golden Rule, they are each bound to do. From this point of view, presumably, they should each accede to the claims of the other. And then we could go on to our second and third convolutions, and so on. But since any stopping-place must be arbitrary, we might as well stop here. Enough has been said, I think, to show that this interpretation of the Golden Rule is impossible, and that the Rule does not really require anyone to think along the lines of the 'if I were he' sort of hypothesis. For, apart from the extreme indefiniteness of this supposition, the reversal of roles that it requires must go on forever.

My conclusion, then, is that the Golden Rule does not require anyone to do for another what he thinks he would want himself to do if he were that other. Such an interpretation makes it equivalent to its Inversion. What the Golden Rule requires is that everyone ought to act in his relations with others on the same standards or principles that he would have them apply in their treatment of him, taking account of and respecting, but not necessarily acceding to, their wishes and desires. This is the most that anyone can reasonably ask, but nothing less will suffice. Naturally, the Golden Rule by itself does not unambiguously and definitely determine just what these 'standards or principles' should be, but it does *something* towards determining this, and it is not necessary that it do everything.

IV

Whately's main point about the Golden Rule is that it does not 'answer the purpose of a complete system of morality', and this is not a point that I am disposed to deny, since it is one with which I emphatically agree. One very commonly expressed opinion about the Golden Rule is that if only everyone were to act on it then everything would be wonderful. This sort of sentimentalism is as harmful and as unwarranted as moral scepticism.

We sometimes hear it stated. . . that the universal adoption of the Golden Rule would at once settle all industrial disputes and difficulties. But supposing that the principle were accepted in good faith by everybody; it would not at once tell everybody just what to do in all the complexities of his relations with others. When individuals are still uncertain what their real good may be, it does not finally decide matters to tell them to regard the good of others as they would their own. Nor does it mean that whatever in detail we want for ourselves we should strive to give to others.[11]

I think that what is said here is perfectly true, and therefore see no need for further comment.

The various difficulties with the Golden Rule with which I have dealt show that it requires interpretation, and is consequently no substitute for an ethical theory, or other moral ideas, in the light of which it must be interpreted. But my method of dealing with it was also designed to illustrate the method appropriate to and necessary for the criticism and examination of a moral principle, or what is put forward as a moral principle, by determining its implications and testing them in the light of the other moral ideas that we have. If we had no moral beliefs to start with, this method would be impossible. But by the same token, any method would be unnecessary.

ADDITIONAL NOTES AND COMMENTS

A. 'The Golden Rule' was published originally in *Philosophy*, 38 (October 1963), pp. 293–314. My statement that no book had ever been written on the Golden Rule turned out to be false; I was informed a year or two later about the publication, just the year before, of the following: Albrecht Dihle, *Die Goldene Regel, Eine Einführung in die Geshichte der antiken und frühchristlichen Vulgarethik* (Göttingen:

---

[11] John Dewey and James H. Tufts, *Ethics* (New York: Holt, 1908), p. 334 (2nd edn., 1932, pp. 309–10).

Vandenhoeck and Ruprecht, 1962). This point was corrected in: (2) 'Golden Rule', *Encyclopedia of Philosophy*, iii. 365–7—an encyclopaedia article, therefore not, as is the essay in this book, a philosophical argument. And I have since written a few others on the subject: (3) 'Defense of the Golden Rule' (modified version of the present essay), in *Morals and Values*, pp. 115–29; (4) 'Golden Rule', *Encyclopedia of Ethics*, i. 405–8—different from item (2); (5) revised—somewhat enlarged—version of (4), in the 2nd edn. of *Encyclopedia of Ethics*, i. 614–19. Extensive bibliographies are included with the three encyclopaedia articles—expanded in (4), expanded further in (5). In *Generalization* (pp. 15–17) I said some things about the relation of the Golden Rule to the Generalization Principle I later came to see were mistaken—indeed, confused.

B. I am now not so sure that 'disputes about the origin of the moral sense are futile'. In *The Descent of Man* (1871), Darwin tried to give an evolutionary account of the origin of the moral sense. Darwin had long accepted the doctrine that the moral sense has a 'rightful supremacy over every other principle of human action', which he had learned from his conversations with James Mackintosh and his reading of Mackintosh's *Dissertation on the Progress of Ethical Philosophy* (1830). As Robert Richards has pointed out in his marvellously illuminating study, *Darwin and the Emergence of Evolutionary Theories of Mind and Behavior*, Darwin was here attempting to provide a naturalistic basis for Mackintosh's theory of the moral sense.[12] Darwin considered the moral sense a species of social instinct—not a developed or acquired capacity—which evolved out of the process of social selection, itself a species of natural selection. Since instinctive actions are not calculated actions, Darwin regarded the moral-sense theory so understood as an altogether distinct ethical theory—and, more to the point, he has here come up with a plausible

---

[12] Robert J. Richards, *Darwin and the Emergence of Evolutionary Theories of Mind and Behavior* (Chicago, Ill.: University of Chicago Press, 1987); see pp. 115–17; James Mackintosh, *Dissertation on the Progress of Ethical Philosophy, Chiefly During the Seventeenth and Eighteenth Centuries*, 2nd edn. (Edinburgh: Adam and Charles Black, 1837), the first book-length history of ethics to appear in English. I should acknowledge that I am here borrowing from my article 'Nineteenth-Century British Ethics', in Lawrence C. and Charlotte B. Becker (eds.), *A History of Western Ethics* (New York & London: Garland, 1992), pp. 101–2, 103–4. I am pleased to acknowledge here my debt to Dr Michael McFall—a specialist in this area—who first drew my attention to Richards's book on Darwin. And I am pleased also to acknowledge my debt to Michael Gershon's ground-breaking book, *The Second Brain* (New York: Harper Perennial, 1998, 1999). Dr Gershon reports that in his investigations he 'began to ask the question: Where does the enteric nervous system come from?' (p. 241). If Dr Gershon, a research physician and scientist, could ask the question of the origin of the enteric nervous system (which Gershon calls the second brain), then a philosopher can enquire about the origin of the sense of justice or moral sense. Only, the question is not properly one for philosophy—though it can be speculated about in speculative philosophy—but one for science, and I am content to leave the matter in the hands of scientists, such as Darwin and his successors. *Vide* Darwin and Richards. Of this I am certain: whatever the origin of the moral sense, its origin does not determine its validity, scope, or function. See also *The Sense of Injustice*, by Edmond Cahn (New York: New York University Press, 1949; 2nd edn. Bloomington, Ind.: Indiana University Press, 1964). It is the sense of injustice, of some felt or sensed injustice done to them, that often brings home to people, otherwise not of a speculative nature, the existence of a moral sense.

theory of the origin of the moral sense—and a dispute about this, though it would be contentious, would not be futile.

C. It has often been claimed that there cannot be a moral sense, since there is no bodily organ corresponding to it. This is a fairly widespread confusion. There are many senses—capacities—that do not have any bodily organ corresponding to them, such as the sense of balance, the sense of decorum, the sense of relevance, and a sense of humour. Unfortunately the latter is missing or undeveloped in a number of people; in others it is perverted. This is also true of the moral sense.

D. As there are various versions of the Golden Rule, there are various perversions of it. Here is one, called 'a schoolchild's version of the Golden Rule': 'Do one to others before others do one to you'. All sorts of variants on this 'version' or perversion are possible, though hardly worth pursuing. Joking and the schoolyard aside, this form of the *lex talionis* seems to be the rule actually operative in Gangland, and also, apparently, in the world of collegiate and professional sports.

E. Two books in English on the Golden Rule have since appeared. (1) *The Golden Rule*, by H. T. D. Rost (Oxford: George Ronald, 1986), is possibly (I cannot be certain of this) the first book-length treatment of the subject in English, though in the tradition of moral theology rather than moral philosophy; it contains an extensive bibliography, especially of religious and theological treatments and discussions in non-western religious traditions. (2) *The Golden Rule*, by Jeffrey Wattles (New York and Oxford: Oxford University Press, 1996), is a thorough if not definitive treatment of the subject, which traces its history in both western and eastern traditions and conscientiously and capably, if only in a summary way, considers a number of recent discussions of it, philosophical, psychological, and religious. Wattles' book contains an inclusive and wide-ranging bibliography of the subject, the fullest yet seen, including listings of some doctoral dissertations from 1966 on, and constitutes a valuable supplement to the book by Rost.

F. My essay on 'The Golden Rule' has been cited with some frequency and has stimulated a certain amount of discussion and also, not surprisingly, some disagreement. It may also have helped stimulate some greater interest in the Golden Rule amongst philosophers, though naturally this interest might have been developing anyway. And there was certainly some interest before; a gem of a paper that I came across only later on is 'The Categorical Imperative and the Golden Rule', by E. W. Hirst, *Philosophy*, 9 (1934), pp. 328–35. As Hirst observes: 'The Rule does not teach that as between two persons there must be similarity in the details of behaviour, but rather impartiality of interest: from that point of view [here responding to one of Kant's examples] the criminal must endorse the verdict of the judge, as the judge must expect and approve the same verdict were he the criminal.' Anyone of opinion that there is no progress in philosophy is respectfully referred to E. W. Hirst's critique of Kant on this point.

Hirst further observes that:

The Golden Rule . . . does not primarily teach impartiality of judgment on acts considered in abstraction from the agents; rather does it inculcate impartiality of regard between the agents themselves. So long as we use the ideas of similarity and equality which pertain to the maxim of Equity, we relate acts and situations rather than persons. The Golden Rule relates to persons, and involves the idea of unity ... [It] implies community of interest, and teaches impartiality of regard.

Another paper I came across only later is 'The Golden Rule', by Paul Weiss, *Journal of Philosophy*, 38(16) (31 July 1941), pp. 421–30. When I wrote the paper, in 1963, although I had been lecturing on and discussing the matter for some years, I had not searched the literature and was unaware of Weiss's paper. It may be just as well; too much delving about in the literature in search of sources and predecessors can be paralysing to philosophical reflection and enquiry. A paper that has appeared since and is of the first importance is 'The Golden Rule: New Aspects of an Old Moral Principle', by Hans-Ulrich Hoche, trans. J. Claude Evans, in Darrel E. Christensen *et al.* (eds.), *Contemporary German Philosophy*, (University Park, Penn., and London: Pennsylvania State University Press, 1982), i. 69–90, which also contains an extensive and useful bibliography.

G. My distinction between the particular interpretation and the general interpretation has come in for some sharp criticism. Lansing Pollock, for instance, has argued that even on the general interpretation the Golden Rule is an 'imprecise directive', that the Golden Rule 'fails as precise statement of the reciprocal ground of our duties and obligations'.[13] But *of course* the Golden Rule is not 'a precise statement of the reciprocal ground of our duties and obligations'; it does not claim to be, that is a merit and not a defect of it, and it is a mistake to interpret it this way.

H. Somewhat similarly, Alan Gewirth has argued that, in its traditional formulations, the Golden Rule is imprecise, fails as an action guide, and if taken literally would lead, he claims, to 'irrational actions'. So, he claims, it needs 'rationalizing' if it is 'to be saved'. But this so-called 'saving' of the Golden Rule involves transforming it into something else; namely, to what Gewirth calls 'the *Rational* Golden Rule', which, lo and behold, is identical with Gewirth's own 'principle of generic consistency'. As Gewirth reformulates it, the Golden Rule is to read: 'Do unto others as you have a right that they do unto you. Or, to put it in its Generic formulation: Act in accord with the generic rights of your recipients as well as yourself.'[14] Gewirth's argument is fascinating, but it is also off the mark. For this 'transformation' combines alchemy with some sleight of hand, and has boomeranged by fooling its formulator. It amounts to a rejection of the Golden Rule altogether, since it fails to capture its essence or intent or meaning. The Golden Rule is misunderstood when it is taken as an attempt to provide a precise action guide or as 'a precise statement of the reciprocal ground of our duties and obligations'. No

---

[13] Lansing Pollock, 'Reciprocity in Moral Theory' (Univ. of Chicago Ph.D, dissertation, 1970), ch. 2, 'The Golden Rule', pp. 6–28, at pp. 16, 27, 2.

[14] Alan Gewirth, 'The Golden Rule Rationalized', *Midwest Studies in Philosophy*, 3 (1978), pp. 133–47, at 137, 139. Gewirth's principle of generic consistency (into which he transforms the Golden Rule) is developed in his much-discussed *Reason and Morality* (Chicago: University of Chicago Press, 1978).

moral principle can serve as a precise action guide, telling us in meticulous detail in each and every set of circumstances just exactly what we ought to do. To understand principles in this way is to confuse moral principles with detailed rules or directives applying to specific sets of circumstances and to leave out of account the morally essential factor of moral judgement, not something deducible from precise 'action guides'. A principle can be in general terms a guide to action without telling us exactly what we ought to do in each set of circumstances. This requires judgement, which in turn requires character, moral sense, and moral discernment (in other words, certain virtues), and to look to precise principles for exact direction is to surrender both autonomy and responsibility for one's own judgements, decisions, and actions.[15] Furthermore, the interpretation that eliminates the phrase 'what you would have' in favour of the language of rights tends to make it appear that the application of the Rule is something mechanical, when what it requires is imagination combined with some measure of both sympathy and empathy. You are not to imagine yourself *being* the other, but you are to imagine yourself 'in the place of the other', and the Rule also calls upon you to think of the principle involved in the action you are contemplating, though the Rule, in its traditional formulations, wisely does not incorporate the language of 'principles', as it does not incorporate the formalized language of 'rights'.

I. I conclude that the general interpretation, on which one has to consider the general ways in which (i.e. the principles on which) one would have others behave in their treatment of oneself, emerges unscathed from these confrontations. For, as I said in the text, 'what I would have them do, in abstraction from any of their particular desires . . . is to take account of my interests [which does not mean—as Gewirth actually suggests at one point—simply note them and then either ignore them or frustrate them] and either satisfy them or at least not wilfully frustrate them'.[16] I am to treat others *on the same principle or standard* as I would have them apply in their treatment of me. A number of writers have pointed out that this does

[15] The text here is paraphrased from my article on the Golden Rule in *Encyclopedia of Ethics*—items (4) and (5) in list above.

[16] Gewirth says: 'The phrase "take account of" is vague; a sadist, for example, takes account of his victim's wishes, since such taking account is necessary to his aim of violating those wishes' ('Golden Rule Rationalized', p. 135). In the context, as Gewirth must realize, this is just silly. 'What Singer means', Gewirth continues,

is that the agent should either 'satisfy' his recipient's wishes or else 'not wilfully frustrate them'. But this then is largely identical with the Inversion conception of the Golden Rule; it requires that the agent always treat his recipient as the latter wishes to be treated, or at least that he not intentionally contravene those wishes. And, as has been emphasized, this is unacceptable as a general principle. It is too permissive for the recipient and too restrictive for the agent.

This argument is more substantial (and I obviously agree with the import of the last two sentences). But, again, I think Gewirth is mistaken. The Golden Rule does not say, nor does it mean, 'Do unto others as [or what] others would have you do unto them'. What it means is what it says: 'Do unto others *as* [not what] you would have others do unto you'. That is, 'Act towards others on the same principles you would have others apply in their treatment of you'. This latter does not imply the Inversion, or any other perversion, of the Golden Rule.

nothing to determine what these standards should be. But of course it doesn't! Why ever should it have been supposed that it should? What standard of conduct would I have others apply in their treatment of me? One who is in a position to ask this question should be in a position to answer it. Well, it is this same standard that I ought to apply in my treatment of others. Children can understand this; apparently some 'thinkers' (to use one of Bradley's favourite phrases) cannot. (Yet I should mention that Professor Hans-Ulrich Hoche's paper on the Golden Rule, just cited, contains a penetrating critique of my concept of the 'general interpretation' of the Golden Rule.)

The point here is akin to a criticism often levelled at Kant's Categorical Imperative, that it provides us with no basis for obtaining or formulating maxims, which are what the Categorical Imperative is meant to test.[17] This point is equally off the mark. A maxim, in Kant's use, is not a rule of conduct telling us what to do or not to do, and contains no element of *ought*. Maxims arise out of inclinations, we act on a maxim whenever we act with a purpose (as, on Kant's view, we always do in voluntary action), and Kant is not using 'maxim' to mean anything like a guide to conduct. One's maxim is a formulation of what one *wills* or intends to do, not a formulation of what one ought to do. (Cf. *Generalization*, ch. 9, esp. pp. 243–9.)

J. Another interesting attempt (there are many others, but not all of them are interesting) to transform the Golden Rule appears in Charles Baylis's *Ethics: The Principles of Wise Choice* (New York: Holt, 1958), in which Baylis proposes what he calls a 'revised Golden Rule [which] says to act toward others in the way which will result in the greatest good for all, giving equal consideration to the good of each' (p. 99). This sounds good, but as with so many other attempts to 'revise' the Golden Rule, it rests on a faulty analysis and consequent misunderstanding of it, in the process transforming it into something other than it is—in this case a qualified form of non-hedonistic utilitarianism. But the Golden Rule is not a utilitarian principle. The Golden Rule, as I said, is a prime instrument of moral education, easily understood by parent and child alike. But this so-called 'revised Golden Rule'—it is really no such thing—would test the patience and the understanding of both parent and child. It might not be so difficult to 'give equal consideration to the good of each', but even one with considerable resources available would be hard pressed to determine which course of action would 'result in the greatest good for all'. If those who are so eager to transform the Golden Rule into something other than it

---

[17] 'Act only on that maxim that you can at the same time will to be a universal law'—that is, can without self-contradiction be willing to have become a universal law, a principle on which everyone acts. And a maxim, which one need not consciously formulate, is a statement of what one wants or intends to do in given circumstances. When generalized, the maxim takes the form: When in circumstances *c* I will do *d* in order to obtain *p*. There is no hint here of an 'ought statement' or a statement of obligation. Now it is the maxim that the Categorical Imperative is to be used to test. A maxim that passes the test—a maxim that one can consistently be willing to have become a universal law—is one that it is morally permissible to act on; *nota bene*, not one that one is morally obligated to act on.

is thought of it explicitly as an instrument of moral education perhaps they would be more hesitant in proposing revisions and transformations of it, some of which are not actually versions but more frequently perversions.

K. In *The New Golden Rule* Amitai Etzioni has a comment on a sentence in my article on the Golden Rule in the Edwards *Encyclopedia of Philosophy*, which is worth some notice as a way of clarifying what was said above. Unfortunately, both his quotation and his comments are a bit out of kilter. Etzioni quotes that article as saying: 'The nearly universal acceptance of the Golden Rule and its promulgation by persons of considerable intelligence, though otherwise of different outlooks, would therefore provide some evidence for the claim that it is a fundamental ethical truth.'[18] The sentence in question is, curiously, the last one in the article, but what the last part of this sentence actually said is not 'would therefore provide', but would therefore *seem to* provide'. This may seem like a subtle difference, but the difference between a conjecture and a categorical assertion is really not very subtle.

Etzioni's comment on this statement is especially choice:

Singer is cautious and very much on the mark: Global endorsement does provide *some* normative accounting. Surely we note that a moral ideal all people respect has a much stronger standing than one that is affirmed by one people or culture or even a handful. Something, though, is still clearly missing: If all societies, for instance, subscribe to a prejudice [in this context 'prejudice' is a question-begging word] that helps them justify treating women (or some other group, such as immigrants or the disabled) as second-class human beings, would this globalism justify the said prejudice? Moreover, when one compares these global values to core values, and the elaborate arguments in their support, found in many religious and secular compositions, such as that of the Old and New Testaments; and in works such as those of Aristotle, Confucius, or Immanuel Kant, the paucity of the empirical list and ethics that build on it stands out.

No doubt. I am always glad to be instructed on the ethical teachings of Aristotle, Confucius, and especially Immanuel Kant, by anyone in a position to provide such instruction. But Etzioni then concludes that:

To the extent that normative globalists rely on empirical observation, their criterion is both rather thin and not well grounded because the data are tricky. The criterion is thin because

---

[18] Amitai Etzioni, *The New Golden Rule: Community and Morality in a Democratic Society* (New York: Basic Books, 1996), p. 231. Etzioni does not cite directly, lists his source (p. 302 n. 64) thus: 'as quoted by James Gaffney, "The Golden Rule: Abuses and Uses", *America*, 20 September 1986, 115'. If Gaffney's article is indeed Etzioni's source, that might explain the misquotation, though not the misdirected comment. But Etzioni, as he indicates, made use of a small brigade of 'young researchers', and it is a pity that not one of these young researchers researched just a bit further in order to see the article in its proper context, in order to get the passage straight, and in order at least to see, and perhaps to understand, what preceded this sentence. And the article was published in *The Encyclopedia of Philosophy*, not in some difficult-to-find out-of-the-way journal, though it might have been out of the way for 'young researchers' who didn't research.

it embraces only a few values, such as murder, theft, and rape. And even here we are on unsure grounds . . . (Outsiders are often fair game in numerous societies.)

This is so elementary, and still so far off the mark, that I find it both amazing and amusing. And my amusement increases when I note that I am labelled an 'empirical or normative globalist'. It never occurred to me that the sentence in question could be so misconstrued for controversial purposes. Here is how Etzioni immediately precedes his comment on the passage in question: 'Some have drawn normative conclusions from data about global uniformities, arguing that *we can hold people of different* cultures to values that all cultures share, because these values are shared by all societies, a global application of the consensus test. A typical statement is one made about the old golden rule. Marcus Singer writes . . .' (emphasis added).

This is, regrettably, shoddy scholarship and worse reasoning. Etzioni takes a statement out of context that he finds quoted or misquoted elsewhere and feels free to comment on it, the article in which it appeared, and the overall view of its author, in blissful ignorance of the true state of affairs, and without stopping to consider whether he might be tilting at a windmill.

What is 'the new golden rule?', you might ask. This is a good question. Unfortunately it is not easy to say. The book's extensive index does not list either this expression or any related expressions, such as 'golden rule', 'golden', or 'rule'. So one must hunt to find out. Here are some candidates: 'Respect and uphold society's moral order as you would have society respect and uphold your autonomy' is one; another is 'the communitarian paradigm entails a profound commitment to moral order that is basically voluntary, and to a social order that is well balanced with socially secured autonomy—the new golden rule' (p. 257). Still another, and possibly the closest one can get to a precise statement in this loosely reasoned treatise, is: 'The basic social virtues are a voluntary moral order and a strong measure of bounded individual and subgroup autonomy, held in careful equilibrium, the new golden rule' (p. 244). Or, to supplement this, the following: 'moral order and autonomy, the twin virtues, crown the communitarian normative account; they provide the final, substantive normative criterion this account requires' (p. 245). I see no criterion here, but perhaps I simply don't understand how the author is using the word 'criterion'. Yet I do notice the next sentence, which says that 'the validity of the dual primary concepts . . . is self-evident'. Even though its meaning is not self-evident, 'self-evidence' does not appear in the index, though 'self-denial', 'self-esteem', and 'self-incrimination' do. Curious this.

With all due respect to Professor Etzioni, this is not a *new* golden rule, in any sense in which a new golden rule is conceived of as something intended to take the place of what he refers to—scornfully, though without analysis—as 'the *old* golden rule'. It is a philosophical thesis about the importance of moral order and individual autonomy and the relations between them. 'The *new* golden rule' is simply a misnomer, though it is admittedly a catchy title, appealing, perhaps, to an interest in whatever is new and up-to-date.

L. What I should say now—some thirty-five to forty years later—about the Golden Rule in connection with its cultural omnipresence is the following (and let this be construed as a whole and in the light of what precedes it in the article from which I am adapting it): An important fact that needs to be explained is why the Golden Rule, in one formulation or another, is involved in the moral codes of nearly every culture known to us. In some of these cultures, as in societies governed by or tracing back to the code of Confucius, it plays a subsidiary role. In others, especially those resting on at least a proclaimed ideal of equality, it serves as a fundamental principle on which more specific rules are based. It is surely curious why the Golden Rule is at the core or at the head of so many codes of conduct in such disparate parts of the world. The fact that it is basic to the moral codes of so many and such different peoples would seem to entail that it is a fundamental normative moral principle, connected inextricably with human nature, and this inference from an *is* to an *ought* surely deserves examination.[19]

We do not need any *new* golden rules, and we need no reformulations or transformations of *the* Golden Rule. We need a better and more balanced understanding of the Golden Rule itself, not cute dialectical attempts to unbalance it. Attempts to improve on it—or replace it—are fruitless, and result from a misunderstanding of its point and purpose. Genuine attempts to understand it and sensibly to teach, inculcate, and act on it, on the other hand, are not fruitless. Think of it, in other words, as a device of moral education, for both children and adults. When thought of in this light, its meaning should not be so difficult to comprehend. And, to repeat what it seems necessary constantly to repeat, the Golden Rule is not an algorithm; it provides no automatic way of distinguishing right from wrong. To search for such an algorithm is to squeeze the life out of morality, by detaching it altogether from traits of character, from moral judgement, and from the virtues. The moral sense can develop only through being used, not by the automatic application of a hard and fast rule.

---

[19] Adapted from the revised article on the Golden Rule in the 2nd edn. of *Encyclopedia of Ethics*.

13

Mill's Stoic Conception of Happiness and Pragmatic Conception of Utility

When I was a bit younger and first starting on the study of philosophy I found great satisfaction in setting out to refute the doctrines of others. This is often the way budding philosophers are trained, and it may be that my graduate training at Cornell, in the late 1940s—at a time when Cornell was regarded in the American philosophical community at large as an offshoot of the linguistic-analysis schools of Oxford and Cambridge[1]—served to reinforce this propensity. But over the years I have acquired a somewhat different outlook and, taking a piece of advice from William James, have come to read philosophers, especially those who are no longer around to defend themselves, with an eye to what they are saying that is true or enlightening rather than solely with an eye for determining where they went wrong or contradicted themselves; that is to say, sympathetically rather than caustically. This has led me over a period of years to come to a view of the moral philosophy of John Stuart Mill that is quite different from the point of view I had of Mill years before and from the view that still seems canonical in the textbooks and the presuppositions of philosophical writers today. So I am going to give an account of some matters in Mill that I have come to think are right, sound, true, or enlightening, even though this goes against the grain of standard philosophical opinion. I make no claims to originality. I do not claim that what I say herein is new, only that it is true, and that it is the result of my own reading of and reflecting on Mill over quite a long period of time. If credit for some fundamental new insight properly belongs elsewhere, then let it be credited elsewhere. We live in a period when philosophical reflection is increasingly being hampered by a rapidly escalating mass of philosophical literature and a proclaimed though rarely defended need to consult all the sources. A pox on it! This

---

[1] So much so that 'Oxford, Cambridge, and Cornell' became for a time, especially in the 1950s, something of an epithet amongst philosophers in America distrustful, or fearful, of what they took to be linguistic or analytic method in philosophy.

attitude, if generalized, would turn philosophers into timid antiquarians constantly looking over their shoulders to see whether someone else might have said it before. If someone else has said it before, so be it; this has the unanticipated benefit that there is then some measure of independent confirmation. Better all told to meditate with an eye to seeing what is true or illuminating. And let us take as our guiding motto a statement by Mill that should be better known:

There is no difficulty in proving any ethical standard whatever to work ill if we suppose universal idiocy to be conjoined with it (*Util.* pp. 30–1, ch. 2, par. 24)[2]

My procedure in what follows will resemble that of a commentary. For present purposes at least I judge it better generally to quote than to paraphrase. So I shall often quote, occasionally at some length, a statement by Mill, emphasizing what in it I think needs emphasis and in the same context also commenting on it.

I

A hedonistic conception of happiness is one that conceives of happiness solely in terms of pleasure—in particular, as pleasure and freedom from pain or as a balance of pleasure over pain—and also conceives of pleasures as sensations or feelings or emotions, and of pleasures and pains as opposites (whether as sensations or feelings) on a commensurable scale. This is what we find in Bentham, to a great extent in Sidgwick, and frequently in Mill, for instance early in the second chapter of *Utilitarianism*, where Mill announces that: 'By happiness is intended pleasure and the absence of pain; by unhappiness, pain and the absence of pleasure' (p. 10; 2. 2).

As the work proceeds, however, Mill develops a different conception of happiness which, if it is not altogether non-hedonistic, is certainly an alternative conception, and contains as essential parts of it some Stoic ingredients. Furthermore, this alternative conception goes along with a conception of the workings of the principle of utility that differs drastically from that found in Bentham and even in Sidgwick, and foreshadows in some ways the sort of pragmatic ethics developed later on by Dewey.

---

[2] J. S. Mill, *Utilitarianism* (London, 1861, repr. 1863; 2nd edn. 1864), abbreviated as '*Util.*'; the page numbers cited are those in the Library of Liberal Arts 2nd edn. (New York: Liberal Arts, 1957); in accordance with a rule that I think should always be followed in the absence of a standard pagination system, I cite also by chapter and paragraph number, using the format 'n. m' to mean 'chapter n, paragraph m'.

Mill in part alerts us to this by observing that: 'To give a clear view of the moral standard set up by the theory much more requires to be said; in particular, what things' are included 'in the ideas of pain and pleasure, and to what extent this remains an open question' (p. 10; 2.2). Only two paragraphs later he goes on to say that to draw out the 'scheme of consequences from the utilitarian principle' in a 'faultless' and 'sufficient' manner 'many Stoic . . . elements require to be included' (p. 11; 2. 4). These 'supplementary explanations', and the Stoic elements in Mill's conception, need to be more adequately appreciated and understood, without worrying about whether by incorporating them Mill is being consistent with his heritage or his self-professed 'Epicureanism'—which we now think of as hedonism— or whether or not it is true, as Mill claims in that same rich paragraph, that 'these supplementary explanations do not affect the theory of life on which this theory of morality is grounded—namely, that pleasure and freedom from pain are the only things desirable as ends'. This is part of what I attempt here. I believe that Mill was right to distinguish different qualities or kinds of pleasure—though I do not think he successfully explained how it can be determined which kinds are better than others—and that Sidgwick and the great bulk of commentators who have derided or ignored Mill's qualitative hedonism,[3] perhaps in their search for a moral algorithm, have been grossly mistaken. I announce this at the outset because I am not here concentrating on this feature of Mill's view, which is really another topic (though I greatly look forward to the distinctive kind of pleasure that would almost certainly accompany a defence of this claim). I add that in developing this alternative theory of happiness Mill is following out consistently the requirements of the quantity–quality distinction his reflections led him to.

II

I shall deal first with the alternative or non-hedonistic conception of happiness. Only later will the different conception of the working of the utility principle come into focus.

---

[3] The expression 'qualitative hedonism' was used by Rem Edwards in the subtitle of his illuminating book *Pleasures and Pains: A Theory of Qualitative Hedonism* (Ithaca, NY, and London: Cornell University Press, 1979), though it should be added that, as Edwards himself brings out, he was not the first to use this self-explanatory terminology. Consider, as a side-light, the following passage from it: 'Probably the most insuperable objection to qualitative hedonism is that if it should turn out to be true that pleasures differ qualitatively as well as quantitatively, practically all the textbooks in ethics that have appeared in over a century would have to be rewritten' (p. 82).

Consider first Mill's statement that 'all human beings possess in one form or another . . . *a sense of dignity*' (p. 13, 2. 6; italics added), which, he says, 'is so essential a part of the happiness of those in whom it is strong that nothing which conflicts with it could be otherwise than momentarily an object of desire to them'. If all human beings possess a sense of dignity and it is an essential part of the happiness of those in whom its strength is at least above the infinitesimal, then happiness can not be merely a balance of pleasurable sensations over painful ones. Further, the idea of a *sense of dignity* is itself a moral idea, one characteristic of what has been called a deontological-type theory, and consequently, given his reliance on a sense of dignity as a determiner (in 'those in whom it is strong') of what is desired on the basis of what is deemed desirable or undesirable, Mill is here recognizing that a moral consideration can determine what certain persons— those with a strong sense of dignity—find pleasurable or painful, hence desirable or undesirable. So there is some evidence that Mill's considered doctrine is not simply or simplistically consequentialist or teleological.[4] Mill also says, a bit further on, that 'the ingredients of happiness are very various', that 'happiness is not an abstract idea but a concrete whole', and that it has various parts (pp. 46, 47; 4. 5, 4. 6). Such statements tell further against the idea that happiness is a mere sum of pleasures over pains. Mill has, of course, been accused of inconsistency on this point, but such a claim is immaterial. It does nothing to help us understand and learn from Mill. Moore had great fun 'refuting' Mill, as he thought he was doing, by ridiculing such statements.[5] But Moore actually understood Mill no better than he understood Bradley, and there is reason to think, since Moore's influence was so extensive, that Moore's alleged 'refutation' set back Mill interpretation for over half a century.

Now notice (pp. 17–20; 2. 12–15) Mill's list of four elements of happiness, which he delineates in part as: (i) moments of 'rapture', (ii) 'in an existence made up of few and transitory pains, (iii) many *and various* pleasures, (iv) with a *decided predominance of the active over the passive*' (p. 17, 2. 12; italics and enumeration added). This of course presupposes Mill's qualitative hedonism, in accordance with which pleasures and pains differ in kind or quality as well as in quantity or degree. Let me direct your attention here to two points. One is that it *makes sense* to speak of various and

---

[4] As indicated earlier in this book, this is a scheme of classification I am not at all happy with, use only for the sake of convenience. A better one would distinguish a consequentialist- or utilitarian-type theory from a teleological theory. Aristotle's ethics is teleological, not consequentialist or utilitarian. But even such a tripartite division is misleading.

[5] G. E. Moore, *Principia Ethica* (Cambridge: Cambridge University Press, 1903), sects. 34–44.

different pleasures—which is a way of speaking of the pleasures arising out of or associated with various experiences and activities—so that Mill's qualitative hedonism is by no means self-evidently false, and indeed quite clearly has something to be said for it. The second is that in distinguishing *active* from *passive* pleasures Mill is distinguishing, what are surely distinguishable even if not separable, the pleasures arising out of activity and those arising out of passivity—which somewhat crudely can be put as the difference between the pleasures experienced by participants and the pleasures experienced by spectators. Mill is already thinking of these as different *kinds* of pleasures.

In addition, Mill speaks of *the foundation of happiness*. The *foundation* of happiness is 'not to expect more from life than it is capable of bestowing'. (Mill's exact words are: 'having as the foundation of the whole not to expect more from life than it is capable of bestowing'.) This provision has a privileged position, since it is '*the foundation of the whole*' and this is the prime (though not the only) Stoic element in Mill's alternative or considered conception of happiness. It is, it should be noted, an *intellectual* and moral element, a characteristic which, if one does not naturally have it, one can develop through mental exercise and exertion, that in other words one can *learn* to acquire. This is surely a far cry from a mere balance of pleasure over pain—it is a prime condition of attaining it.

Note now Mill's reference to the 'present wretched education and wretched social arrangements' (p. 18; 2. 12). The context is one in which Mill says, right after delineating the four elements of happiness and observing that the foundation of happiness is 'not to expect more from life than it is capable of bestowing', that

such an existence is even now the lot of many during some considerable portion of their lives. The present wretched education and wretched social arrangements are the only real hindrance to its being attainable by almost all.

Mill then goes on to speak of 'The main constituents of a satisfied life'. In this phrase 'satisfied' should be replaced by 'happy', since Mill tends to use the terms 'satisfied', 'contented', and 'happy' (or 'happiness') in ways that sometimes lead to trouble—sometimes he uses them equivalently and sometimes not—so he is here saying that the main constituents of a happy life 'appear to be two . . . tranquillity and excitement'. I think it apparent that Mill is associating passive pleasures with tranquillity, or thinking of the passive pleasures as those arising out of or associated with tranquillity, and also that he is associating active pleasures with excitement, or thinking of active pleasures as those arising out of or associated with excitement—only in referring to tranquillity and excitement there is of course no explicit mention of pleasure. The following sentence also needs interpretation: 'With much tranquillity, many find that they can be content with very little pleasure.' Here Mill falls into using 'pleasure' as a surrogate for *excitement*, or active pleasures; what he is actually saying, though, is that with much tranquillity, or with much in the way of passive pleasures, many find that they can be content with very little excitement, or very little in the way of active pleasures, and this gloss eliminates the appearance of contradiction in what Mill actually wrote. The remaining part of the sentence reads: 'with much excitement, many can reconcile themselves to a considerable quantity of pain'. This can be glossed as: much absorbing activity can absorb or diminish pain.

This is true, and we are even beginning to have some understanding of the physiological basis for it: much excitement, or engaging activity, releases endorphins, which are natural pain fighters. The generation of adrenalin has much the same effect. Thus we have the phenomenon of the athlete who continues to play with a broken leg and feels no pain until the game is over.

Mill goes on to say:

There is assuredly no inherent impossibility of enabling even the mass of mankind to unite both [that is, both tranquillity and excitement), since the two are so far from incompatible that they are in natural alliance, the prolongation of either being a preparation for, and exciting a wish for, the other. It is only those in whom indolence amounts to a *vice* that do not desire excitement after an interval of repose; it is only those in whom the need of excitement is a *disease* that feel the tranquillity which follows excitement dull and insipid, instead of pleasurable in direct proportion to the excitement which preceded it. (p. 18; 2. 13; italics added)

It seems clear that Mill is here using the terms 'vice' and 'disease' interchangeably, and could with the same meaning, though perhaps not with the same rhetorical effect, have spoken of those in whom indolence amounts to a disease and those in whom the need of excitement is a vice. It is also evident that Mill is quite openly using these terms in a normative way, to express an evaluation of the character of such persons. After all, a vice is a moral defect. A clue to this point is provided by the next two sentences:

When people who are tolerably fortunate in their outward lot do not find in life sufficient enjoyment to make it valuable to them, the cause generally is *caring for nobody but themselves.* To those who have neither public nor private affections, the excitements of life are much curtailed, and in any case dwindle in value as the time approaches when all selfish interests must be terminated by death; while those who leave after them *objects of personal affection*, and especially those who have also *cultivated a fellow-feeling with the collective interests of mankind*, retain as lively an interest in life on the eve of death as in the vigor of youth and health. (p. 18; 2. 13; italics added)

Thus selfishness—self-centeredness, egocentricity, egotism—is picked out as the chief cause of unhappiness in those 'who are tolerably fortunate in their outward lot'. What follows adds substance to this:

Next to selfishness, the principal cause which makes life unsatisfactory is *want of mental cultivation*. A cultivated mind . . . [a] mind to which the fountains of knowledge have been opened, and which has been taught . . . to exercise its faculties— finds sources of inexhaustible interest in all that surrounds it: in the objects of nature, the imaginations of poetry, the incidents of history, the ways of mankind, past and present, and their prospects in the future. It is possible to become indifferent to all this, and that too without having exhausted a thousandth part of it, but only when one has from the beginning no moral or human interest in these things and has sought in them only the gratification of curiosity. (pp. 18–19; 2. 13; italics added)

Of course, this 'only when' clause is implausible in the light of present knowledge, but Mill was writing at a time before depression had been identified as a clinical entity, capable of medical treatment, even though Mill knew and associated with a number of people who were regarded at that time as 'melancholic'. But this is only a momentary interruption in our story.

Thus we find Mill saying that the chief cause of unhappiness, at least for those 'who are tolerably fortunate in their outward lot', is selfishness, caring for no one but oneself. And the second main source of unhappiness is 'want of mental cultivation'. Consequently, caring for others, 'cultivating a fellow-feeling with the collective interests of mankind', is another essential ingredient in or source of happiness, as is mental cultivation, developing one's mind and sensitivities, and these are two further elements of happiness, to be added to the four distinguished before (p. 18; 2. 13). Of course, as we in this century in particular know, it can also be a source of sympathetic misery, since the lot of humanity in so many places in the world is one of unremitting and ceaseless misery.

Mill now says that:

there is absolutely no reason in the nature of things why an amount of mental culture sufficient to give an intelligent interest in these objects of contemplation should not be the inheritance of everyone born in a civilized country. (p. 19; 2. 14)

If there is no such 'reason in the nature of things', then the reason must lie
in something else, and it does. It lies in the 'present wretched education and
wretched social arrangements' (p. 18; 2. 12); in other words, in economic,
cultural, educational, and political institutions, all of which are within the
control of human beings—at least human beings collectively—to modify.
Mill now amplifies this theme. There is no 'inherent necessity', he tells us,
that 'any human being should be a selfish egotist, devoid of every feeling or
care but those which center in his own miserable individuality' (p. 19; 2.
14):

Genuine private affections and a sincere interest in the public good are possible . . .
to every *rightly brought* up human being. (italics added)

'*Every rightly brought up human being*', Mill says. Upbringing, not nature, is
the key, and upbringing, in turn, depends on social arrangements of the sort
just mentioned, not on the nature of things—within limits to be mentioned
in a moment. We come now to a passage almost poetic in its passion:

In a world in which there is so much to interest, so much to enjoy, *and so much
also to correct and improve*, everyone who has this moderate amount of moral
and intellectual requisites is capable of an existence which may be called enviable.
(p. 19; 2. 14; italics added)

Such a person, Mill goes on, 'through bad laws or subjection to the will of
others', may be 'denied the liberty to use the sources of happiness within . . .
reach'. However, if not, the person 'will not fail to find this enviable existence, if he escape the positive evils of life, the great sources of physical and
mental suffering'. What are these 'positive evils of life'?

They include 'indigence, disease, and the unkindness, worthlessness, or
premature loss of objects of affection', and 'it is a rare good fortune entirely
to escape' from 'these calamities' (p. 19; 2. 14). 'The main stress of the
problem', Mill continues, 'lies . . . in the contest with these calamities from
which it is a rare good fortune entirely to escape; which, as things now are,
cannot be obviated, and often cannot be in any material degree mitigated'.
Yet, Mill adds,

most of the great positive evils of the world are in themselves removable, and will,
if human affairs continue to improve, be in the end reduced within narrow limits.
(p. 20; 2. 14)

'[I]f human affairs continue to improve'. Let us suppose they will—a very
large assumption, to be sure—and see what Mill says about these positive
evils that can be 'in the end reduced within narrow limits'.

These positive evils are 'poverty, in any sense implying suffering . . . disease . . . [and] vicissitudes of fortune and other disappointments connected with worldly circumstances'. But these vicissitudes of fortune, Mill claims, are 'principally the effect either of gross imprudence, of ill-regulated desires, or of bad or imperfect social institutions' (p. 20; 2. 14). Consequently, Mill concludes:

All the grand sources . . . of human suffering are in a great degree . . . conquerable by human care and effort; and though their removal is grievously slow . . . yet every mind sufficiently intelligent and generous to bear a part . . . in the endeavor will draw *a noble enjoyment from the contest itself which he would not for any bribe in the form of selfish indulgence consent to be without.* (p. 20; 2. 14; italics added)

It scarcely needs remarking that the noble enjoyment drawn from the contest itself is an *active* pleasure, a pleasure intrinsically bound up with an activity in which obstacles are to be overcome and there is no guarantee in advance that the goal will be achieved. It is the process itself that is enjoyable, to anyone with sufficient mental culture who is not a 'selfish egotist'; that is to say, who has the requisite social concern. For this is a 'world in which there is so much to interest, so much to enjoy, and *so much also to correct and improve*' (p. 19; 2. 14; italics added). Mill has already spoken of the 'present wretched education and wretched social arrangements' (p. 18; 2. 12); he now goes on to speak of the 'imperfect state of the world's arrangements' (p. 21; 2. 16), and to add that

in this condition of the world . . . the conscious ability to do without happiness gives the best prospect of realizing such happiness as is attainable. For nothing except that consciousness can raise a person above the chances of life by making him feel that, let fate and fortune do their worst, they have not power to subdue him; which, once felt, frees him from excess of anxiety concerning the evils of life and enables him, *like many a Stoic in the worst times of the Roman Empire*, to cultivate in tranquillity the sources of satisfaction accessible to him, without concerning himself about the uncertainty of their duration any more than about their inevitable end. (pp. 21–2; 2. 16; italics added)

I have here deliberately emphasized the explicit reference to Stoicism, which may be added to the implicit reference remarked on before; namely, 'not to expect more from life than it is capable of bestowing' (p. 17; 2. 12). It is apparent that, as Mill had forewarned us earlier (p. 11; 2. 4), these Stoic virtues are essential elements in Mill's conception of happiness and consequently in Mill's utilitarian programme. And Mill is not troubled philosophically, though he is troubled morally and politically, by the fact that, as he puts it:

Unquestionably it is possible to do without happiness; it is done involuntarily by nineteen-twentieths of mankind, even in those parts of our present world which are least deep in barbarism. (p. 20, 2. 15).

And this is 'a very imperfect state of the world's arrangements' (p. 21, 2. 16).

Now a world in which nineteen-twentieths of the inhabitants are involuntarily in misery is not a good world or a desirable state of affairs; and, it might be added, a world in which the same proportion of people were *voluntarily* in misery would be a very weird one, practically unintelligible. As Mill had stated earlier in response to the happiness sceptics, even 'if no happiness is to be had at all by human beings . . . utility includes not solely the pursuit of happiness, but the prevention or mitigation of unhappiness, and if the former aim be chimerical, there will be all the greater scope and more imperative need for the latter' (p. 17, 2. 12).

The goal of all this activity, or one main goal, is to make the world 'all that, if will and knowledge were not wanting, it might easily be made' (p. 20, 2. 14). Let us now see how Mill thinks that this can be done.

III

First, it is essential that:

laws and social arrangements should place the happiness or (*as speaking practically, it may be called*) the interest of every individual as nearly as possible in harmony with the interest of the whole. (p. 22, 2. 18; italics added)

I want to dilate for a moment on the phrase I have just emphasized. Mill is saying that 'the *happiness* of a person' can, *speaking practically*, serve as a surrogate for 'the *interest* of a person', where this latter phrase refers not to what a person is curious about, but to what is in that person's interest, or for that person's own good. There is here no necessary reference to hedonism in any form whatever, and it is my considered judgement that Mill uses the term 'happiness' here purely out of long-standing hedonistic habit. For here Mill is concentrating not on defending the tradition in which he was raised, but on the facts as he sees them, and his capacity for doing this is what helps make him such a fascinating philosopher. So, let the 'laws and social arrangements' do what they can to place 'the interest of every individual as nearly as possible in harmony with the interest of the whole'. Why? Because 'as between his own happiness [that is to say, interest] and that of others, utilitarianism requires [the individual human being] to be as strictly impartial as a disinterested and benevolent spectator'—and here Mill incorporates into his own developed moral philosophy the prime element of another and ostensibly incompatible ethical tradition with (it seems clear to me) no incoherence whatever. How the laws and social arrangements are to bring this about is another matter, which Mill does in fact turn to.

Second, 'education and opinion', Mill holds, have a vast 'power over human character', so let

education and opinion . . . so use that power as to establish in the mind of every individual an indissoluble association between his own happiness and the good of the whole . . . so that not only [may the individual] be unable to conceive the possibility of happiness to himself, consistently with conduct opposed to the general good, but also that a direct impulse to promote the general good may be in every individual one of the habitual motives of action, and the sentiments connected therewith may fill a large and prominent place in every human being's sentient existence. (pp. 22–3, 2. 18)[6]

This will be quite a task for education and opinion and for those, if any, who direct them. Proper education can have a vast power over human character, if started at an early enough age, and so can opinion. But, even if it be granted that education can be centrally directed to this end, how can it be supposed that opinion—that elusive thing called public opinion, often manifested in customs and mores and, in this period, supposedly measured by public-opinion polls—can be centrally directed to this end, at least in a liberal state that respects the 'freedom of thought and opinion' that Mill had defended so eloquently in his *On Liberty* of two years earlier? Mill has something of an answer to this which we must now consider. Whether his answer is adequate is something else.

Mill's answer is that 'by the improvement of education' (p. 35, 3. 2)— and let us not forget his earlier references to 'the present wretched education and wretched social arrangements' (p. 18; 2. 12)—by the improvement of education and presumably also by the improvement of opinion and institutions,

the feeling of unity with our fellow creatures shall be . . . as deeply rooted in our character . . . as the horror of crime is in an ordinarily well-brought-up young person. (p. 35, 3. 2)

---

[6] I am deliberately ignoring Mill's reliance in this passage on the theory of psychological association. It plays no essential role here.

The foundation for this process is actually a natural one, 'the social feelings of mankind—the desire to be in unity with our fellow creatures, which is already a powerful principle in human nature' (p. 40; 3. 10).

The social state is at once so natural, so necessary, and so habitual to man, that, except in some unusual circumstances or by an effort of voluntary abstraction, he never conceives himself otherwise than as a member of a body . . . Any condition . . . which is essential to a state of society becomes more and more an inseparable part of every person's conception of the state of things which he is born into, and which is the destiny of a human being. Now society between human beings, except in the relation of master and slave, is manifestly impossible on any other footing than that the interests of all are to be consulted. Society between equals can only exist on the understanding that the interests of all are to be regarded equally. And since in all states of civilization, every person, except an absolute monarch, has equals, everyone is obliged to live on these terms with somebody; and in every age some advance is made toward a state in which it will be impossible to live permanently on other terms with anybody. In this way people grow up unable to conceive as possible to them a state of total disregard of other people's interests. (p. 40; 3. 10)

This may seem unduly optimistic, especially when we consider the horrendous crimes against humanity that have been such a marked feature of our own age; we must recognize, however, that Mill is not engaged in sociological description, but in normative ethics and politics. As he says, 'whatever amount of this [social] feeling a person has',

he is urged by the strongest motives both of interest and of sympathy to demonstrate it, *and to the utmost of his power to encourage it in others,* and *even if he have none of it himself, he is as greatly interested as anyone else that others should have it.* (p. 41, 3. 10; italics added)

Thus Mill takes care of the problem of egotism and 'the selfish egotist'; even a person who has none of this social feeling, who is a selfish egotist *in extremis,* is required by prudence and self-interest 'to encourage it in others . . . and . . . is as interested as anyone else that others should have it'. The shortsighted—that is to say, the stupid—egotist, will not see this, but the intelligent egotist will, and this therefore becomes something people are capable of learning through education and the reform of other institutions—and perhaps, Mill hopes, if institutions are made less wretched, even the shortsighted egotist can be brought to see this. So in the end self-interest, prudence—even selfishness—dictates that everyone try to encourage the development of this social feeling in others, and the most effective way of bringing this about, apart from personal example, is by the reform of social institutions to this end. So even though Mill appears to talk in the language of descriptive or predictive fact, and thus to speak of what is, he is actually talking about what ought to be and how it can be brought about. This is the way, for instance, to read the passage in which Mill says that 'This mode of conceiving ourselves and human life', that is to say, as members of a body all members of which are equal and have equal rights to have their interests consulted,

as civilization goes on, is felt to be more and more natural. Every step in political improvement renders it more so, by removing the sources of opposition of inter-est and leveling those inequalities of legal privilege between individuals or classes, owing to which there are large portions of mankind whose happiness it is still prac-ticable to disregard. *In an improving state of the human mind,* the influences are constantly on the increase which tend to generate in each individual a feeling of unity with all the rest. (p. 41, 3. 10; italics added)

What Mill is setting forth here he is setting forth as a desirable goal, which the arrangements of society ought to aim at achieving. But in order for this to be brought about, an educational and social revolution is neces-sary. Mill actually asks us to

suppose this feeling of unity to be taught as a religion, and the whole force of education, of institutions, and of opinion directed, as it once was in the case of religion, to make every person grow up from infancy surrounded on all sides both by the profession and the practice of it. (p. 42; 3. 10)

And he has no doubt that this can be brought about, some time in the future. What Mill is proposing here is nothing less than a revolution in the condition of society. I remind you again of Mill's references to 'the present wretched education and social arrangements'; he now observes that we live in a 'comparatively early state of human advancement'. Mill was writing about England and the world of 1860, at a time when slavery was still legal in the United States and elsewhere, something he was well aware of, and there may be some question how much advancement there has been towards attaining Mill's ideal goal since that time. But, even if there had been none—something that Mill would not accept and that is really too pessimistic—that would not diminish the validity of Mill's goal as an ideal. That would call for an entirely different kind of argument. But 'already', Mill says:

a person in whom the social feeling is at all developed cannot bring himself to think of the rest of his fellow creatures as struggling rivals with him for the means of happiness . . . The deeply rooted conception which every individual even now has of himself as a social being tends to make him feel it one of his natural wants that there should be harmony between his feelings and aims and those of his fellow creatures . . . This feeling in most individuals is much inferior in strength to their selfish feelings, and is often wanting altogether. But to those who have it, it possesses all the characters of a natural feeling. (pp. 42–3; 3. 11)

The writer of these last statements cannot fairly be regarded as a pie-in-the-sky optimist, because this same writer two years earlier had published *On Liberty*, in which he said, among many other things, that 'in political and philosophical theories, as well as in persons, success discloses faults and infirmities which failure might have concealed from observation', and also that 'The likings and dislikings of society, or of some powerful portion of it, are . . . the main thing which has practically determined the rules laid down for general observance, under the penalties of law or opinion'.[7] The latter phenomenon is one Mill set out to combat, in *On Liberty*, in *Utilitarianism*, and in other works. The former phenomenon (that is, 'success disclosing faults and infirmities which failure might have concealed from observation') brings into prominence a phenomenon that Mill is helping to exhibit in Benthamite utilitarianism, a theory that he had once espoused as well. In the *Liberty* Mill claims about the liberties he enumerates that:

No society in which these liberties are not, on the whole, respected, is free, whatever be its form of government; and none is completely free in which they do not exist absolute and unqualified. *The only freedom which deserves the name, is that of pursuing our own good in our own way, so long as we do not attempt to deprive others of theirs or impede their efforts to obtain it.* Each is the proper guardian of his own health, whether bodily, or mental and spiritual. Mankind are better gainers by suffering [i.e. allowing] each other to live as seems good to themselves, than by compelling each to live as seems good to the rest. (*Liberty*, pp. 75–6, 1. 12; italics added)

The author of this passage was not supposing that the society of which he was writing was free in the sense he was delineating. And the author of this passage was also the author, ten years later, of a book whose opening paragraph contains the memorable lines:

The principle which regulates the existing social relations between the two sexes—the legal subordination of one sex to another—is wrong in itself, and now one of the chief hindrances to human improvement; and . . . ought to be replaced by a

---

[7] J. S. Mill, *On Liberty* (1859), in *Utilitarianism, Liberty, and Representative Government*, Everyman edn. (London: J. M. Dent, 1910), p. 67, ch. 1, para. 4 and p. 70, ch. 1, para. 7.

principle of perfect equality, admitting no power or privilege on the one side, nor disability on the other.[8]

So Mill cannot fairly be accused of unrealistic optimism about the state of society and the world at the time in which he was writing. He definitely had a theory of moral progress, of social improvement, partially delineated in the following passage near the end of *Utilitarianism*:

The entire history of social improvement has been a series of transitions by which one custom or institution after another, from being a supposed primary necessity of social existence, has passed into the rank of a universally stigmatized injustice and tyranny. So it has been with the distinctions of slaves and freemen, nobles and serfs, patricians and plebeians; and so it will be, and in part already is, with the aristocracies of color, race, and sex. (*Util.* p. 78; 5. 36).

Some questions, however, can fairly be raised about whether the principle of freedom, the principle 'of pursuing our own good in our own way, so long as we do not attempt to deprive others of theirs, or impede their efforts to obtain it',[9] coheres with Mill's religion of social unity, in which the 'feeling of unity' would be 'taught as a religion, and the whole force of education, of institutions, and of opinion directed . . . to make every person grow up from infancy surrounded on all sides both by the profession and the practice of it' (*Util.* p. 42; 3. 10). There is something here that smacks of being forced or induced to be free, of teaching people from infancy what their own good is, about which some questions can legitimately be raised. We have just witnessed the gross and utter failure of one such large-scale social experiment, aimed at getting all individuals to identify their own individual interests with the interests of the whole, in the collapse of communism in the Soviet Union—something which some far-sighted prophets had predicted. Is what communism practised, or professed to be practising (we know that the profession was accompanied by an immense amount of fraud, cheating, special privileges, and lying, along with monstrous cruelties), an approximation of what Mill is calling for in the passages I have been quoting? To put it another way, is Mill's religion of social unity consistent with rational autonomy? I only raise the question here, will not attempt to answer it, want now to go on to bring out what I meant earlier when I characterized Mill's alternative conception of utility as a forerunner of pragmatism.

---

[8] J. S. Mill, *The Subjection of Women* (1869), in *On Liberty, Representative Government, The Subjection of Women*, World's Classics edn. (London: Oxford University Press, 1912), p. 427; 1. 1.

[9] Note the resemblance of this principle to Herbert Spencer's law of equal freedom: 'Every man has freedom to do all that he wills, provided he infringes not the equal freedom of any other man' (*Social Statics* (London: John Chapman, 1851), ch. 6, sect. 1).

IV

Here I shall be more sketchy, but a sketch can at least provide a picture.[10] First, recall Peirce's conception of truth as that opinion which is fated to be agreed to by all who enquire if enquiry is carried on far enough and long enough. It is not any actual opinion, but that end point, never actually reached, towards which scientific investigation in the long run tends to converge.[11] Now there is an analogy here to Mill's conception of the ideal social unity, in which each individual comes to identify his or her interest with the interest of the wider whole. For this ideal goal can be thought of as just that, an ideal goal, something not to be literally or totally attained but rather a state of society towards which social progress tends to converge if it is carried on long enough. The ideal end of the one process is truth, which depends on enquiry; the ideal end of the other process is the mitigation and eventual elimination of (eliminable) human misery and some progress towards the attainment of the sort of happiness Mill has delineated—which 'nineteen-twentieths of mankind' are presently forced to do without—through progress towards social harmony, which depends on measures being taken to reform 'the present wretched education and wretched social arrangements' and social institutions generally.

This is an analogy with Peirce, the founder of pragmatism. But it was Dewey who developed pragmatism into a comprehensive social doctrine and programme. It is characteristic of Dewey's moral theory that, on its terms, all actions and all judgements—since judgements are construed as themselves actions—are to be judged and evaluated by their consequences. That means that Dewey is not interested in a spectator's point of view, in which one looks back and judges the morality of actions, persons, and practices of the past—unless such judgements can play a significant role in altering the future. Dewey's ethics is the ethics of agents, of participants, its

---

[10] Pragmatism was first introduced to the world—though the world at the time took no notice—in Peirce's papers of 1877–8 ('Illustrations of the Logic of Science', *Popular Science Monthly* (November 1877–August 1878); repr. in Morris R. Cohen, (ed.), *Chance, Love, and Logic* (New York: Harcourt, Brace, 1923)). The world took no notice until James's 1898 Berkeley, California, lecture, 'Philosophical Conceptions and Practical Results', *University Chronicle* (September 1898); repr. in James's *Collected Essays and Reviews* (New York: Longmans, Green, 1920), pp. 406–37—which used the term 'pragmatism' for the first time and attributed the idea to Peirce—so Mill anticipated this development by from sixteen to thirty-seven years.

[11] Charles Sanders Peirce, 'How to Make Our Ideas Clear', *Collected Papers*, ed. Charles Hartshorne and Paul Weiss (Cambridge, Mass.: Harvard University Press, 1934), v. 268 (5.407). Also in Cohen, *Chance, Love, and Logic*, pp. 32–60.

perspective is always prospective, and the aim is social and personal change and improvement, which Dewey characterizes (when he characterizes it at all) under the comprehensive term 'growth'. For Dewey the process always and only begins from the inception of a problem, an indeterminate situation, and then goes through the stages of the definition of the problem, the formation of hypotheses about what actions or policies would solve the problem, and then the carrying out in action of the hypothesis that seems most promising; it is verified if it works, disproved if it doesn't; if it doesn't work, drop it and try another, but *do* something. Consequently, on this instrumentalist view of moral judgements, every moral judgement is a hypothesis proposing a way of solving a problem and requiring action to test it. To the extent it resolves the problem, it works; to the extent it does not, it does not work and is to be dropped in favour of another one.[12]

Now Mill, as I have been interpreting him, is saying, in quite different language, something very like this. In the passages I picked out to emphasize, Mill is not thinking of the principle of utility as a principle to be used by a spectator, in a retrospective perspective, merely to judge situations, actions, and practices of the past—except in so far as such use of intelligence can teach us valuable lessons for reforming the present and improving the future. For otherwise there is no future pay-off. On the contrary, Mill is thinking prospectively, from the perspective of the agent, and also the statesman, of ways of making life better through alleviating the many problems he described in his rapid progress through the topics dealt with in his *Utilitarianism*—improving 'the present wretched education and wretched social arrangements', mitigating and preventing avoidable misery, bringing about social harmony and a state of more perfect equality, relieving and conquering the 'grand sources . . . of human suffering', and reducing 'the great positive evils of the world' to 'within narrow limits'. This ongoing and never-ending process will tend towards a situation in which human beings will be better able to identify their own true good—their own best interests on the whole—and a form of government and a state of society in which 'the freedom to pursue our own good in our own way, so long as we do not attempt to deprive others of theirs' will be honoured and protected. To put it in more Deweyian language, Mill is thinking of an adverse moral judgement of a social arrangement as one prompted by a problem about that arrangement and consequently as a proposal for so changing the arrangement as to help bring about this

---

[12] Although there are many places in which this Deweyian view is delineated, the best single source is Dewey's *Human Nature and Conduct* (New York: Holt, 1922; Modern Library, 1930).

better state of affairs; and alleviating the evils in the present arrangement is itself a process that constitutes a better state of affairs.

It is no wonder, then, that William James, that other great pragmatist and the founder of the doctrine called radical empiricism, dedicated his *Pragmatism*, of 1907, 'To the memory of John Stuart Mill From Whom I First Learned the Pragmatic Openness of Mind and Whom My Fancy Likes to Picture as Our Leader Were He Alive Today'.[13] The wonder is that the significance of this dedication had not been previously recognized; I myself did not recognize it until I embarked on the present enquiry.[14]

V. AFTERWORD

One other problem arises, which a fuller treatment of this topic must deal with: Does Mill's stoic conception of happiness entail or imply his pragmatic conception of utility? When this question was first raised (by Andrew Levine) my initial reaction was that it does not. On further reflection, however, it came to seem to me that there could very well be a logical relationship between the two, that the Stoic conception of happiness may very well imply the pragmatic conception of utility. Stated very informally, the consideration is this: this conception of happiness requires that one pay attention to the situation of others, that one try to alleviate the sufferings of others, that one be prepared to do without happiness for oneself. Given this, it seems but a short step to the consideration that utility be conceived of in pragmatic terms. However, this is only what seems, and it may be a very long step indeed.[15]

[13] William James, *Pragmatism* (New York: Longmans, Green, 1907).

[14] I said earlier that I was not claiming priority of any kind (except in the way of truth—which, to be sure, is an important priority) for any of the ideas contained herein. I was anticipated in some ways on the interpretation of Mill's conception of happiness by Edward Walter in three papers which deserve to be better known, and which I list accordingly: (i) 'Revising Mill's Utilitarianism', *Journal of Social Philosophy*, 12(2) (May 1981), pp. 5–11; (ii) 'Mill on Happiness', *Journal of Value Inquiry*, 16 (1982), pp. 303–9; (iii) 'A Concept of Happiness', *Philosophy Research Archives*, 13 (1987–8), pp. 137–50. Another paper that departs from the beaten track is David O. Brink, 'Mill's Deliberative Utilitarianism', *Philosophy and Public Affairs*, 21(1) (winter 1992), pp. 67–103. On Mill's qualitative hedonism, in addition to the book by Rem Edwards cited in n. 3 above, two useful papers come to mind: Rex Martin, 'A Defence of Mill's Qualitative Hedonism', *Philosophy*, 47 (1972), pp. 140–51; and Henry R. West, 'Mill's Qualitative Hedonism', *Philosophy*, 51 (1976), pp. 97–101. West's paper is a reply to Martin, and actually a bit more of a defence of Mill.

[15] This paper was originally prepared for presentation to the Birkbeck College Philosophy Society, 5 March 1993—where the discussion was very stimulating. A later version was presented

APPENDIX: FURTHER ON HAPPINESS[16]

On the conception of happiness presented, happiness is not a fixed end in which, once achieved, we can rest, but a complex process consisting of activity combined with periods of tranquillity, all resting on certain conditions.

Despite Mill's occasional lapses into the standard talk embedded in the Benthamite tradition, such as references to 'the greatest amount of happiness altogether', Mill's qualitative hedonism makes it manifest that the orthodox utilitarian standard cannot be the one he is actually using and employing. Even if, as Bentham supposed, it is possible to quantify different amounts of pleasures and pains, it is impossible to quantify different *kinds* of pleasure. The idea is incoherent.

I spoke of Mill's Stoic conception of happiness. By this I do not mean that Mill's conception of happiness is a form of Stoicism, but rather that it embodies key elements of the Stoic tradition, the ones Mill himself explicitly mentioned. There are, to be sure, aspects or forms of Stoicism that Mill came nowhere near adopting. Thus Mill was very far from being a fatalist, and the Stoics never talked about improving the world. But the elements Mill delineated are enough, and it is clear enough that this feature of Mill's view has been almost universally overlooked in the drive to refute, akin to a philosophical 'take no prisoners' strategy.

Mill says that 'the foundation of happiness' is 'not to expect more from life than it is capable of bestowing'. This condition is essentially and distinctively Stoic, and also essentially Millian, but it might be regarded as a trivial point, on the ground, say, that 'not expecting more from life than it is capable of bestowing is a vital strategy for being able to enjoy what we get'.[17] That is true; the opposite is a recipe for continual frustration. Nonetheless the point is not trivial; it was not acknowledged by orthodox utilitarians such as Bentham or by quantitative hedonists such as Sidgwick, and, unless I have overlooked some important exception, it is not to be found in the works of classical hedonism.

It might be claimed that, for example, 'endorsing a strategy to gain happiness is not changing one's idea of it'. But on Mill's view of happiness this seems to me manifestly false. The point in question presupposes a fixed and rigid distinction between happiness, as some fixed end to be attained at the end of a journey, and the means or roads to it. And such a conception of happiness does not accord with

at the University of Illinois (Urbana), 29 April 1994, and a penultimate version as the invited 'keynote address' to the Tennessee Philosophy Association at Vanderbilt University, 10 November 1995, where the discussion, opened by John Lachs, also was very beneficial. I was pleased that in all these places the usual 'defend your thesis' attitude was replaced by an atmosphere of common enquiry.

[16] The comments of Professor Lachs at Vanderbilt in November 1995, as well as some questions that arose during the session, have prompted me to add some further remarks.

[17] Here and in the next paragraph I use, with some modification, the words of Professor Lachs.

Mill's (*Util.*, pp. 17–20; ch. 2, paras. 12–15). Mill, remember, delineates four elements of happiness: '(i) moments of rapture, (ii) in an existence made up of few and transitory pains, (iii) many *and various* pleasures, (iv) with *a decided predominance of the active over the passive*' (*Util.* p. 17, 2. 12), 'having as the foundation of the whole not to expect more from life than it is capable of bestowing'. Mill's succeeding claim is that 'A life thus composed, to those fortunate enough to obtain it, has always appeared worthy of the name of happiness'. To me it is clear that Mill did not regard these essential elements merely as means to happiness, but *also* as essential components of it. Moore was puzzled, actually puzzled himself, over how something said to be a means to happiness could also be a part of it. He puzzled himself because he was thinking of happiness or pleasure on the model of physical events or objects. Mill knew better than to think of the infinite on the model of the finite. Happiness is not like anything else; it is *sui generis*. There is no sharp distinction between happiness and the so-called means to it. The means merge into and become part of the whole. The notion of happiness is amorphous vague and fleeting, as is the feeling of happiness itself. No wonder then that traditional attempts to delineate the concept have failed.

In addition to the four elements of happiness just delineated Mill speaks of two more: (v) 'cultivating a fellow-feeling with the collective interests of mankind', and (vi) mental cultivation, developing one's mind and sensitivities. Thus there are at least six elements in or sources of happiness, together with the foundation of the whole—not expecting more from life than it is capable of bestowing (p. 17; 2. 12). And there is also, it should be recalled, a sense of dignity involved, which brings in a moral element (p. 13; 2. 6). Happiness, on Mill's view, is a very complex process and phenomenon, not a mere balance of pleasure over pain, and certainly not a mindless balance of pleasure over pain. The happiness Mill is describing is a distinctively human sort of happiness, not the sort of happiness that can be enjoyed by a pig that has more than enough to eat and no worries to cause sleepless nights. (So much for Carlyle's ill-tempered talk of a 'pig philosophy'. Cf. *Util.*, pp. 11–14; 2. 3–6.)

To put the point another way, happiness is not a destination towards which we can head by various means. With destinations, as ordinarily understood, one can know when one has arrived, one can disembark and stay there for a while. Happiness is not at all like that. There is no way in which anyone can reach it and stay there a while. Once one decides to stay one is there no longer.

One might think that what is needed here is a distinction between a strategy for attaining happiness and happiness itself. But in this context, a very special context, this distinction presupposes a sharp distinction between means and ends, which *in the case of happiness* is not operative. This is one of the things so peculiar and so distinctive about happiness. To be sure, the distinction between means and ends is important and central in our lives and thought. But that does not mean that it is always and everywhere applicable.

Dewey held that in conduct and in life there is a melding of means and ends, that means tend to become ends and ends to become means, so that there is nothing that is in itself a means and nothing that is in itself an end. There is much in this that is worthy of careful attention. But, perhaps because I do not understand it very well, I do not accept this doctrine in its sweeping generality. Yet it is precisely my point that the supposed sharp distinction between the necessary *means for* happiness and the *elements or constituents of happiness* (the end) is spurious and deceptive. This is one important thing that Mill's doctrine brings out. Once we get over the prejudice that nothing can be both a means to and a part of the same thing, and that all things are physical and material, we have a chance of seeing this.

Let me allude once again to the question whether the Stoic conception of happiness implies or is necessarily connected with the pragmatic conception of utility. I add to what little I said above on this matter that, given Mill's considered and complex conception of happiness, his view that everyone is entitled to equal treatment, and his adherence to a 'Greatest Happiness Principle'—not any of the traditional ones but a complex one that is not easy to formulate, though I have attempted to characterize it above—he would have to develop something like that which he did develop (or rather, hint at): the pragmatic conception of utility. However, I still do not see how to *prove* this. On the one hand, it seems dubious that the denial of the pragmatic conception of utility would entail the denial of the Stoic conception of happiness. On the other hand, that is surface thinking only, and appropriately superficial. So until further notice I shall take it as a hypothesis, to be tested by how well it works, that the Stoic conception of happiness entails, or at least practically requires, the pragmatic conception of utility. One virtue of this hypothesis is that it will enable us to see that the traditional and standard division of ethical theories into teleological and deontological, or into consequentialist, teleological, and deontological, is superficial and misleading, and not a good device for discovering ethical truth. For John Stuart Mill's complex moral philosophy, here described, incorporates all three, which shows that the classification is not mutually exclusive, and it is almost certainly not exhaustive.

And it seems to me fitting, appropriate to the ideal character of philosophy, for a philosophical enquiry to end with a question.

ADDITIONAL NOTES AND COMMENTS

A. 'Mill on Happiness and Utility' was originally published in *Philosophy*, 75 (January 2000), pp. 25–47; reprinted here as it was published there, with a few phrases slightly modified.

B. In Mill's Stoic-like conception of happiness one can find the explication of Aristotle's doctrine that happiness is activity in accordance with virtue—that is, excellence. For Aristotle, happiness *is* activity. I was always puzzled by this, from the very first time I studied Aristotle's ethics a number of years ago. How can happiness, which I had always thought of as a feeling of some kind, *be* an activity. Well, another way of saying this is that it is *found in* activity, though the activity must not be engaged in for the sake of the happiness, or it will not be happiness. It must be engaged in for the sake of something else. And this is unquestionably one side of Mill's conception, in which activity and passivity alternate and interact and require each other, in somewhat the way of polar terms.[18]

To recap: for Mill, happiness is found in activity, though not only in activity: (i) moments of rapture, (ii) an existence made up of few and transitory pains, (iii) many and varied pleasures, (iv) with a decided predominance of the active over the passive, with (v) the foundation of the whole being 'not to expect more from life than it is capable of bestowing'.

It occurred to me later on that this Millian account is somewhat Aristotelian in character. As I said, I had been puzzled for a very long time about why Aristotle said that happiness *is* activity, and this puzzlement was alleviated by a better understanding of Mill's conception of happiness.[19]

---

[18] I am thinking of polar terms (or concepts or phenomena) in the sense in which an instance of one cannot exist unless an instance of the other exists also. Thus, buying and selling, or buyer and seller. There is only an analogy, however; I said 'in *somewhat* the way of polar terms'. The relation between activity and passivity is empirical, not conceptual.

[19] Aristotle, *Nicomachean Ethics*, 1. 13. 1102ª. Some experts on Aristotle claim that 'happiness' is not an accurate translation of Aristotle's term 'eudaemonia', that the Greek term has no accurate counterpart in English. This may well be so, but I am not here engaging in Aristotelian scholarship, and 'happiness' happens to be the English word almost invariably used in translations of Aristotle's work.

INDEX

References to the Golden Rule are, typically, abbreviated 'GR'

abortion: treated as an example 247–8, 260–1

Abrams v. *United States*: dissent in 149

absolutism and relativism 140–1

abstraction: institutions as abstractions, though nonetheless real 219–20

action guide: no, can be complete 23; the Golden Rule (GR) is not to be regarded as a precise 287–9

Acquisitive Society, The (Tawney) 185 & n., 214; *see also* Tawney

Adams, James Truslow (*The Epic of America*) 248–9

Adlai Stevenson: A Study in Values (Muller) 138 & n.

Adler, Felix 153 n.

adultery 277

Adventures of Huckleberry Finn (Twain) 115–16, 115 n.

After Seven Years (Moley) 244 n.

algorithm: GR not an 292

Als, Hilton: on Chester Himes and racism 189

altruism: Kant on perfect 267–8

America: Coolidge on the business of 186

American: pragmatism as typically 243–4

American: Spaniel Club 145; Rocket Society on GR 266

American civilization: pragmatism and 244

anarchic idea: of right and wrong 27

Anastasoff v. *United States of America* 212

And Even Now (Beerbohm) 257 & n.

Anglo-Saxon, The: A Study in Evolution (Boxall) 162–4, 163 n.

anti-Semitism: a form of racism 188

appellate courts: characteristically hand down opinions 192–3

appeals: apparatus of, essential to justice 202

appearance and reality 87

approving: distinguished from liking 148–9

a priori: a relativized 31

Ardrey, Robert: on race 174–6; mentioned 179, 184

'Are Fundamental Moral Principles Incapable of Proof?' (H. Jones) 21

argument: form of, to ultimate principles 20–1

Aristotle: saw that slavery needed justification 117; ethics of, not consequentialist 132; mentioned 290

Nicomachean Ethics: quoted 105, 106

Aristotle's: distinction between moral and intellectual virtue 154; conception of happiness 313–14

arithmetic: principles of, not applicable to goods 63–4

Austin, John (*Province of Jurisprudence Determined*) 190

Autocrat of the Breakfast Table, The (O. W. Holmes, sen.) 112 & n.

axiology 131, 133; *see also* theory of value; value theory

bad metaphysics, particularly, 188

Baier, Kurt: on value judgements 142 n; mentioned 153 n.

The Moral Point of View 5 n., 277–8

Ball, George W. ('The Disenchantment with Kissinger') 60 n.

Barzun, Jacques: on race 164–6; alluded to by Benedict 171; on Marxist doctrine being racist 182–3; felicitous phrase of 187; quoted 167; mentioned 176

Race: A Study in Superstition 160

baseball: example from, used by Rawls 217

Baton Rouge: judicial seat of distinguished Judge Daniels 200

Baylis, Charles (*Ethics: The Principles of Wise Choice*): 'revised golden rule' of 189–90

Beerbohm, Max (*And Even Now*): on the sense of justice 257

beliefs: examples of true common sense 93

Benedict, Ruth: on race 170–2; on conflicts between classes 182

Race: Science and Politics 160

beneficence: duty of, established by GR 276–7

Bentham, Jeremy: ethics of 132–3; mentioned 294

Bentham's utilitarianism: idea distinctive of 133 n.
Bergson, Henri: on common sense 88
Berreby, David ('Race Counts') 188 n.
Best Defense, The (Dershowitz) 213
Beyond Deduction (Will) 31
Black, Max (*Problems of Analysis*) 121
Black's Law Dictionary 110 & n.
Blackwell's: an institution (though not an abstraction) 221 n.
Bock, Philip K. (*Modern Cultural Anthropology*) 224 & n.
Bosanquet, Bernard (*Implication and Linear Inference*) 20 n.
Boxall, George E.: on race 162–4
Boyd, William C. (*Genetics and the Races of Man*) 162
Bradley, F. H.: apposite phrase of 85; mentioned 289
  Collected Essays 12 n.
  Ethical Studies 12 & n.
Brandeis, Justice Louis D. 202
Brondigmalian trait 177
Burger, Chief Justice Warren: on the Watergate Scandal 136
Burke, Edmund (*Reflections on the Revolution in France*) 16 n.
business: the, of common sense 97, 98, 99
Business Ethics (Sharp and Fox) 272
business men: standards of, alleged by Sharp and Fox 272
Bury, J. B. (*A History of Freedom of Thought*) 156

Caligula 141
Cardozo, Benjamin Nathan: on customary morality 102
care: prudence is defined as due 110–11
Castell, Albury (*An Elementary Ethics*): on the grading problem 215
casuistic questions: cannot be decided in advance 251, 252
casuistry: the, of common sense 111–12
'Casuistry of Common Sense, The' (Pollock) 109–10, 109 n., 111–12
Categorical Imperative, the: what, was put forward as 80; formulations of 135; is to be used to test maxims 289 n.; two forms of 226–7, 227 n.
'Categorical imperative and the Golden Rule, The' (Hirst) 286–7
cause: chief, of unhappiness 298–9

'Celebration of Intellect' (Emerson) 117 & n.
Challenge and Response: Justification in Ethics (Wellman) 35 & n.
Chamberlain, Houston 182
'changing our minds': a deceptive phrase 12–13
character: the moral importance of 163, 154–5; is at stake in a moral problem 245
'Checkers speech' 145
choice: mere, does not commit 58; not applicable to values or ethics 145–6; relation between, and morality 261
choice and contract: in Rawls 57–60
choosing: can, make an action right? 261
churn: case of a broken 193–4
circularity: proof in ethics available without 22
'citizen': a political not a moral term 62
claiming a right: does not prove that one has a right 155
classes: Benedict on conflict between 182
Cohen, Brenda 27 n.
Cohen, Felix S. (*Ethical Systems and Legal Ideals*) 133 n.
Cohen, Morris R.: on common sense and common knowledge 91–2
  The Faith of a Liberal 262–3
Cohen, Morris R. and Ernest Nagel: on facts 139 n.
Collected Essays (Bradley) 12 n.
Collected Legal Papers (O. W. Holmes, jun.) 149 & n.
Collected Papers (Peirce) 41 & n., 120
commercialism: the Tawneyesque account of 186
commitment: not generated by a choice 58
common knowledge: and common sense 91–2; two broad kinds of 92–3; the meaning of, in the law 93
common law: and common sense 102; fundamental maxim of the 191
Common Law, The (Holmes) 137, 138 n.
common moral sense: must be supplemented by moral theory 117
common sense: the 'natural mother-tongue of thought' (James) 85; and ordinary language 87; is more than one thing 87; a practical capacity 89, 96–7; original conception of the 90; an anomaly of 90–1; two main senses of 90–1; the philosophy of 93; intimately connected

with morality 95; the local, links with public opinion 95, 99; necessity of 95, 96; cannot get along without ethics 96; limitations of 96–7; not a reliable source of metaphysics 96–7; compatibility between, and science 97; the business of 97, 98, 99; distinguished from folklore 97–8; does not attempt to provide answers to philosophical question 98–9; what, is liable to be confused with 99–100; and common law 102; value of, lies in application 103; not innovative or creative 103; systematic ambiguity of 104; lessons of, in ethics 105–8; not infallible 108; not a system 108; casuistry of 109–10, 111–12; as, understood in the law 110; contains intrinsically a normative standard 111; implies standard of impartiality 111; what passes for 112–13; counterfeit, not always easy to discern 113; dictates nothing on the death penalty 113; appeals to, can be fallacious 113–14; is in touch with different kinds and degrees of wrong 17–18; cannot be defined on any standard model 121

Broad on 87; Bradley on 87–8; Bergson on 88; Moore on 88; Ayer on 90; M. R. Cohen on 91–2; Sidgwick on 94; Malinowski on 95; Emerson on 96; James on 96–7; Morgenthau on 97; Whitely on 98; Twain on 109; Pollock on 111–12

common-sense: belief: examples of true 93; definition of 94

morality: and positive morality 100–2; has changed over time 113; not a system 114

moral philosophers 105, 106

view of the world 88, 93

Communist Party: of the United States 30 n.

concurrence: necessary for resolution, not sufficient; *see also* moral issues

Concept of Law, The (Hart) 102 n., 115 n., 190, 191 n., 192 n.

conception: pragmatic, of utility 310

concrete embodiment: of an institution 219–20

Condemned to Freedom (Pfaff) 42 n.

condition: a, is different from a means 62 n.

conflict: *see* moral issue; social conflict

conflicts: in-group/out-group 183–4

Confucius 290

confusion: Russell involved in a 10

consequences: important irrespective of consequentialism 259

consequentialism: of John Dewey 133–4; further difficulty with 137; has no monopoly on considering consequences 259

consequentialist: and deontological theories distinguished 130–8

consistency: a foolish ix–x n.; in the sense of conformity to the past 244 n.

contract; original, metaphorical, not hypothetical 58–60; does not generate principles of justice 59

contract model: limitations on the generalizability of the 54

contrary to reason: Baier's concept of 278

Coolidge, Calvin: on 'the business of America' 186

Cornell University 293 & n.

correspondence: not necessary for truth 38

courts of law: functions of 193–4, 256

crime: a, against philosophy 216 n.

criminal justice: basic principle of a system of 204; utilitarian theory of 206–7

criminal justice system: must be weighted in one direction or another 204–5

Crisis of the Old Order, The (Schlesinger) 244 n.

criterion: maximin, not identical with maximin rule 65 n.

cultural: generalizations: explained 177–8; unlike ordinary factual generalizations 178

relativism: curious fate of all forms of 184

omnipresence: of GR 290, 292

culture: relation of philosophy to 240–1

Dance to the Music of Time, A (Powell) 24

Daniels, Judge William H. (Hawk): contribution to jurisprudence of 200

Darwin, Charles: on race 165 & n.; the moral theory of 285–6

The Descent of Man: quoted 165 & n.

Darwin and the Emergence of Evolutionary Theories of Mind and Behavior (Richards) 285 & n.

Data of Ethics (Spencer) 80 & n.

dead: promises to the, Melden on 114; Sidgwick on 114

death penalty: common sense dictates nothing on the 113

deduced decision: is no decision at all 24

deduction: is truth-preserving 37

'Defence of Common Sense, A' (Moore) 88 & n.

definition: common sense cannot be defined on the standard model of 121; of 'race' 161–2

Definition (Robinson) 121

Democracy in America (Toqueville) 19 n.

depublication: of judicial opinions 213

depublished opinion: a, cannot determine a precedent 213

derivation: a, is not a proof 47

Dershowitz, Alan M. (*The Best Defense*) 213

Descent of Man, The (Darwin) 165 & n., 285–6

destination: happiness not a 312

determinism: the true home of 13; curious fate of all forms of 184

Dewey, John: on intellectual progress 129; consequentialism of 133–4; on the distinctive national colour of philosophies 243; on melding of means and ends 312–13; quoted 248
    and James F. Tufts (*Ethics*) on GR 284

Dewey's ethics: an ethics of agents not spectators 308–9

Dictionary of Modern English Usage, A (Fowler) 218 & n., 220–1

difference principle, the 65 & n., 81

dignity: *see* sense of dignity

'Discrimination and Irrelevance' (Lucas) 23 n.

disinterestedness: most indispensable intellectual virtue 41

disputes: about race 161–2; war can be a means of settling 254–5

Dissertation on the Progress of Ethical Philosophy (Mackintosh) 285 & n.

distinctions: certain essential 147–9

Dobzhansky, T. B.: *see* Dunn, L. C.

Douglas, Mary (*How Institutions Think*) 236

Douglas v. *Jeannette* 196–7, 197 n.

due care: the common law standard of 110–11

Dunn, T. C. and T. B. Dobzhansky: on race and races 168–9 n.

duties: moral agent has both rights and 158

duties and responsibilities: must be primary goods 62–3

duty: imperfect, defined 26

Duty and Inclination (Reiner) 18–19, 19 n., 146 n.

Dworkin, Ronald: on the fundamental right 155; definition of natural right 156; paraphrased 191

education: GR an instrument of moral 280–1; Mill on the 'present wretched' 297, 300, 301, 303, 305, 308
    and opinion: Mill on 303–4

Edwards, Rem (*Pleasures and Pains: A Theory of Qualitative Hedonism*) 295 n.

efficiency: has no value by itself 15 n.

egotism: problem of 104

egotist: self-interest requires even the selfish, to be prudent 304–5

Elementary Ethics, An (Castell) 215

'Elements of Ethics, The' (Russell) 39 & n.

Elements of Logic (Whately) 89 & n.

Elements of Morality Including Polity, The (Whewell) 208–9

Emerson, Ralph Waldo: on foolish consistency ix–x n.; on common sense 96, 117

empiricism in ethics 126

Encyclopedia of Ethics 292

Encyclopedia of Philosophy, The: not a difficult-to-find-out-of-the-way journal 290 & n.

enlightenment: the distinctive sort of, philosophy can bring 259–60

enquiry and intelligence: presuppose common sense 97

Epic of America, The (J. T. Adams) 248–9

epistemological theories: distrusted by common sense 112

epistemology and ethics: significant disanalogy between 24

epitome of racism, the 185

equal: Law of, Freedom (Spencer) 307 n.

Equality (Tawney) 81–2, 81 n.

equity: common sense more akin to, than to law 109–10

Essays on the Intellectual Powers of Man (Reid) 88 & n.

Essays on Truth and Reality (Bradley) 87–8, 88 n.

ethical generalizations: some true universal 35–6

'Ethical Paradox, An' (Brenda Cohen) 27 n.

Ethical Philosophy of Life, An (Adler) 153 n.

Ethical Studies (Bradley) 12 & n.

ethical: theories, types of 126, 127; traditional classification of 313
theory: GR no substitute for an 284
truth: traditional classification of ethical theories not a good device for discovering 313
ethics: disanalogy from epistemology 24; two main senses of the term 86; relation of, to morality 104; Parmenidean 106–8 *passim*; rationalism and empiricism in 126; practical use of the term 150; teaching of, a moral responsibility 151; an often overlooked role of 247–8; *see also* Dewey; institutional ethics
Ethics (Dewey and Tufts) 284; (Nowell-Smith) 155 n.
Ethics: the Principles of Wise Choice (Baylis) 289–90
'ethnic group': proposal to substitute, for the term 'race' 168–9 & n.
Etzioni, Amitai (*The New Golden Rule*) 290–1
Evans, Bergen (*The Natural History of Nonsense*) 97–8, 100 & n.
'evil': used precisely, the worst term of opprobrium imaginable 211 n.
evils: Mill on the positive, of life 300–1
exactness: fallacy of delusive 119
Existentialism and Human Emotions (Sartre) 24–5, 25 n.
Experiments in Living (MacBeath) 224 & n.

fact: politicized questions of 39–40; concept of a, ambiguous and complex 138–40, 139 n.; and law 139
facts: paradigm theory-laden 45
facts and values 124–5, 139–40; Murphy on 140
faddism 117
Faith of a Liberal, The (M. R. Cohen) 262–3
fallacy: of delusive exactness 119; a, in normative reasoning 144–5; in Barzun's discussion of race 164–5; in Montaagu's reasoning on race 179–81; *see also* institutional fallacy, Zionist fallacy
Feibleman, James K. (*The Institutions of Society*) 236–7
Fielding's Guide to Europe 177 n.
Fields, W. C.: recipe for curing insomnia 129
Flew, Antony ('The Jensen Uproar') 176 n.
flipping coins: as a method of deciding cases 199–200, 201

folklore: of human society 40; what, consists of 97–8; confused with common sense 99–100; masquerading as common sense 112
Following the Equator (Twain) 109
fool: what any, knows 207
foundation of happiness: Mill on the 311
Fowler, H. W. (*A Dictionary of Modern English Usage*) 218 & n., 220–1
Fox, Philip G.: *see* Sharp, Frank C.
Fredonians 177
Frank, Jerome (*Law and the Modern Mind*) 195–7
free: thought not naturally 156–7
freedom: moral, explained 23–6; Law of Equal 307 n.
freedom of speech: not entailed by freedom of thought 156–7; restrictions on, always require justification 158
freedom of thought: does not entail freedom of speech 156–7
freedom of thought and conscience: right to, is fundamental 155–6
Fuller, Lon 190–1
functions: of courts of law 193–4, 200–1 of legal system as a whole 201–4
fundamental right: the, is a natural right 156

Gauthier, David 23 n.
generalization argument: defined 18 n.; presupposed by Rawls's theory 55–6; used by James 254
generalization in ethics: some problems connected with 26; examples of hasty 28
generalization principle: presupposed in Rawls 55–6; applied 155; defined 215 & n.; accepted by James as a formal condition 254; relation to GR 273; mentioned 17–18
generalizations: cultural 177–8
generalized principle of consequences: defined 18 n.
General Theory of Value (Perry) 256–8
genes: racism not concerned with 162
Genetics and the Races of Man (Boyd) 162 & n.
'genocide': term came into use about same time as the word 'racism' 161
Gershon, Dr Michael (*The Second Brain*) xii n., 285 n.

Gewirth, Alan ('The Golden Rule
    Rationalized') 287–9, 287 n.
God: is incapable of having opinions 149
Go Gentle into the Night (Sulzberger)
    249 & n.
Golden Rule, the (GR): what, directs us to do
    17; a principle both of positive and of
    rational morality 19; version of 138;
    prime source of justice 157; biblical
    formulation of 264; positive and
    negative formulations of 264–5;
    inversion of 265; must be distinguished
    from its denial 265; must be understood
    as a moral principle not a moral rule
    265–6; not a specific directive 265–6;
    does not presuppose a uniformity of
    human nature 269–70, 271; a distinc-
    tion vital to understanding 270; general
    and particular interpretations of 270–1,
    287–9; implies a uniform standard the
    same for all 271; requires that the same
    standard be applied irrespective of
    persons 272–3; sort of case condemned
    by 273–4; formulates a fundamental
    requirement of justice 273–4; condemns
    injustice not heroism 274; no logical
    difference between the negative and
    positive formulations of 275–7; at the
    basis of the principle of justice 279; an
    instrument of moral education 280–1,
    289; what, requires 283; by itself no
    substitute for an ethical theory 284;
    requires interpretation 285; perversions
    of 286; not intended as a precise
    statement of the reciprocal ground
    of our rights and duties 287–8;
    application of, not mechanical 288–9;
    not a utilitarian principle 289; cultural
    omnipresence of 290, 292; not an
    algorithm 292; a so-called 'new' 291;
    fact about, that needs explaining 292;
    see also inversion of GR
  Hans Reiner on 18–19; L. J. Russell on
    268–70; Lippman on
    269; Whately on 278–83; Dewey and
    Tufts on 284
Golden Rule, The: A Universal Ethic (Rost)
    286
Golden Rule, The (Wattles) 286
'Golden Rule, The' (Weiss) 287
'Golden Rule, The: New Aspects of an Old
    Moral Principle' (Hoche) 287

'Golden Rule Rationalized, The' (Gewirth)
    287–9, 287 n.
Golden-Rule thinking: essential component
    of moral reasoning 18
goods: the principles of arithmetic do not
    apply to 63–4
good sense and good judgement: essential
    107
good society: necessary condition of a 158
good will, the: defined 135; meaning of
    153–5
grade inflation: causes and effects of
    216 n.
grading: institution of 216 & n.
  case 231
  the, problem: detailed 215–16
Greek philosophers: B. Russell on the 107–8
Green, Thomas F.: on positive morality and
    norms 121; conception of value and
    disdain for values-talk of 151
Greider, William (*Secrets of the Temple: How
    the Federal Reserve Runs the Country*)
    225–6, 225 n.
Gresham's Law 103
Grundlegung zur Metaphysik der Sitten (Kant)
    134–6, 134 n.; first proposition of 153–4
Gulag Archipelago, The (Solzhenitsyn)
    210 & n.

Hamerton, Philip Gilbert: on disinterested-
    ness 41; on common sense 99
Hamlet: quoted 203
happiness: hedonistic conception of 294;
    Mill's list of four elements of 296–7; not
    a mere sum of pleasures over pains 296,
    297; Mill on the foundation of 297; Mill
    on the main ingredients of 299–300;
    further essential elements of 299–300;
    relation of Stoic conception of, to
    pragmatic conception of utility 310; not
    a fixed end but a complex process
    311–12; elements of, not merely means
    to, but parts of 312; no sharp distinc-
    tion between, and the means to 312; not
    a destination 312; Aristotle's conception
    of 313–14
Hare, R. M. 31, 125, 126, 215 n.
harm: intentional, felt as more grievous than
    unintentional 199
Harris, William T., on American thought
    242
Harrison, Jonathan, on proof in ethics 21

Hart, Henry M., jun. ('Holmes's Positivism')
on the importance of judicial opinions
197–8; mentioned 199

Hart, H. L. A. (*The Concept of Law*): cited
102 n.; on Huckleberry Finn 115 n.;
mentioned 190–1, 192 n.

Hart v. *Massanari* 212–13

Hayek, Friedrich A. (*The Road to Serfdom*)
155 n.

hedonic calculus 133 & n.; Hutcheson's early
version of the 133 n.

hedonism: defined 131; qualitative 295,
295 n., 296–7

hedonistic conception of happiness 294

Henle, Paul: on James as 'representative
American philosopher' 243

Henry IV: the time of 14

Heredity, Race, and Society (Dunn and
Dobzhansky) 168–9, 168–9 n.

heroism: not condemned by GR 274

Hetherington, H. J. W. and J. H. Muirhead
(*Social Purpose*) 224 & n.

Highet, Gilbert: quoted 4

Himes, Chester: on racial oppression 189

'Historical Roots of Racism, The' (Bernard
Lewis) 188–9

Hirst, E. W. ('The Categorical Imperative and
the Golden Rule') 286–7

Historical Consciousness (Lukacs) 181 & n.

History of Freedom of Thought, A (Bury)
156 & n.

'Hitch your wagon to a trend': not a maxim
worth following 117

Hitler, Adolf: on truth 42; Montagu's view
implies (perhaps unwittingly) that,
not a racist 180; mentioned 166, 168,
255

Hitler's Germany: absence of rule of law in
192

Hitler Speaks (Hermann Rauschning) 42 n.

Hobbes, Thomas (*Leviathan*) 79, 264–5,
265 n.

Hobhouse, L. T.: on common sense 97;
Liberalism essential minimum statement
of the rule of law 157

Hoche, Hans-Ulrich ('The Golden Rule: New
Aspects of an Old Moral Principle')
287, 289

Holmes, Oliver Wendell, jun.: on a rationalized legal system 14–15, 15 n.; Vermont
churn case 193–4; quoted 137, 149,
199; mentioned 202

Holmes, Oliver Wendell, sen. (*The Autocrat
of the Breakfast Table*) 112 & n.

'Holmes's Positivism' (Henry M. Hart, jun.)
197–8, 198 n.

Hook, Sidney ('Pragmatism and the Tragic
Sense of Life'): on the method of
creative intelligence 255

Hoover, Herbert: quoted on the Prohibition
Amendment 249

How Institutions Think (Mary Douglas) 236

Huckleberry Finn, Adventures of: lessons of,
for moral theory 116–17; H. L. A. Hart
on 115 n.; Tice on 116; Trilling on 116

'Huckleberry Finn' (D. J. Tice) 116 & n.

Human Intercourse (Hamerton) 99 & n.

Human Nature and Conduct (Dewey) 133–4,
134 n.

Human Zoo, The (Morris) 183–4, 184 n.

Hume, David: on natural or instinctive beliefs
93; in relation to common sense 95; on
importance of motives 137, 154;
Treatise of Human Nature quoted 11;
mentioned 124, 125

Hume's Law 125

Hutcheson, Francis: a pre-Benthamite
version of hedonic calculus 133 n.

'Hypostatic Ethics' (Santayana) 39 & n.

hypothesis: moral judgement as 128

Iannone, A. Pablo (*Philosophy as Diplomacy*):
on moral issues 262

Idea of Race, The (Montagu) 169–70, 170 n.

Idea of a Social Science, The (Winch) 226 n.

ideal: of a rationalized legal system 15 n.;
meaning of 15–16; a fundamental moral
158

ideal theory: constructed by Rawls 52

ideologies: can distort basic aims of a legal
system 104

ideology: definition of 30

Idi Amin 172

idiom: often a guide to common sense 87;
can enshrine a standard fallacy 119–20

'Illustrations of the Logic of Science' (Peirce)
308 & n.

illusion: money as 225–6

impartiality: intrinsic part of common sense
111

imperfect duty situations: fall within the area
of moral freedom 26

Implication and Linear Inference (Bosanquet)
20 n.

importance: judgements of 150–1
'Impossibility of Ethical Egoism, The' (Gauthier) 23 n.
incapacity: trained, to make relevant practical distinctions 109–10
inclusiveness: ideal of 253
incoherence: not the same as inconsistency 234 n.
incoherent: does not mean self-contradictory 30–1
inconsistency: not the same as incoherence 30–1, 234 n.; when there is moral, and there isn't 237–8
'Independence of Moral Theory, The' (Rawls) 67 n.
industry: Tawney on the purpose of 228–9
inequalities: not an index of inequities 70–1
inequities: not inequalities require redress 70–1
infinite regress: proof in ethics available without 22
inflation: of grades 216 n.
Influence of Darwin on Philosophy, The (Dewey) 129 & n., 248
inference-gap thesis 230–6; as first principle of institutional ethics 236
inquiry: *see* enquiry
Inquiry Concerning Moral Good and Evil (Hutcheson) 133 n.
insight: how, into moral issues can be obtained 249
institution: positive morality an 9; rational morality not an 9; an unjust, can be justified 77–8; racism an 189; the term, not replaceable by 'practice' 217 n.; an, not same as an organization or association 218; as an abstraction 219; a complex conception 218–19; definition of 219; concrete embodiment of an 219–20; different conception of an 220; alternative accounts of 223–5; money as an 225–6
institution-constituted action 218
institutional ethics: questions of 74–7; a main question of 214; is, a distinct branch of ethics? 226–7; first principle of 236
institutional evaluation: sort of principles needed for 227; standards for 227–30; *see also* Tawney
institutional fallacy: defined 234–5
institutional questions: when, arise 216–17

institutions: distinguished from associations and organizations 214; society a network of interrelated 230; moral relevance of 217–18; examples of 221–2; logical relations between 222; different kinds of 222; precise ground of distinction between two categories of 223; in abstract sense, cannot act yet can have effects 223
Institutions of Society, The (Feibleman) 236–7
instrumentalism: view of moral judgements taken by 309–10
Intellectual Life, The (Hamerton) 41 & n.
intellectual life: James on 250
virtue: disinterestedness the most indispensable 41
intelligence: *see* enquiry
intentions: essential to determining morality 137
interests: answer to all the, involved 253–4
interstices: in the law 193–4
Introduction to Logic and Scientific Method, An (Cohen and Nagel) 139 n.
Introduction to Metaphysics, An (Whitely) 98 & n.
Introduction to Social Anthropology (Mair) 188–9
intuitionist: the author of this book not any kind of 82; *see also* rationalism in ethics
inversion of GR 265; absurd consequences of the 267–8
'is': a valid move from an, to an 'ought' 138
ism-words: Tawneyesque account of 185–7
is/ought distinction: overcome 138; tends to break down in relation to institutions 230
is/ought problem, the: Kant's way of dealing with 136; mentioned 126
issue: the, point of view 248; settling the, 253–7; other uses of the term 260; *see also* problems
issues and problems: taxomony of, needed 259

Jackson, Justice Robert H.: opinion in *Douglas* v. *Jeanette* 196–8; mentioned 199
James, William: on obligation 52, 252; not a utilitarian 83; on common sense 96–7; 'Remarks at the Peace Banquet' quoted 239 & n.; connection between, and Franklin Roosevelt 244 n.; 'The Moral

Philosopher and the Moral Life'
discussed 250–3; 'Philosophical
Conceptions and Practical Results'
mentioned 308 n.; and Mill 310; Henle
on, 243; Royce on 243
James's account: distinctive feature of 253
Jaques 71
Jones, Hardy: on proving fundamental moral
principles 21
judgemental: definition of a, person 27
judicial opinions: role of 204; importance of
207; depublication of 212–13; Frank on
196; *see also* depublication; depublished
just: prime condition of, government 157
justice: Rawls's principles of, not object of
contract 59; the public sense of 201;
apparatus of appeals essential to 202;
basic principle of a system of criminal
204; system of criminal 211–12; basic
demand of 211–12; Rawls's two
principles of 230; GR formulates a
fundamental requirement of 273–4; *see
also* criminal justice; law; law and justice;
pure procedural justice
Justice (Spencer) 79
justice and justification: not identical
77–8
'Justice as Fairness' (Rawls) 53, 78, 79 n.
'Justice as Reciprocity' (Rawls) 78–9, 79 n.
justification: when, required and when not
23–4; Rawls on 45–6; distinguished
from proof 47; different from persuasion 49; a, always required for
restrictions on freedom of speech 158
justified: a, action not necessarily right 40–1;
has wider range than true 48

Kant, Immanuel: opening sentence of the
Grundlegung 134–5; on the uncondi-
tional good 153–4; on perfect altruism
267–8; quoted 170; mentioned 78, 79,
290
Kantian: conception of a maxim 289 & n.
'Kantian interpretation of Justice as Fairness,
The' (Rawls) 79
Khan, Genghis: a gay philosopher 254, 255
King, Martin Luther, jun.: moral outlook of
209
Kinsley, Michael (*The New Republic*) 234
Kirchwey, Freda: quoted 9–10, 10 n., 35 n.
knowledge: of the truth not identical with the
truth 38; *see also* common knowledge

Kuklick, Bruce (*The Rise of American
Philosophy*) 239, 240, 241; on James
250–1; on Perry 258
Ku Klux Klan: affected the laws of several
states 209

Lachs, John: paraphrased 311–12
Ladd, John (*The Structure of a Moral Code*)
22 n.
law: rule of 157; perennial questions in
philosophy of 190; common sense as
understood in the 110; positive 190;
one way in which, essentially related to
morality 207; how, affects morality 208;
see also morality; philosophy of law
law and facts 139
law and justice: necessary connection
between 211
law and morality: one difference between
14–15; relations between 208–9;
intersection of 212
Law and the Modern Mind (Frank) 195–7
Law of Equal Freedom (Spencer) 307 n.;
Law of Peoples, The (Rawls) 48–9, 82–3
legal institution: two different senses of 222–3
legal positivism: Austin and H. L. A. Hart
190
legal realism: maintained by J. Frank 195–7
legal system: essential elements in a 190 & n.;
aims and functions of a, as a whole
201–4; explanation of philosophical
differences about a 203; standing
possibility of conflict between aims of a
203
legislative bodies: basic function of 194
Lessons on Morals (Whately) 278–83
Lewis, Bernard: on the roots of racism
188–9
Lewis, C. S. (*Mere Christianity*) 5 n.
lex talionis: not to be confused with GR 265;
operative in Gangland 286
Liberal Imagination, The (Trilling) 116 & n.
Liberalism (Hobhouse) 197 & n.
liberties: Rawls on 62
Liebling, A. J. (*The Press*) 229 n.
Life of Reason, The (Santayana) 27 n.
Lincoln, Abraham: went well beyond the
common sense of his time 119
Lippmann, Walter (*Public Opinion*): on GR
269–70
litigants: reasons can matter even to 199
Living in Europe (Lanier) 177 & n.

lobbyists: endlessly hampering attempts to draft statutes fairly and precisely 223 n.

logical structure: proof that rational morality has a 22

logic of moral judgements 40–1

lost-soul hypothesis (of William James) 251–2, 253, 256–7

Lucas, J. R.: 'Discrimination and Irrelevance' 23 n.; on facts and values 139; mentioned 27 n.

Lukacs, John: quoted 181

MacBeath, A. (*Experiments in Living*) 224 & n.

Mackintosh, James (*Dissertation on the Progress of Ethical Philosophy*): influence on Darwin 285 & n.

McMullin, Ernan 3

McWilliams, Carey (*A Mask for Privilege*) 188 n.

Madden, Edward H.: on the history of the philosophy of common sense 120

Magic, Science and Religion (Malinowski) 95 & n., 96

Mair, Lucy: on race 188–9

Malinowski, Bronislaw: on common sense and the rudiments of science 95–6

Malvolio 71

Man's Most Dangerous Myth: The Fallacy of Race (Montagu) 166–70, 167 n.

Man's Responsibility for Nature (Passmore) 130 & n.

Man's Unconquerable Mind (Highet) 4 n.

Marx, Karl: mentioned 159

Mask for Privilege, A (McWilliams) 188 n.

matter of fact: solution of conflict (issue) not a simple 258

matter of opinion: mere, defined 149–50

Maugham, Somerset ('Sanatorium') 69–70 n.

maxim: the Categorical Imperative is to be used to test a 289 n.; in Kant's use a, is not a prescriptive rule 289 & n.; generalized form of a 289 n.

maximin: rule not identical with, criterion 65 n.

means: a, differs from a condition 63 n.

means and ends: Dewey's theory of 312–13

Medlin, Brian: on ultimate principles 19–21

Melden, A. I.: on what 'passes' for common sense 112–13; on promises to the dead 114; mentioned 102 n.

memory: essential for enquiry and intelligence 97

Mere Christianity (C. S. Lewis) 5 n.

merits: in principle ascertainable in any criminal case 205

metaphor: a burned-out 240–1; a, for human society 257

Metaphysical Elements of Ethics (Kant) 267–8, 268 n.

metaphysics: particularly bad 188

Metaphysics and Common Sense (Ayer) 90 & n.

Methods of Ethics, The (Sidgwick) 100–2, 100 n., 114 & n.

Midas 63, 65

Mill, John Stuart: not guilty of foolish consistency ix–x n.; *Representative Government* quoted 75–6 n.; some overlooked passages in *Utilitarianism* of 134; on motives 137; on rules of conduct 141; on national character 179; vitally important statement by 294; considered doctrine of, not simply consequentialist 296; a fascinating philosopher 302; analogy with Dewey 309–10; and James 310; complex moral theory of 313; mentioned 9

On Liberty 156, 157 n.

Mill's: principle of utility 131; resemblance of, account of happiness with Aristotle's 313–14

Mind and its Place in Nature, The (Broad) 87 & n.

misnomer: designation of a 'new' GR a 291

mist: plenty of 175

mobs: when people become members of 98

Modern Cultural Anthropology (Bock) 224 & n.

Moley, Raymond (*After Seven Years*) 244 n.

Moline, Jon 59 n.

money: as illusion 225–6

Montagu, Ashley: on race 166–70; fallacious reasoning in 179–81; on Hitler 180; mentioned 176

Montesquieu, Charles de: parody of racist arguments 172–4

Moore, G. E.: *Principia Ethica* 39 & n.; 'Defence of Common Sense' 88 & n.; on common sense 88, 92–3; extreme moral conservatism of 108; understood Mill no better than he understood Bradley 296

'Moore's Defence of Common Sense' (Murphy) 120

moral agent: a, must have both rights and
duties 158
conflict: solution to 257; not every, can be
solved 258
education: a terrible precedent for 24; GR
a prime instrument for 280–1, 289
facts: can be discovered only through
moral theory 44
fanaticism: defined and refuted 23–4
freedom, area of: circumscribed by moral
principles 23; illustrated by Pierre's
dilemma 25; includes perfect duty
situations 26
ideal: a fundamental 158
inconsistency; *see* inconsistency
issue: distinguished from moral problem
246–9; when a, becomes a social
problem 248; pragmatic method for
setting a 253–4; conditions to be met by
solution of a 258–9
issues: the task of moral philosophy with
respect to 247–9; how insight into
nature of, can be obtained 249; one
condition for resolution of 250
moralistic reasoning: in Benedict and
Montagu 169–72
morality: systematic ambiguity of 5, 86; a
person's, not just a set of principles 6,
94–5; how, can be an institution 8–9; a,
essential to a society 9; test of proposed
changes in 9; intimately connected with
common sense 95; not identical with
positive 102; relation of, to ethics 104; of
common sense has changed over time
113; not an object of choice 146; one way
in which, essentially related to law 207;
question of relations between law and, is
multiple 208–9; question whether, can be
legislated 209 & n.; three senses or kinds
of 211; moral sense essential to, but not a
reliable guide to 280; how to squeeze the
life out of 292; *see also* law
and law: one difference between 14–15
Morality of Law, The (Fuller) 190–1, 191 n.
moral judgement: not a matter of taste or
preference 7–8; place of value theory in
26; logic of 40–1; not simply deducible
from general principles 41; a, is an
answer to a moral question 128; must
rest on reasons to be genuine 149; a
morally essential factor of 288; capacity
to make a genuine 273

Moral Judgment of the Child, The (Piaget)
137 n.
moral judgements: critical, presuppose ideal
of rational morality 12; are judgements
not deductions 20, 231; defined 127–9;
presuppositions of 127–8
motivation: moral sense theories are
theories of 280
necessity: a 212
neutrality: not desirable on all matters
262–3
parochialism: the mistake of 10
Moral Philosopher and the Moral Life, The
(James) 52, 83, 250–3
moral philosophy: a problem of 95;
relevance of institutions to 217–18; the
role of 244–5; the task of, with respect
to moral issues 247–9; moral relevance
of 260
Moral Point of View, The (Baier) 5 n., 142 n.,
277–8, 277 n., 281 n.
moral principle: how a, can be proved 19;
application of, not an automatic matter
227; definition of 265
principles: are *sui generis* 31; circumscribe
an area of moral freedom 23
problem: defined 128–9, 130, 245; types of
128–9 n.; how a, arises 128, 245; value
judgements involved in existence of
130; distinguished from a moral
question 245–6; a second-order 247
progress: instances of 115; not inevitable
117
question: not every, has a unique and
definitive answer 106; *see also* moral
problem
questions; not all, are problems 246–7
reasoning: essential component of 18
relevance: of moral philosophy 260
rights: concept ineliminable in favour of
wants or interests 155
rules: fundamental, essential to survival
and welfare 9; local, vary across time
and space 9; fundamental, distinguished
from local 104; definition of 265
scepticism: defined 126–7 n.
'Moral Scepticism' (Harrison) 21 & n.; *see
also* scepticism
moral sense: Pollock on the 110; in James
251–2; referred to by Perry 257;
origins of the 279, 285 & n.; not a
reliable guide to morality 280;

moral sense (*cont.*):
  Darwin on the 285–6; requires no
    corresponding bodily organ 286;
    can develop only through being used
    292
moral-sense theories: are theories of moral
    motivation 280
moral theory: Rawls on 43; essential for
    discovering moral facts 44; can
    supplement and correct common sense
    117; complex, of John Stuart Mill 313;
    see also ethical theory
moral truth: common-sense morality as a
    body of 101–2
  truths: necessary, essential to Sidgwick's
    ethics 51
  value: objects can have no 153; what has
    153
'Moral Value and Moral Worth' (Baier)
    153 n.
moral values: a social structure in which, can
    flourish 158
  worth: conception of, introduced by Kant
    134–5; used most often for the moral
    value of character 153; what has 154;
    concept of, explained 154–5
Moreland: a rather special literary character
    24
Morgenthau, Hans: perspicuous conception
    of common sense 97
Morris, Desmond: on racial and group
    conflicts 183–4
motives: Hume and Mill on, 137; importance
    of, emphasized by Aristotle, Hume,
    Kant, and Whately 154–5
Muirhead, J. H.: *see* Hetherington
Muller, Herbert J. (*Adlai Stevenson: A Study
    in Values*) 138 & n.
Murdoch, Iris: on philosophy 242–3
Murphy, Arthur E.: on ideology 30; on
    common-sense judgements 109–10; on
    epistemological theories 112; on facts
    and values 140; *The Theory of Practical
    Reason* 104 n.
Mind Your Own Business (MYOB) principle,
    the: fundamental 24
'myth of "race", the': expression bandied
    about by Montagu 166–7

Nagel, Ernest: *see* Cohen, Morris R.
national character: concept of 177–9;
    relation of, to race 179–80; Mill on 179;

the question whether philosophy can
    have a distinctive 141–4
natural facts: are neither just nor unjust
    69–70
  inequalities 70–1
  right: Dworkin's sound conception of 156
Natural History of Nonsense, The (Evans)
    97–8, 97 n., 100 n.
naturalistic fallacy: instance of the 169–70,
    171–2
natural-law theory: stems from the Stoics
    190
Nature of the Judicial Process, The (Cardozo)
    102 & n.
necessity: a moral 212
negative GR: logically and morally equivalent
    to positive GR 276
negotiation: a form of pure procedural justice
    73
'new golden rule': a misnomer 291; not clear
    what the, is 291
New Golden Rule, The (Etzioni) 290, 290 n.
Nicomachean Ethics (Aristotle) 105, 106;
    quoted 132, 314 n.
'Nigger': what the abusive word, imports 116
Nineteen Eighty-Four (Orwell) quoted 22 n.
nonsense: examples of 146; philosophical
    98, 170
normative claim: defined 123–4
'normative globalist': concept employed by
    Etzioni 290–1
normative reasoning: a fallacy of 144–5
  standard: a, is built right into the very
    conception of common sense 111
norms: Frederick Will on 31; Thomas Green
    on 121
'no-truth' theorists 42
Nowell-Smith, P. H. (*Ethics*) 155

Oberdiek, Hans ('Review of Rawls: A Theory
    of Justice') 61 n.
objective: when a value judgement is, 143
objectivity and truth 143
obligation: James's conception of 52, 252
Ockham's razor 233
On Liberty (Mill) 9, 156, 157 n., 303,
    306 & n.
'On Not Worshipping Facts' (Lucas) 139 &
    n.
opinion and preference 147–8
opinions: God incapable of having 149; are
    typically issued by appellate courts

193–4; essential importance of judicial 212; *see also* judicial opinions

ordinary language: often a guide to common sense 87

Orwell, George (*Nineteen Eighty-Four*) 22 n.

Ortega y Gasset, Jose: quoted 98

ought: the psychological, can be binding 25; a valid inference from an 'is' to an 138; *see also* is/ought distiction; is/ought problem

Our Changing Morality (Kirchway) 35 & n.

Our Knowledge of the External World (B. Russell) 92 & n., 107–8, 108 n.

Paine, Thomas: acute observation of 117

Paley, William (*The Principles of Moral and Political Philosophy*) 206–7

Paley's Moral Philosophy (Whately) 137, 137 n., 154, 155 n.

paradox: only minds can generate a 184

Parmenidean: type of ethics 106, 107, 108

Parmenideanism: in ethics 108

parochialism: 141–2

parody: by Montesquieu 172–4

Passmore, John: on solving a social problem 130

'Path of the Law, The' (Holmes) 15 n., 193 & n.

Peirce, Charles Sanders ('Illustrations of the Logic of Science') 308 & n; quoted 41

perfectly rational being: Kant's conception of a 136 n.

permissible wrongs: category of, recognized by common sense 117–18

Perry, Ralph Barton: *The Thought and Character of William James* 250 & n; *General Theory of Value*, on moral issues and the lost-soul hypothesis 256–8; Kuklick on 258

personal morality: what, consists in 5–6; *see also* positive morality

persuasion: is different from justification 49

Peters, Richard (*Reason and Compassion*) 5 n.

Pfaff, William (*Condemned to Freedom*) 42 n.

philosopher: what makes Mill such a fascinating 302

'Philosophers are Back on the Job' (P. Singer) 107

philosophic nonsense: examples of 170

'Philosophical Conceptions and Practical Results' (James): introduced Peirce to the world 308 n.

philosophically: what it is to consider moral issues 259–60

philosophical proof: what, is provided by 19; does not conform to conventional pattern of proof 31

philosophy: the task of 159; a crime against 216 n.; can be culturally relevant 240–1; relations of, to a culture 240–1; can, have a distinctive national character? 241–4; the distinctive character of 242–3; can be personal, national, and impersonal all at the same time 243; the distinctive sort of enlightenment, can bring 259–60; cannot be neutral on the distinction between good and evil 263; Kuklick on one crucial dilemma of professional 241; Iris Murdoch on 242–3; *see also* moral philosophy

Philosophy: Encyclopedia of, The 290 & n.

Philosophy as Diplomacy (Iannone) quoted 262

Philosophy: Its Scope and Relations (Sidgwick) 38 & n.; 94 & n.

Philosophy of Bertrand Russell, The 34 & n.

philosophy of common sense: stems from Reid developed by Sidgwick and Moore 93

'Philosophy of Common Sense, The' (Sidgwick) 120

philosophy of law: perennial question in 190; relations of, to political philosophy 191–2; peculiar province of 192

Piaget, Jean (*The Moral Judgment of the Child*) 137 n.

Pincoffs, Edmund L. (*Rationale of Legal Punishment*): on 'practice' and 'institution' 217 n.

Plato: Russell on 108

pleasures: active, distinguished from passive 296–7, 298

Pleasures and Pains: A Theory of Qualitative Hedonism (E. Edwards) 295 n.

'Poetry and Imagination' (Emerson) 96 & n.

point of view: internal, distinguished from external 101–2

polar terms 31, 314 & n.

political philosophy: relation of, to philosophy of law 191–2; curious dichotomy within 192

politicized: questions of fact 39–40; issues 261–2

Pollock, Frederick: on 'the Casuistry of Common Sense' 109–10; on common sense 111–12; on deficiencies of common sense morality 115

Pollock, Lansing (*Reciprocity in Moral Theory*) 287–8

positive and personal morality: distinction between, refined 94; alluded to 208–9

positive evils of life: Mill's account of the 300–1

positive GR: *see* negative; *see* Golden Rule

positive law (Austin) 190

positive morality: meaning of 5; other names for 5; existence of, a social fact 8; distinguished from common-sense morality 100–2; overlaps with positive law 102; rules of, often narrow stupid and cruel 104; Thomas Green on 121; *see also* personal morality; morality

postulate of concurrence 256–7

Powell, Anthony (*A Dance to the Music of Time*) 24

'practice': one ordinary sense of 217; not a workable substitute for 'institution' 217 & n.

pragmatic conception of utility 310

pragmatic method: of settling moral issues 253–4

pragmatism: respects in which, typically American 243–4; and American civilization 244

Pragmatism (James) 85 n., 96–7, 96 n.

'Pragmatism and the Tragic Sense of Life' (Hook) 255

precedent: where opinion is depublished, is unascertainable 213

precise action guide: *see* action guide

preference and opinion 147–8

preferences: change in, not a change of judgement 7–8; cannot be true or false 148

prejudice: can be enshrined in idiom 119–20

presuppositions: of Rawls's theory 54–7, 68–70; of moral judgement 127–8

Press, The (Liebling) 229 n.

price: reasonable, defined 111

primary goods: discussed 62–4; most important of social 64

Principia Ethica (Moore) 39 n., 131 & n.

principle: of coherent principle 16 & n.; of conscience defined 26–8; of desert

rejected by justice as fairness 67–8; of factual relevance 24; of fairness 54–5; of fair opportunity (Rawls) 81; of freedom 307; of generic consistency (Gewirth) 287 & n.; of redress accepted by justice as fairness 68–9; of utility 21

of justice: GR at basis of the 279; mentioned 273

of reversibility (Baier): relation of, to the generalization principle 277–8

principles: various senses or kinds of 31; legal, not creatures of the law 191; require judgement in application 288; *see also* moral principles

Principles of Moral and Political Philosophy, The (Paley) 206–7

priority of right: in Rawls 52–3

Prisoner Without a Name, Cell Without a Number (Timerman) 210 & n.

problem: of the inference gap 230–6; *see also* moral problem

problems: different levels at which, arise 247–8

Problems of Analysis (Black) 121

professional philosophy: Kuklick on one crucial dilemma of 241

prohibition: serious moral issue of 248–9

promises: *see* dead, the

proof: of a moral principle 19–22; distinction from justification 47; every, presupposes a standard of 23; that there are rights 155

proof and truth: sufficient for the rationality of morality 34; are inextricably connected 48

proof in ethics: available without circularity or infinite regress 22

propositions: how, differ from statements 37 n.

Province of Jurisprudence Determined, The (John Austin) 190

prudence: defined as reasonable or due care 110–11; not the same as selfishness 111; what, requires even of the selfish egotist 304–5

psychology of character: what the, studies 151

Public Opinion (Lippmann) quoted 269–70

punishment: capital, controversial 210

pure procedural justice: defined 73 n.

purpose: Tawney on the, of industry 228–9

Purpose of American Politics, The
   (Morgenthau) 97 & n.
Pythagorean theorem, the 125

qualitative hedonism: *see* hedonism

race: fallacies about, can cause great trouble
   120; controversy over the term 161–2; a
   highly emotive word 161, 162; defined
   161–2; the term, is obscure, elastic, and
   slippery 166; a lethal area 176, 179; the
   term has been used to cover multitudes
   of differences among people 176;
   relation of, to national character
   179–80; claim that, is an artificial social
   construct 187–8, 189; Ardrey on 174–6;
   constitutional question about 199
'Race Counts' (Berreby) 188 n.
Race, Science and Humanity (Montagu)
   167 & n., 168 & n., 169, 180–1
Race: A Study in Superstition (Barzun) 160,
   164–6, 164 n., 182–3
Race: Science and Politics (Benedict) 160,
   170–2, 170 n., 182
racemania: what, is 187
races: manifest that there are different 166;
   the claim that, do not exist is philosophical nonsense 170; are found in nature
   187; existence of different, not essential
   to racism 182, 188
racial conflict: Morris on 183–4; Lucy Mair
   on 188–9
racialize, to: discussed 184–5
racializing: very much with us 184–5, 186
racism: the term 159–60; term, came into use
   about the same time as the word
   'genocide' 161; not concerned with
   genes 162; does not depend upon the
   existence of different races 167; really
   independent of race 182, 188; epitome
   and paradox of 185; Tawneyesque
   account of 185–7; essence of 186–7;
   when we have, incarnate 187; anti-
   Semitism a form of 188; Bernard Lewis
   on the root of 188–9; an institution, as
   was slavery 189; is one of the legacies
   of slavery 238; an institution 238;
   Hilton Als on 189; Chester Himes
   on 189
racist: different senses of the term 162–4
racists: tend to stereotype 163; not all who
   speak of races are 164

Rationalia: not the residence of rational
   morality 15
rationalism in ethics 126
rational intuitionist 82; *see also* intuitionist
rational morality: explained 6–8; central
   provision of 13–14; not resident in
   rationalia 15; existence of 15–16; ideal
   of a 15–16; not the same as 'ideal
   morality' 16; proof that, has a logical
   structure 22; what has no place in a 24;
   where we can get a glimpse of 101;
   relation of, to law 209–11; basic
   demand of 211–12; *see also* personal
   morality; positive morality
Rationale of Legal Punishment, The (Pincoffs)
   217 n.
Rauschning, Hermann (*Hitler Speaks*) 42 n.
Rawls, John: on moral theory 43–4; on
   justification 45–6, 47, 48; *The Law of
   Peoples* 48–9; baseball example used by
   217; *A Theory of Justice* discussed 50–78,
   229–30; two principles of justice of 230
Rashdall, Hastings *The Theory of Good and
   Evil* 131 n.
Reagan, Ronald: deduction by 140
realism: *see* legal realism
reason: *see* contrary to reason
reasonable care: the same as prudence
   110–11
Reason and Compassion (Peters) 5 n.
Reason and Nature (M. R. Cohen) 91–2,
   91 n.
reasonable care: definition of prudence
   110–11
   price: defined 111
reasoning: shoddy scholarship and worse 291
reasons: a moral judgement must rest on
   149
Rechtslehre (Kant) 79
'Reciprocity in Moral Theory' (L. Pollock)
   287–8
Reflections on the Revolution in France
   (Burke) 16 n.
reflective equilibrium: explained 67
Regents of the University of California v. *Bakke*
   198–9, 255–6, 255 n.
regional characteristics: exist 177
regress: proof in ethics obtainable without
   circularity or infinite 22
Reid, Thomas: on common sense 88
Reiner, Hans: (*Duty and Inclination*) on the
   Golden Rule 18–19; cited 146 n.

Reiter, Michael: on the publication of judicial opinions 212

relativism: and absolutism 140–1; an incoherent form of 141–2

relevance: moral, of moral philosophy 220

religion: of social unity (Mill) 307

religious bigotry and superstition 238

'Reply to Alexander and Musgrave' (Rawls) 58 & n., 65 n.

Representative Government (Mill) 75–6 n.

reversibility: *see* principle of reversibility

'Review of Rawls: A Theory of Justice' (Oberdiek) 61 n.

Revolt of the Masses, The (Ortega y Gasset) 98 & n.

Richards, Robert J. (*Darwin and the Emergence of Evolutionary Theories of Mind and Behavior*) 285 & n.

Riggs v. *Palmer*: quoted 191

right: Dworkin's sound conception of a natural 156; the fundamental 155–6

right and wrong: an anarchic idea of 27

rights: proof that there are 155; a moral agent has both, and duties 158

Rights and Persons (Melden) 112–13, 112 n., 114

Right and the Good, The (Ross) 155 n.

right to freedom of thought and conscience: the basis of all other rights 156–7; of value by itself 156–7

right to life: not fundamental but derived 157–8

rigor: of rigor mortis 105

Rise of American Philosophy, The (Kuklick) 239, 240, 241

Road to Serfdom, The (Hayek) 155 n.

Robinson, Richard (*Definition*) 121

Roe v. *Wade* 247, 255, 256

Rome: fiddling while, burns 240–1

Roosevelt, Franklin Delano: Oglethorpe University speech of, on experimentation 244; connection between, and William James 244 n.

Ross, W. D. (*The Right and The Good*) cited 155 n.

Rost, H. T. D. (*The Golden Rule: A Universal Ethic*) 286

Royce, Josiah (*William James and Other Essays on the Philosophy of Life*): on James 243

rule: *see* moral rule

Ruritanians 177

Russell, Bertrand ('Styles in Ethics') 4, 9–10; involved in a confusion 10–11; on truth in ethics 34–5; ethical scepticism of 34–5, 38–9; on common knowledge 92; on the Greek philosophers 107–8

Russell, L. J. ('Ideals and Practice'): on GR 268–70

Ryle, Gilbert xii–xiii, 17 n.

sagacity: one sense of common sense 90

'Sanatorium' (Maugham) 69–70 n.

Santayana, George (*The Life of Reason*): quoted 27 n; critique of Russell 39 n.

Sartre, Jean-Paul (*Existentialism and Human Emotions*): famous example of 24–5

sceptical: arguments: all embracing, are fallacious 21

ethical theories: some minor vindication for 28

scepticism: moral, defined 126–7 n.

Schlesinger, Arthur, jun. (*The Crisis of the Old Order*) 244 n.

scholarship: shoddy, and worse reasoning 291

Second Brain, The (Gershon) xii n., 285 n.

Secrets of the Temple: How the Federal Reserve Runs the Country (Greider) 225–6, 225 n.

selfish egotism: Mill on 304–5

selfishness: prudence not the same as 111; Mill on, as a chief cause of unhappiness 298–9

'Self-Reliance' (Emerson) ix–x n.

sense of dignity: itself a moral idea 296; Mill on the 296

justice: Beerbohm on 257; *see also* moral sense

settlement: of moral issues 250

settling: war can be a means of, disputes 254–5

sex slavery: not just wicked but evil 211 n.

sexual morality: not fundamental but variable 10–11

Shakespeare, William: sonnet 129; Hamlet 203

Sharp, Frank Chapman and Philip G. Fox (*Business Ethics*): on standards 272

Sidgwick, Henry: doctrine of esoteric morality of 16–17 n.; on the principle of utility 21; on the principle of conscience 26–7; *Methods of Ethics* contrasted with Rawls's *Theory of Justice* 51–2; *Methods of Ethics* 78 & n., 80; on common sense 92; *Philosophy: Its Scope and Relations* 94 & n; on common-sense morality and positive morality 100–2; where, went astray 108; on promises to the dead 114; rigorous formulation of the principle of utility 131; quoted 38, 78; mentioned 294

Singer, Peter: quoted 107

slavery: situations in which, is tolerable 76–7; Aristotle and 117; no question about the immorality of 210; main objection to 229; *see also* sex slavery

social conflict: when we have a solution to 257

Social Contract, The (Ardrey) 175–6, 175 n.

social contract theory: in ethics and politics 53

problem: when a moral issue becomes a 248

Social Purpose (Hetherington and Muirhead) 224 & n.

social relations: concept of, difficult to characterize 226

Social Statics (Spencer) 79, 79 n., 80 & n., 307 n.

social unity: Mill's religion of 307
wisdom: Rawls's view of 72

society: no, can do without a morality 9; a network of interacting institutions 230

solution to social conflict: when we have a 257

solved: when a conflict has been, not a simple matter of fact 258

solving: complexity of notion of, a moral problem 129–30

Solzhenitsyn, Alexander (*The Gulag Archipelago*) 210 & n.

'Some Reasons for the Maximin Criterion' (Rawls) 65 n.

Sovereignty of Good, The (Murdoch) 242–3

speed: a contest of, 165

Spencer, Herbert: resemblance of moral philosophy of, to Rawls's 78–80; *Social Statics* Law of Equal Freedom 307 n.

Spirit of the Laws, The (Montesquieu) 173–4, 173 n.

standard: implied in GR 271

standard of proof: a, is presupposed in every proof 23

standards: connect facts with value judgements 143, 145

statements: of fact, of value, of logic 124–5

statements of fact: can be false 124

stem-cell research: embryonic, already politicized 261–2

Stevenson, Adlai: quoted 138

Stoic: elements in Mill's ethics 295, 297, 311; relation of, conception of happiness to pragmatic conception of utility 310

Stoicism: explicit incorporation of, by Mill 301

Stoics: originated natural-law theory 190

Structure of a Moral Code, The (Ladd) 22 n.

'Styles in Ethics' (B. Russell) 5, 9–10

Subjection of Women, The (Mill) 9, 306–7, 307 n.

Sulzberger, C. L. (*Go Gentle into the Night*): quoted 249 & n., 254

Supreme Court, the: deals with large issues of national interest 256

survival: necessity of common sense for 95, 96

System of Logic, A (Mill) 179 & n.

Taking Rights Seriously (Dworkin) 155–6, 156 n., 190–1, 191 n.

Tawney, R. H.: on ism-words 185–6; on institutional evaluation 227; on the purpose of industry 228–9; quoted 81–2, 214

Tawneyesque criterion: for institutional evaluation and criticism 228–9

taxonomy: of issues and problems needed 259

teaching of ethics: itself a moral responsibility 151

teleological theories: 132

Teller, Edward: moral acuity of, 136

Territorial Imperative, The (Ardrey) 174 & n.

Theory of Good and Evil, The (Rashdall) 131 n.

Theory of Justice, A (Rawls) 43, 50–78; *see also* Rawls

Theory of Knowledge, The (Hobhouse) 97 & n.

Theory of Practical Reason, The (Murphy) 104 n., 109–10, 140

theory of value: defined 144

think: we cannot change what we 152

Thompson, Clark C.: on Nixon 145

thought: not naturally free 156

Thought and Character of William James, The (Perry) 250 & n.

Tice, D. J.: on *Huckleberry Finn* 116
Timerman, Jacobo (*Prisoner Without a Name,*
    Cell Without a Number) 210 & n.
Tocqueville, Alexis de: quoted 19 n.
torture: as an instrument of national policy
    210–11
Tractatus Logico-Philosophicus
    (Wittgenstein): opening sentence of
    139 n.; 11 & n.
travel books: quotations from 176–8
Treatise of Human Nature, A (Hume)
    11 & n., 93 & n.,137 & n., 154
Trilling, Lionel: on Huck's moral crisis 116
truth: formal properties of 36–7; not
    identical with knowledge of the 38; may
    have different meanings in different
    applications 40; Hitler on 42; no
    infallible guide to philosophical 98–9;
    common-sense morality as a body of
    moral 101–2; Peirce's conception of,
    analogous to Mill's conception of social
    unity 308; *see also* ethical truth
truth and falsity: not dependent on what we
    think 152
truth and objectivity 143
truth and proof 48
true or false: preference cannot be 148
Tucker, Carll: quoted 146
Tufts, James F.: *see* Dewey
Twain, Mark: on common sense or the lack
    of it 109; *Huckleberry Finn* passage
    exemplifying conflict between personal
    and positive morality 115–16
Two Sources of Morality and Religion, The
    (Bergson) 88 & n.

ultimate principles 19–22
understanding: the precondition of intelligent
    change 159
unfair to oneself: discussion of the idea 274
unhappiness: chief causes of 298–9; utility
    includes mitigation of 302
United States: Communist Party of the 30 n.
United States Law Week 213 n.
universalizability 215 n.
universal moral laws: without exceptions
    22
Uses of Reason, The (Murphy) 30 & n., 147 n.
utilitarian: James not a 83; GR not a,
    principle 289
utilitarianism: a form of empiricism in ethics
    126; has no monopoly on consideration

of consequences 259; a qualified form of
    non-hedonistic 289; James's moral
    philosophy not a version of 250, 253;
    can accept the lost soul at the far-off
    edge of things 253
Utilitarianism (Mill) 141, 294 n.
utility: formulations of principle of 131;
    includes also mitigation of
unhappiness 302; pragmatic conception of
    310

value: forms of 136; theory of, defined 144;
    T. Green's conception of 151; different
    kinds of 152–3; what has fundamental
    155
value and worth: difference between
    153 & n.
value judgement: when a, is objective 143
value judgements: defined 122, 127; are
    involved in the existence of moral
    problems 130; how, can be verified
    142–3; can be true or false 152
'Value of "Values", The' (T. Green) 151
values: definition of 123, 150; not objects of
    choice 145–6; how, can be modified
    150–1; are judgements of importance
    152
value theory: place of, in moral judgement
    26
verification: of value judgements 142–3
virtue: the most indispensable intellectual 41;
    see also intellectual virtue
Voices: The Educational Formation of
    Conscience (Green) 121, 151

war: can be a means of settling disputes
    254–5
Watergate scandal 136
Watkins, John: acute question raised by
    237
Wattles, Jeffrey (*The Golden Rule*) 286
weighting: necessary in any genuine system of
    criminal justice 204–5
Weiss, Paul ('The Golden Rule') 287
welfare: good healthy concern for one's own,
    is not selfishness 111
Wellman, Carl: on true universal ethical
    generalizations 35
Whately, Richard: on common sense 89; on
    the importance of motives 137, 154–5;
    Lessons on Morals on GR 278–83;
    paraphrased 284

Whewell, William (*The Elements of Morality, Including Polity*) 208–9
Whitely, C. H.: on common sense 98–9
Will, Frederick L.: on norms 31
William James and Other Essays on the Philosophy of Life (Royce) 243
Wilson, Woodrow: phrase made famous by 257
Winch, Peter (*The Idea of a Social Science*) 226 n.
Wisconsin: peculiar occurrence in a town in 193–4
Wittgenstein, Ludwig (*Tractatus Logico-Philosophicus*) 11, 139 n.

word magic: an instance of 168–9
world: both one and many 97
worth and value: difference between 153 & n.
wretched: Mill on the present, education and, social arrangements 297, 300, 301, 303, 305, 308
wrong: different kinds and degrees of 17–18
wrongs: category of permissible 117–18; instances of never permissible 118

Zionist fallacy: expression coined by Ardrey 174